CAMBRIDGE LATIN AMERICAN STUDIES

EDITORS
DAVID JOSLIN   TIMOTHY KING
CLIFFORD T. SMITH   JOHN STREET

13

BOLIVIA:
LAND, LOCATION, AND POLITICS
SINCE 1825

THE SERIES

BOLIVIA:
LAND, LOCATION,
AND POLITICS
SINCE 1825

BY

J. VALERIE FIFER

Principal Lecturer in Geography,
Goldsmiths' College, University of London

CAMBRIDGE
AT THE UNIVERSITY PRESS
1972

Published by the Syndics of the Cambridge University Press
Bentley House, 200 Euston Road, London NW1 2DB
American Branch: 32 East 57th Street, New York, N.Y.10022

Library of Congress Catalogue Card Number: 72–139713

ISBN: 0 521 07829 6

Printed in Great Britain
at the University Printing House, Cambridge
(Brooke Crutchley, University Printer)

CONTENTS

Contents

Contents

MAPS

PLATES

Between pages 80 and 81

ACKNOWLEDGEMENTS

Grateful acknowledgement is made to the staff of library and archive collections in Bolivia, Britain and the United States who have afforded me every assistance in the preparation of this book. I am similarly greatly indebted to the many members of staff in Bolivian Government Ministries, and to transport and other officials in Bolivia and neighbouring States for their interest and practical assistance, and for the opportunities provided to examine documentary and statistical material. In addition to members of the Bolivian Embassy staff in London and those of the British and U.S. Embassies in Bolivia, my thanks are due in large measure to the many local officials, private individuals and friends throughout Bolivia and its adjacent territories who gave so freely of their time in discussion, and willingly shared with me the benefits of their own indispensable knowledge and experience.

Further appreciation is expressed for grants in aid of research from the Central Research Fund of the University of London and the Delegacy of Goldsmiths' College. The book has been published with the help of a grant from the Latin American Publications Fund. I am also indebted to Professor W. G. East who supervised early research, to the editors of this series, Dr J. Street and the late Professor D. M. Joslin, and to the editorial adviser Professor C. T. Smith for their advice and helpful comment. Finally, and especially, I thank my husband for his ready assistance and encouragement at all times.

September 1971   J. V. F.

ABBREVIATIONS

Bol. Soc. Geog. Sucre   *Boletín de la Sociedad Geográfica e Histórica 'Sucre'*, Bolivia

B.M.   British Museum

Col. Trat. Vig. Bol.   *Colección de Tratados Vigentes de la República de Bolivia – Convenciones Bilaterales*, Ministerio de Relaciones Exteriores y Culto, La Paz

F.O.   Foreign Office Archives, London

Geog. Journ. (*Journ. Roy. Geog. Soc.*), (*Proc. Roy. Geog. Soc.*)   *The Geographical Journal*, London, 1893– ; (formerly *The Journal of the Royal Geographical Society*, 1831–80; *Proceedings of the Royal Geographical Society*, 1856–78; *Proceedings of the Royal Geographical Society* (New Series), 1879–92)

Geog. Rev. (*Bull. Am. Geog. Soc.*), (*Journ. Am. Geog. Soc.*)   *The Geographical Review*, New York City, 1916– ; (formerly *Bulletin of the American Geographical and Statistical Society*, also *Journal of the American Geographical and Statistical Society*, and *Proceedings of the American Geographical and Statistical Society* variously between 1852 and 1872; *Journal of the American Geographical Society of New York*, 1873–1900; *Bulletin of the American Geographical Society of New York*, 1901–15)

Hisp. Am. Hist. Rev.   *The Hispanic American Historical Review*, Duke University, Durham, North Carolina

P.R.O.   Public Record Office, London

Scott. Geog. Mag.   *The Scottish Geographical Magazine*, Edinburgh

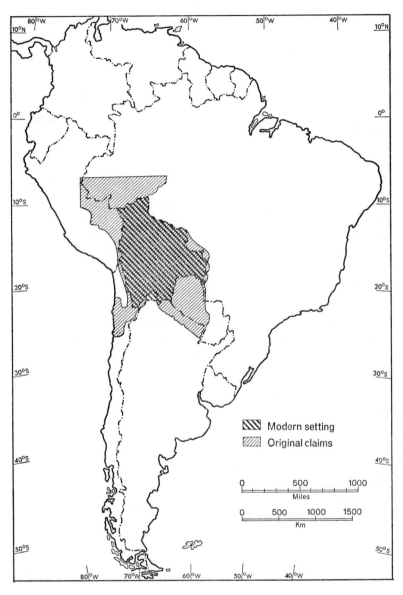

Bolivia: modern setting and original claims

INTRODUCTION

The disadvantages of an interior location in South America have remained apparent for nearly five hundred years. By the end of the fifteenth century, Spain's maritime exploration of the Americas had already become the skilful and free-ranging coastal reconnaissance whose discoveries were to provide the framework of the first great European empire in the New World. Subsequently, the style and pattern of Spain's imperial organisation were to emphasise the significance of sea routes and port cities, and confirm the hegemony of the coastal regions.

In the northern section of Spain's American empire, the imperial structure remained centred upon the Mexican plateau, set between spheres of interest in both the Atlantic and Pacific basins. The European endorsed the indigenous power focus, and Mexico City rose upon the ruins of Tenochtitlán. Whereas islands and isthmus had sketched an initial ground-plan of empire, however, the conquest of Peru represented the first major assault upon the continental land mass, and soon thrust the Spaniards into some of the highest and most rugged terrain in the Americas. Deeper penetration of the interior rapidly intensified the isolation of a mainland frontier whose supply-lines were extended from the west coast ports – ports already two thousand miles beyond the Caribbean and six thousand miles from Spain. Thus, although the central Andean cordilleras became primary sources of wealth, they never located the real centres of power. Lima, not Cuzco, was Pizarro's City of the Kings; the coast, not the plateau nor the high mountain basin, was to focus Spain's authority and prestige in South America, and reap the more lasting benefits from the resources of the interior. The Inca highways had constituted an elaborate system of overland circulation, one which tied both coastal valley and *montaña* fringe to the highland centres of empire. The pre-Columbian trackways would best survive, however, where they assisted Spain's new primary purpose – to link the mountain regions not internally, but to the sea lanes of the empire.

The mining centres in the Viceroyalty of Peru were serviced for the most part by the Pacific ports. Although to stray very far from the west coast increased both the sense and the burden of isolation, and demanded existence at altitudes to which neither the Spaniards nor their cavalry were ever comfortably adapted, yet the richness of such silver strikes as Potosí in Upper Peru impaled the administrative machinery of empire upon the highest and most inaccessible regions of the central Andes. Efforts to minimise the isolation from the ports were responsible for the close trading and commercial ties which were maintained between Lower and Upper Peru after the latter's transfer to the Viceroyalty of the Río de la Plata. The export of unminted gold and silver from Upper Peru was officially diverted to Buenos Aires and the Atlantic route in 1777, but legitimate trade in such items as fish and guano, and in agricultural produce from the irrigated coastal valleys, for example, as well as the movement both of legally imported manufactured goods and of contraband, continued to underline the reliance on Pacific exchange.

Above all, there were overwhelming advantages to be gained, wherever possible, in shortening the overland lines of communication. Longer sea routes, even additional transhipments, were rarely critical factors in Spain's imperial organisation of South America. Within limits, routes were more frequently evaluated in terms of the additional time and inconvenience they involved in travelling overland, provided that military or strategic considerations were of lesser concern. Although the trails through the central Andes westward to the Pacific were forced to negotiate the continent's highest, roughest and most barren terrain, such trackways in general provided Upper Peru's shortest and cheapest overland routes to the coast. Moreover, despite the steep gradients and physical hardships they imposed, the Pacific trails were spared the savage attacks by plains Indians, untamed by Inca or Spaniard, which endangered the *pampas* and trans-Chaco routeways. Given the opportunity of free movement and exchange of goods, therefore, and disregarding the temporary late eighteenth-century realignment of trading patterns dictated by the Viceroy in Buenos Aires, Upper Peru's economic dependence upon the most accessible Pacific ports was unchallenged.

Nevertheless, in other respects, the links between the four provinces of Upper Peru and the major administrative centres of both Lower Peru and the Río de la Plata were tenuous, and weakened by distance; both viceregal capitals were more than one thousand miles from Potosí and Chuquisaca. When the opportunity was presented, the effects of physical separation were expressed in political terms, although Upper Peru – the Audiencia or Presidency of Charcas – was ill equipped and poorly sited to support political independence in economic terms. The post-Revolutionary period produced few fundamental changes in economic or social patterns, and the southern continent's reliance on the overseas export of primary products continued with little modification after the break-up of the Iberian empires. The prosperity of the newly independent States was to be closely tied to their continuing ability to participate in overseas trade. Colonial interdependence had rarely been fostered by Spain; there were few durable patterns of regional integration, communication and mutual dependence within Spanish America. Notable exceptions, such as the *pampas* mule trade with Peru, tended to strengthen the truth of the generalisation. Thus, the routine of a long-established overseas-exchange economy offered few antecedents and little scope for future flexibility or innovation.

In seeking political separation in 1825 from both Peru and Argentina, Bolivia was obliged by the application of the principle of *uti possidetis de jure 1810* to accept a singularly inappropriate distribution of territory – one whose frontiers, though ill-defined, reflected patterns of internal administrative convenience rather than those which would be required for successful participation in overseas trade. The centrifugal lines of movement to the ports and shipping lanes were recognised and safeguarded by the viceregal boundaries – soon, in this instance, to be abandoned. The future viability of any region plucked from the broader framework of the viceroyalty was uncertain, but it would inevitably depend to a great extent, and with few exceptions, upon how favourably the new State was placed in relation to sea routes, and to overseas contacts and influences. Around the early wealth of Potosí, Spain had shaped and reshaped many of its most important administrative frontiers – judicial, ecclesiastic and military. Internal sub-divisions, however, based with varying degrees of precision on the jurisdiction of intendants, *oidores* and provincial governors, would not necessarily combine to function as a political unit; nor, in external relations, would they provide a satisfactory setting for the unfamiliar and competitive role into which an independent Bolivia would be cast. The principal routeways from Upper Peru to the coast lay outside the jurisdiction of the Presidency or Audiencia of Charcas. In losing its rights to the most readily accessible Pacific ports, Bolivia had shed the advantages as well as the disadvantages of colonial dependence.

Paradoxically, therefore, Bolivia emerged in practice as a non-maritime Pacific State, a situation which was to be confirmed politically with the subsequent loss of the remote Atacama province. If the choice of independence was Bolivia's to make in 1825, such initiative was not long retained; the country was to survive as a unitary State on terms dictated elsewhere.

From the outset, internal and external communications formed one of the weakest aspects of Bolivia's political and economic geography, and the greatest single obstacle to further development. There was no marked determination in South America in the nineteenth century to link opposing coasts by transcontinental railways, lines from which the continental interior might well have derived some benefit. Occasional attempts or proposals to substitute shorter canal or rail linkages between stretches of navigable waterway in central South America ended, for the most part, in failure. In sharp contrast, the increasing number of transcontinental railroads linking the Atlantic and the Pacific seaboards in the United States and Canada between 1869 and 1886 demonstrated the intention to promote coast-to-coast national unification and, at the same time, provided the stimulus and the means to achieve greater economic development of the western interior. In South America, however, political fragmentation, rival national interests, the lack of available capital, and the persistence of widely dispersed peripheral population clusters combined with the physical difficulties to make transcontinental railways impracticable. Circulation revolved around separate and selected coastal foci; the landlocked State of Bolivia reflected the stagnation of the continental interior, its disadvantages intensified by non-participation in the economic growth of the coastal zones. The inner Andean centres no longer offered sufficient inducement to the speculator; mines in Bolivia and Peru failed to attract the early replacement investment of British capital necessary to revive their declining output and to stabilise conditions. Political uncertainty and technical difficulties aside, the excessive delays and high cost of mineral transport to the coast remained severely limiting factors. The risks were great, the returns inadequate.

Under these circumstances, the landlocked State stood back from those areas which tempted both the foreign investor and the overseas immigrant to South America during the nineteenth century. It failed to share the advantages of direct contact with new ocean steamship routes and the effective world-wide lessening of distance they initiated. It failed to experience or benefit directly from the increased mobility afforded by the first phase of railway construction in South America. In both respects, therefore, a landlocked location represented serious isolation from two of the most important technological advances bearing on the growth of State organisation and State power during the nineteenth century.

Access to the coast, by direct or indirect means, thus became a priority in the conduct of Bolivia's external affairs, and was attempted in various ways: by the proposed exchange of territory, by improved access to the navigable portions of international waterways (suggested or confirmed), by demands for a corridor to the Pacific, and by free port and free transit agreements. Protracted effort and legal argument, however, met with little success. Indeed, Bolivia's long catalogue of nineteenth- and twentieth-

4

century boundary disputes was closely linked to the country's attempts to secure internationally recognised, free and permanent access to the sea. Much was to depend, therefore, on the attitudes of the immediate neighbours, and in an era of vigorous continental economic exploitation and territorial expansion, enclosure by as many as five other newly created States was an added burden – a restraint plainly lacking the advantages of competition and cooperation that such a location can, in other circumstances, afford. Bolivia negotiated from a position of weakness, and was to discover to its cost that compromise was thereby denied. The guaranteeing of unimpeded access or transit to the high seas remained one of the most sensitive areas in foreign relations within South America, and one over which attitudes tended to harden most readily. Despite the various transit agreements which subsequently eased the communications problem in part, the legacy of persistent early failure survived in many forms.

For almost a century, Bolivia's physical and cultural isolation emphasised internal weakness, accentuated grievances, and stifled economic development. To the extent that in the attraction of investment, and in the siting of many growth and development projects the continental interior still competes unsuccessfully with the peripheral areas, the country's position has remained unfavourable. With few exceptions, major undertakings sponsored by the coastal States within their own national interiors have primarily been in response to the demands of the urbanised fringe. Indeed, whatever the future nature of the continent's interior development, the coastal and near-coastal city regions in South America will probably continue to focus population growth and migration, thus locating perhaps the last as well as the first major settlement frontier upon the continent's periphery. As always, the effectiveness of resource exploitation within the interior, and particularly within the landlocked State, is likely to remain closely linked to external forces and external communications. The gradual improvement of Bolivia's internal transport system will finally be measured in relation to external exchange: on the extent to which it may be possible to minimise the disadvantages of location by drawing the country into a wider continental circulation.

CHAPTER I

THE INDEPENDENCE OF BOLIVIA

I. ACHIEVEMENT

Bolivia was created when the provinces of Upper Peru declared their independence in August 1825 – an independence not only from Spain but, in some respects even more significantly, independence from Argentina and Lower Peru at the same time. The new State adopted the name *República Bolívar* and amended it two months later to *Bolivia*. It was a prudent choice determined not, as might be thought, by the desire to acknowledge with gratitude Bolívar's support and sympathy for Upper Peru's independence movement. Indeed, the reverse was true for, ironically, an independent Bolivia was never part of the Liberator's grand design for the post-Revolutionary political map of Spanish South America. Bolívar's evident anxiety and displeasure at being forced to condone as a *fait accompli* the breakaway of a colonial *audiencia* from the Viceroyalties of both Peru and the Río de la Plata were not surprising, for he opposed Upper Peru's unilateral declaration of independence on two grounds – legal and geographical. Not only did the breakaway flaunt the principle of *uti possidetis de jure 1810*; in Bolívar's opinion, an independent Upper Peru, outside any proposed federation, was palpably not a viable unit. Its location, he observed, would never permit it to survive. Unduly pessimistic though this view was to prove, Upper Peru's situation in the South American land mass undoubtedly placed its successor State in a uniquely vulnerable position. The pattern of events both before and after Bolivia's independence continually reveals the interplay of political and economic factors against a background dominated by immutable problems of location – a remote mid-continental hinterland of extreme physical difficulty, its core secluded to the point of isolation within the lofty Andean cordilleras.

In one respect, the fact that an independent State emerged at all in this most massive and intractable section of the Andean system, two-and-a-half miles above sea level, was one of the long-term effects of the extraordinary silver strike made at Potosí. Spain's momentous discovery in 1545 of the great 'silver mountain' (15,600 feet) swiftly focused imperial attention upon one of the highest, bleakest and most inaccessible sites in all Latin America. Yet, by any standards and despite fluctuations in output, the enormous wealth derived for almost two centuries from this legendary Cerro Rico confirmed it as one of the greatest mineral strikes of all time, a prodigious source of revenue which thrust Potosí into sudden prominence, supplied the language with a new synonym for riches and established its location in the Spanish empire as 'the axis of an immense world' as Bolívar later described it.

Despite the harsh physical conditions, such exceptional prosperity resulted in the rapid influx and concentration of population which characterises the 'boom-town' of any age – miners, speculators, adventurers and merchants – the diverse, foot-loose elements of a silver *bonanza* whose magnitude eclipsed anything the Western Hemisphere had ever experienced. Accompanying them were those who set this 'boom-town' apart as a peculiarly Spanish enterprise: the Crown assayers, comptrollers and hierarchy of officials employed in the Royal Treasury and the Royal Mint. Around the city, inevitable adjunct of Spain's imperial administration, sprawled the camps of the many gangs of Indians transported under the system of forced labour in the mines known as the *mita*. Transport and supply networks, indeed all the complex logistics of organisation on the grand scale, were forced to penetrate this wild country – and not only to penetrate it, but to operate within it successfully despite the difficulties of sustained physical effort, of over-stretched lines of communication and of remoteness from the ports and sea routes to Spain. Imperial ambition, sustained in large measure by the extraction of precious minerals from its New World empire (in theory as much as one-fifth of total production was claimed by the Crown), had thus secured for Potosí a unique importance. Gratefully designated the Villa Imperial de Potosí by Charles V in 1553, it held at the close of the sixteenth and for much of the seventeenth century an unchallenged position as the largest city in the whole of the Americas.[1]

The impact of Cerro Rico upon the population pattern of the region was not confined, however, to the cold, barren, windswept site of Potosí. In fact, the very dreariness and hardship of life at over 13,000 feet favoured a complementary growth of settlement in some of the warmer Andean intermontane basins, set apart from the Imperial City's more immediate orbit. These provided a welcome haven for officials and entrepreneurs inevitably committed to long spells of duty in Potosí and consequently within more congenial environments, there developed small, attractive

---

[1] The vigorous, turbulent character of cosmopolitan Potosí has been vividly described by Lewis Hanke, *The Imperial City of Potosí*, The Hague, 1956. See also Bartolomé Arzáns de Orsúa y Vela, *Historia de la Villa Imperial de Potosí*, edit. L. Hanke and G. Mendoza, 3 vols., Providence, R.I., 1965.

'garden cities' such as Chuquisaca (modern Sucre, 9,500 feet), Cocha-bamba (8500 feet) and Tarija (6250 feet). These 'garden cities', with their surrounding estates, prospered as administrative, university or agricultural centres or, as in the case of Chuquisaca, in all three capacities. Potosí's role in stimulating the early growth of the principal intermontane urban centres of Upper Peru was therefore a fundamental one, for while they quickly exploited their agricultural advantages in response to the demands of the mining settlements, some of these centres gradually assumed a political awareness also, sustained, both directly and indirectly during the peak of its prosperity, by the economic stature of Potosí.

This developing sense of regionalism, intensified by location and topo-graphy, should be reviewed against the administrative patterns gradually evolved by Spain for the organisation of its South American empire. West of the Tordesillas line, a broad initial division of Spanish territory had been made among the first *conquistadores*. South of the equator, early land grants or *adelantazgos* between 1529 and 1548 divided much of the western part of the continent into broad bands, variously assigned to Francisco Pizarro (New Castile or Castilla del Oro), Diego de Almagro (New Toledo), Pedro de Mendoza and Pedro de Valdivia (New Estre-madura, as far south as 41° S). In order to control the activities of the *conquistadores*, however, and identify the Crown as the centralised authority in all colonial adminstration, Spain divided its vast new empire into viceroyalties, directed by the Royal and Supreme Council of the Indies, founded in 1524 and subject only to the king. Of the two original viceroyalties – New Spain and Peru – the latter contained nearly the whole of Spanish South America until the eighteenth-century Bourbon reforms.

The immense size of the Viceroyalty of Peru soon dictated its progressive internal sub-division, and a series of *audiencias*, as well as the Captaincy-General of Chile, were gradually carved out of the whole. The original function of the *audiencias* was purely judicial. They were courts composed of judges (*oidores*) who, by tradition, were usually Spaniards born in Spain, not in America, i.e. *peninsulares*, not creoles. The post of *oidor* demanded keen professional ability and bestowed considerable prestige, for the *audiencias* long comprised one of the most important elements in the complex organisation of Spain's empire. Nominally, *oidores* were subordinate to the viceroy, although in practice the exercise of power by any individual was checked and balanced by the intricacies of administrative procedure. The location of the *audiencias*, too, had an important bearing on the measure of autonomy which they could achieve, for the increased isolation imposed on some by time and distance could render many of the prescribed channels of communication too slow and cumbersome to be operated effectively. Thus, the power of the *audiencia* tended to increase with distance from the viceregal seat and while still forming the highest chambers of appeal, subject only to the Crown veto, these courts in time added political, economic, ecclesiastic and military functions to their judicial ones. Moreover, they provided a continuity of administration during the interregna between viceregal appointments and in some measure acted as a controlling influence upon the viceroy himself. *Audiencias* (the term applied both to the tribunals and to the areas over which they had jurisdiction) were established at intervals throughout the colonial period;[1] of these, the Audiencia of Charcas became the eventual territorial basis of nineteenth-century Bolivia.[2]

So great had been the influx of population into Potosí after 1545 that only six years later, as the astonishing potential of the Cerro Rico began to be realised, the Council of the Indies was moved to recommend the establishment of a new *audiencia* in the general vicinity of the busy mining town. Chuquisaca, known also as Ciudad de la Plata and occasionally as Charcas, was selected, having been founded as early as 1538, only three years after Lima itself – Pizarro's City of the Kings. By 1551 Chuquisaca, Potosí's 'garden city', had become the seat of a bishopric, later an archbishopric, while in 1559 its importance was enhanced still further by Philip II's official creation of the Audiencia. It was given the regional name of Charcas, after the local groups of Charcas Indians; Chuquisaca was to be its centre. Towards this sheltered basin contained by a jumble of Andean sierras the *oidores* slowly made their way from Spain. Even with the long voyage to Lima/Callao safely accomplished, their final destination, and usually the worst part of the journey, still lay several weeks ahead – a tedious, uncomfortable progress following desert and mountain trails into the heart of the continent. As they penetrated ever more deeply into the interior, the *oidores* had ample time to reflect that Chuquisaca had provided them with one of the remotest assignments in the empire.

Initially, in the absence of any detailed information on settlement and topography, the jurisdiction of the *oidores* at Charcas was prescribed within

---

[1] Santo Domingo 1511, Mexico 1527, Panamá 1535, Lima 1542, Guatemala 1543, New Galicia 1548 (based at Guadalajara after 1560), Bogotá 1549, Charcas 1559, Quito 1563, Manila 1583, Santiago de Chile 1609, Buenos Aires 1785, Caracas 1786, Cuzco 1787.

[2] Specific studies of the Audiencia of Charcas may be found in: (i) G. René-Moreno, 'La Audiencia de Charcas, 1559–1809', *Revista Chilena*, Santiago, no. xxix, May 1877, pp. 93–142; (ii) A. Jauregui Rosquellas, 'La Audiencia de Charcas', *Bol. Soc. Geog. Sucre*, vol. xxx, 1933, pp. 1–53.

a radius of one hundred leagues around Chuquisaca. The limits of *audiencias*, however, were frequently rearranged by a stream of royal *cédulas* from Spain, which augmented or reduced the administrative regions. The Audiencia of Charcas, no exception to this rule, expanded and contracted around its highland core; at one period it extended nearly two thousand miles from Arica to Buenos Aires, straddling the continent from the Pacific to the Atlantic Ocean and incorporating regions which had been explored and colonized from both these points of penetration. In 1776, however, the new Viceroyalty of the Río de la Plata was created, and the Audiencia of Charcas was transferred from the Viceroyalty of Peru. Other internal administrative reforms followed, notably the establishment of the intendant system in 1782, which introduced the first important curb upon the power of the *oidores* in Chuquisaca, as indeed it did elsewhere. Eight new intendancies were set up in the extensive and territorially unwieldy Audiencia of Charcas, the head of each being responsible directly to the Viceroy. As a result, the *oidores* lost much of their gradually assumed political and administrative power, reverting rather more to their original function as a court of appeal. The President of the Audiencia was also the Intendant of the province of Chuquisaca (La Plata); the judicial power of the President now, however, became purely nominal. This late eighteenth-century reorganisation of Spain's bureaucratic structure is seen to have had significant political repercussions: 'the introduction of intendants into Upper Peru provoked a reaction on the part of the *audiencia* which completely shattered the united front of Spanish government in this part of the empire, and created a tension which contributed in no small part to the undermining of the colonial régime in Upper Peru'.[1]

The creation of two new *audiencias* – Buenos Aires in 1785 and Cuzco in 1787 – pared away still further Chuquisaca's sphere of influence. But these, and other, adjustments did nothing to lessen the relative isolation of Charcas, situated at the north-western extremity of the Viceroyalty of the Río de la Plata, and even farther from Buenos Aires than from Lima. Although the limits of the Audiencia of Charcas had been modified many times during its history, enclosing a vast area just before the establishment of the intendant system, its effective centres had always remained firmly within the central Andes, where a distinctive regionalism gradually emerged in the four Upper Peruvian provinces of Chuquisaca, Potosí, La

[1] J. Lynch, *Spanish Colonial Administration, 1782–1810. The Intendant System in the Viceroyalty of the Río de la Plata*, London, 1958, p. 241. Chapter x, 'The Intendant and the Audiencia', examines growing tensions and attitudes of independence at this period, with particular reference to the Audiencia of Charcas.

Paz and Cochabamba, together with Santa Cruz de la Sierra.¹ It was a regionalism which moved subtly from economic to political self-consciousness, from regional awareness to a pronounced regional intro-spection which has been dubbed *la mentalidad altoperuana*. In time, these attitudes hardened and found expression in the ultimate determination for political independence.

Chuquisaca, as the administrative, ecclesiastic and judicial focus of Upper Peru, was thus the headquarters of the President-Intendant, the Archbishop and the *oidores*. It became the central arena for political and philosophical debate, particularly within the walls of its own university. The Jesuit Universidad Pontífica y Real de San Francisco Xavier, founded in 1621 and functioning by 1624, had established a considerable reputation in the Spanish colonies, contributing to the recognition of Chuquisaca as one of the principal university towns in the Viceroyalty. The expulsion of the Jesuits in 1767, however, resulted in a perceptible shift of emphasis from theological to legal studies, and in 1776 a new post-graduate law school, the Real Academia Carolina, was established under the direction of the Audiencia's *oidores*, who comprised the entire teaching faculty. Although a declaration of loyalty to the king of Spain and to the Roman Catholic faith remained obligatory for entry, the Academia Carolina soon became a forum for the exchange of liberal ideas and radical thought.² Within this cell of localised but intense activity, the articulate aired their views in printed broadsheets and interminable discussions, isolated but not insulated from contemporaneous revolutionary developments in North America and Europe.

In time, the concentration of creole law graduates in the Academia Carolina exacerbated a situation of increasing resentment and dissatis-faction which, while not of course confined to the Audiencia of Charcas, was particularly well illustrated by conditions at Chuquisaca. Throughout the empire, the prestige appointments to *oidor* tended to remain the per-quisite of *peninsulares*, who had always in consequence formed a locally distinct and envied élite. Until the colonial law schools had become firmly

¹ 'In 1793 Intendant Viedma of Cochabamba requested that an additional intendancy should be created for Santa Cruz in order to strengthen government there, and control a tyrannous and independent creole class of *alcaldes ordinarios*. His suggestion, however, made no pro-gress.' J. Lynch, *ibid*. p. 67.

² C. W. Arnade, in *The Emergence of the Republic of Bolivia*, Univ. of Florida Press, 1957, traces the growth of radical and revolutionary thought and action in Upper Peru up to 1825. Political events in Chuquisaca and Potosí, particularly in the first decade of the nine-teenth century, were examined by Gabriel René-Moreno in *Ultimos Días Coloniales en el Alto-Perú*, Santiago, Part I, 1896, Part II, 1898; and *Documentos Inéditos sobre el Estado Social y Político de Chuquisaca en 1808 y 1809*, Santiago, 1897 and 1901.

and reputably established, appointments to *oidor* had inevitably to be distributed among suitably qualified peninsular Spaniards. Long after the necessity for this had disappeared, however, the practice had tended to be perpetuated by tradition so that, in general, it remained the exception rather than the rule to find a creole in such an office. This loading of the system against Spaniards born in America – and by the second half of the eighteenth century these included many long-established, able and influential creole families – brought increasing discontent. In Chuquisaca the juxtaposition of the two groups of lawyers, peninsular and creole, in the Academia Carolina, readily emphasised mounting tension and frustration.

Early nineteenth-century events in Europe accelerated many eighteenth-century trends. The abdication of the Spanish king Charles IV, the detention of his son Ferdinand VII by Napoleon, the resulting claims of Charles' daughter Carlota and the establishment of the rival *juntas* in Spain together combined to provide fertile ground for intrigue and opportunism among the colonial territories. Clearly, the dilemma of divided loyalties could be turned to advantage. An early manifestation of this occurred in Chuquisaca when the *oidores*, supported by a number of radicals who for the moment saw their own cause indirectly strengthened by such action, elected to disregard a directive from the Viceroy at Buenos Aires requiring the Audiencia of Charcas to acknowledge the *junta* at Seville. Instead, a group of *oidores* assumed control on 25 May 1809 in the name of the imprisoned Bourbon king, Ferdinand VII, deposing the President of the Audiencia while the Archbishop fled from the city towards Potosí. As far as the traditional view is concerned, this marks the beginning of the country's fight for independence but in fact the attempted *coup* was short-lived, and firm control was later restored by the Viceroy in Buenos Aires. In July of the same year, the President of the Audiencia of Cuzco quickly put down a second, more open declaration of independence by radicals who had infiltrated into La Paz and deposed the Intendant and the Bishop. The central square, Plaza Murillo, today commemorates that rebellion which likewise enlisted no widespread support, its ringleaders snuffed out by public hangings and imprisonment. Indeed, over the next fifteen years, the struggle for independence from Spain, where it existed at all in this region, was confined to sporadic mountain guerrilla activity, punctuated by the abortive attempts of the newly independent United Provinces of the Río de la Plata, later to become Argentina, to liberate their north-west frontier in Upper Peru.

Not unnaturally, Buenos Aires had refused to recognise the return of

Upper Peru, and its mining revenues, to the Viceroyalty at Lima after its own break with Spain in 1810. Encouraged by the revolutionary demonstrations in Chuquisaca and La Paz the previous year, Buenos Aires dispatched a liberating force in August 1810, which was subsequently decisively defeated by Royalist troops at Guaqui, the small lake port on the shores of Titicaca. Relations between the Argentine troops and the Upper Peruvians were strained and broken by the former's disregard for life and property, and by their over-estimation of anti-Royalist sentiment in Upper Peru. The public execution of the President of the Audiencia of Charcas and the Intendant of Potosí in the early part of the campaign was ill-conceived and locally unpopular, so that the total mismanagement of the first Argentine expedition ensured a hostile reception for the successive campaigns in 1812–13 under General Belgrano, and in 1815 under General Rondeau. After their last defeat at Sipesipe near Cochabamba, the would-be liberators withdrew for good from Upper Peru in an atmosphere of mutual distrust, and evinced little further interest in the region. The Argentine failure is not surprising when it is recalled that the Royalist army was well established in Upper Peru. The relatively peaceful conditions which prevailed for so long in Lower Peru had not necessitated any major withdrawal of auxiliary forces from the more remote provinces beyond the Desaguadero. Moreover, unlike the *porteños*, Royalist troops stationed for some time in Upper Peru had become better adjusted to the altitude, a factor which gave them a considerable edge over their opponents in the rigours of military campaign.

Eventually, as the wars for the emancipation of Spanish South America moved into their final phase, the liberating armies of Bolívar and San Martín converged to prepare for the final onslaught upon Peru. Within the provinces of Upper Peru, meanwhile, a further complication had been introduced by the Spanish General Pedro Antonio de Olañeta who, dissociating himself from the authority of the Constitutionalist Viceroy in Lima, had assumed the Absolutist line of direct and unquestioning obedience to the king of Spain. Indeed, by so doing, he had split Royalist support in the two Perus even to the point of armed conflict for, despite the critical state of events elsewhere, Viceroy La Serna felt constrained to dispatch troops into Upper Peru between January and August 1824 in a vain attempt to bring the General into line. Not surprisingly, the Revolutionaries regarded Olañeta with some ambivalence, partly convinced at one stage that he had become sympathetic to the Patriot cause and was, in consequence, engaged in some elaborate secret stratagem of double bluff. After the decisive battles of Junín in August 1824 and Ayacucho in

December 1824, however, Olañeta remained within his moutain eyrie, making a final stand for Spain and displaying a bravado largely nourished by distance from the real centres of power. Upper Peru's excessively difficult terrain had been avoided during the principal campaigns of liberation; the successful southern invasion of Lower Peru had been achieved through Chile, not through Charcas. Now it was to provide a postscript to the Revolutionary war.

At the very end of 1824, Marshal Antonio José de Sucre was commissioned by Bolívar to proceed into Upper Peru and subdue the pockets of Royalist resistance there under Olañeta. For the first time, Sucre approached the region with whose future he was to be briefly but so significantly linked. With the victory of Ayacucho behind him, Sucre's progress into Upper Peru became a triumphal march along the Andean *altiplano* – by the western shores of Lake Titicaca, across the Desaguadero and on to an ecstatic reception in La Paz. Addressing the crowd massed before him in the Plaza Murillo, a site which had witnessed many of the separatist aspirations of Upper Peru, Sucre announced his famous decree of 9 February 1825, calling upon the provinces to elect a council of delegates to deliberate and decide upon the region's future. Although his audience was reminded of former and variously existing ties with both Buenos Aires and Lima, Sucre's decree unequivocally stated Upper Peru's right to self-determination.

The extreme probability that Upper Peru would vote for its own independence thus violated the fundamental principle of *uti possidetis 1810* whereby Bolívar had established that the major administrative divisions then obtaining were to provide the blueprint of the newly independent States after the Revolutionary wars. Admittedly, the boundaries of most of Spain's colonial divisions were loosely determined. Where delineated at all in the Laws of the Indies, it was usually only in the vaguest of terms. Systematic demarcation was deemed unnecessary while the whole territory was united as part of the Spanish empire; even the more important boundary between Spanish and Portuguese claims (the San Ildefonso line of 1777) was incompletely surveyed. Imprecise as they were, however, the colonial divisions had achieved a degree of acceptance and internal organisation which had become familiar through nearly three centuries of usage; as such, they had no obvious substitute as a pattern of reference when the former dependent territories began to go their separate ways. The provinces of Upper Peru – Chuquisaca, Potosí, La Paz and Cochabamba, together with Santa Cruz – had always been administered either by Lima or by Buenos Aires and legally, therefore, were to abide by the decision of one of these, strictly the latter, as to their future commitment. Bolívar's reaction to the news of Sucre's February decree was swift and unambiguous. In a letter to the Marshal later the same month, Bolívar observed:

It seems to me that the matter of Upper Peru offers no problem from a military standpoint, and in regard to the political aspect, it is a very simple matter for you. You and the army that you command are under my orders, and you have only to follow my instructions... Neither you, nor I, nor the Congresses of Peru and Colombia can violate or disregard what had come to be recognised as a principle of international law in America, namely: that the republican governments are founded within the boundaries of the former viceroyalties, captaincies general, or presidencies, such as Chile. Upper Peru was a dependency of the Viceroyalty of Buenos Aires – an immediate dependency, as Quito was of Santa Fe...Neither Quito nor Charcas can lawfully be independent unless a treaty is arranged between the parties concerned, either as the result of a war or by the resolution of a congress...by this action you will at once incur the disapproval of the Río de la Plata, of Peru, and of Colombia herself.[1]

But nearly three months later, as the provinces of Upper Peru went about the election of their delegates, it had become patently obvious that nothing less than complete political independence would satisfy the most determined and eloquent group of creoles in Upper Peru.

Sucre meanwhile set about the remainder of his official task, to eradicate the last remnants of Royalist resistance under Olañeta. Leaving La Paz, he marched on across the *altiplano* to Oruro and still higher into the sierras to Potosí. Spanish resistance crumpled in the face of the advancing force and disintegrated completely with the death of Olañeta at Tumusla early in April 1825, but the march drew Sucre more deeply into Upper Peru. Thus, as one of the very last areas in Spanish South America to be emancipated from colonial rule, Upper Peru's way was now clear to assemble and settle its own future. By that time, Bolívar appears to have accepted grudgingly that the independence of Upper Peru was inevitable, but admonishing Sucre in a letter dated 15 May 1825, the Liberator declared, with considerable irritation: 'I am convinced that everyone will be displeased...I must tell you frankly that I do not believe I am authorised to issue this decree; only the power of circumstances has forced it from me in order to sanction your conduct, to placate Upper Peru, to please the Río de la Plata, to prove the liberal sentiments of the Congress of Peru, and to defend my reputation as a supporter of popular sovereignty and of free institutions.'[2]

[1] Bolívar to Sucre, Lima, 21 February 1825, *Selected writings of Bolívar*, compiled by Vicente Lecuna, Vol. II, *1823–1830*, New York, 1951, pp. 469–70.
[2] *Ibid.* Arequipa, 15 May 1825, p. 493.

There was no going back, however, and delegates from Chuquisaca, Potosí, La Paz, Cochabamba and Santa Cruz were sent, appropriately enough, to the University of San Francisco Xavier at Chuquisaca in July 1825. The delegates took their places within the small university debating hall and doctoral examination centre, beneath the exquisite opulence of gold and carving that decorated this former Jesuit chapel. In an atmosphere heavily charged with emotion and a sense of history, the orations were delivered. Almost two-thirds of the deputies seated together in this crucible of Upper Peru's independence had themselves been trained at San Francisco Xavier, absorbing and preserving its isolationism and separatist attitudes. Debate prolonged throughout July displayed both self-interest and the apparently more disinterested conviction that an independent Upper Peru would preserve a balance of power between Buenos Aires and Lima.

Eventually, a decision was reached to compose a Declaration of Independence: 'The Provinces of Upper Peru, firm and unanimous... declare that their irrevocable will is to be governed by themselves.' This, Bolivia's 'birth certificate', was signed on 6 August 1825, the first anniversary of the Battle of Junín, with only one of the two delegates from Santa Cruz arriving after a long and tedious journey in time to record his approval! Throughout the discussions by the forty-seven delegates, no enthusiasm whatsoever had been evinced for union with Argentina. Two delegates from La Paz, however, had voted for union with Lower Peru, although these were later persuaded to sign the Declaration of Independence in order to make it a unanimous document.[1] A decree on 11 August 1825, five days after independence had been announced, established amid acclamation the Republic of *Bolívar*.

Evincing considerably less enthusiasm for his namesake, Bolívar himself hastily rode up into the country later the same month, travelling to La Paz, Potosí and Chuquisaca between August and November 1825, issuing directives and preparing a new model constitution. Although somewhat mollified by his rapturous reception, Bolívar refused to recognise Upper Peru's unilateral declaration of independence until it had been ratified by both Buenos Aires and Lima. Even so, he continued to entertain doubts about its wisdom and about the viability of Bolivia as a unitary State: 'We must set an example by joining Bolivia and Peru in a federation, and when I proceed to Colombia I shall see what can best be done... *Bolivia cannot remain as she is, because the Río de la Plata and the Emperor of Brazil would eventually bring about the destruction of that*

[1] C. W. Arnade, *The Emergence of the Republic of Bolivia*, pp. 203–4.

Republic.'[1] So much then for Bolívar's opinion of Bolivia's self-appointed future role as a successful buffer State.

Marshal Sucre, however, at least initially, harboured none of the Liberator's gloomy forebodings about Bolivia, remaining its first President until 1828 and working indefatigably to lay the foundations for its successful survival. The old 'garden city' of Chuquisaca, cradle of Bolivian independence, assumed yet another name, Sucre, in his honour, the name by which the town is now more usually known. Today, in the central Plaza 25 de Mayo, a large statue of Sucre stands with arms outstretched towards the old Jesuit chapel where independence was declared. Thereafter named la Casa de la Libertad, it remained Bolivia's legislative hall until the end of the nineteenth century. Below the statue, Sucre's words to the country's new administrators are inscribed: 'Aun pediré otro premio á la nación entera y á sus administradores: El de no destruir la obra de mi creación, de conservar por entre todos los peligros la independencia de Bolivia.' To regard Sucre as the founder or even as the chief architect of Bolivian independence, however, is to ignore the prolonged and complex combination of factors to which the country's separatism should more accurately be imputed. Nevertheless, his genuine sympathy to the cause of a small, but intensely active and articulate group of creoles in Upper Peru, his status in the ranks of the South American military emancipators, and the energy and resolute purpose he displayed, were vital to the final stages of Bolivia's struggle for independence – as much in their timing as in their degree. The years 1825 to 1828 were critical in the initial establishment and recognition of an autonomous Upper Peru, and Sucre's active support at that period was indispensable in tipping the balance in Bolivia's favour.

Bolivia, however, was nothing if not self-confident in its own future. Certainly, a study of the orations delivered by the independence assembly in July and August 1825 reveals how lightly the forty-seven delegates assumed the burdens of the new republic they added so determinedly to the map of South America. But optimism over the republic's future prosperity appears to have lessened with distance from the sheltered urbanity of Chuquisaca. Bolívar's doubts had been forthrightly expressed, while others also noted that, once the gesture of independence had been made, Bolivia's connexions with Peru would, and should be maintained and strengthened. The British Consul-General in Lima, C. M. Ricketts, in his report to

---

[1] Bolívar to Sucre, Magdalena, 12 May 1826, *Selected writings of Bolívar*, p. 591 (my italics). Bolívar was also depressed by the 'lack of talent and pure feelings in public affairs...he despairs of meeting, especially in Upper Peru, men of sufficient weight and character in whom he could entirely repose'; part of Bolívar's conversation with C. M. Ricketts reported in the latter's dispatch to George Canning, Lima, 18 February 1826, *F.O.* 61/7.

Canning dated 30 May 1826[1] upon the economic potential of the new republic, observed that future commercial and financial prospects appeared to be extremely promising, although he stressed repeatedly that the commercial consolidation of Peru and Bolivia was greatly to be desired: 'political relations may safely be entered into with both these Republics', Ricketts assured Canning; 'I speak here of *both* as their interests are inseparable'.

The Consul-General declared his intention of dispatching his secretary, J. B. Pentland, into Bolivia as soon as possible, with instructions to record the first detailed description of the country, to compile a map and make a collection of specimens for the British Museum – no small undertaking. Bolívar himself had expressed great interest in such a scientific reconnaissance and urged its commencement with all speed. How conscientiously Pentland carried out his laborious commission can be seen in his voluminous report to Ricketts, dated 2 December 1827, which is valuable principally as a contemporary survey of the centres of settlement and the mines.[2] Pentland estimated the total population to be about 1,100,000, nearly three-quarters of them Indian, and as many as one-third of the total living between 12,500 and 14,000 feet, a fact which caused the observer considerable astonishment. During his slow and painstaking survey, Pentland enjoyed the full cooperation of President Sucre though, somewhat bleakly, he had to record that: 'The roads throughout Bolivia are only adapted for mules and lamas [*sic*] – a cart or carriage road does not exist in any part of the Republic, and with the exception of one or two carriages used in religious ceremonies at Chuquisaca, a wheeled vehicle does not exist in any part of Bolivia.'

Some of the imponderables, the overwhelming problems facing the newly independent Upper Peru, introduce a fresh note of caution into Pentland's appraisal as he proceeds. Certainly, Ricketts' accompanying letter to London becomes more qualified in its enthusiasm than his earlier,

---

[1] *F.O. 61/7.* (See also R. A. Humphreys, edit., *British Consular Reports on the Trade and Politics of Latin America, 1824–1826*, Royal Historical Society, London, 1940, pp. 207–25.)

[2] *F.O. 61/12.* Pentland's report was divided thus: (*a*) an historical review of the events which preceded the independence of Bolivia; (*b*) a geographical and statistical description of the Republic; (*c*) the state of the mines; (*d*) a review of commercial relations, foreign and domestic; (*e*) a view of its government, laws and institutions. Population statistics for the chief towns were approximated as follows: Chuquisaca 12,000; La Paz 40,000; Cochabamba 30,000; Potosí 9,000; Santa Cruz 9,000; Oruro 4,600.

A second report was later requested by the Foreign Office and Pentland accordingly presented 'A Review of the Rise, Progress and Actual State of the Republick of Bolivia', 24 October 1831. *F.O. 61/20.* But by this time, Pentland had been back in Europe for nearly four years and this shorter survey contains little new material, and much hearsay. Pentland, an Irishman, held the post of British Consul-General in Bolivia between 1836 and 1839.

more superficial knowledge had permitted, for Pentland noted that feelings for strict independence in Bolivia were stronger than those for any kind of alliance. 'If Bolivia could be secured exactly in the position in which she is at present placed,' the Consul-General observed, 'or if even she were placed on the non-intercourse system of Paraguay, the expectation of her becoming the favoured spot in South America might not be Utopian; but,' he added prophetically, 'I fear that the tranquil state of her horizon is threatened to be overcast.'

2. ASSESSMENT

Far from being placed in a 'favoured spot', Bolivia in several respects had inherited a most unenviable position. The very act of establishing an independent State on the groundplan of the formerly dependent territory of Upper Peru immediately aggravated problems of location which hitherto had been ignored, or parried fairly successfully within the wider protective limits of the Viceroyalty. Leaving aside the existing problems of internal organisation bequeathed to the republic, it was soon apparent except to the most ardent separatists that new problems in external relationships would be no less formidable.

The area claimed by Bolivia as the Presidency or Audiencia of Charcas on the basis of *uti possidetis de jure 1810* comprised an extensive, very irregularly shaped mass of approximately 850,000 square miles – almost exactly twice the area of Bolivia today. Such size, however, was largely the result of inherited claims to the continental interior, not to the coastal fringe (Fig. 1). Behind the Andes, more than two-thirds of the territory claimed lay in the central landlocked plains of South America. Distances of well over two thousand miles separated lowland Bolivia from the Atlantic Ocean, but distance itself was aggravated by other severe physical limitations. Direct access to the Amazon waterway was interrupted for more than two hundred miles by the hazardous Madeira–Mamoré rapids and falls; access to the navigable reaches of the Paraguay remained seriously impeded by shallows, seasonal flooding, and extensive swamps.

Across this vast wedge of the South American hinterland claimed by Bolivia at independence, only two tenuous links between the Andes of Upper Peru and the Amazon and Paraguay routeways had been maintained under Spain's colonial administration. From the sheltered basin of Cochabamba (8500 feet), the route to the Amazon trailed north-eastwards overland for one hundred and fifty miles to reach Todos Santos at the head of navigation above the Mamoré. This river, more frequently followed

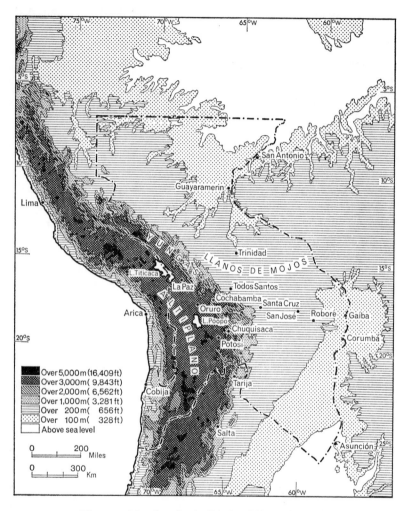

1   The area claimed as the Audiencia of Charcas 1810: relief

than the Beni, flows northward across the plains, meandering for about six hundred miles through the heart of the old Jesuit Mission-Reserve Province of Mojos – the effective north-eastward limit of Spanish penetration. Eventually, in the cataract section, the Mamoré enters the river Madeira, principal south-bank affluent of the Amazon and at that point still two thousand miles from the Atlantic.

2 The area claimed as the Audiencia of Charcas 1810:
location in relation to watershed

The second trail, that to the Paraguay and Asunción, picked its way
eastwards through the sierras to the town of Santa Cruz, seat of the seventeenth-century bishopric, and the only important ranching and regional
centre of the plains. From Santa Cruz de la Sierra, the trail skirted the edge
of the Chaco for about four hundred miles through the Jesuit Province of
Chiquitos. Linking San José and Roboré, it ran out eventually on to the

Paraguay river at either Gaíba or Corumbá. Apart from these two very slender lines of movement, Upper Peru's penetration and exploration of the low eastern lands had been minimal; routes to the north and east received little attention within the viceregal organisation. After 1776 the principal trails to the Atlantic were to Buenos Aires, and led southward from the *altiplano*, the intermontane basins and the piedmont settlements, *via* Salta and Tucumán.

Westward, the problem of access to ocean transport was placed in a contrasted environment. The only outlet to the Pacific which Upper Peru could inherit under the terms of *uti possidetis de jure 1810* was a relatively narrow corridor included in the Intendancy of Potosí – an awkward panhandle running away south-westwards to the sea across three hundred of the worst miles of the Atacama desert – a panhandle, moreover, which contained no irrigated settlement save at a scattering of tiny interior oases, and no port of any consequence whatever. In every direction, therefore, legally inherited routeways to the coast were long, difficult and dangerous – an inauspicious beginning for any newly independent State struggling to develop an overseas trading economy.

What most of the Upper Peruvian creole separatists had persistently discounted, consciously or unconsciously, was the very real dependence of the area upon Lower Peru. Its major communication links were with that Pacific coast, as two of the delegates from La Paz to the 1825 independence assembly had stressed. There, amid the general insistence on complete political independence, these *paceños* had counter-proposed a union with Lower Peru, on the grounds that the Audiencia of Charcas lacked the resources, the stature and the organisation for successful separation and, in particular, that it lacked a good seaport. The complementary role of the two Perus was emphasised, but such a realistic assessment ran against the prevailing mood. Arguments based on commerical considerations carried little weight in Chuquisaca; enclosed and characteristically self-centred, creoles largely confined within the intermontane basins were more attracted by the idea than by the practicalities of independence.

To some extent, the political and trade reorganisation which had operated during the final years of empire had diminished, even partially obscured, the importance of the Pacific routeways. The prohibition in 1777 by the Viceroy of the Río de la Plata on the export of unminted gold and silver from Upper Peru except through Buenos Aires had had the effect of seriously reducing trade between Upper and Lower Peru. European manu- factured goods formed a large part of the return cargo from the Río de la Plata: 'In 1800 the import capacity of the Potosí market was assessed at

2,806,700 pesos: imports from Lower Peru accounted for 308,700 pesos, while as much as 600,000 pesos was accounted for by European merchandise arriving by way of Buenos Aires.'[1]

Nevertheless, despite the increased traffic through Buenos Aires which followed the viceregal ruling on the movement of bullion, trade through Lower Peru was obviously not extinguished. A comparison of transport costs (per 100 lb. of merchandise) from Buenos Aires and Arica to the principal Bolivian highland centres in 1826–7, clearly reveals the long-term advantage of the Pacific routeway:

Buenos Aires to:		Arica to:	
Potosí	$16.4	Potosí	$16.4
Chuquisaca	$19.0	Chuquisaca	$16.4
Oruro	$22.0	Oruro	$13.4
Cochabamba	$25.0	Cochabamba	$13.4
La Paz	$26.0	La Paz	$7.0[2]

Whatever commercial links had been forged with Buenos Aires during the period of its Viceroyalty, however, political as well as economic factors combined to weaken them after independence. Both in Upper Peru and in the United Provinces of the Río de la Plata, as already shown, enthusiasm for perpetuating the northern boundaries of the Viceroyalty had quickly faded upon closer acquaintance. The unsuccessful liberating campaigns dispatched from Buenos Aires between 1810 and 1815 had brought significant numbers of Argentines into Upper Peru for the first time, and had served to emphasise the physical and cultural differences between the two areas. The military outcome of the campaigns was failure; the political sequel was to confirm the lack of cohesion between the central cordilleras and the plains, and to delimit Argentina's effective sphere of interest within its northern foothill zone.

After independence, Bolivia's trade links with Buenos Aires rapidly declined whilst those with the Pacific, never completely broken, regained their importance. The trails from the Pacific ports climbed into the high sierras by way of Cuzco, Arequipa or Tacna: supply centres, rest and acclimatising centres and oases punctuating the routes to and from the Titicaca basin and the mining areas beyond. As noted earlier, the Pacific ports had retained a substantial share of Upper Peru's trade despite its transfer to the Viceroyalty of the Río de la Plata in 1776. There was the legitimate dispatch of foodstuffs from Lower Peru, the through-trade in

---

[1] J. Lynch, *Spanish Colonial Administration, 1782–1810. The Intendant System in the Viceroyalty of the Río de la Plata*, London, 1958, p. 44.

[2] From statistics supplied to J. B. Pentland by the Bolivian Minister of Finance, 1827. *F.O. 61/12.*

imported manufactured goods, and the export of small quantities of minted gold and silver. Several officials also had continued to approach western centres in the Audiencia of Charcas by way of Arica, rather than undertake the 1500-mile journey from Buenos Aires. Commenting upon the revival and advantages of the Pacific routeways for the newly independent Upper Peru, C. M. Ricketts had reported from Lima in 1826:

> I speak of Arica and Arequipa together, as the trade of both places is chiefly connected with Bolivia, and as the foreign merchants who conduct it are the same individuals, though they reside at present at Arequipa.
>
> During the latter period of the Spaniards the trade of Arequipa was monopolized by a Spanish merchant, Cotero, owing to his influence with the Viceroy La Serna; and the consequence of the high prices which he charged on his goods was that the merchants of Buenos Aires were enabled to supply the articles required in Upper Peru at a cheaper rate. Since the trade has been declared free, and the port of Arica has been opened, the demand for European goods has been considerable, and has latterly still further increased by the blockade of the Río de la Plata.[1]

Significantly, throughout the colonial period, the *Lower* Peruvian ports from Islay, even from Pisco southward had been familiarly known and frequently designated as the ports of *Upper* Peru. The basis of the broad communications network with which Spain had loosely tied its land and sea empire for nearly three hundred years had been viceregal, and laid across many internal administrative divisions. Yet any assumption or impression that the well-established lines of movement of colonial times would automatically be maintained for an indefinite period across new international boundaries was rudely dispelled. Centuries of reliance upon the imperial routeways linking the mining centres, the *altiplano* and the Pacific coast had caused one vital factor to be largely overlooked. It was that the ports of Upper Peru, and Arica in particular, did not lie within the Audiencia of Charcas.

In 1825, however, it was generally assumed that Peru, i.e. Lower Peru, would cede the Pacific coast, from Arica southward, to Bolivia – in other words regularise politically the long-established colonial circulation pattern. Indeed, both British and United States diplomats in Lima, reporting the 1825 breakaway of Upper Peru, were confident that Bolivia's Pacific seaboard would be extended; Tudor even recommended a man for the new post which would be created in Arica when this port was transferred to Bolivian ownership.[2] Some of the hard facts of political

---

[1] C. M. Ricketts to George Canning, Lima, 27 December 1826, *F.O. 61/8*.

[2] P. W. Kelly to George Canning, 10 October 1825, *F.O. 61/6*; W. Tudor to Secretary of State Henry Clay, 23 February 1826, Consular Despatches from Lima, *General Records of the Department of State, National Archives, Record Group 59*, Washington, D.C.

independence were soon exposed, however, and nowhere was this more true than in the field of communications. Bolívar was opposed to any distortion of the boundary between the two Perus, and quite determined that Bolivia should not rearrange matters to suit itself; any violation of Lower Peru's rightful territorial claims was out of the question. As the suggested federation had proved unpalatable, and Upper Peru had voted to go its own way, then it would have to make the best of what could legally be salvaged from the colonial administrative boundaries.

Reasonably or otherwise, Bolívar was inevitably and bitterly blamed for this contretemps which marred the general euphoria of independence celebrations. In vain the Liberator was reminded that Arica was not just *a* port, it was *the* port. At the end of the most direct route down to the sea from the Bolivian *altiplano*, *via* the Tacna oasis, it continued to handle the bulk of the trade to and from La Paz, Cochabamba and the most densely populated sections of the country. Geographically a part, in the wider sense, of the Upper Peruvian region, Arica's sudden political amputation quickly came to be regarded by a number of Bolivians, in moments of candour, as a major disaster; and not only by Bolivians, but by many *ariqueños* also. The dependence was, after all, mutual. Arica had never been anything more than the port for Upper Peru. Although founded in 1535, its own growth began dramatically in 1546 after the discovery of Cerro Rico, and in 1574 it was officially designated by the Viceroy in Lima as the port of Potosí.

Thus, in 1825–6, Bolivia was confronted by the 'Problem of the Pacific' – how quickly it became known as this to those who had only just ceased to call themselves Upper Peruvians! The country's very first diplomatic mission was directed to Lima, but the offers for Arica made there fell upon deaf ears. Indeed, the failure of this errand contained a sombre portent for the future, since Bolivia was to bargain interminably for the cession, exchange or purchase of Arica from Peru or Chile for more than a century. The unavoidable fact remained, therefore, that Bolivia had perforce to select the least difficult site for a port within its own panhandle. Little success was ever achieved, however, in identifying as Bolivian this 350-mile section of the Pacific littoral before its absorption by Chile fifty-four years later. The panhandle port of Cobija never competed economically with Arica. Given the available methods of transport before the railway era, and the harsh nature of the intervening terrain between coast and cordillera, the overwhelming advantages of the *shortest* route between them proved unbeatable.

The problems of political and economic survival in Bolivia were not confined to the impracticability of legally inherited routeways, nor to the uncertainty over the legally inherited frontiers through which they passed. River courses and, to a lesser extent, mountain crests were heavily relied upon to give respectable definition to the Audiencia's perimeter, although most of this remained *terra incognita*, an oblivion of desolate peaks, desert, savanna, swamp and rain forest. With certain notable exceptions, such as the more densely populated Titicaca section, frontiers were almost completely unknown and unexplored, sparsely peopled, if not actually uninhabited, and remote from the Charcas core region which, to all intents and purposes, had nothing in common with any of them. To make matters worse, it was in the core region that some of the most serious difficulties of communication were to be found, and Bolivia's intrinsic problems of circulation and organisation emerged most clearly. The central Andes displayed little continuity in its settlement patterns. Although the mountains contained more than three-quarters of the total population, the inhabited areas were poorly connected, and remained separated from one another by steep, rugged, unoccupied tracts.

The principal colonial administrative centre of Chuquisaca owed its selection as the seat of the Audiencia of Charcas to its relative proximity to Potosí. The initial delimitation of the *audiencia*'s authority had traced a circular boundary centred upon Chuquisaca. Confirmed as the capital of Bolivia in 1825, however, Chuquisaca (Sucre) was not only very poorly located in relation to La Paz and the Pacific ports, but also extremely difficult to reach from other widely dispersed intermontane and piedmont centres in Upper Peru such as Cochabamba, Tarija and Santa Cruz. The mountain valleys sheltered their own small, discrete clusters of population within the most massive portions of the central Andes, here at their broadest extent in South America. Distinctive regional attitudes, emphasising the poverty of land communication, were already apparent during the colonial period despite an outward semblance of unity under Spain. The tedium and delay involved in travel between small, scattered mountain settlements was reflected, for example, in matters of routine organisation: 'In 1787, Intendant Viedma of Cochabamba explained that on his appointment as intendant he had had to decide between making a visitation, a task which in a province like Cochabamba would take two years, and pushing ahead with immediate problems of administration.'[1]

Movement within the central Andes, however, was not everywhere equally difficult and time-consuming. In Upper Peru, the severely dissected eastern sierras comprised by far the most isolated and inaccessible

[1] J. Lynch, *Spanish Colonial Administration*, p. 150.

portion of the cordilleras. Westward, the *altiplano* presented considerably less of an obstacle to movement, for although the plateau (12,000–13,000 feet) is much higher than the eastern valleys and intermontane basins, its topography offers little hindrance to long-distance passage, particularly along the eastern side. The *altiplano*, with its settlement-focus around the Titicaca basin, had provided a high, north–south corridor of communication within the Andes since pre-Columbian times, and during the colonial period it continued to channel the increased transverse movement – that between the mining and administrative centres lodged within the eastern sierras, and the staging posts and checkpoints strung along the trails to the Pacific ports. Despite the attention and prestige which had been accorded to Chuquisaca as the seat of the *audiencia* for nearly three hundred years, La Paz had long been the largest city in Bolivia when the country achieved its independence.

Subsequently, political rivalry between the plateau and the intermontane centres increased. Cochabamba attempted a compromise: 'it is in contemplation to make Cochabamba the capital', wrote Ricketts of Bolivia in 1826. 'It is more central, it has a ready communication with Arica, its climate is mild and it has long been the granary of Upper Peru.'[1] The advantages of shorter trails to La Paz and the Pacific had contributed to Cochabamba's growth; the size of its population, estimated at 30,000 in 1826–7, compared favourably with that of La Paz (est. 40,000), and emphasised the very limited development that Chuquisaca (est. 12,000) had been able to achieve.[2] The latter was to struggle unsuccessfully throughout the nineteenth century against the growing political and commerical dominance of La Paz – a dominance which was eventually confirmed by new railway links between the *altiplano* and the Pacific coast.

The disintegrative forces within the Bolivian highland core area quickly became stronger and more apparent once the common objective of independence from Spain had been accomplished. When applied to Bolivia, therefore, Ratzel's theme of the 'State-Idea' – a body of traditions and clearly defined purposes to which the majority of the population willingly subscribe, and which help to unify and distinguish a group of people within a politically organised nation-state – clearly underlines the lack of stability and fresh, positive direction encountered by the newly independent Upper Peru. Simply to draw the map of a State, Ratzel observed, gives not the slightest hint of the political idea which inspires it, and which furthers the progressive organisation of the territory through ever-closer integration of

[1] C. M. Ricketts to George Canning, Lima, 30 May 1826, *F.O. 61/7*.
[2] Population estimates, see above, p. 18 n. 2.

the land and the people. There is need for the population as a whole to support, and gain fellow-feeling (*Gemütlichkeit*) from a unifying concept and purpose; where serious conflict of spirit, of ethos exists, the cohesion of the body politic is completely destroyed. 'The strongest States', Ratzel concluded, 'are those in which the political idea completely fills the body of the State in all its parts. Those sections of the State in which the idea does not gain acceptance fall away.'[1]

In the case of Bolivia, the winning of independence had fulfilled the one outstanding political purpose evident within Upper Peru. Subsequent unanimity, or comparative unanimity of aim and outlook, involving Bolivia as a whole, was very much more difficult to achieve. There was pronounced cultural as well as physical diversity; few policies commanded widespread loyalty or support. Creole rivalry and separatist aspirations within the country remained divisive elements. Indeed, the failure of further separatist movements in Bolivia after independence owed more to the lack of encouragement they received from contiguous States than to any positive and successful internal organisation.

Under these circumstances, the core area could do little to withstand the disintegrative forces on the perimeter. Highland Bolivia forms a complex watershed region, deeply scored by headwaters of the great Amazon and Paraguay–Paraná river systems whose middle and lower courses have always lain outside Bolivian territory (Fig. 2). Given the inadequacy of internal communications, the economic effects of these waterways, despite their navigational hazards, tended to become centrifugal rather than centripetal. Physically, the asymmetry of the principal continental divide results in nine-tenths of Bolivia draining towards the Atlantic; even the city of La Paz, astonishingly, lies within the Amazon basin. But at the same time, proximity to the Pacific seaboard dictates that Bolivia be classed and regarded as a Pacific state. Penetration of lowland Bolivia – the ultramontane tract – was to be most successfully achieved by *up*stream rather than *down*stream movement; movement upstream by way of the extensive middle courses of the Amazon and Paraguay systems, and controlled by the countries that contained them. Bolivia was not alone in experiencing this pressure from the riverine States beyond its own ill-defined frontiers. Nor was it a characteristic only of the post-Revolutionary period, for the position of the San Ildefonso line as delimited in 1777 between Spanish and Portuguese territory clearly acknowledged Portugal's domination of the Amazon and middle Paraguay river routes. Admittedly it was always a

[1] Friedrich Ratzel, *Politische Geographie, oder die Geographie der Staaten, des Verkehres und des Krieges*, Munich and Berlin, 2nd edit., 1903, pp. 3–8, *passim*.

tenuous line of movement punctuated by forts and trading posts, but it was significantly related for much of its length to the Amazon watershed, and to the Madeira–Guaporé and the Paraguay river courses. As such, the Ildefonso line often combined the functions of both frontier and routeway, a combination potentially troublesome for many of the successor States to the Spanish empire in their subsequent relations with Brazil.

Exposed, therefore, by the very events of 1825, Bolivia's location resulted in its subsequent external policies being dominated, rightly or wrongly, by the struggle to secure ports and establish practicable outlets to the sea. For a weak buffer State this would have been a sufficient task, but the twin dilemma presented by Bolivia's essentially Andean location was that the securing of outlets directly to the sea or to the continent's major navigable waterways would at the same time involve it in the control and organisation of the most remote and alien sections of its national territory. Efforts to establish routes to the sea, and efforts to sustain historical claims to peripheral areas were facets of the same problem. As long as these peripheral areas remained unknown, unexplored wastes of desert, rain forest or savanna scrub, the inherent weakness of Bolivia's position was to some extent concealed. Fringe areas could provide frontiers of separation, conveniently insulating rival national interests. Indeed, for the stronger powers, there were obvious advantages to be gained in the avoidance of detailed boundary decisions until more was known of the frontiers' economic potential. Where these regions, and the routes they contained, acquired economic and thus political significance, however, former wastelands were reappraised and *de jure* claims to ownership had to be supported by a degree of internal territorial organisation which Bolivia could never produce. The exploitation of guano, nitrate, rubber and petroleum were all at some stage to become economic flashpoints on Bolivia's borderlands, and emphasis tended to shift from the ports and routeways vital for Bolivia's trade to the sudden economic revenue the frontiers could yield when the world shopped for their resources. Even so, the two interests were linked, often inseparably. Despite the considerable geographical contrasts of terrain and environment characterising Bolivia's outlets to the Pacific, to the Amazon, and to the Paraguay–Paraná routeways, and despite marked contrasts in the timing and development of the various economic *bonanzas*, it is the similarities between them which, in the overall view, stand out most clearly. The facts differ only in detail.

In the years shortly after independence, preoccupation with the Pacific outlet did not lead to the eastern borderlands being completely ignored.

Bolivia's own small population remained concentrated within the Andes, but the immigration of foreign settlers into 'the fertile but extensive deserts of the interior' was officially encouraged under various administrations. It was stressed, for example, that these far-flung peripheral wastelands had the advantage of greater proximity to Europe. At irregular intervals between 1830 and 1930 a variety of European and North American colonization projects in the Oriente were enthusiastically supported by Bolivia. The majority involved settlement or homesteading schemes, steamboat navigation or railway construction, and were frequently influenced in their aims and dreams by the enviably successful westward expansion of the nineteenth-century frontier of settlement in the United States. Many of the Bolivian schemes, in context, were astonishingly ambitious and disastrously impractical. Some, although these were in fact a minority, were never designed to be more than temporary concessions for the brief but intensive 'get in, get out' type of economic exploitation, rather than for permanent agriculturally based settlement. But both in their timing and their location on or near Bolivia's periphery, such European and North American schemes frequently became the test cases of boundary claims, and the triggers of subsequent boundary conflict.

Even the modest initial programme of eastern exploration and navigation mounted or supported by the Bolivian Government in the 1830–50 period was, however, viewed with scepticism by the British Vice-Consul in Chuquisaca (Sucre). Future European traffic up and down the rivers of Bolivia he regarded as totally absurd, and its encouragement as entirely mischievous.

He reported:

A mighty fuss is made about the navigation of the rivers of Bolivia, but that consummation so devoutly to be desired is far, very far, from realisation. The rivers rise, it is true, in Bolivia, but not one of their mouths in the Paraguay, Paraná or Amazons, belong to this republic...and the neighbouring states are decidely opposed to the conclusion of treaties for the arrangement of river navigation... The Bolivian Government is *highly culpable* in permitting its agents to conclude contracts with foreigners for navigating the Amazons, *not a drop of whose waters belongs to Bolivia.*

Earlier, he had informed London: 'Be assured that nothing awaits emigrants in Bolivia but sorrow and hopeless disappointment...they will not only plunge into a sea of trouble themselves, but entail on their descendants the miseries inseparable from a state of society proceeding from bad to worse.'[1]

[1] C. Masterton to J. Bidwell, Chuquisaca, 13 May 1843 and 8 January 1843, *F.O. 11/1* and *F.O. 126/11.*

It was quite clear that the colonization projects depended, apart from anything else, on navigation of the interior waterways, and this in turn depended on the permissive attitudes of Brazil, Paraguay and Argentina. The attempts made by Bolivia to delegate economic development of its territory to foreign concession were strenuously resisted by the surrounding States. Brazil was not alone in projecting an early and determinedly national (even nationalist) interest in the future exploitation of resources close to its own borders, and these interests effectively discouraged Bolivia's tentative efforts to introduce European and North American agents into peripheral areas. While other neighbours pursued similar policies in this respect, however, the fact remained that virtually half the Bolivian perimeter was flanked by Brazilian territory. Although the line of separation of Spanish and Portuguese interests in the Americas had originally been placed far to the east, it was in the upper Paraguay and, more especially, in the upper Amazon basin that the interests of Brazil and the Spanish successor States would eventually collide. 'Brazil, unfortunately, borders upon all our states', wrote Bolívar in 1825. The vigour with which Bolivia could pursue settlement and navigation schemes was limited, the timing of international agreements on waterways was unpropitious and, in consequence, foreign colonization projects for Bolivia's eastern lands were stillborn. It quickly became evident that future economic development and territorial security in the South American interior, as on the west coast, would remain in the hands of the South American States themselves or, if delegated, would still reflect their relative strengths in controlling major routeways – whether to the Atlantic or Pacific seaboard.

Thus the readjustment of old colonial frontiers,[1] ill-defined and largely undemarcated as they were, demonstrated more sharply perhaps than any other single indicator the influence of communications upon the emerging balance of power in South America during the nineteenth and twentieth centuries. Inevitably, individual sovereignty was to emphasise spatial relationships on a national basis far more distinctly than colonial groups, broadly unified under the Spanish Crown, had ever done. In the disastrously protracted period of boundary disputes which ensued, no new nation remained immune, while Bolivia's own unsuccessful involvement with its neighbours became total.

[1] Frontier implies a *zone*, boundary a *line*.

CHAPTER 2

THE WESTERN SECTOR: ROUTES
TO THE PACIFIC

BOLIVIA'S RELATIONS WITH CHILE AND PERU

In 1825, Bolivia could claim approximately 350 miles of the 5000-mile Pacific coast of South America. Maps of the Spanish colonial period had placed the southern limit of the Audiencia of Charcas' littoral province variously along the river Salado (26° 20' S), or the river Copiapó (27° 20' S), although there was frequent confusion over the placing of the rivers and the parallels. The 1833 Constitution of Chile declared vaguely that its territory extended 'from the desert of Atacama to Cape Horn'.[1] Notwithstanding this obvious ambiguity, the mouth of the Salado river appears to have been the most generally accepted southern limit of Bolivian territory (Fig. 3). Yet there were further problems and uncertainties in the early years of independence. Chile was able to claim a zone some eighty miles north of the Salado since a small group of Chilean fishermen and graziers had settled at Paposo (25° S) at the very beginning of the nineteenth century, and had been placed under Chilean jurisdiction. Just over twenty miles south of Paposo was Hueso Parado – the Vertical Bone or Stone. At this point, it was claimed, a whale's rib or jaw-bone had been set upright in the ground to mark the nearby boundary of the river Salado, but as the mouth of this river lies about sixty miles farther south, it seems likely, if indeed any connexion existed between them at all, that Hueso Parado gave no more than a general indication of the frontier, though it may have helped to locate Paposo.[2] Nevertheless, perhaps the most realistic limit of effective Chilean settlement at independence was the well-watered valley of Copiapó at 27° 20' S. Chile evinced little interest north of this point except for the tiny Paposo cluster and a few scattered copper workings.

[1] Certain Chilean writers, e.g. Jaime Eyzaguirre, *Chile y Bolivia: esquema de un proceso diplomático*, Santiago, 1963, have stated that no Pacific outlet was inherited by Bolivia on the basis of *uti possidetis de jure 1810*, and that the coastal strip was included for the first time at independence. This argument must, however, be rejected on the ground that the Intendancy of Potosí extended through a part of the Atacama desert to the Pacific after 1782.

[2] Investigation of the coast at Hueso Parado suggests that the name is more likely to have been derived from a steep fold in the rocks clearly visible off-shore and which, from a distance, resembles the shape of a whale's rib or jaw-bone.

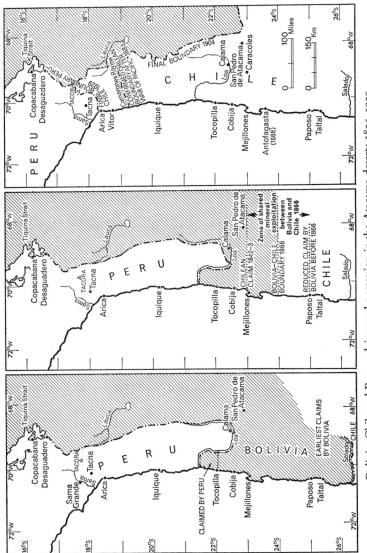

3 Bolivia, Chile and Peru – claims and possession in the Atacama desert: 1825–1929

Bolivia's frontier with Peru, by contrast, was extensive and even in that southern section, considered here as part of Bolivia's western sector boundary, it included highly varied terrain between the Titicaca shores, the cordilleran peaks and the sea. The desert boundary was generally accepted to be the river Loa, although Peru had laid a claim to the coast as far south as Tocopilla. The Loa opens a steep cleft in the almost featureless scarp of the Coast Range (El Sistema Cordillerano de la Costa) and has always formed an easily discernible landmark to shipping (Plate 1). As movement overland across the wastes of Atacama was negligible, movement coastwise assumed considerably more importance, so that the deep gullies which at rare intervals slash the Coast Range were an obvious choice for territorial delimitation.[1] Inland, the river Loa possessed an additional advantage for, as the only permanent stream to cross the Atacama in nearly five hundred miles, it could serve as a useful interior boundary between Bolivia and Peru. Its gorge, floored by a narrow glaucous ribbon of scrub vegetation, is frequently incised seventy feet or more below the barren surface, and today still provides a striking break in the monotony of miles of unrelieved desert. The Loa thus fulfilled the important role of an existing, continuous and instantly recognisable feature demarcating the wasteland. North of the Loa, the old frontier between Upper and Lower Peru followed the central chain of peaks and principal watershed in the Cordillera Occidental before descending to the source of the Desaguadero.

Bolivia thus claimed a broad desert corridor between the Loa and Salado rivers in which more precise boundary definition was judged unnecessary, as well as impossible, given the ignorance of the terrain. Not surprisingly, the Atacama was shunned in favour of more congenial environments and formed an insulating zone of negative country shared unequally and uncompetitively between Peru, Bolivia and Chile. The physical aspects of this Pacific littoral were, and still are, harsh and uncompromising. The steep fault scarp of the Coast Range soars abruptly out of the ocean to

[1] The significance of the location and shape of these gullies along an almost uninhabited coast is shown, for example, in the excellent sketches made by officers of the *Beagle* survey, and others, 'to assist in the identification of the ship's position along the most featureless sections of the Pacific coast'. These sketches accompany the carefully annotated 'Survey of the West Coast of South America: Chile, Bolivia and Peru', by Capt. Robert Fitzroy, R.N. and officers of *H.M.S. Beagle* in 1836 (with plans and other later additions to 1894). Sheets IX, X and XI show the coast of Bolivia at the time of the 1835/6 survey, *B.M. Map Collection SEC. 10 (1276); ibid. (1277); ibid. (1278); ibid. (1301).*

A chart of this coast published for the Admiralty by James Imray, London, in 1851 marks the Chile–Bolivia boundary at Hueso Parado in Nuestra Señora bay, and the Bolivia–Peru boundary at the Loa river mouth, *B.M. Map Collection 83100 (2).*

plateau levels of between approximately 3000 feet and 6000 feet, and rarely concedes any point of easy exchange between land and sea. Although marine terraces occasionally offer some slight modification of slope, the gradient is almost everywhere severe. Access to the interior, as noted earlier, is restricted to the remarkably few openings through this great longitudinal tabular range, either by valley or low-altitude pass. Few of the early anchorages could be dignified by the name of port. Shipping had mostly to lie in dangerously open roadsteads or shallow coastal indentations, pounded by strong south and south-west winds and heavy seas, so that traffic between ship and shore by lighter and raft remained a perilous undertaking.

Hazard was further increased by the shortage of wood and water for ships' supplies – in fact their absence in some instances rendered valueless an otherwise possible anchorage since the Atacama is unquestionably one of the driest regions on earth. Along the immediate coastal fringe, temperatures are somewhat reduced by the regular sea breeze blowing by day from a surface cooled by the Peru Oceanic and Coastal currents[1]. These cold currents, particularly the irregular swirls of the Peru Coastal current close inshore, are also responsible for the development of advection mist and fog (known in Peru as *garúa* and in Chile as *camanchaca*) which form locally during the low-sun season, occasionally lifted by turbulence as a dense stratus pall less than 2000 feet above sea level, and maintained for long, dismal spells under a pronounced upper-air inversion. Darwin described the bleak conditions he encountered along this coast in July, referring in particular to a six-weeks' sojourn in Callao: 'A dull heavy bank of clouds constantly hung over the land...during almost every day of our visit there was a thick drizzling mist, which was sufficient to make the streets muddy and one's clothes damp: this the people are pleased to call Peruvian dew.'[2] Where persistent, this moisture supports a thin cloud

[1] *Rainfall*: Antofagasta averages (although this has little real meaning in such an environment) $\frac{1}{2}''$ (12 mm.) annually. Arica averages $\frac{1}{40}''$ (0.5 mm.) annually.

Temperature: °F (°C) monthly average:

	Jan.	Feb.	Mar.	Apr.	May	June
Antofagasta	70 (21)	70 (21)	68 (20)	64 (18)	61 (16)	59 (15)
Arica	70 (21)	71 (22)	70 (21)	68 (20)	64 (18)	63 (17)

	July	Aug.	Sept.	Oct.	Nov.	Dec.
Antofagasta	57 (14)	57 (14)	59 (15)	61 (16)	64 (18)	67 (19.5)
Arica	61 (16)	61 (16)	62 (17)	65 (18.5)	67 (19.5)	68 (20)

[2] Charles Darwin, *Journal of Researches into the Geology and Natural History of the various countries visited by H.M.S. Beagle under the Command of Captain Fitzroy, R.N. from 1832 to 1836*, London, 1839, p. 446.

3-2

flora and is responsible for a few high-level oases perched on the Coast Range, of which the grazing grounds belonging to the early Chilean settlement at Paposo was one (Plate 1).

From maximum heights of over 7000 feet, the Coast Range descends eastwards relatively gradually, when compared with its steep Pacific front, to the interior *pampa*, a continuation of the longitudinal valley of central Chile. Here, without the coastal fog or cloud, aridity is almost total. Streams from the Andean foothills disappear into its surface. Huge fans of detrital material, seamed by gullies, form rugged country along the margins of the *pampa*, white glistening *salares* shimmer in the heat, and cinder cones and lava flows compose a landscape both stark and unyielding.

1. COBIJA...OR ARICA?

The very nature and location of the Atacama had always made it more of a barrier than the comparatively narrow width would suggest. Mileage alone gives little indication of the true sense of physical and mental separation which has always existed between the *altiplano* settlements and the sea. As far as Bolivia was concerned, this separation was aggravated by the long oblique approach to the Pacific across the panhandle. The coast itself was practically uninhabited. Cobija, huddled on a low marine bench at 22° 32′ S, had originally been founded in 1587 as Santa María Magdalena de Cobija, a tiny seamen's sanctuary on a particularly inhospitable stretch of shoreline. It soon became deserted, but was re-established early in the eighteenth century as a customs control-point for the silver export from Potosí, a small part of which would occasionally be carried by mule train down to Cobija, a journey of nearly six hundred miles. Its importance had steadily declined, however, until after independence, and following a preliminary reconnaissance, Bolívar designated Cobija as Bolivia's Pacific port.

Sucre, President of the new Republic, had been instructed to survey the coastal strip inherited from the Audiencia of Charcas, and his aide Burdett O'Connor investigated the littoral in 1825 at Sucre's direction:

There are three ports and of these you may select the best. They are Atacama (or Cobija), Mejillones and Loa. The first two have no water and the last, as it is a river, is said to have no depth. This, however, is the one that the Liberator prefers, because the river is there and because it is the nearest to Potosí. Should it not be desirable, you will survey the other two, or any other, with a view to establishing thereat a large city.

Upon O'Connor's return, Sucre duly reported back to Bolívar:

> O'Connor arrived yesterday and informed me that he estimates it will cost 120,000 pesos to supply Cobija with water, and a further sum to construct a waggon road to within 20 leagues of Potosí – about 300,000 pesos in all. It will be advantageous if you can inform the Peruvian Congress of our desire for the cession of Arica, emphasising that Arica is a port which functions solely as a point of access to Bolivia.[1]

Sucre's persistent requests to Bolívar, urging him to reconsider the Arica 'question', merely evoked the response that clearly, outside Bolivia, no such question existed. Sucre was peremptorily roused to set about the improvement of Cobija, henceforth to be known, the Liberator decided, by the additional name of Puerto La Mar, in honour of General José de la Mar of Guayaquil, a hero in the wars of independence. Beyond dispatching one government official and a small army garrison down to Cobija, however, Sucre expended no more effort in its direction. In May 1826, he again wrote to Bolívar: 'The port of La Mar (Cobija) will open with more sensation than actual benefit...Bolivia's acquisition of Arica is of the utmost importance. It will be a magnificent port for Bolivia, especially with a good road to Cochabamba. But if Peru retains it, we may declare Cobija a free port which will cause Arica to decline.'[2] Despite the ominous sound of this last thrust, it was stated without conviction and received imperturbably in Lima.

As soon as Bolívar had left Peru, Sucre sought a quick resolution to the problem of Bolivia's Pacific outlet with the proposal that Bolivia's frontier with Peru be shifted northward from the Loa for about two hundred and fifty miles to Cape Sama at 18° S. This and other suggestions were incorporated in a treaty signed on 15 November 1826.[3] From 18° S, the suggested boundary was to follow the river Sama as far as the town of Sama Grande, proceeding thence by the deep ravine to the Tacora range. Investigation reveals contradictions and ignorance of the actual ground here, and it is obvious that this early delimitation was pegged to a few points easily recognisable from a distance, without detailed exploration. Beyond Sama Grande, the deep Estique ravine runs, not to the Tacora range, but into the Cordillera de Barroso, rising to nearly 17,000 feet. The Cordillera de Tacora lies beyond, well separated by the Piscullani gorge. Tacora's magnificent volcanic cone, however, nearly 20,000 feet above

---

1 Sucre to Bolívar, Chuquisaca, 27 January 1826, *Cartas de Sucre al Libertador*, vol. I, *1820–1826*, edit. D. F. O'Leary, Madrid, 1919, p. 390. Other references to Arica are made in letters from Potosí dated 28 February and 9 March 1826, *ibid.* pp. 400 and 404.

2 Sucre to Bolívar, Chuquisaca, 11 May 1826, *ibid.* vol. II, *1826–1830*, pp. 8–9.

3 *F.O. 11/1.* See also Jaime Mendoza, *El Mar del Sur*, Sucre, Boliva, 1926, pp. 44–7.

sea level, dominates the whole mountain group in this region and is easily visible through a col in the Cordillera de Barroso. Tacora provided the essential peak on which the boundary was to pivot towards Lake Titicaca; it was merely that the surrounding complex of ranges and gorges was unknown, and therefore confounded attempts even at accurate delimitation in such rugged terrain. Beyond Tacora, the boundary was to trace the old provincial division between Pacajes (Bolivia) and Chucuito (Peru) as far as Lake Huiñaimarca, the southern extension of Titicaca and the source of the Desaguadero river. Peru was to take the whole of Lake Titicaca north of the Tiquina Strait, together with the Copacabana peninsula, and part of the unexplored *montaña* forest country in Apolobamba or Caupolicán province.

By this arrangement, Bolivia would have gained not only the port of Arica but the provinces of Tacna and Tarapacá as well, thereby laying claim to some six hundred miles of Pacific seaboard between 18° S and 26° 20′ S (river Salado). The promise of 5 million pesos payable by Bolivia to overseas creditors, fortified by territorial adjustments in Peru's favour at Lake Titicaca and beyond, did nothing to alter the fact that the proposals were regarded, not surprisingly, with extreme disfavour in Lima, and Peru, under Andrés Santa Cruz, refused to ratify the treaty in December 1826. Thwarted first by Bolívar and then by Santa Cruz, in what both considered meddlesome interference on Bolivia's part, Sucre may well have begun to doubt the wisdom of his own impetuous decision to champion an independent Upper Peru under circumstances he now found he could not change. In 1827, Sucre toyed with the idea of a Federal League between Bolivia, Chile and Argentina and a statement to this effect was published by the Bolivian Government on 4 April of that year;[1] but neither Santiago nor Buenos Aires responded.

In the critical early years of Bolivia's independence, however, it seemed on more than one occasion that Arica and Tacna might, after all, be incorporated into the country with which their economic ties were already well established. As late as 1836, the port still declared, 'La ciudad de Arica en la parte que le toca se une a la Nación Boliviana y forma una porción de su familia.'[2] Peru's refusal to ratify the November 1826 treaty was followed by a period of strained relations and open hostility during the next thirteen years while Sucre's successor, Andrés Santa Cruz, held the political reins in Bolivia. Elected in 1828, after Sucre's withdrawal, the former President of Peru thus became the new President of Bolivia and it

[1] *F.O. 61/11.*
[2] *Acta de Arica*, 25 March 1836. (See Jaime Mendoza, *El Mar del Sur*, p. 93.)

was soon apparent that Santa Cruz' ideals of a confederation between the two Perus conformed much more closely with Bolívar's than with those of his immediate predecessor.

Santa Cruz, Bolivian by birth, had initially remained loyal to Spain during the early years of the revolutionary wars, but abandoned the Crown in favour of Bolívar in 1821. His record as a military strategist was uneven but his administrative ability was unquestioned. His determination upon taking office in Chuquisaca to establish a confederation between Bolivia and Peru was substantially aided by the protracted period of political intrigue and unrest in the latter. Armies were still at strength after the wars of independence from Spain; men were mobile and ready for action, their marshals impatient for political as well as military power. In 1828, the Peruvian General Gamarra crossed the Desaguadero on a marauding expedition to eradicate Colombian troops still remaining in Bolivia, and found many pro-Peru sympathisers in and around La Paz. There, threats of a breakaway became more frequent and a few years later Peruvian exiles in La Paz were causing so much trouble that the Bolivian Government ordered their removal to Cochabamba, with the decree that such exiles must not remain within a hundred leagues of the Bolivia–Peru boundary. But in 1828, sporadic fighting achieved little, and treaties were drawn up in July 1828 and again in August and November 1831.[1]

None of these settlements, however, involved any transfer of Arica to Bolivia. Santa Cruz' request for the port by exchange or purchase, made early in 1831, was refused and thereafter abandoned. Instead, he proposed that Arica should remain available to both countries. In the treaty decisions to appoint a Joint Commission for the purpose of drawing a topographical map of the southern zone and compiling a statistical record of the settlement found within it, it was clear that both parties referred only to the Titicaca basin, not to the remote Atacama section of the Peru–Bolivia frontier. While for President Sucre, the desert had focused the problems of Bolivia's 'southern frontier', for Santa Cruz the southern frontier now stopped short for all practical purposes of negotiation on the *altiplano*. There, the comparatively dense settlement, pre-dating the Spanish era, provided features unique along the entire Bolivian perimeter. The Titicacan shore, the plateau and associated foothills were carefully divided and terraced by the Indian communities and creole landowners, property boundary cairns were already part of the landscape, and grazing rights were strictly observed. Under these circumstances, precision was called for – generalisations and astronomical lines would not do. Both

---

[1] At Piquisa, Tiquina and Arequipa, *F.O. 61/14* and *F.O. 61/19*.

countries agreed that the boundary should be drawn along easily recognisable physical features and that adjustment and exchange of land, reciprocally agreed upon, would have to be made so that the physical boundary could be continuous. But even so, times were too uncertain, other problems were more pressing, and no action resulted from the decision to map the frontier across the *altiplano*.

More significantly, there was neither action nor intention to institute any further demands for Arica, for Santa Cruz was imbued with a vision – myopic, his critics considered – in which Bolivia formed but a part of the much greater whole. Accordingly, Santa Cruz launched a series of determined efforts to build up Cobija, visiting it in 1832, even residing there for a period in 1833, and endeavouring to keep its needs before the National Assembly. He remained, nevertheless, one of the very few Bolivians who had ever seen, or indeed would ever see, the port. In 1831 he addressed the delegates:

The political existence of Bolivia was problematical whilst it was unprovided with a convenient port...The Government therefore directed its earnest attention to the formation of such a port, undismayed by obstacles which appeared to be insurmountable. A local Coast Authority was established by a decree. The contributions paid by the inhabitants and the proceeds of the Customs have been appropriated to the levelling of the roads, the erection of a pier, and the warehouses and other buildings necessary for business and the encouragement of a population. Peculiar and exclusive advantages have been held out by the Customs house regulations in order to attract merchants to Cobija, and various measures have been adopted for the establishment of posts and for facilitating the transport and conveyance of goods...In the year 1830 no less than three-quarters of our articles of consumption were entered at that port... and very beneficial and important results may reasonably be expected from it hereafter. I must not omit to inform you that, believing it to be desirable both for the encouragement of the port and the benefit of the Republic to attract industrious foreigners to settle amongst us, I have declared that they shall receive such special protection as all good men are entitled to.

This last statement was to gain a sombre significance in the next few decades.

Some of the more immediate results of the President's efforts to develop Cobija, however, as well as the difficulties encountered there, are recorded in a brief but valuable description of the Bolivian port in 1831–2 made by a visiting United States naval surgeon.[1] Noting the difficulty not only of landing at Cobija but even of finding the port from sightings along the coast, Ruschenberger continued his narrative once ashore:

---

[1] W. S. W. Ruschenberger, *Three Years in the Pacific: including notices of Brazil, Chile, Bolivia and Peru*, Philadelphia, 1834, pp. 163–74.

We walked towards the governor's house, which fronts the landing, and turning to the left, found ourselves in the main and only street of Cobija. It is perhaps a quarter of a mile long, but not closely built. The houses are all one story high, and constructed of wood and of adobes in the simplest style, and very few of them have patios. The plastering is mixed with salt water, and very soon blisters and peels off, from the effects of the sun, and therefore constant repair is necessary. Wood, all of which is brought from Chiloe and Concepcion, is a cheaper material for building than adobes, both on account of repairs and the original cost. A great proportion of the houses are occupied as stores, where a great variety of foreign goods, both European and American, are exposed for sale...

The oldest building here is a church, said to have been erected a hundred and fifty years ago. It is built of adobes of a small size...a temple very small and mean in appearance, which opens to the sea by the only door in the building, which is double, and secured by a common padlock; in fact, unless attention were called to it, it would be overlooked as some stable.

Amongst the inconveniences of this port, perhaps the greatest is the scarcity of water, which is barely sufficient for the daily consumption of the present small population, and even this is so brackish, that strangers are unable to drink it without a pretty free admixture of wine or spirits...The springs from which it is obtained are in the side of the hill and secured by lock and key, except a small tube of the size of a gun barrel, from which a stream as large as a swan quill issues; and this is carefully stopped when not running into the bottles or other vessels of those who come for water. At the end of the street, and within ten yards of the surf, is a well, said to contain the best water in the place: this the governor has appropriated to his own use, and that of the garrison, not exceeding in all, servants included, fifty persons. About a half a mile from the town is a spring, which is used for washing and for watering the cattle. A barrel of sweet water from Valparaiso or Peru is esteemed no small present, and the favor is frequently asked of vessels arriving in the port...

There is a tavern here, where all the foreign residents eat...Some idea of the trouble of housekeeping may be had from a knowledge of the fact that everything, except butcher's meat, is brought from Chile and Peru. Every vessel, particularly the coasters from both countries, brings large quantities of vegetables and livestock for this market, and a part of that is sent off to the interior! Meat and fodder for the cattle are brought from Calama; and between it and the coast, I am told, there is not a habitation, a tree, nor a blade of grass, nor a spring of wholesome water!

Ruschenberger recorded Cobija's population in 1831–2 at between six and seven hundred persons, although this included copper miners working in the immediate vicinity. Following President Santa Cruz' directives to divert business to the port, the writer noted that an estimated half a million dollars-worth of foreign imports had passed through Cobija in a year, bound for the interior: mostly European dry goods, cottons, silks, quicksilver, flour, tobacco, teas, wines and American 'domestics'. The duties were low and the possibility of making Cobija an entirely free port was being urged by President and Congress. All kinds of provisions, Ruschenberger observed, except luxuries such as wine, were already admitted free of tax. Manufactured goods, such as furniture and American cottons paid an *ad valorem* duty of 10 per cent, which was the highest duty levied in the port at that time; silks and similar goods paid 5 per cent. Exports from Cobija, however, remained very limited – only small quantities of copper and copper ores, together with a little coined gold and silver, on which a 2 per cent duty was charged. Bullion export remained illegal. Nevertheless, for a while, Arica's trade suffered a setback.

The improved fortunes of Cobija in the early 1830s, though precarious, had prompted President Santa Cruz to deliver a glowingly optimistic report to Congress in 1834, following his tour of inspection of the desert panhandle made in the previous year:

The Litoral and the port of Cobija have made rapid progress in every respect... Their population and institutions have wonderfully increased, and by the impulse already given, we may indulge the hope that before 10 years have elapsed the province will become one of the richest in the Republic. The copper of its mines is one of its most valuable productions. The Government, which has been always convinced of the necessity of maintaining a secure means of communication with the exterior, has continually afforded Cobija the assistance to which it is so much entitled and which may be considered as indispensable to our very independence.

As time went on, however, repeated assurances as to the steady progress of Cobija were in fact quite groundless. The population of the entire Bolivian desert province in the late 1830s and 1840s was probably not more than five thousand, and at most only about one-fifth of these lived permanently in the port.[1] Oasis settlement lay in the desert interior, its major axis along the Andean foothills, where villages were located close to the the short snow-fed mountain torrents, or at well sites above a water-table often no more than four feet below the surface. 'So far as their daily life is concerned, the coast might as well be a thousand as a hundred miles away', wrote Isaiah Bowman in 1924, finding the pattern of centuries still persisting.[2] Chief among these wet-point settlements was San Pedro de Atacama, 8000 feet above sea level and one of the oldest settlements in the desert. It lay on a traditional north–south line of movement, which had

---

[1] There is no general agreement as to the designation, as Province or as Department, of Boliva's Atacama region at this time. Initially, the province, *El Litoral*, was upgraded to Department status by President Santa Cruz' decree of 1 July 1829. The Bolivian Constitution of 1831, however, still refers to the *Provincia Litoral*. The creation of the Department is recorded again in 1839, while on 9 June 1843 the British Vice-Consul in Chuquisaca (Sucre) informed London that Cobija had 'henceforth' been made a Department, and that the port itself contained about 1000 souls. *F.O. 11/1*.

The first National Census of Bolivia was undertaken at the direction of Andrés Santa Cruz in 1831, and recorded a population of 1,088,768. In 1845, the census figure was 1,378,896 (Archives, Dirección General de Estadística y Censos).

[2] Isaiah Bowman, *Desert Trails of Atacama*, American Geog. Soc. Special Publication No. 5, New York, 1924, p. 64.

been important in pre-colonial times and which had been followed by Spanish *conquistador* penetration into Chile.

Apart from the foothill oases, a few scattered settlements lay on the river Loa. Although its water tends to be saline, it can be used for irrigation at selected localities and of these, Calama was an important victualling and mule supply-centre three days inland along the Cobija–Potosí trail. Its function in this connexion meant that, whilst a site on the right bank of the Loa strictly placed it inside Peruvian territory, the town and its region were more usually regarded as Bolivian. Map-makers, in consequence, frequently positioned the whole of the middle and upper Loa region inside the Bolivian panhandle (Fig. 3 b).[1] After independence, however, emphasis was placed upon the coast, and the significance of the interior settlements was measured by their contribution to the survival of one much more precariously situated. Cobija, for instance, still lacked one essential; although brackish water could be obtained from the well close to shore and from the few springs behind the town, it was all virtually undrinkable. During the colonial period, casks of water had always been imported coastwise, or carried from the interior oases of Calama and San Pedro de Atacama, whenever a brief period of activity connected with a silver shipment occurred. These practices were forced to continue since Cobija's water supply remained totally inadequate – 'the trail into the miserable little village is marked only by the carcasses of asses, mules and horses lying in the drifting sand' commented one traveller. Even from the sea, as Ruschenberger had observed, the port was difficult to find, its site constricted and backed by no clear landmarks. The approach recommended in the *Beagle* survey, illustrated by appropriate sketches (Plate I), ran: 'Cobija bay is not easily distinguished at a distance, the mountains behind it (2000–3000 feet) affording no sufficiently marked feature to point out the position of the town at their base. Hence it is recommended to make the coast some miles south and run down close in until the houses are seen.'[2]

[1] For example, Hugo Reck's *Mapa Topográfico de la Altiplanicie Central de Bolivia, trabajado en los años 1860–1 para el proyecto de Canalización y Ferrocarril a la Costa del Océano Pacífico*, San Joaquin, 1862. This records a scheme for a navigable channel to link the river Desaguadero, Lake Poopó, the river Lacajahuira and Lake Coipasa to a railway terminating at Iquique.

[2] Well over a century later, a modern instruction manual adds little to this: 'the orange-coloured church with two white octagonal towers is an excellent mark, it looks like a large shed. There is a small pier in need of repair. Landing is dangerous when a heavy swell is running...but in any case the town is practically deserted.' *South America Pilot*, vol. III, current edition, Admiralty, London, p. 355.

   A sketch of the site of Cobija was made by Alcide d'Orbigny in 1833 as part of a set of maps and sketches of Bolivia compiled between 1830 and 1833 and printed in Paris, many of which were dedicated to President Andrés Santa Cruz.

Arica, by contrast, both in terms of site and situation, was located on one of the few really good points anywhere along the desert coast. North of the blunt sandstone headland of El Morro, the steep front of the Coast Range buckles and disappears for a few miles as the Cordilleran system swings round, pivoting to take up a new alignment. Within this hinge, the interior *pampa*, known locally as Pampa sin Nombre, extends uninterruptedly to the sea. Unlike the restricted 'ledge settlements' characterising so much of this coast, Arica was thus established at the corner of an extensive plain, and with abundant supplies of fresh water readily accessible from shallow wells. Indeed its water supply was, and still is, quite superb, causing it to be pinpointed during the colonial period as the best-watered site anywhere along this coast between Callao and Valparaiso. Regular supplies of fruit, olives and sugar from the irrigated gardens of the Azapa valley behind the town augmented other agricultural produce (and quicksilver from Huancavelica), sent coastwise to Arica and pack-muled into Upper Peru. Far better facilities than Cobija could offer were necessary to compete with advantages such as these (Plate v).

Meanwhile, President Santa Cruz pursued his ideal of confederation between the two Perus. In June 1835 Bolivia invaded its neighbour and a treaty proposing the union was concluded later the same month.[1] The following year came the formal partitioning of a defeated Peru with the establishment, in March 1836, of the State of South Peru comprising the department of Arequipa, Ayacucho, Cuzco and Puno.[2] The Declaration of Independence expressed its conviction 'by long and sad experience of the extreme inconvenience of association with the people of the North'. Certainly a strong sense of regionalism had long existed around the Titicaca basin, tied by the old-established route between Islay, Arequipa, Cuzco, Puno and La Paz, as well as by that of Arica and Tacna. The presence of an international frontier had done little to disturb this exchange. Indeed, it had been observed many years earlier that if Cuzco or Arequipa had become the viceregal capital instead of Lima, an independent Upper Peru would never have emerged. Although this is improbable, one might for the sake of argument suggest that, had it been so, Upper Peru's boundaries could well have excluded La Paz. However, when in March 1836 the provinces of Moquegua, Tacna, Arica, Locumba and Tarapacá expressed a desire to separate from Peru, Santa Cruz used this to foster a political division of Peru leading to confederation, rather than as an opportunity to extend Bolivian territory.

[1] 15 June 1835, F.O. *61/33* and F.O. *61/84*.   [2] F.O. *61/39*.

44

The independence of the State of North Peru was announced five months later and consisted of the departments of Amazonas, Junín, Libertad and Lima.[1] Bolivia, North Peru and South Peru were each to maintain a President and Congress; Santa Cruz was established as the Supreme Protector of the Confederation in October 1836, guiding foreign policy and all military matters. Each of the three member States was to maintain at least one principal port, Cobija being that of Bolivia. It is interesting, if idle, to speculate on the possible turn of future events had this larger political unit eventually succeeded in welding the rich coastal valleys of Peru with the high plateau areas, as the pre-Columbian period had to some extent achieved. But the displeasure of both Chile and Argentina had been incurred by this shifting of the power balance in South America. Chile in particular regarded a possible union of Peru and Bolivia with some alarm. Together, they constituted a serious threat to any future Chilean expansion – even perhaps to Chilean survival. With the aid of dissatisfied sections in the Peruvian army, Chile succeeded in defeating Santa Cruz in January 1839 at the battle of Yungay. The Confederation was dissolved after a brief three years of life, and Article vi of the treaty signed in Santiago on 6 August 1839 stipulated that no further attempts to dismember or incorporate States by federation, or any other means, would be tolerated.[2] The Supreme Protector was later exiled to Europe, dying in France in September 1865, aged seventy-two.[3] A century later, his remains were exhumed at Versailles and transferred with great ceremony to South America aboard a French warship. They now lie in La Paz, in a newly constructed tomb facing Plaza Murillo.

Andrés Santa Cruz has been variously judged as an inspired visionary and a ruthless fanatic. The opposition of Chile and Argentina to the emergence of a potential power bloc on their northern flank proved the deciding factor, however, and Bolivia's future as a unitary State was confirmed. Even without outside intervention, it may be argued that Peru, infinitely more favoured by location, size of population and variety of accessible resources, would not have remained contented indefinitely with its supporting role. The northern departments had frequently expressed their strong aversion to Santa Cruz, stating that any partition of Peru, confederation with Bolivia, or existence under his protection would not be

[1] *Ibid.*

[2] *F.O. 61/63* and *F.O. 126/8.*

[3] While in Europe, however, Santa Cruz represented Bolivia in various ministerial capacities. A personal letter to B. H. Wilson from Andrés Santa Cruz, Paris, 29 April 1852, is signed 'Envoy Extraordinary and Minister Plenipotentiary to France, England, Belgium and Rome, formerly President of Bolivia and Protector of the Peru–Bolivian Confederation', *F.O. 11/10.*

tolerated.[1] The Confederation as envisaged by Santa Cruz was doomed to founder from within if outside forces had not destroyed it first. It was indeed the last attempt at such a political union of States in Latin America. As Kendall has commented, 'Although advocated by many leading South American thinkers, such projects have always failed, largely because Hispanic pride and Hispanic individualism demand for themselves complete independence or else complete subordination'.[2] But to such an assertion one must also add, and take into account, the enormous number of practical difficulties facing any attempt of this nature, whether political or economic, not least the overwhelming problems of internal circulation and communication which help to make such associations workable.

Bolivia itself was very far from united, and certainly not over confederation with Peru. The general determination for independence in 1825 did not signify national unity on other issues, even if it implied it. The line between *regionalismo* and *separatismo* in Bolivia particularly was always a fine one. Deep schism existed between Chuquisaca and La Paz. As a *paceño* (he was born at Huarina), President Santa Cruz had threatened to remove Bolivia's capital permanently to La Paz, the larger and more convenient city proudly boasting even then that 'La Paz es Bolivia, y Bolivia es La Paz.' Despite its altitude, it was infinitely preferred by foreign diplomats who feelingly described La Paz as fifteen days nearer to North America and Europe. 'Chuquisaca is so far in the interior – almost beyond the sphere of civilisation', complained one British Chargé d'Affaires[3] to a Foreign Office already frequently acquainted with the fact by a succession of Ministers hoping to account satisfactorily for the very high cost of living in Bolivia. Considerable extra expense was undoubtedly involved in following Presidents and Government on their regular itinerary between Chuquisaca, La Paz and Cochabamba. Throughout Santa Cruz' administration in particular, the imminent loss of income, patronage and prestige facing Chuquisaca resulted in his downfall in 1839 being received there as a timely reprieve, and happy deliverance from a man rarely trusted in central Bolivia. Interested parties in Chuquisaca, Potosí and Tarija had shown little real enthusiasm for the Peru–Bolivia Confederation, while the Department of Santa Cruz was so poorly linked to the capital by trail that its representatives often arrived too late to be counted.

What emerges quite clearly is that, in general, Andrés Santa Cruz

---

[1] B. H. Wilson, Consul-General in Lima, to Lord Palmerston, 23 June 1836, *F.O. 61/38*.

[2] L. C. Kendall, 'Andrés Santa Cruz and the Peru–Bolivian Confederation', *Hisp. Am. Hist. Rev.*, vol. XVI, 1936, pp. 29–48. This reference p. 47.

[3] J. A. Lloyd to the Earl of Malmesbury, Chuquisaca, 11 October 1852, *F.O. 11/10*.

enlisted more support among his contemporaries outside than inside South America. To European and North American governments, he embodied generally well-reasoned policies and stable administration. Britain's first official recognition of Bolivia, for example, was delayed until 1837 when it was formally made, not of Bolivia, but of the Peru–Bolivia Confederation under Santa Cruz.[1] His subsequent overthrow was regarded as a calamity, and resulted in considerable loss of confidence in Bolivia at the Foreign Office. Occasional efforts made outside Bolivia to reinstate him, however, proved unsuccessful.

Despite Santa Cruz' commitment to maintain Cobija as Bolivia's port, so long as political relations with Peru were in flux, and while Arica considered its own interests better served by Bolivia, the 'Arica para Bolivia' movement flourished, persistently if modestly. Then in 1841, Gamarra again invaded Bolivia. Fighting was concentrated on the *altiplano*, but Peruvian troops landed and occupied the port of Cobija in October 1841, only to abandon it two months later. Bolivia's decisive victory against Peru at Ingavi, about thirty miles from La Paz, encouraged a sweeping advance into Arica, Tacna, Puno and Moquegua. It was the first and last time that Bolivia was ever to occupy Arica. In the early months of 1842 General, also President, Ballivián of Bolivia was forced to withdraw gradually to Juliaca, and in a report to London, the British Vice-Consul recorded that although Ballivián no longer appeared to consider seriously any further inroads into Peru, while the Bolivian army still held Arica he was offering to purchase the port and offset part of Peru's debt to Britain. Would Britain be willing to guarantee Bolivia's possession of Arica in the event of any outside intervention?[2] Such a guarantee was not supplied, Peru rejected all purchase offers and Bolivia withdrew once more behind the Desaguadero. If Bolivia's victory at Ingavi marks the final confirmation of the country's independence, it also marks the end of any real chance there may ever have been of Arica's incorporation into Bolivia.

Attention once again turned to Cobija. Since 1839, thirty thousand dollars had been voted annually for its improvement, but the many

[1] In Lima, 5 June 1837, *F.O. 94/161*. J. B. Pentland (see above, p. 18 n. 2) had been appointed as Britain's first Consul-General to Bolivia in August 1836, after it appeared certain that the Peru–Bolivia Confederation would become established. After the dissolution of the Confederation, recognition of Bolivia and a treaty exchange took place in Chuquisaca, 29 September 1840, *F.O. 94/344*. The United States recognised the Peru–Bolivia Confederation in June 1838, but delayed recognition of Bolivia until 1848.

[2] C. Masterton to J. Bidwell, Chuquisaca, 2 January 1842, *F.O. 126/11*.

attempts to boost Cobija's trade on a permanent basis were defeated by the gruelling six hundred-mile trail between it and the centres on the *altiplano*. 'It is a benighted spot separated by an immense desert of sand from the inhabited part of the country', observed Masterton, lugubrious as ever, for at best the trail to La Paz took well over three weeks, in contrast to a journey of seven or eight days from Arica. Even when, in 1843, a 40 per cent *ad valorem* duty was temporarily imposed on goods entering Bolivia *via* Arica, compared with one of only 5 per cent *via* Cobija, merchants in La Paz complained that losses on transport, wear and tear, and delay in receipt of merchandise all combined to render Cobija totally uneconomic under any circumstances.[1] Their extra costs when routed through the panhandle more than outweighed the extra tariff imposed, and many continued to boycott Cobija. Merchants in Cochabamba similarly rejected the port from which consignments took never less than six weeks to arrive. In the country as a whole, Cobija, however inadequately, could only serve the southern sector; its links had been with Potosí and Chuquisaca, not with La Paz and Cochabamba. Indeed, the only sub-stantial body of support ever to exist inside Bolivia for such generous injection of aid into Cobija came from Chuquisaca. Paradoxically, it was one point on which there was agreement with the policy of Andrés Santa Cruz, since the acquisition of Arica, Chuquisaca was certain, would only strengthen the power of La Paz and precipitate its promotion to the capital city. 'Chuquisaca is without resources or commerce of any kind,' wrote Masterton; 'if Arica becomes included in Bolivia, then the government will move to La Paz and this city must inevitably perish and dwindle to little more than a deserted village – a small provincial town.'[2]

Chilean circles also had privately expressed the opinion that Cobija should be maintained. Although it was too insignificant ever to become competitive as a port of call for European vessels, it was closer to Valparaiso than Arica. Almost all Cobija's imports were sent coastwise from Lima or Valparaiso and broken up there into small packages suitable for mule transport into the mountains. In March 1846, thirty-five camels were landed

---

[1] C. Masterton to J. Bidwell, Chuquisaca, 10 August 1843, *F.O. 11/1*. Several earlier attempts had been made to increase Cobija's trade by means of preferential tariffs, but all were equally unsuccessful as long-term measures. In 1827, for example, J. B. Pentland had re-ported (*F.O. 61/12*) that a special *ad valorem* duty of only 2 per cent was levied on goods entering Bolivia through Cobija, compared with 55 per cent *via* Buenos Aires, and 45–92 per cent *via* any Peruvian port. In 1831–2 Ruschenberger (*Three Years in the Pacific*) had noted much duty-free traffic passing through Cobija, although certain specified items carried a 5 per cent or a 10 per cent import duty. By comparison in the same period, duties at Arica on goods bound for Bolivia were between 5 per cent and 15 per cent.

[2] C. Masterton to the Earl of Aberdeen, Chuquisaca, 13 February 1846, *F.O. 126/13*.

at Cobija for use on the trail to the *altiplano*, but they were not a success and mules remained the basis of transport.[1]

While most overseas trade to and from Bolivia thus continued to move through Arica[2] (all other lines being negligible in comparison), tariff adjustment seesawed in a vain attempt to modify the pattern. Immediately after independence, Peru had regularly disputed Bolivia's claims to the right of free transit through Peruvian territory, but after the defeat at Ingavi in 1841, the right of such transit was written into the 1847 treaty. In addition, pressure from the merchants of La Paz successfully led to Arica being declared a free port for Bolivian trade. The abolition of all port and transit dues on both imports and exports became effective on 1 January 1850 and *ariqueños* went wild with excitement.[3] Recording the general jubilation, the U.S. Consul at Arica estimated that the population of between four and five thousand in the port would quickly double.[4]

[1] The use of camel transport was tried experimentally in other parts of the American continent in this period in desert, or supposedly desert, areas. About seventy-five camels were landed on the Texas coast between 1855 and 1857, and one caravan crossed into California. The effort attracted much attention but the experiment was dropped.

[2] 'Arica would seem naturally to belong to Bolivia', wrote U.S. Secretary of State James Buchanan to John Appleton, 1 June 1848. The new American Minister to Bolivia was instructed to encourage, discreetly, the transfer of the port of Arica: 'Without attempting to interfere with the domestic concerns of either of these Republics [Peru and Bolivia], you might, should an opportunity offer, by your counsel and advice promote this cession.'

[3] *Ad valorem* duties on imports entering Bolivia *via* Cobija in 1850 were between 3 and 20 per cent (H. A. Weddell, *Voyage dans le nord de la Bolivie et dans les parties voisines du Pérou*, Paris and London, 1853, p. 251). Peru confirmed free commercial transit for Bolivia through Arica in 1864 and 1870, but with agreed tariff adjustments.

[4] F. M. Ringgold to Secretary of State John M. Clayton, 1 March 1850, Consular Despatches from Arica, *General Records of the Department of State, Record Group 59*, Washington, D.C. Ringgold reported large quantities of pure silver brought annually into Arica from both Peruvian and Bolivian mines. For the year 1849, i.e. *before* the 1850 agreement came into force, he recorded:
Silver: $214,440-worth of silver, and $9,704-worth of silver plate ('old silver') which merchants considered almost as good since most plate was made without alloy and hammer-beaten. In addition $250,000-worth of 'hard' dollar pieces made for export.
Gold: $153,578-worth from Tipuani in Bolivia.
Copper: copper dust (70–80 per cent pure copper): 9,769,050 lb.; copper bars (from Corocoro): 954,450 lb.
Tin: from Oruro and Iuanani: 691,800 lb.
Alpaca wool: 3000–4000 bales, and a few hundred bales of *sheep's wool*.
Chinchilla skins: 3740.
Cow hides: 1200.   *Vicuña hides*: 670.
Coffee: small quantities from the Bolivian Yungas.
Peruvian bark: In terms of value, *Cinchona* headed the list. At this time, Arica was handling a virtual monopoly export of the product, which was wrapped in hides and brought from the Bolivian Yungas to La Paz, the market for all foreign buyers. Ringgold noted that recent increased demand in Europe and the U.S.A. had lifted the price from $20–$80 per 150 lb. to a record $200 per 150 lb. In 1849, Arica exported $607,650-worth of bark.

Such a boost was timely, for it enabled Arica to withstand the sudden drain of population into California; even Cobija supplied its own small band of 'forty-niners' from an already meagre population.

The lack of vigilance and general supervision along the trail, however, particularly between Tacna and La Paz, led to serious abuses of the free port–free transit agreement by both Peruvians and Bolivians as duty-free goods destined for Bolivia were smuggled away for Peruvian home consumption. In July 1853 Peru renounced the existing agreement and imposed a 40 per cent duty on all traffic in transit to or from Bolivia. Incensed, the Bolivian Government retaliated by imposing a complete ban on all trade through Arica and for one year, 1854, Cobija basked in unaccustomed attention while no Bolivian cargo was shipped officially through Arica at all. But there was violent opposition in the latter port, as well as in La Paz and Cochabamba where merchants had previously shown, as in 1843, that they would favour Arica under almost any circumstances. Combined pressures led to the rescinding of the ban on the port in 1855. Despite the heavy duties which remained,[1] only two years later the U.S. Consul reported that Arica was again riding high, so high indeed that in terms of foreign imports it had completely cornered the trade, not only of Bolivia but of much of south Peru. It was now Peru's second port, and the third port on the entire Pacific coast south of Panamá.[2] Down at Cobija, however, Lewis Joel, an Englishman acting as U.S. Consul and British Vice-Consul, complained of illness caused by drinking imperfectly distilled sea water and continued to criticise the lack of organisation and facilities in the port. A trickle of imported goods for Cobija's own needs and for southern Bolivia was received coastwise from Valparaiso, while vessels

[1] Information on these is incomplete and occasionally conflicting, but from separate returns made to the State Department, Washington, D.C., by the U.S. Consuls at Arica and Cobija, *General Records of the Department of State*, *Record Group 59*, import duty *ad valorem* at Arica on manufactured goods for Bolivia is given, for example, in 1856–7 as 40 per cent on shoes, 30 per cent on furniture, 15 per cent on cotton goods. Duty at Cobija was sometimes as little as one-third of this, although in 1858 the Consul at Cobija reported a 12½ per cent import duty on grey shirting, adding that he had great difficulty in obtaining reliable records of any sort at Cobija. The place was even then without proper quays and quayside accommodation; for despite President Santa Cruz' assurances in 1831 (see above), the Government was still advertising for tenders from engineering firms for the construction of a pier and water-supply installation ten years later, and adequate facilities were never completed. Cobija's extra trade in 1854, however, increased its population to over 5000.

    In 1862, in an effort to restrict smuggling, it was agreed that all Customs duties at Arica would be recovered by Peru, which would then pass to Bolivia a share (about half a million dollars annually) every three years. Never wholly satisfied, Bolivia established its Custom Houses at La Paz and Oruro in March 1878.

[2] J. L. Lansing to Secretary of State Lewis Cass, 3 November 1857, Consular Despatches from Arica, *General Records of the Department of State*, Washington, D.C.

generally departed with locally derived cargoes of guano and copper ore.[1]

At this stage of Arica's prosperity came technological advances in transport which were later to have a profound effect on the relative merits of Bolivia's Pacific outlets. Railway construction as a business proposition was attracted to growth areas, and it is no coincidence that one of the earliest railways ever built in South America was constructed in 1851–6 to replace the trail between Arica and Tacna, and form the first phase of a projected railway up to La Paz. In Tacna, carriers advertised mules of particular strength and endurance which could be specially commissioned for heavy loads – pianos, sofas and printing-presses were often quoted – at rates of $80–$100 per animal. Beyond the town, the mule and llama trail continued to wind along the floor of the San Francisco *quebrada*, before climbing precariously by narrow paths in the sides of the ravines to approach the 15,000-foot pass *en route* for La Paz. This eight-day journey remained the quickest route into Bolivia from the Pacific for almost another twenty years.

The Amazon and the Plate could justifiably be ignored as Bolivian trade outlets in this period, for exchanges by these routes were almost entirely local in character. Then, temporarily overriding Bolivia's continual agitation for possession of Arica, came a revaluation of the Atacama. Bolivia's Pacific boundary problems were submerged, only to be tossed up again as part of the economic reappraisal of the desert.

2. EXPLOITATION OF THE DESERT PANHANDLE BEGINS. THE GUANO BOOM: 1840–1870

Large-scale economic development in the Atacama commenced with exploitation of the rich guano deposits along the coastal fringe, for although guano is not confined to the desert edge of the Pacific, nowhere else in the world was it found in such vast quantity in the early nineteenth century. The millions of sea birds inhabiting the islands and headlands had led to an accumulation of dung sixty or more feet thick in places, and its value

---

[1] The volume of Cobija's trade has occasionally been much exaggerated – e.g. 'Cobija handled something like one-third of Bolivia's international trade by the 1850s', H. S. Klein, *Parties and Political Change in Bolivia, 1880–1952*, Cambridge, 1969, p. 4. Such proportions are not substantiated by foreign consular reports. The basis for isolated contemporary statements of this nature, however, made in the mid-1850s by those unacquainted with the port over a number of years, may well be chance reference to the trade figures for 1854 which, as shown above, were temporarily inflated by the ban on Arica.

The Foreign Office invariably refused to consider a salaried consular post at Cobija on the ground that 'Bolivia's trade is carried by the shorter and much cheaper route through the Peruvian port of Arica.' *Memorandum relative to the appointment of a Consular Agent at Cobija,* 1 March 1861, *F.O. 16/118* and 18 April 1862, *F.O. 97/93.*

as a fertiliser had been known locally for centuries. Pre-Columbian agricultural communities frequently sprinkled crushed guano around the roots of their plants, while the islands and cliffs where young birds were hatching were strictly protected by the Incas. Humboldt brought specimens to Europe in 1804 and gradually its use as a fertiliser was recognised there, ushering in a period of exploitation along the South American west coast which had been dubbed the 'Golden Age of Manure'.

Export of guano from the tiny islands of Chincha (13° 32′ S, 76° 28′ W) and Lobos (6° 38′ S, 80° 59′ W), off the Peruvian coast, began seriously about 1840. The Chincha Islands, three rocks only about two miles each in circumference, were State-owned, and within a few years guano had become Peru's chief source of income, responsible for almost three-quarters of the total national revenue – indeed, for a time, guano became South America's largest single export. In 1859 Peru earned U.S. $16 million from the sale of this fertiliser, with nearly three hundred vessels calling regularly to load it by lighter from the jetties to which it was trundled in barrows, or conveyed down wooden chutes, by gangs of Indian and Chinese labourers. Guano ships taking on fresh water supplies begin to figure prominently in Arica's port returns during the 1850s. The guano was blasted loose, or chipped and prised away with picks and spades. The smell was so intense that sailors familiar with this coast have described how, at night or in fog, ships were often able to locate and avoid the larger guano islands lying hazardously in the sea lanes by the stench surrounding them.[1] Guano became the cause of that last attempt by Spain, between 1863 and 1866, to regain some of its old imperial glory by seizure of the Chincha Islands.[2] Both Peru and Chile were active in exploiting the wealth in guano, and Bolivia found its own deposits within the panhandle frequently poached by more energetic neighbours. All were suddenly enthusiastic about the possibilities of such unexpected but much-needed revenue; the British Vice-Consul in Bolivia reported the good news:

[1] A brief commentary upon guano exploitation following an Englishman's visit to Peru in the early 1870s is found in A. J. Duffield's *Peru in the Guano Age*, London, 1877. Duffield observed (p. 73) that Peru had by then already sold twenty million tons of guano at £12–£13 per ton, and estimated (p. 101) that a further seven-and-a-half million tons remained. Much of Peru's guano revenue was used in an intensive period of prodigal railway construction, notably between 1868 and 1874, of which Meiggs' line Mollendo–Arequipa–Puno was one famous example and the Oroya railway another. Duffield was shocked by the conditions under which the guano was extracted and loaded – 'No hell has ever been conceived...that can be equalled in the fierceness of its heat, the horror of its stink, and the damnation of those compelled to labour there, to a deposit of Peruvian guano when being shovelled into ships' (pp. 77–8).   [2] See W. C. Davis, *The Last Conquistadores*, Univ. of Georgia Press, 1950.

On the coast of Bolivia between Cobija and Iquique [Bolivia did not in fact claim the coast north of the Loa mouth], there are several small islands which have the appearance of being covered with snow...Guano has been sold in the Port of London for £25 a ton, and now a company of French and English speculators have approached Bolivia for a monopoly in the trade. The terms are likely to be 60% profits annually to Bolivia – perhaps i.e. one and a half million dollars and an initial (or like that) half a million dollars...This sudden influx of wealth to the present attenuated Treasury of Bolivia is a subject of universal national exultation, and as wealth is power it may before long place Bolivia in a political point of view in a very different position to that which it has hitherto held in the scale of South American nations.[1]

In 1842 Peru made such new and particularly rich discoveries that Chile dispatched an exploratory group to examine the Atacama coast as far north as Mejillones (23° 2′ S). The mission was highly rewarding, and President Bulnes of Chile introduced a bill which 'established' the Mejillones parallel, taken as 23° S, as the northern boundary of Chile. All *guaneras* south of this line were declared national property, while Bulnes observed:

I am inclined to believe that the profit derived from them will be of relatively short duration, but none the less this does not imply that the exploitation of these deposits should be left free to foreign commerce, thus depriving the nation of a resource which, without adding any burden to the public, may serve to supply subsidiary funds that may be applied to many objects of common utility urgently required.[2]

Deserts, he declared, like rivers, should be divided by the median line and as such, 23° S was selected. For the first time in this region, the astronomical line was suggested as a boundary in little-known country. No mention was made of Bolivia. In the same year the Bolivian Minister of Finance wrote to the Prefect of Cobija: 'Stringent measures must be adopted to prevent incursions by the parties holding guano concessions outside the limits of the rivers Loa and Paposo which comprise the littoral of this Republic.'

In 1846 the Bolivian Foreign Minister, Tomás Frías, added: 'In the desolate state of our coast between the two republics it will be very difficult to prevent the guano extractors of Chile from extending their illegal inroads to our territory, unless we can obviate that difficulty by a treaty between the two governments.'

The Bolivian Government dispatched five separate diplomatic missions to Santiago over the next twenty years, and resorted to exhaustive

[1] C. Masterton to J. Bidwell, Chuquisaca, 15 March 1842, *F.O. 126/11*.
[2] Quoted by Gonzalo Bulnes, *Chile and Peru: the causes of the War of 1879*, Santiago, Chile, 1920, p. 4.

research to prove ownership of the disputed territory under *uti possidetis de jure 1810*. Both countries unearthed archive evidence in support of their claims although these were already, in practice, passing beyond arguments based on *de jure* ownership to those more forcibly presented by *de facto* possession.[1] Contrary to Bolívar's fears that an independent Upper Peru would be extinguished by Argentina or Brazil, in the event it was Chile which set the pace.

Bolivia maintained a custom house at Paposo (now supported as the southern Bolivian boundary in place of the river Salado eighty miles farther south), in order to control its guano trade. A small brig with two guns, the *General Sucre*, and two other vessels, patrolled the Bolivian coast after 1843, but the Chilean captains ignored the administrative authorities in Cobija quite blatantly, despite the 'Lacaw incident', when the Bolivian Consul in London later brought a successful action against a Chilean frigate charged with guano smuggling. Chile offered no objection to this verdict, but continued to defy the feeble show of Bolivian authority. The Bolivian panhandle appeared to be characterised chiefly by a number of relatively thin deposits of guano which were quickly worked out under foreign concessions. By the late 1840s the only rich *guanera* in operation in Bolivia was on the north side of Cape Paquica (San Francisco), about 36 miles north of Cobija, where beds of between 50 and 75 feet thickness remained. But even this had been contaminated with spray and falling sand during its accumulation, and yielded about £3 a ton less profit on the London market than the high-quality guano quarried, for example, from the Chincha Islands.

Interest, in consequence, was once again directed farther north, and by 1857 Chile felt sufficiently in command of the local situation to move along the coast of the panhandle to 23° S and occupy the bay of Mejillones, one of the finest natural harbours on South America's west coast. An American ship, *Sportsman*, loading copper ore in the bay was challenged and possessed, charged with illegal activity in Chilean territory. Mejillones was not only a superbly sheltered site, its great chalk-like cliffs were also thickly crusted with guano. Alerted early in 1863, the U.S. Consul in Cobija reported the passage northward of the Chilean war vessel *Esmeralda*, carrying twenty guns. It stationed itself in Mejillones bay to protect the loading of Chilean guano vessels there bound for Europe, and Joel acquainted the State Department in detail with the American concessionary interests already

---

[1] Systematic exploration of the desert was officially commissioned by Chile. See, for example, 'Abstract of a Report made by Dr. R. A. Philippi to the Government of Chile, of a Journey into the Desert of Atacama in 1853–54', *Journ. Roy. Geog. Soc.*, vol. xxv, 1855, pp. 158–71.

obtained from the Bolivian government which were now in danger of Chilean expropriation.[1] The resources around latitude 23° S were currently estimated to be anything up to ten million tons and in London the Board of Trade was recommending the Foreign Office to establish a British Consul in Mejillones.

In 1866 the guano dispute was temporarily suspended following the Spanish aggression in the Chincha Islands and the bombardment of Valparaiso in March of that year. Bolivia joined in a defensive Pacific alliance with Ecuador, Peru and Chile, in spite of having broken off diplomatic relations with the last-named three years earlier. The tension had temporarily eased in the face of the old common enemy Spain, and a Treaty of Territorial Limits was signed in Santiago in August 1866 by Chile and Bolivia,[2] both declaring that in 'the old question pending between them as to the settlement of their respective territorial limits in the desert of Atacama and the working of the guano deposits on the coast of that desert...both have determined to renounce a part of the territorial rights, which each, with good reason, believed themselves to possess'. By Articles I and II the new boundary between the two States was placed along the 24° S parallel, although the proceeds from the exploitation of guano at Mejillones and any other guano deposits which might be discovered each side of this line, between parallels 23° S and 25° S, were now, together with all mineral export duties derived from the same zone, to be divided equally between Chile and Bolivia (Fig. 3 b). Chile was to check customs administration at Mejillones, and Bolivia could do the same at any post Chile might establish between 24° S and 25° S. A beacon was later erected fifty feet above sea level at 23° 58′ 11″ S to demarcate the 24° S boundary.[3]

Chile had thus pushed an extreme claim of 23° S and subsequently agreed to 24° S with an air of compromise. Certainly, it was generally agreed by foreign observers in Santiago that such a settlement would not have been entertained for a moment by Chile without the prevailing sentiment along the whole coast of the need to preserve a Pacific 'good neighbour' policy. But the terms of Article II in fact permitted Chilean penetration as far north as 23° S and this at once became a focus of Chilean activity. Within the 23°–24° S zone lay not only the very rich guano deposits of Mejillones, but other mineral wealth soon to be discovered. The 24°–25° S zone offered little in comparison. The 1866 treaty was

[1] Lewis Joel to Secretary of State William H. Seward, Cobija, Bolivia, 25 January 1863, Consular Despatches from Cobija, *General Records of the Dept. of State, Record Group 59*, Washington, D.C. (Joel also acted as French Consul at Cobija from 1863 to 1866.)

[2] *F.O. 16/141*.

[3] This beacon is marked on the later editions of the *Beagle* charts (see above, p. 34 n. 1).

greeted with anger in Bolivia, whilst the request by President Melgarejo for one hundred Chilean troops to form the garrison at Cobija because of his greater faith in their discipline and reliability further incensed that small proportion of the Bolivian population aware of events in their Litoral Department. The year 1866 was indeed a fateful one, for in that year two Chilean prospectors discovered nitrate behind the future site of Antofagasta, a discovery of greater significance in the economic and political geography of Atacama than guano had ever achieved.

3. THE NITRATE BOOM (1870–1918): THE INITIAL PHASE

The guano trade had been confined to the immediate coastal strip, leaving most of the desert as negative a zone as before. But while the extraction and loading of guano had rarely called for any penetration inland, nitrate exploitation swung the focus of attention into the most arid region of Atacama – the interior *pampa*, particularly the Pampa del Tamarugal. Here in this 30-mile-wide plain, secluded between the Coast Range and the Andean piedmont, aridity and very high evaporation rates have preserved a wide variety of salts in depressions along its broadly undulating surface.[1] *Salares*, pans of predominantly sodium chloride, are common, and on the gentle western slopes particularly, sodium sulphate, potassium nitrate and sodium nitrate are among the considerable range of other salts which have been deposited. Of these, sodium nitrate (Chile saltpetre) became of outstanding economic importance along a discontinuous belt between 19° 30′ S and 26° S. Its origin is still debated but the *caliche* (rough gravels cemented by sodium nitrate and other salts), 3 to 6 feet thick, below an overburden of 1 foot to 6 feet, extended over wide areas.[2] Outcrops were rare, but early prospectors could often detect its presence below by a characteristic puffy appearance of the surface, and shallow pits were dug in all likely stretches. Thousands of these trial pits and the small mounds of overburden beside them may still be seen along the Pampa del Tamarugal, which was to become the centre of a world monopoly in natural nitrate on a commercial scale.

[1] Average solar evaporation rate recorded at Coya near the María Elena nitrate plant of the Anglo-Lautaro Co. is 7 litres per square metre per day. This can soar under windy conditions to the phenomenal figure of 13 litres per square metre per day.

[2] George E. Ericksen, 'Rhyolite Tuff, a source of the Salts of northern Chile', *Geological Survey Research Paper No. 230*, Washington, D.C., 1961, pp. 224–5. Investigations, in co-operation with Chilean research centres at María Elena, Santiago and Iquique, lead this author to suggest that surface and ground waters have carried the salts west from the Andes, where precipitation in Pleistocene and Recent times has been sufficient to leach the widespread rhyolitic tuffs occurring there which are rich in these same constituent salts.

The *caliche* was blasted loose by a nitrate–sulphur explosive, gangs then breaking the blocks down by pick to lumps of manageable size which were carried by mules to the refineries (*oficinas*). Here the lumps were pulverised and boiled for about eight hours until the impurities sank to the bottom. The solution, often as much as 97 per cent pure, was run into large evaporating tanks whence the white crystals of sodium nitrate were bagged, ready for movement to the coast. Thousands of mules from Argentina were originally used for this transport, but the difficulty of providing feed and water, as well as the need for large quantities for the latter for processing (piped as time went on both from the river Loa and from the Andes), soon necessitated a network of tramways and railways. These quickly spread across the *caliche* zones, and probed an often precarious route through the Coast Range, before winding down its steep face to the sea. The preparation of the nitrate was thus more lengthy than that for guano, but the technical knowledge required was not great, given the very high-grade ore used in the nineteenth-century development of the industry. The first important production began in Peru in the 1830s at La Noria, twenty-five miles south-east of Iquique, and until about 1860 output was significant only in the Peruvian section of the desert, where over fifty *oficinas* were located in the province of Tarapacá.

The first major find in the Bolivian desert was made in 1866 at Salar del Carmen. Significantly, the discovery had been recorded by two Chileans, working north of the 24° S boundary, within the 'shared' treaty zone. At its nearest Pacific outlet, on a marine bench, the port of Antofagasta was officially founded in 1868, growing rapidly in the next few years to become the largest settlement in the Bolivian Litoral, although it was always characterised by a predominantly Chilean population.[1] The Custom

---

[1] Alcides Arguedas, *Historia General de Bolivia, 1809–1921*, La Paz, 1922, p. 349. The author gives Antofagasta's population in 1874 as 93 per cent Chilean and 2 per cent Bolivian. Antofagasta replaced Cobija as capital of the Litoral in 1875. Although the U.S. State Department continued to receive occasional dispatches from Cobija until 1874, other foreign consular representation had been withdrawn from Cobija in 1869 (if not earlier), by which time the settlement was practically deserted. It had suffered severe earthquake damage in 1868. Brief observation of the appearance and decline of Cobija about the year 1860 is recorded by H. W. Baxley, *What I saw on the West Coast of South and North America, and at the Hawaiian Islands*, New York, 1865, pp. 180–2.

Cobija in 1873 is also the subject of a short and disparaging reference by B. S. Dingman, *Ten Years in South America*, part 2, *Bolivia, Complete in Itself*, Montreal, 1876, pp. 19–24. Invited to attend the inauguration of work (30 January 1873) on the Mejillones–Caracoles railway (Bolivian Govt concession, July 1872), Dingman failed to disembark at Mejillones and was carried on to Cobija, where he spent a miserable four days awaiting another ship. Dingman is a superficial and somewhat inaccurate writer on Bolivia, but his survey and anecdotes are not without interest. The inaccessibility of Cobija overland was noted by others: the approach to the port was usually made *via* Arica and coastal steamer south.

House and Consulate at Mejillones, built by Chile under the 1866 treaty terms, was dismantled and re-erected in Antofagasta about 1873. Today it is that town's oldest public building and, except for the period of its transfer from one port to the other, has been in continuous use as a Custom House for more than a century (Plates III and IV).

Throughout the Atacama, nitrate was almost always worked by private concessions, unlike guano, which had often been State-exploited. Behind Antofagasta, scattered operations combined in 1872 to form the Compañía de Salitres y Ferrocarril de Antofagasta, a Chilean company incorporated in Valparaiso, which secured generous concessions from the Bolivian Government. The latter was to receive in exchange a payment of 10,000 pesos, the contruction of a road with water depots (which would have been required by the company in any event), and of a mole at the port of Antofagasta. A length of railway was substituted for the road, reaching Salar del Carmen in 1873 and forming the first part of what was to become the famous Antofagasta and Bolivia Railway. Although the concession was modified, too much capital (largely English) was tied up in the Compañía de Salitres y Ferrocarril de Antofagasta for it to be withdrawn entirely. Chile meanwhile was pouring population, money and enterprise into the 'shared' zone to such an extent that, not only in Antofagasta but in the whole region between 23° S and 25° S, probably at least 95 per cent of the inhabitants were Chilean.

Chile's initiative in the exploration of the 'shared' zone had promoted an irreversible build-up of population and capital investment. Both States, for various reasons, regretted the 1866 agreement, especially as the 23°–24° S section was proving so much richer. Quite apart from the saltpetre beds, one of the best strikes ever made sparked off a new silver *bonanza* at Caracoles in 1870. It had been discovered on the Antofagasta–San Pedro de Atacama trail and by 1872, not less than ten million dollars, and nearly as much more in credit transactions, had been invested in the mines by Chileans who comprised almost the whole population of approximately 10,000, exchanging Chilean currency and, although in Bolivian territory, applying and maintaining Chilean law and order. Caracoles was hailed as 'the modern Potosí' and advertisements for new Chilean limited liability companies in the Caracoles region appeared regularly in the Santiago and Valparaiso press. By 1874, over 4000 mines had been registered in the vicinity. Clearly, Chile regarded it as iniquitous that companies should be obliged to share any part of the proceeds of this extraordinarily rich zone with a 'sleeping partner', and announced that any necessary steps would be taken 'to protect' Chilean nationals in

Antofagasta and elsewhere. Even the British Minister, expanding upon the wealth of the region, now described it as having been ceded to Bolivia by the Chilean Government in 1866. 'Chile may well be tempted', he observed, '*to take back* that which once belonged to her.'[1]

Bolivia, anxious about Chilean encroachment, concluded a treaty with Peru in 1873,[2] guaranteeing each other's territorial integrity and assuring mutual defence against aggression by a third party. An additional twelfth article declared that the treaty should be kept secret as long as both signatories deemed its publication unnecessary, and Chile was later to make some play over this 'treachery'. It is open to question, however, whether Chile was unaware of its existence: 'it was one of those diplomatic jokes', wrote W. H. Russell later, 'called a "Secret Treaty", which is known to everybody'.[3]

In 1872 a convention between Bolivia and Chile[4] had confirmed the 24° S parallel from the sea to the highest summits of the Andes as the boundary, while by the treaty of 6 August 1874,[5] '*divortia aquarum*' was substituted for 'highest summits', and Bolivia agreed (Article IV) not to increase the taxes and duties on the existing Chilean enterprises in Bolivian territory between 23° S and 24° S for the next twenty-five years. All Chilean produce imported into Bolivia was to be exempted from import duties over the same period. These favourable terms prompted even the Chilean Chargé d'Affaires in Chuquisaca to observe to his own Foreign Minister that Chile might well appear as 'a crafty speculator' as a result of it, although to the Bolivian Foreign Minister he wrote:

> To the narrow-minded and suspicious persons who have reproached your Excellency with having ceded immense tracts of Bolivian territory...it would be well to reply that *the Republic of Chile desires nothing further than to shut herself in between the sea and the mountains* in order to obtain that which is her ambition – peace, well-being and progress...*My government intends for its eastern boundary in the district of the desert of Atacama only the high peaks of the mountain range and nothing else.* I think this declaration is clear enough and will leave no room for doubts.[6]

Foreign observers doubted whether the 1874 treaty would be sanctioned by the Bolivian Congress as its terms were so favourable to Chile,[7] and

---

[1] J. de V. Drummond-Hay to Earl Granville, Valparaiso, 2 October 1872, *F.O. 16/172*.

[2] *F.O. 16/202.*

[3] W. H. Russell, *A Visit to Chile and the Nitrate Fields of Tarapacá*, London, 1890, p. 302.

[4] *F.O. 16/178.*   [5] *F.O. 16/202.*

[6] It is difficult to understand how this was intended to provide an assurance to the Bolivian Foreign Minister of Chilean integrity, since its literal interpretation effectively severs Bolivia from the Pacific, and in fact summarises the future political division of this territory (my italics).

[7] H. Rumbold to the Earl of Derby, Santiago, 15 September 1874, *F.O. 16/181.*

indeed the treaty was not ratified. On 14 February 1878 the Bolivian Government passed a resolution disputing Article IV and ordering the imposition of a new tax of 10 cents on each quintal (100 pounds) of nitrate exported from the 23°–24° S zone, claiming arrears from the date of the signing of the 1874 treaty. The Bolivian authorities in Antofagasta were directed to claim an immediate payment of $90,000 from the Compañía de Salitres y Ferrocarril de Antofagasta and when ten months later the English manager of the company, a Mr George Hicks, still refused such payment, the Bolivian Prefect ordered the sale by auction of sufficient of the company's property to cover the sum required. Hicks, who was to be placed under arrest, fled to a Chilean vessel lying off port.[1] The British Minister in Santiago informed London of an imminent *coup*, noting that the desperate lack of funds in the Chilean treasury strengthened the resolve to retain all available nitrate revenues and take possession of the area once and for all: 'Chile will endeavour to retake the strip of coast which of her own accord she gave to Bolivia in 1866 for the sake of peace and quietness, and to put an end to apparently interminable bickering on the subject of boundaries.'[2] Exactly one year after the original imposition of the 10-cent tax, Chile made an unopposed landing at Antofagasta at 7 a.m. on 14 February 1879 and seized the town before the impending auction of company property could be held.

The War of the Pacific was now almost inevitable, for the richest prizes lay beyond the Bolivian panhandle, in the Peruvian desert. Despite the 'Secret Treaty' of 1873, it was noted somewhat cynically that Peru did not rush to Bolivia's aid. Peru was not formally involved in the conflict until war was officially declared by Chile on both Bolivia and Peru on 5 April 1879, by which time the Bolivian Litoral had already fallen and the Chilean blockade of Iquique begun. As Russell wrote upon visiting Antofagasta some years later: 'Here arose the quarrel – a cloud not larger than the hand of Mr. Hicks – which, charged with the thunder of war, spread over Tarapacá, burst in storm on Peru, and when it receded left the Chilean flag waving all along the coast northwards up to Arica.'[3]

---

[1] Background to these events is found in the records and correspondence of Hicks and other officials of the Compañía de Salitres y Ferrocarril de Antofagasta (Milbourne, Clark & Co., partners of William Gibbs & Co., of Valparaiso), held in the archives of Antony Gibbs & Sons, Ltd, Guildhall Library, London; *Mss. 11,128; 11,138; 11,033B*.

[2] F. J. Pakenham to Lord Salisbury, Santiago, 10 February 1879, *F.O. 16/202*. No British Minister in Chile at this period ever appears, even in confidential correspondence, to have acquainted himself accurately with the sequence of historical ownership of the Bolivian panhandle.

In a somewhat similar manner, of course, Bolivia would occasionally demand the 'restoration' of Arica.

[3] W. H. Russell, *A Visit to Chile*, p. 136.

4. THE WAR OF THE PACIFIC: 1879–1882

The value of naval strength had been visibly demonstrated to Chile during the three-hour bombardment of Valparaiso by Spanish ships in the war thirteen years earlier. The American Civil War too was fresh in the memory. Successive Chilean governments had needed little persuasion upon the merits of sea power as the basis for a bid for leadership on the west coast of South America. The 'Nitrate War' would be fought and won on the greater mobility offered by sea transport, and the greater flexibility of attack possessed by the country which controlled it. The isolated railway nets, all single-track and metre-gauge or less, which were growing behind the nitrate ports from Pisagua to Taltal, were not yet linked by the continuous longitudinal line through the Pampa del Tamarugal, so that overland movement was localised, and followed the short east–west railways or ravines to the coast. Forced marches north–south through intolerable conditions of heat and drought were a poor match for the initiative of attack held by sea power. Although the spoils of war were the rich nitrate deposits of the desert interior, the War of the Pacific was aptly named.

Chile had recently taken delivery of two ironclads built at Kingston-upon-Hull, both of nearly 4000 tons and commanded by a number of English officers. They were supported by two corvettes and several smaller gunboats. Peru's naval strength consisted primarily of two Birkenhead-built vessels, both inferior in weight and armament to the larger Chilean ships. To these were added two wooden corvettes and two monitors. Bolivia had never possessed ships of any consequence and could field only a small army, which consisted mainly of poorly equipped Aymara Indians from the *altiplano*.[1]

The *coup* of 14 February 1879 found Bolivia comparatively powerless. Six hundred Chilean troops sailed into Antofagasta early that morning to be greeted with flag-waving and general rejoicing by the largely Chilean populace. Two days forced march brought the troops to the Caracoles silver mines,[2] whence the advance continued towards the Calama oasis. There, in March 1879, a small band of just over one hundred Bolivians, under the command of Ladislao Cabrera and Eduardo Abaroa, defended their ground, Abaroa in particular emerging as the young Bolivian war hero whose name is so prominent today in any ceremonial associated with

[1] Details of the naval and military strength of the three republics at the outbreak of war may be found in Clements R. Markham, *The War between Peru and Chile 1879–1882*, London, 1883, pp. 93–101. Markham was strongly sympathetic to Peru.

[2] Only a few miles of the Mejillones–Caracoles railway (Meiggs *et al.*) were completed. Work was abandoned in 1877.

the lost Litoral. Meanwhile the Chilean fleet captured Cobija and Toco-pilla without difficulty. Cobija, along with some other coastal settlements, had already recently suffered very severely from a series of earthquakes and tidal waves in 1866, 1868 and 1877:

This unhappy little place presents a sad example of the effects of earthquakes along the coast...the ground was so shaken that the bones from the shallow graves were scattered over the surface. The place looked as if it had been exposed to a severe bombardment, and we at first imagined that we were viewing the effects of the war. This occurred as recently as 1877 and was evidently a severe one.[1]

The main centres in the Bolivian Litoral had fallen, only the most isolated settlements around San Pedro de Atacama remaining undisturbed. In little more than a month the Bolivian flag had been lowered on the Pacific coast to leave Peru in jeopardy, for the War was now quickly carried north into the rich nitrate province of Tarapacá. The blockade of Iquique, Peru's principal nitrate port, continued and Pisagua and Mollendo were bombarded.

At the end of April 1879, the Bolivian President sent a 4000-strong army to Tacna, as well as two battalions to Pisagua. But the long marches across the desert and the lack of railways hindered any fast communication and effective joint cooperation between the Peruvian and Bolivian generals. At Iquique, Patillos and Tarapacá their forces were isolated and cut down. On 23 April 1879 the Bolivian Government requested the British Foreign Office to stop arms shipments from New York bound for Valparaiso *via* Glasgow, adding that it did so because nearly all the transit trade along the South American west coast was in English hands. Bolivia, lacking any merchant navy of its own, stated its intention to coopt privateers under the Bolivian flag by letters of marque, in order to seize Chilean property of any description being carried aboard neutral vessels. The Admiralty reacted immediately by letting it be known that it would not sanction such 'organised and legalised piracy',[2] and the Government instructed the Commander-in-Chief Naval Forces Pacific to prevent any such attempted seizures aboard British vessels, by force if necessary.[3] The English Pacific Steam Navigation Company, whose virtual monopoly of the west coast transit trade was based on a fleet of forty-six steamships, was careful, in its own interests, to preserve strict neutrality. Its major repair yards were in Peru and the company refused a Chilean request to carry Chilean troops into any part of the disputed territory of either Bolivia or Peru.

[1] R. Nelson Boyd, *Sketches of Chili and the Chilians during the War 1879–1880*, London, 1881, p. 179.
[2] W. H. Smith to Lord Salisbury, Admiralty, 9 June 1879, and H. H. Gibbs to Lord Salisbury, Admiralty, 14 July 1879, *F.O. 11/27*.
[3] Lord Salisbury to Lords Commissioners of the Admiralty, August 1879, *ibid.*

Once Iquique had surrendered to the blockade, the Chileans lost no time in putting this key point back into production. 'From the appearance of the place', wrote Boyd, 'it would have been difficult to imagine that it had only recently been surrendered and was then occupied by enemies. As a matter of fact, almost the entire population is Chilian, and they feel more at home under their own flag than under that of Peru.'[1] *Oficinas*, railways, water depots and distillation plants were captured and carefully preserved so that output continued without serious interruption during the war period.

By the end of 1879, in less than a year, Chile was in control. It was considered vital, however, to carry the offensive well beyond the nitrate zone, making victory so decisive that future possession of the region would be indisputable. Arica was never a nitrate port but it was still southern Peru's most important centre of resistance, despite the havoc caused by recent earthquakes. The port of Arica was therefore blockaded and shelled and the Arica–Tacna railway cut, for its first few miles lie close to the beach. After Tacna eventually fell with the defeat of a combined Peruvian–Bolivian army, a rear assault on Arica in June 1880 deprived Peru of its main defence focus south of Callao. Arica was almost immediately reopened for Bolivian transit trade and La Paz ran agog with rumour that the Chileans were on the point of invading the city.[2] The Bolivian Government prepared to evacuate to Oruro, and Peru launched two gunboats on Lake Titicaca. But the triumphant Chileans pursued a consistent policy, swept north along the coast and confirmed their supremacy with the occupation of Lima in January 1881. Only sporadic guerrilla fighting inland prolonged the war until 1882.

5. THE POST-WAR PERIOD: BOLIVIA RENEWS ITS DEMANDS FOR ARICA

As far as Bolivia was concerned, the Nitrate War was both an ending and a beginning, for it heralded an important new phase in the 'Problem of the Pacific'. While it had obviously resulted in the loss of the panhandle, it had also involved the defeat of Peru, whose resolute grip on Arica had tightened over the years until shaken free with such apparent ease in 1880. Suddenly, the related problems of boundaries, ports and outlets called for new solutions in a Chilean context. It seemed unlikely, Bolivia reasoned,

[1] R. Nelson Boyd, *Sketches of Chili*, p. 181.
[2] Charles Adams to Secretary of State W. M. Evarts, La Paz, 3 August 1880, Diplomatic Despatches from Bolivia, *General Records of the Department of State, Record Group 59*, Washington, D.C.

that Chile would wish to remain in permanent possession of territory thus far north, particularly as it lay outside the valuable nitrate belt and placed excessive strain on Chile's longitudinal lines of communication. What seemed more certain was that the shock waves which Chilean expansion had sent surging all along the Pacific coast would at last toss Arica Bolivia's way.

In April 1884 Bolivia signed a truce of undetermined duration with Chile, and a temporary boundary was drawn until such time as a detailed survey could take place.[1] This new line linked the volcanic cones of Zapalegui, Licancaur (Licancabur) and Cobana; the most southerly whirlpool in Lake Ascotan; the peaks of Ollagüe and Túa, and thence continued northward to follow the former boundary between the Peruvian province of Tarapacá and Bolivia. Officially, Bolivia became landlocked as a result of the truce. Peru meanwhile had concluded the Treaty of Ancón with Chile in 1883,[2] recognising permanent Chilean ownership of Tarapacá province as far north as the Camarones ravine, Chilean occupation for a period of ten years after ratification as far north as the Sama river, and agreeing a plebiscite to determine the eventual possession of the provinces of Tacna and Arica. This plebiscite, due to be held in 1894, never took place but in May 1895 two treaties were simultaneously concluded between Chile and Bolivia. One confirmed permanent Chilean ownership of Bolivia's Litoral Department while the second, a secret Transference of Territory Treaty, was designed to allow Bolivia a corridor to the sea. Article I stated that:

If in consequence of the plebiscite which was to take place in conformity with the Treaty of Ancón, or if by virtue of direct arrangement, Chile should acquire dominion and permanent sovereignty over the territories of Tacna and Arica, she undertakes to transfer them to Bolivia in the same form and to the same extent in which she may acquire them, with the stipulation that (Art. II) Chile, at the same time, shall advance her frontier north of the Camarones ravine to that of Vitor. While using the utmost effort, either separately or jointly with Bolivia, to obtain definite possession of Tacna and Arica, if (Article IV) Chile cannot obtain sovereignty of the zone in which are situated the cities of Tacna and Arica, she binds herself to cede to Bolivia the roadstead of Vitor or another analogous one, in addition to the sum of $ US 5 million.

Bolivia was to have paid a similar amount if the Tacna–Arica territory was transferred to it as a Pacific corridor, but although ratifications were

[1] *F.O. 16/229.* Under Article v of the truce agreement, Bolivia was forced to accept the *duty-free* import of Chilean products and manufactured goods. It was a reciprocal arrangement, but Bolivia in fact could derive little benefit from it. Other foreign manufacturers exporting to Bolivia frequently found themselves unable to compete with cheaper Chilean imports.

[2] *F.O. 16/229.*

exchanged in 1896, the exchange was well outside the six-month period stipulated in Article VIII, and none of these proposals, so obviously favourable to Bolivia, went any further than the conference table. It has been suggested that some understanding may have existed between Chile and Bolivia in 1866 that if Chile ultimately gained the Bolivian Litoral, the Peruvian nitrate zone of Tarapacá and beyond, then the provinces of Tacna and Arica would go to Bolivia.[1] Other considerations aside, however, negotiations between Chile and Bolivia were complicated at this time by the involvement of Argentina. Part of the high Puna de Atacama, adjacent to the former Litoral, had been ceded by Bolivia to Argentina in 1889 and 1891–3, and a further section was to be the subject of a United States arbitration award in 1899.[2] Bolivia, anxious to conclude the Pacific corridor agreement temporarily offered by Chile, found itself unable to do so in the face of opposition variously from Peru, Chile and Argentina.

In August 1900 the Chilean Minister in La Paz, on instructions from Santiago, repudiated the suggestions outlined five years earlier and reminded Bolivia of the weakness of its supposed bargaining position. While the official statement observed that 'the ancient Bolivian sea coast is and will be for ever Chilean', mention was made of monetary compensation and railway construction from at least one Chilean port into Bolivia. But in turning to examine the proposals for the cession of a strip of territory with a port, the document expanded Chilean arguments so as to leave no ambiguities:

Where could we find such a zone and a port? From the valley of Camarones to the south as far as the Straits of Magellan all the cities are Chilean, formed, developed and sustained with our own nationals, with our capital, with the sweat and the courage of the Chilean nation. In those populations...are almost no Bolivians. To grant a zone and a sea port in those places will be to give up to foreign countries thousands of Chilean families...Premature contracts were concluded in 1895 since when Chilean public opinion has modified. It is necessary to declare that Bolivia cannot rely upon the transference of the territories of Tacna and Arica, notwithstanding if the plebiscite is favourable to Chile...North of Arica there is no sea port and no division of Chile can be contemplated. *It must be asked if it is of vital necessity for Bolivia to have a seaport on the Pacific?* Antofagasta and Arica will be terminal points of railway lines...

In time of war Chilean forces will take the only Bolivian port with the same ease with which it occupied all the Bolivian sea ports in 1879. This is no vain boast. Bolivia must see things as they are, not as they could be. The friendship and goodwill of Chile are of great advantage to Bolivia, more than a narrow band of unfruitful territory with a port attached. There is no possibility of a port in compensation for the sea coast; Chile has occupied the Bolivian sea coast and has taken possession of it with

---

[1] See Victor M. Maúrtua, *The Question of the Pacific*, English edit., Philadelphia, 1901, pp. 20–1 and 256–63.   [2] See below, p. 187.

the same title with which Germany annexed Alsace and Lorraine, and the United States of North America has taken Puerto Rico. Our rights arise from victory, the supreme law of the nations.

That the Bolivian sea coast is rich and worth many millions we have always known. We keep it because of its worth; if it had no value there would be no point in keeping it.[1]

6. OLD PORTS AND NEW RAILWAYS

It was made clear that Chile's intention was to compensate for territory lost in 1879 by much-needed railway construction, and events moved slowly forward to the Treaty of Peace, Friendship and Commerce of 20 October 1904.[2] Elaborating the simplified line of the 1884 truce agreement, ninety-six points in the Andean Cordillera Occidental were listed in Article II as forming the boundary between the two republics. Demarcation of the 1904 boundary began in 1906 and over the next few years eighty-three of the ninety-six points mentioned in the treaty were fixed and marked with metal tripods. Some of the peaks, considered unnecessary or too difficult to climb, or even inaccessible, by the Mixed Boundary Commissioners, remain without artificial demarcation, while supplementary tripods have in some cases been added in the field to clarify the position of the boundary. By Articles VI and VII, Bolivia was guaranteed commercial transit rights through Chile and facilities at selected ports, notably Arica and Antofagasta.[3] A cash payment of £300,000 to Bolivia was provided for in Article IV and, within stipulated limits, up to a 5 per cent guarantee was made on capital which Bolivia might borrow to construct five railways over a thirty-year period.[4]

The core of the agreement, however, was considered under Article III, by which Chile undertook to construct a railway between Arica and Alto La Paz. Work began in 1906, although Chile was technically still only an occupying force in the region through which nearly half the total length of track would run. The London firm of Sir John Jackson had secured the

---

[1] Extracts from the 'Ultimatum' presented to Bolivia by the Chilean Minister, Abraham König, La Paz, 13 August 1900. (Enclosed in United States' Diplomatic Despatches from Bolivia, *General Records of the Dept. of State, Record Group 59*, Washington, D.C.) Two weeks later, a copy was also forwarded to the Foreign Office by the American Minister in La Paz, G. H. Beidgman, 2 October 1900, as Britain maintained no diplomatic representative in Bolivia between 1853 and 1903. *F.O. 11/37.*

[2] *F.O. 16/348.* Also *Col. Trat. Vig. Bol.*, vol. IV, pp. 394–415.

[3] Further details were included in a Commercial Convention 1912, protocols February and August 1928; and Conventions on Transit Trade 1937, 1953 (Arica Declaration), and 1955 (Chilean–Bolivian Economic Coordination Treaty), Foreign Ministry files, La Paz.

[4] Article III listed these railways as: Uyuni–Potosí; Oruro–La Paz; Oruro–Cochabamba–Santa Cruz; La Paz–Beni region; Potosí–Sucre–Lagunillas–Santa Cruz.

contract and work proceeded without undue incident, despite a series of complaints by Peru that the railway was being laid through Peruvian territory, i.e. territory over which Peru still held sovereign right and where in consequence any railway construction was completely unauthorised.[1] The colonization, irrigation and railway programs which Chile was by now energetically promoting, however, were regarded as a clear indication that Chile did not intend to relinquish the territory, and the work went ahead without interruption. The steepest section on the 275-mile line was negotiated by twenty-five very difficult miles of rack rail (maximum gradient 6 per cent), as well as by considerable cutting and two tunnels. Inaugurated in 1913, the 145-mile Bolivian section was handed over to that country after a further fifteen years, in accordance with the treaty terms. Thus a Chilean railway, built for Bolivia, in Peruvian territory, by a British company, put Arica within twenty-four hours of the edge of La Paz.

The long-awaited completion by rail of the traditional link between the *altiplano* and its port had now to be reviewed against a sequence of events which had slowly been changing Bolivia's Pacific outlet problem. One could note, for instance, that the new railway did not follow the historic trail into Bolivia by way of the Tacna oasis. The old Arica–Tacna railway still terminated at that point for although contractors had been engaged to extend the track to La Paz in 1871, and work was scheduled to begin in October 1872, the whole enterprise had been shelved and never revived after the War of the Pacific. No agreement was made to build on to this already existing track, probably because Chile never seriously considered the likelihood of retaining Tacna on a permanent basis, despite the Chileanization policy pursued there during the occupation. A completely separate and more southerly track, on the other hand, immeasurably strengthened Chile's political claims to Arica, as subsequent events were to prove.

The Arica–La Paz railway had been surveyed along a new, steeper and more direct route and one which was unquestionably the shortest (Fig. 4), but by the time it was inaugurated in 1913 it had become the *third* rail link between the Pacific and the *altiplano*, the third and the last. Henry Meiggs had already extended a 325-mile railway from Mollendo to Arequipa by 1870 and to Puno by 1874 (p. 52 n. 1). This famous American entrepreneur from Catskill, N.Y., had developed wide-ranging interests in railroads, guano, agriculture (in the Cochabamba area), and in various banking

---

[1] See correspondence between the Peruvian Legation, London and the Foreign Office, April 1909, *F.O. 371/720.*

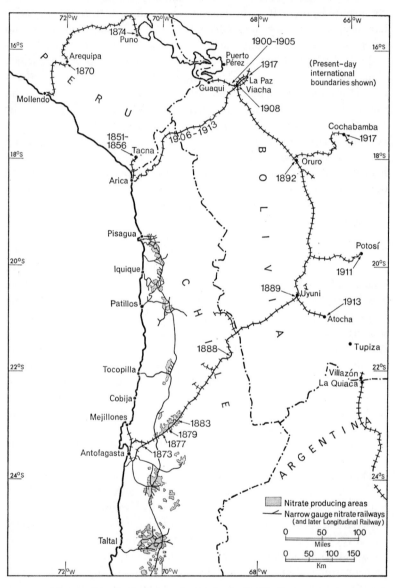

4   The growth of rail communication in the Pacific Sector: 1851–1917

and credit houses in Peru, Bolivia and Chile in the 1860s and 1870s. Immediately Meiggs' railway reached Puno on the shore of Lake Titicaca, Mollendo became competitive with Arica for the Bolivian trade. Two steamers plied across the lake to Chililaya (Cachilaya), where heavy wagons especially imported from the U.S.A. loaded cargo for the 40-mile journey into La Paz. Bolivia renamed Chililaya Puerto Pérez, and after Antofagasta, Arica and Mollendo were captured by Chile during the Pacific War, for a time declared the small lake settlement to be Bolivia's only port. Washington even established a U.S. consular agency there. This route claimed to put La Paz as little as four days from the Pacific, while by 1905 the wagon trail had been replaced by a railway to La Paz from Guaqui, to which the steamers were rerouted. This 60-mile Guaqui–La Paz line was subsequently purchased from the Bolivian Government by the British-owned Peruvian Corporation. Thus, after 1874, the Mollendo rail-and-water route was faster than the Arica trail, even though nearly twice as long.[1]

Five hundred miles farther south, the early nitrate railway behind Antofagasta belonging to the Compañía de Salitres y Ferrocarril de Antofagasta had been extended through and then beyond the Pampa del Tamarugal. No longer simply a nitrate railway, it had rapidly been pushed up towards the new Chile–Bolivia trucial boundary after the War of the Pacific, and after the formation in London of the Antofagasta (Chili) and Bolivia Railway Co. in 1888, the line had been continued into Bolivia under concession to reach Uyuni in 1889 and Oruro in 1892. La Paz itself was linked in 1917. It was admittedly a long route (at 729 miles, over two-and-a-half times as long as the Arica–La Paz railway) but serious gradients and tortuous curves were avoided.

Thus, in the period just before the outbreak of the Pacific War, Mollendo and Arica together were reported by the U.S. consul in La Paz to have been handling not less than 90 per cent of Bolivia's trade,[2] and not

[1] The advantage gained by Mollendo in this period, at the expense of Arica, is illustrated, for example, by a North American pharmacist describing his expedition to Bolivia in 1885-7 on behalf of Parke, Davis & Co. of Detroit, to investigate new sources of coca and other drugs: 'At the time of our arrival, Arica seemed to be walled in. Upon closer approach, we found the wall to consist of cases, bales and casks of merchandise awaiting transportation to the interior, because of the closing of the port of Mollendo...on account of rebellion at the time...But there was daily expectation that Mollendo would again be thrown open to commerce. Merchants therefore shipped from Arica to the interior only the most necessary merchandise, holding the remainder awaiting developments.' H. H. Rusby, *Jungle Memories*, New York and London, 1933, p. 10.

[2] Charles Adams to the Second Assistant Secretary of State, 5 January 1881, Consular Despatches from La Paz, *General Records of the Dept. of State, Record Group 59*, Washington, D.C.

until the Chilean blockade had temporarily closed these two Peruvian ports was any appreciable volume diverted to the Argentine (Tupiza) route. In such an emergency, despite a journey of over fifteen hundred miles, export through Argentina at least offered greater security for cargo, mostly out-going metals.[1] But by 1895 the emphasis had shifted again quite dramatically. The railway from Antofagasta had reached Oruro to tap the principal mining centres, and suddenly this more remote Pacific port dominated Bolivia's western outlets. Not only did it handle more than twice the tonnage of imports *via* Mollendo, and well over one hundred times the tonnage *via* Argentina (excluding 35,762 imported live animals); in terms of export volume the Antofagasta railway had clearly captured the lion's share of the Bolivian bulk-ore carrying.[2] Without rail communication to the *altiplano*, Arica's trade had slumped catastrophically and it was not even included in the official trade returns submitted to Washington by the American Legation. These clearly stated the entry points handling Bolivian imports to be Antofagasta and Mollendo/Chililaya (Puerto Pérez).

The completion of the Arica–La Paz railway in 1913 did not lead to any sudden salvation for the port. With its chronic shortage of rolling stock, steep curves and rack section, high freight rates and maintenance costs, and later its dual administration, the problems were severe. Neither the Peruvian Corporation nor the Antofagasta (Chili) and Bolivia Railway Co. considered that it presented them with serious competition. Indeed, Bolivia was rumoured to be anxious to overcome the pitfalls of joint ownership with Chile after 1928 by declaring it an international railway under U.S. ownership, a suggestion always strongly resisted by Chile.

In time, however, although Antofagasta retained undisputed command

[1] In 1883, official Argentine sources recorded the following export from Buenos Aires of Bolivian materials (all tons quoted are metric tons): Silver: 1,036.362 tons; *Silver bars*: 204.606 tons; *Tin*: 727.784 tons; *Bismuth*: 60.868 tons. (Quoted by W. A. Seay to W. Hunter, 20 October 1885, Consular Despatches from La Paz, *op. cit.*)

[2] 1895 imports into Bolivia

    via Antofagasta all-rail route as far as Oruro: 12,849 tons
    via Mollendo rail–lake–wagon road to La Paz: 5367 tons
    via Tupiza (representing all Argentine traffic), rail to Jujuy and trail into Bolivia: 108 tons, plus 15,692 sheep, 9557 asses, 7404 cows, 2368 mules and horses, 443 llamas, 298 mares.

1895 exports from Bolivia

    via Antofagasta: 233,381 tons
    via Mollendo: 3518 tons
    via Tupiza: 82 tons

(Report on the Commerce of Bolivia submitted by G. Zalles to Assistant Secretary of State W. Rockhill, 19 February 1897, Consular Despatches from La Paz, *General Records of the Dept. of State, Record Group 59*, Washington, D.C.)

of Bolivia's Pacific trade, Arica was able slowly to overhaul Mollendo. The delays due to the breaks of load at each end of Lake Titicaca, and the innumerable opportunities for pilfering, were crippling, since the nineteenth-century proposal to continue the railway around the lake had unfortunately never been implemented.[1] The Mollendo route declined, so that by 1922, although still a very poor second to Antofagasta, Arica was handling nearly three times more import tonnage for Bolivia than Mollendo. Arica was also more popular for passenger traffic, more so than Antofagasta, for even at that period the Arica railway claimed to have put La Paz within twelve hours of the Pacific.

The American Minister accordingly advised his Government in 1923 to disregard the Mollendo route, as goods were taking anything from two weeks to two months to arrive in La Paz. The Southern Peruvian Railway Co. complained in reply that their line would never be competitive as long as it was severed by the lake, and proposals for a Puno–Guaqui line were reconsidered. But competition from the two all-rail routes was now too strong, besides which the rail-building era, on the *altiplano* at least, was almost over. Already the thought of eventual competition from motor transport was sufficient to turn down any further rail construction on the Pacific–La Paz run. Indeed, by then, rail freight rates were so high that in 1922, two bids to re-canalise the Desaguadero were seriously considered by the Bolivian Government in the forlorn hope of finding a practicable alternative for the movement of ores.

7. NEW PACIFIC BOUNDARY CONSIDERATIONS: BOLIVIA CLAIMS ITS 'RIGHTS' TO THE SEA

What the rail links through Chile, Chilean-occupied territory and Peru had done in terms of Bolivia's 'Problem of the Pacific', among all other considerations, was to rob the country of its claim to be without transport outlets to the sea. The plea for access had been answered in terms of transit concessions. Treaties and conventions, transit agreements, port

[1] Although a link between Puno and Guaqui along the western side of the lake would have been considerably shorter (it would in fact have followed one of the old, colonial trails into Upper Peru), the proposed line had been routed around the northern and eastern shores: Juliaca–Puerto Acosta–Carabuco–Achacachi–Viacha. It was stated that this was done for strategic reasons as these shores were less vulnerable (to attack from the Pacific sector). The proposal for railway extension was linked to the Peruvian Corporation's plan to capture a more profitable share of Bolivia's trade by the development of barge navigation on the Desaguadero river, involving only short overland hauls from the Corocoro and Oruro mining areas. But, in the event, this failed to survive competition from the Antofagasta and Arica railways.

and warehouse facilities and competitive rail routes, with all their un-doubted problems and limitations, had undermined many of Bolivia's traditional arguments. The side effects, however, of the reciprocal trade agreements involved in the transit and other treaties were often serious, for Bolivia's domestic manufacturing was unable to make much headway against the resulting flow of imported foreign goods.

As the rail links relieved, in some measure, one aspect of the problem, new emphasis was placed upon intrinsic 'rights' of access to the Pacific – i.e. the 'right' of every State, whenever continental location made this at all feasible, to possess its own independent outlet to the high seas. To be forced to plead and negotiate transit terms was thus held to be at variance with a nation's intrinsic sovereign status. This shift in the argument, if Bolivia was determined to pursue such a line, was necessitated by the three existing rail links to the Pacific. But it was also given new impetus by President Woodrow Wilson's message to the United States Senate, delivered on 22 January 1917. This included the statement that every country had the right of direct outlet to the sea 'either by the cession of territory...or by the neutralisation of direct rights of way under the general guarantee which will assure peace'.[1] When news of this announce-ment reached La Paz, its effect was electrifying. The city was jubilant, and the idea immediately gained ground that Bolivia might acquire, even demand, an Arica corridor, and that in so doing it could simultaneously provide a buffer zone between Chile and Peru.

President Wilson's statement proved the decisive factor in Bolivia's breaking off diplomatic relations with Germany later that year. Deference to the wishes of the U.S.A. had become of paramount importance, although the influential German element in the Bolivian population made it an extremely unpopular move domestically. Indeed, it was noted by the Allies' Ministers in La Paz, somewhat wryly, that great care continued to be taken not to stress the diplomatic rupture with Germany at any business or social functions. The French Minister to Bolivia, congratulating the Government on its decision, promised France's official support in sub-sequent negotiations for a port, although which port was not specified.

Such a mood of optimism encouraged Bolivia to prepare and present an impassioned plea to the Secretariat of the League of Nations in 1920 for possession of Tacna and Arica.[2] It was the product of long and exhaustive research by ex-President Montes, than Bolivia's Minister in Paris. No

---

[1] National Archives, Washington, D.C.; also *A Compilation of the Messages and Papers of the Presidents*, Bureau of National Literature, New York, vol. XVI, p. 8202; and *F.O. 371/2899*.
[2] I. Montes, *Blue Book Memorandum on the Rights of Bolivia to Tacna and Arica*, Paris and London, 1920 (encl. in *F.O. 371/4428*).

attempt was made to conceal the fact that Bolivia's acquisition of Arica was the basis of the country's entire foreign policy. All external relations were measured against the yardstick of how far the actions might assist or impede this realisation. Despite the strong pro-German sentiment obtaining in Bolivia at the time, the Treaty of Versailles was ratified and all hopes pinned upon the League of Nations. After the Armistice, Chile became aware that it might be pressured into yielding a Pacific corridor and accordingly the Bello Mission proposed a zone for this purpose in territory still only occupied, not owned, by Chile, namely a strip *north* of Arica and the Arica–La Paz railway, as far as the river Sama. Arica, it was suggested, might become a free port under joint Chile–Bolivia control and in it, Bolivia would be permitted to construct its own wharves and warehouses.[1] But in return Chile was to be granted such favourable trade preferences that Bolivia complained it could never hope to be more than a commerical annexe of the other.

Agitation for Arica continued, particularly as part of the periodic anti-Chilean movements which punctuated the long Liberal administration of 1899–1920. Then in July 1920, a revolutionary *coup* brought the Republicans into power, and as a party more consciously pro-Peruvian in outlook, Bolivia's demands for Arica were softened and a call made instead for the return of Antofagasta. This was not in fact pursued for long, as its chances of success were remote, even in the opinion of the Republicans themselves. But it was an interesting manœuvre in the light of a century of Pacific boundary controversy. Throughout this period, Bolivia had never agitated with any real conviction for the return of its original panhandle; strict irredentism was not sustained as part of Bolivia's demand for a 'window' on to the Pacific. The Republicans' short-lived plea for the return of Antofagasta serves to point up how little effort was ever made to retrieve the panhandle. In part, this was a result of its inconvenient location when compared with the Arica outlet; in part, because of the extraordinarily vigorous growth achieved there under Chile, which made its ownership incontestable.

8. CHILEAN DEVELOPMENT OF BOLIVIA'S 'LOST LANDS'

After the War of the Pacific, the Bolivian Litoral Department had become the Chilean Province of Antofagasta which, together with the Province of Tarapacá, was known as the Norte Grande. Nitrate production boomed during a thirty-year 'Golden Age' in the Atacama desert. Although out-

[1] G. Haggard to Lord Curzon, Annual Report on Bolivia for 1919, La Paz, *F.O. 371/4428*.

put fluctuated in certain years, Chile's control of the nitrate zone coincided with a *bonanza* period in world demand. The invention of dynamite by Nobel in 1867 had stimulated an era of feverish activity among the nitrate *oficinas*, while at the same time the needs of agriculture in a world of rapidly expanding population became more insistent. Natural methods of maintaining the nitrate content of the soil in the more exhausted regions of Europe and North America were insufficient under conditions of continuous heavy cropping, and Chile saltpetre provided nitrate in an easily assimilable form. It had rapidly replaced copper as Chile's main source of revenue, allaying any post-War depression, attracting British capital investment, and wiping out the National Debt. What had once been regarded as one of Spain's poorest and remotest possessions now became one of the great South American powers.

The nitrate ports of Pisagua, Iquique, Tocopilla, Mejillones, Antofagasta and Taltal – particularly Iquique and Antofagasta – grew phenomenally as urban foci on the inhospitable coast. Nitrate clippers rounded Cape Horn to load the valuable cargo, while the isolation of life on this barren coast was made tolerable by the many amenities of Europe and North America which could be imported quite economically during this period of unprecedented prosperity. Like many 'boom-towns' in harsh surroundings, these ports happily pursued an existence rendered bizarre only by their extraordinary location. Iquique, for example, managed to engage many famous theatrical performers, including Sarah Bernhardt and the entire D'Oyly Carte Opera Company, while during its boom years the town had the reputation of consuming more champagne per head than any other city in the world! In Antofagasta's Plaza Colón, peacocks strutted over green, tree-shaded lawns. It was, and still is, difficult to realise the artificiality of these ports in an environment of such extreme aridity.

The age was typified by the Nitrate Kings, none more famous than the flamboyant John Thomas North, a great Victorian entrepreneur, who controlled, in addition to his extracting plants, a large proportion of the nitrate railways and the provision-, water- and coal-supplying companies in north, central and south Chile.[1] Foreign investment, particularly English and German capital, continued to flow into the region, so that by the end of the nineteenth century only 15 per cent of the nitrate exploitation remained directly in Chilean hands, although this was to rise to 51 per cent by 1921. Nevertheless, between 1880 and 1900 Chile collected £81 million in export taxes and another £40 million up to 1918 from the 'lost

---

[1] An interesting account of his activities is given by H. Blakemore, 'John Thomas North, the Nitrate King', *History Today*, vol. XII, 1962, pp. 467–75.

lands' of Peru and Bolivia. As much as 71 per cent of the total value of Chile's exports was from nitrates in this period, although the desert zone accounted for only 7.3 per cent of the nation's population.

But World War I, while temporarily increasing nitrate production for explosives and fertiliser, ended Atacama's 'Golden Age'. The blockade which cut Germany's supply line from Chile (Germany was one of the biggest nitrate importers) stimulated the discovery by Professor Fritz Haber of nitrogen fixation from the air, a discovery for which he later received a Nobel Prize in recognition of its value to world agriculture. Now that nitrate could be produced so cheaply in Europe and North America, an area so remote as Atacama suffered severely. The trade crashed, *oficinas* closed, railways were abandoned, and numbers of mules used for preliminary loading were turned loose into the desert to die.

New systems of recovery, using low-grade *caliche* (8.0 to 9.0 per cent), notably the Guggenheim process in 1926, were introduced to replace the simple Shanks method which had demanded high-grade ores (often up to 30 to 50 per cent). Production is now concentrated at two giant, fully mechanised plants – Pedro de Valdivia and María Elena – owned outright until 1968 by the Anglo–Lautaro Company. More significantly, nearly 40 per cent of the world's iodine is produced here as part of the total process, the entire nitrate and iodine output being shipped from Tocopilla. Other nitrate-producing centres today, on a very much smaller scale, are at Victoria (export from Iquique), and two other small *oficinas* behind Taltal.[1] Pedro de Valdivia and María Elena together employ over 12,000, and are both in the former Bolivian Litoral.

Also in former Bolivian territory (i.e. as claimed a few miles north of Calama, Fig. 3 *b*) lies Chuquicamata, the biggest single opencast copper mine in the world and part of the Anaconda group. In June 1969 Anaconda finally agreed to sell to Chile 51 per cent of the Chuquicamata (and El Salvador) mines by 1 January 1970 for approximately U.S. $200 million,

---

[1] Nitrate production in recent representative years (thousands of metric tons):

	Pedro de Valdivia and María Elena	Victoria	Taltal
1962/3	927	121	58
1963/4	975	119	51
1964/5	1000	110	43
1965/6	992	113	56
1966/7	780	126	42

Total output from all five centres is nevertheless only about 3 per cent of world nitrate production. Iodine, however, per kilo, sells today at approximately U.S. $5.0, nitrate at $0.05.

and to sell the remainder after 1972 at a price still to be determined. Chuquicamata employs nearly eight thousand in the works alone, and approximately 280,000 metric tons of refined copper are exported annually, entirely through Antofagasta: 80 per cent to Europe, Japan, and elsewhere in South America, and 20 per cent to the U.S.A. Re-discovered in 1910, and developed by Guggenheim, Chuquicamata has at least a thousand million tons of ore reserves, among the largest in the world. Events thus disproved the statement made by Clements Markham in 1883 after the War of the Pacific when, referring to Chile, he observed: 'But what is her real net gain? She has got some manure that belongs to her neighbours. That is all!'[1] It was not all, but even so it was enough to promote the reappraisal of Atacama, *res nullius* during the Spanish colonial period and in the early days of independence, and to establish Chile securely in the emergent Latin American power hierarchy.

Yet such had been the catastrophic effect of World War I upon the natural nitrate industry, that when the final arbitration discussions began once more in the 1920s to attempt to settle the old Tacna–Arica problem, the nitrate revenues – the original cause of the controversy – were in decline. Out of 150 Chilean *oficinas*, 111 had closed, and by the time agreement was achieved, only twenty were still working. In such circumstances, the concluding settlement of the Pacific's Atacama boundaries began.

9. 1921–1929: BOLIVIA'S FINAL ATTEMPT TO GAIN ARICA

At the end of 1921 the long stalemate of disputed ownership in Tacna and Arica was submitted to the United States for arbitration. This sore on South America's west coast had been festering for almost forty years, and as the U.S.A. assumed its somewhat thankless role, it was generally felt that if the Monroe Doctrine was not already dead, the Tacna–Arica question would provide its grave. Investigation and deliberation upon the

---

[1] Clements R. Markham, *The War between Peru and Chile*, p. 273. For a general commentary on contemporary conditions in Bolivia's old desert panhandle, see W. E. Rudolph's illus-trated description of Chile's Antofagasta province (approximating to the former Bolivian Litoral), based on many years' residence in the region, in *Vanishing Trails of Atacama*, Am. Geog. Soc. Research Series No. 24, New York, 1963. Rudolph notes (p. 55) that 'their change in nationality from Bolivian to Chilean in 1884 made no difference to the Indians... As recently as the 1920's and 1930's, *comuneros* of the smaller settlements (in the desert's eastern fringe) were wont to refer to the world outside, "over there in Chile", as they pointed a finger to the west.' Note is also made (pp. 82–3) of a minor adjustment to the boundary made in the 1920s near Ollagüe in order to place a branch railway to Collahuasi entirely within Chilean territory, in exchange for an area ceded to Bolivia farther north.

problems of a plebiscite continued until, in 1926, after General Pershing had been replaced by General Lassiter as President of the Plebiscite Commission, the idea of any solution by this means was finally abandoned. It boiled down, Lassiter acknowledged, to the fact that while Arica was being demanded by all three neighbouring States, Chile was in possession of it.

Rumours that U.S. capital would back Bolivia's purchase, not only of the Arica–La Paz railway, but of the port of Arica itself, and even of Easter Island in order to provide a U.S. naval base, were eagerly fanned by Chile in a mood of rising anti-Americanism. Secretary of State Kellogg's 1926 suggestion that the neutralisation of the two provinces, or their cession to Bolivia, might resolve the deadlock which discussions had then reached was greeted in Chile with the comment that Bolivia would shortly become a second Panama or Cuba. Thus as Chile continued to forecast that neutralisation would result in permanent U.S. dominance of the zone, both Chile and Peru declared vehemently that they would each prefer the other to own the provinces rather than allow them to be ceded to Bolivia.

Eventually, one suggestion which had previously been rejected in 1926 was successfully revived, to be announced with some relief by President Hoover on 14 May 1929.[1] Peru retained Tacna; Arica was acquired officially by Chile and the Arica–La Paz railway was selected as a convenient line of reference in the desert *north* of which to set out the new Chile–Peru boundary. Delimited in the treaty which followed the award, and starting from a point on the coast to be called 'Concordia', 10 kilometres north of the bridge over the river Lluta (just outside the port of Arica), the boundary was to run eastwards, paralleling the Arica–La Paz railway as far as possible, 10 kilometres north of the track. Adjustments were made in the north-east to include Mt Tacora's rich sulphur deposits within Chile, although Chile agreed to cede in perpetuity to Peru rights over the Uchusuma and Mauri (Azucarero) canals. Proposals for, and construction of, the first of these had been pioneered by Peru before the War of the Pacific in one of the several nineteenth-century schemes to divert the headwaters of eastward-flowing streams such as the Mauri and Lauca westward into the desert, particularly towards the Tacna–Arica area. Chile had developed the idea to some extent during the occupation with the construction of the Mauri canal, and in relinquishing both of

---

[1] Details of the background and course of the American arbitration were recorded by W. J. Dennis in *Documentary History of the Tacna–Arica Dispute*, Univ. of Iowa, 1927, and in the same author's *Tacna and Arica*, Yale Univ. Press, 1931. See also *F.O. 371/4448*, *F.O. 371/11105*, *F.O. 371/11106*, *F.O. 371/11107*, *F.O. 371/11950*, and *F.O. 371/13452*.

these canals in 1929, granted to Peru full rights of access in those sections which would pass through Chilean territory, together with rights to widen, modify and utilise the canals and their waters, only excepting supplies to the river Lluta and the Tacora sulphur beds.

Chile was also to construct within 1575 metres of Arica bay, for the exclusive use of Peru, a wharf, a Peruvian Custom House, and a terminal station for the Arica–Tacna railway which has, therefore, since 1929 crossed an international boundary. A further payment of six million dollars was to be made to Peru upon the exchange of ratifications. Port and warehouse facilities already established for Bolivia in Arica, under earlier agreements, were maintained. No specific mention of Bolivia, however, had been made in the U.S.A.'s arbitration announcement, although in order to avoid Bolivia's complaint that it had been shut away from the Pacific by America's attitude, the Hoover arbitration stated that its proposals in no way affected any future disposition of the disputed territory by either party.

The treaty incorporating the proposals was concluded between Chile and Peru at Lima on 3 June 1929,[1] but it was accompanied by a supplementary protocol.[2] Article 1 stipulated that neither Government might, without the previous agreement of the other, cede to any third country all, or any part of, the Tacna–Arica territory. Nor were any new international railway lines to be constructed through it. Bolivia's Pacific boundary was thus finalised at the triple point in the Cordillera Occidental; almost exactly one hundred and four years after the creation of an independent Upper Peru, the failure of the protracted 'Arica para Bolivia' movement was irrevocably confirmed.

10. REMAINING BOUNDARY SETTLEMENT WITH PERU: THE DISTINCTIVENESS OF THE TITICACA REGION

The southern section of Bolivia's boundary with Peru had been shortened by over five hundred miles as a result of Chilean expansion. By the time the uncertainties bequeathed by the War of the Pacific had been finally

---

[1] *F.O. 371/13452.* The return of the province of Tacna to Peru necessitated new boundary negotiations between Peru and Bolivia in this section which, between 1906 and 1929, had been provisionally demarcated between Chile and Bolivia. Minor disagreements between Peru and Bolivia over the placing of the boundary posts at Mauripalca still await final settlement. Failure to complete demarcation of this portion of the boundary is linked to a revival of interest, on the part of Peru, in westward diversion of some of the Mauri headwaters for irrigation and power projects in the Tacna region. (For related aspects of this problem, see below, pp. 89–90 and p. 263.)

[2] *F.O. 371/13452.*

resolved in 1929, only the Titicaca and adjacent sections of the boundary, which included therefore the most densely populated portion, remained undelimited. A number of attempts, it is true, had been made to resolve the intricacies of this southern section across the *altiplano*. In 1842, 1847 and 1848 proposals originally put forward in 1831 were revived, stressing again the tangle of land ownership around Lake Titicaca and the need, by careful exchange, for simplification of the international boundary. Physical features were still to form the basis of division, and adequate indemnity was assured for plots exchanged in order to avoid excessive twisting of the line around scattered claims. A treaty in November 1863 and another in April 1886 (but without exchange of ratifications) reiterated these intentions yet again, their wording clearly demonstrating that neither the long-awaited topographic maps nor the population data required for the boundary delimitation and demarcation in this particular area were yet forthcoming. Most of the villages and estates were in fact already openly recognised as either Bolivian or Peruvian according to the nationality of the *patrón*, and points of friction where they existed provided insufficient incentive for arduous survey and demarcation.

In September 1902, however, renewed attention was given to the Bolivia–Peru boundary as a whole, and the southern section was divided into three parts:

(i) from the snow peaks of Palomani (later changed to the confluence of the Pachasili and Suches rivers 15° 15′ 32″ S, 69° 8′ W) as far as the bay of Coccahui,

(ii) from the bay of Coccahui, across Lake Titicaca as far as the opening of the Desaguadero river,

(iii) from the opening of the Desaguadero river in Lake Titicaca as far as the confluence of the river Mauri with the river Ancomarca.[1]

No very serious difficulties were encountered in sections (i) and (iii) of the line, that is to the north and south of Lake Titicaca, but across the massive peninsula of Copacabana the well-established pattern of land ownership was so complex that it was inevitable that a compromise would have to be accepted. The greater part of the peninsula was clearly Bolivian, including the famous pilgrimage town of Copacabana itself which contains the seventeenth-century Spanish Basilica and the renowned Dark Aymara Virgin, whose alleged miraculous powers have drawn pilgrims many hundreds of miles. While the beautiful Islands of the Sun and Moon were always important centres of Incan worship throughout that extensive

---

[1] *Col. Trat. Vig. Bol.*, vol. v, pp. 406–12.

empire, Copacabana's Christian shrine became rather more narrowly associated with Bolivia and its ownership was not questioned.

A little farther south and east, however, the distribution of the estates (*fincas* in Bolivia, *comunidades* in Peru) was more irregular, as the Mixed Boundary Commission's map illustrates (Fig. 5). After the signing of an

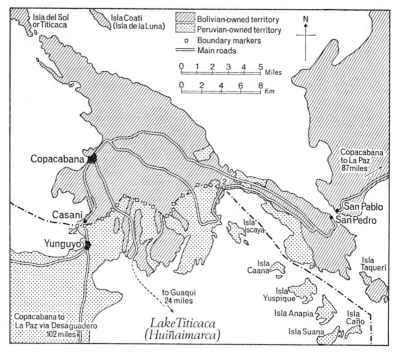

5 Land ownership and boundary demarcation in the Copacabana peninsula: 1932

additional treaty in June 1925, many more detailed plans and maps extending three or four miles each side of any contested village were drawn, until the final decision was incorporated in a protocol in January 1932.[1] The intricacies of this boundary when followed in the field, and the knowledgeable detail incorporated into the terms of its delimitation are unique in the whole history of Bolivian boundary record. It is doubly unique in respect of the high density of population through which it passes,

[1] *Ibid.*, pp. 479–84, Protocolo Ratificatorio de la Demarcación de la Segunda Sección de la Frontera (Península de Copacabana).

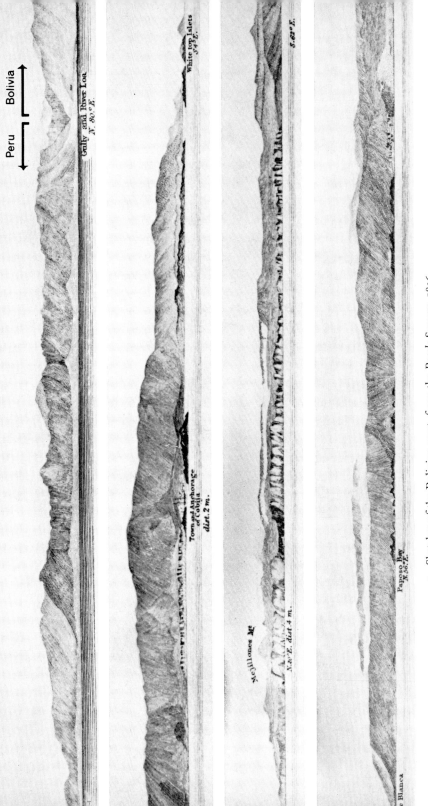

Peru   Bolivia

Gully and River Loa
N. 80.° E.

White top Islets
54.° E.

Town and Anchorage
of Cobija
dist. 2 m.

S. 62° E.

Mejillones Mt.
N. 2.° E. dist. 4 m.

Papeso Bay
N. 56° E.

Blanca

1   Sketches of the Bolivian coast, from the *Beagle* Survey, 1836.

II The Pacific port of Cobija, Bolivia, about 1870 (from Bresson, *Bolivia. Sept Années d'Explorations...* 1886).

III The guano port of Mejillones, Bolivia, about 1870 (from Bresson, *Bolivia. Sept Années d'Explorations...* 1886). The Custom House and Consulate was built in the Bolivian port by Chile in 1866, in accordance with the 'shared zone' treaty of that date. A Chilean guard-ship is shown anchored in the bay.

IV The Custom House in Antofagasta. Dismantled and transferred from Mejillones to the busier nitrate port of Antofagasta, Bolivia, about 1873, the same Custom House still operates in the port, which was lost to Chile in 1879. It stands beside the Antofagasta Railway yard.

V Looking north over Arica, Chile, from the headland of El Morro. New port facilities extend to the left; industrial, commercial and residential developments spread across the Arica plain.

VI Batallas, one of the new roadside market towns on the Bolivian *altiplano*, developed since the 1952 Social Revolution. Set within the densely populated agricultural region close to Lake Titicaca, the weekly market at Batallas attracts *campesinos* and vendors from distances of up to 80 miles, including the valleys of the Yungas, and Peru. The new market and the school (opened in 1954) have stimulated urban growth, although some new buildings are still occupied only periodically.

VII Part of the steeply terraced Copacabana peninsula, Lake Titicaca, Bolivia and Peru.

for nowhere else does Bolivia's perimeter pick its way so carefully through closely settled country, peopled well in advance of the international political divides of the nineteenth and twentieth centuries.

Thus in this final portion of the Bolivian–Peru frontier still awaiting delimitation, the Commissioners in 1932 applied the principle of *uti possidetis de facto*. A protocol in October 1941[1] considered the properties left on the wrong side of the line in 1932, and both countries agreed to recognise the rights of ownership established legally before 2 December 1939 in the exchanged areas. In addition, individuals were to retain their old nationality, unless they recorded a desire to change it within three months of the protocol's announcement. Demarcation across the Copacabana peninsula, therefore, is aided by property boundaries, and frequently employs existing features of the cultural landscape, such as walls, buildings, bridges and roadways, to assist location of the international line (Plate IX). Elsewhere, numbered iron posts of variable height, but usually inter-visible, are employed – all, however, without any State name-plate.

The predominantly Aymara Indian population is clustered along much of the central part of this boundary section, particularly around the Titicaca shore (Plates VII and VIII). The advantages afforded by the lacustrine soils, periodically enriched by flooding where close to the lake fringe, the moister air, and consequently slightly modified local climates all combine to encourage as close a distribution of farms around Titicaca (and Huiñai-marca) as the crop yields and grazing capacity will support. Remnants of old pre-Columbian ridged fields at or near the lakeside, reclaimed from marshland or from zones subjected to periodic inundation, suggest with other evidence an earlier, even higher, population density. So too do the magnificent Incan and pre-Incan terrace flights which climb in some instances to the summits of the neighbouring sierras, or to their upper limit of cultivation. Such ridges and spurs around Titicaca and Copacabana, rising locally to well over 13,000 feet, represent strongly folded Palaeozoic, Mesozoic and Tertiary sediments half-buried by enormous quantities of Pleistocene and Recent infill; together with local volcanics, they provide a sharp contrast to the generally level expanses of the *altiplano*.

Titicaca thus remains the great focus of activity for farmer and fisherman alike on both the Bolivian and Peruvian *altiplano*. Yet, despite the similarity of ethnic groups, culture, language and occupation around the lake's numerous embayments, it is now possible to detect subtle differences between the Bolivian and Peruvian sections. These spring largely from the Agrarian Reform program which followed the Bolivian National

---

[1] Foreign Ministry files, La Paz. Also *F.O. A.6412/182/35*(1942).

81

Revolution of 1952. Peasant ownership of land on the Bolivian side contrasts with the old *hacienda*-type tenure system still widely maintained in Peru, although future events there are likely to weaken these contrasts. In June 1969 Peru introduced a new Agrarian Reform law involving proposals for widespread land expropriation and redistribution. It remains to be seen, given time, what effects these objectives may achieve.

Meanwhile, until existing contrasts are reduced with the progress of Peru's Agrarian Reform, a political boundary which originally ran through a socially and culturally homogeneous area, at present draws attention to the results of Bolivia's earlier revolutionary land policies and socio-political reorganisation. Since 1952, such differences have often been most clearly expressed in the border landscape. Material changes can be noted: the more widespread use in Bolivia of galvanised iron roofing sheets which are replacing the old thatch of *paja brava* or *totora* reed, for example; the greater frequency in Bolivia of two-storeyed construction, and of windows, with or without glass, in small domestic buildings; and the increasing evidence of ownership by the Bolivian *campesino* of factory-made products, particularly items of clothing, bicycles, and transistor radios.

In addition, the Bolivian Agrarian Reform has introduced certain new features in settlement siting, particularly in the La Paz–Titicaca–Peruvian border region, which are likely to show further modest development. New marketing procedures, initiated by the break-up of the large estates, sponsored new fairs and new out-of-town markets, often situated by the sides of main roads or in some other convenient location. These in turn, together sometimes with new schools, sponsored about a dozen small new towns in and after the late 1950s, which are permanently or periodically occupied (Plate VI). Thus, although contrasts in this uniquely densely populated section of Bolivia's borderland are by no means abrupt, and exceptions to what is generally observed can still readily be found, changes due to a politically inspired Agrarian Reform in Bolivia in 1952–3 are by now unmistakably evident as one moves through the Titicaca basin between Bolivia and Peru.

II. COMPETITION WITHIN THE WESTERN SECTOR: THE RELATIVE MERITS OF BOLIVIA'S LAND ROUTES TO THE PACIFIC

Although Chile dominates Bolivia's lines of Pacific communication, the most important crossing point farther north, on the Bolivia–Peru boundary, is at present still made on Lake Titicaca between the ports of Guaqui and Puno. Overland, it most commonly occurs at Desaguadero, at the source of this river, which slowly drains Titicaca southward into Lake Poopó. The Desaguadero crossing is one of the oldest lines of movement in South America; for centuries a pontoon bridge of reed *balsas* linked the two river banks, and at this point the traditional and most-frequented entry into Upper Peru was sited.

For the exchange of local products, the Desaguadero crossing is supplemented by that on the Copacabana peninsula at Casani–Yunguyo which carries an important lorry route from La Paz *via* the narrow three-quarter-mile Tiquina Strait to Puno (Fig. 5). Considerable quantities of oranges, bananas, and other tropical produce, including dried coca, make their way from the Yungas through La Paz and into southern Peru to compete effectively with Peru's own products. Indeed at times this route from the tropical valleys behind the Cordillera Real has proved preferable to that through Guaqui and Desaguadero, owing to the better condition of the road. Decisions made jointly by Peru and Bolivia, however, in the 1950s are concentrating attention once again on the Desaguadero crossing and, for the first time, on its extension to the Pacific Ocean.

A metalled highway from La Paz to Ilo on the Peruvian coast was first mooted in Lima on 19 November 1955, during a period of investigation into how communications along the western side of Lake Titicaca could be improved. This highway was selected in place of railway extension along the west Titicaca shore, and Conventions for the routing and construction of the Carretera Internacional La Paz–Desaguadero–Ilo were signed by Peru and Bolivia on 19 February 1957, and 7 February 1964. The Bolivian Government showed particular enthusiasm for the project, claiming that it would put the La Paz region 'only seven hours from the sea'. It was mutually agreed that transit agreements already operating between the two States should be applicable to the new highway connexion, sections of which would form part of the Pan-American Highway net.[1] Costs of construction between La Paz and Moquegua are to be shared equally by Peru and Bolivia, including those for the new toll bridge over the Desaguadero river which was completed in 1964. The old bridge close by, almost awash when Lake Titicaca's level is high, continues to be frequented by the Indian population living each side of the Desaguadero river in settlements of the same name. The Peruvian town is larger, but both consist largely of Aymaras who cross freely over the narrow bridge, pausing

[1] Commercial treaties and protocols on transit trade variously through Mollendo, Ilo, Puno, Santiago de Huata and Cojata were concluded by Peru and Bolivia in November 1905, January 1908, September 1911; further agreements were exchanged in 1917, 1936, 1937 and 1948. A Joint Declaration agreeing to freedom of navigation by Peru and Bolivia on Lake Titicaca was concluded in October 1966.

only for an occasional cursory check of their enormous bundles for coca, gold or firearms being brought illegally from Bolivia into Peru.

Peru is responsible for the existing sixty-mile highway beyond Moquegua down to Ilo, and thus the completion of Bolivia's first La Paz–Pacific road link will in this instance entirely depend upon both States' willingness and ability to finance the expensive section between Moquegua and Desaguadero.[1] Pressing demands in Peru for additional finance to improve the old Mollendo–Arequipa–Puno railway are continually made, fortified by the argument that while Ilo on average handles as little as 75,000 tons of cargo annually (two-thirds of which is cabotage), Mollendo–Matarani moves about six times that amount. Ilo's site is constricted and virtually unprotected from the very heavy swell along this coast; any significant increase in traffic will demand a new breakwater pier and extended berthing facilities to replace the need for lighterage.

The new port of Matarani, in contrast, was completed in 1947, and by 1962 had taken over almost all the functions of the old port of Mollendo, a little farther south. Although many of the port workers still live in Mollendo, travelling by 'bus each day until new housing schemes are completed, Matarani is now firmly established as Bolivia's only port in Peru. Its three new deep-water berths are carved out of the base of a high rocky bluff, and protected by a long breakwater. Out of the approximately 420,000 tons handled at Matarani in 1967, 145,500 tons moved to or from Bolivia – a figure which is controlled by the capacity of the railway up to Puno, and particularly by the steamer capacity of the three small vessels crossing Lake Titicaca. Continuance of the congestion at this age-old bottleneck has led to the introduction of a fleet of lorries to help shift cargo along the western lake shore between Puno and Guaqui, while perhaps 20,000 tons a year move from Matarani to La Paz entirely by the existing road, such as it is. At present firmly rejecting proposals revived in 1955 for new railway extension around the lake, the Peruvian Corporation plan instead to introduce three freight-train ferries on Titicaca in the early 1970s, in order to eliminate the time-consuming breaks of load, and to fend off the increasing competition of road transport in the Puno–La Paz section. Rail gauges, however, at Puno and Guaqui are not yet standardised. The total 388 miles by rail and 127 miles by water make the Matarani route the slowest and clumsiest of the established connexions between Bolivia and the Pacific. Yet it represents an existing and long-standing capital investment which may well continue to attract financial support.

---

[1] Peru and Bolivia agreed jointly in July 1968 to approach the Inter-American Development Bank for credit for basic work on the Desaguadero–Ilo highway.

Where money is short, and vested interests powerful, the Matarani route may even contrive to divert funds from new ventures such as the Ilo road and Ilo port schemes.

Farther south, the two Chilean ports of Arica and Antofagasta compete with each other, as well as with Matarani, for the Bolivian transit trade (Fig. 6). Twentieth-century commercial and transit agreements between Chile and Bolivia were concluded at intervals between 1904 and 1955[1] and, on average, the two Chilean ports may be reckoned to handle nearly two-thirds of Bolivia's overseas trade. Of these two Chilean transit ports, indeed of the three Pacific transit ports for Bolivia, it has already been shown that Antofagasta went quickly into the lead once the Antofagasta and Bolivia Railway had taken the sting out of the long, oblique route across the desert. Antofagasta has dominated Bolivia's Pacific outlet since the line's extension to Oruro in 1892 and to La Paz in 1917, despite the fact, as already noted, that at 729 miles its railway is more than two-and-a-half times as long as that to Arica, and more than 200 miles longer than the combined rail–lake–rail route to Matarani. Even so, superior port facilities, the uninterrupted flow of goods along a gently graded track (without the steep rack section of the Arica railway), and the coordinated operation and maintenance of the line by British administration combined with powerful tariff controls to assert Antofagasta's superiority.[2]

Only now is this under growing challenge from Matarani and, more recently, from Arica, which has sought to retrieve its traditional role as Bolivia's Pacific outlet by the construction of a new port. This has greatly increased Arica's handling capacity by the introduction of four new, sheltered, deep-water berths to replace the old mole and lighterage system, as well as by the reorganisation of scattered warehouse facilities. Plans are

---

[1] See above, p. 66 n. 3. The 1955 Additional Protocol agreement involved Chilean consent to the construction of a Bolivian oil pipeline to the port of Arica, in return for Chilean preference in the sale of petroleum from the pipeline. The line was completed in 1960 and runs close to the Arica–La Paz railway for much of its length. Later developments concerning the use of the pipeline are noted on p. 228. (Suggestions made in 1957 for a Bolivian oil pipeline to be run to Ilo in Peru were not developed.) Agreement between Chile and Bolivia on transit by road was negotiated in 1970.

[2] The Chilean section of the railway is still owned by the Antofagasta (Chili) and Bolivia Railway Company, but the Bolivian section was handed over to the Bolivian Government in February 1959. After the railway's rapid deterioration, however, the Company agreed in April 1962 to take over again until the end of April 1964 – not as owners but as managing agents for the Bolivian Government. At the latter's request, this two-year period was extended for a further six months. At the end of October 1964, the operation and administration were handed over to the Bolivian Government which now coordinates the western system of railways under a single management. Negotiations for an agreed compensation to the Company of £2,524,277 were completed in December 1967.

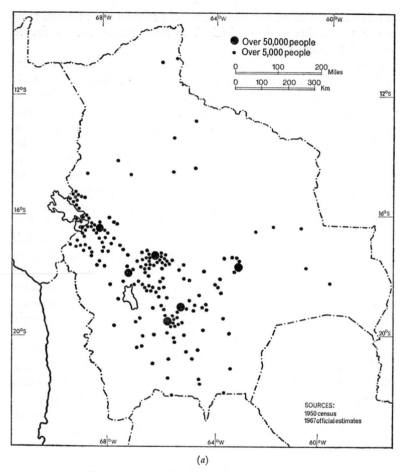

(*a*)

6   The dominance of the Western Sector: (*a*) population
distribution, and (*b*) rail freight traffic flow

prepared for the electrification of the Chilean section of the Arica–La Paz
railway and the elimination of the very steep, 25-mile rack section between
Central and Puquios.[1] For in 1962 Arica handled only 45,222 tons of cargo
to and from Bolivia, and in 1966 about 84,000 tons. By 1967, however,

[1] The Chilean Government's decision since 1953 (i.e. after the Bolivian Revolution of 1952),
to sponsor major improvements in the port and rail facilities at Arica rests both on the desire
to *increase* the port's share of Bolivian trade, and at the same time to diversify Arica's
activities and *decrease* its dependence on Bolivia in terms of overall economy. See J. V. Fifer,
'Arica: a desert frontier in transition', *Geog. Journ.*, vol. cxxx, 1964, pp. 507–18.

(b)

this figure had risen to 110,500 tons, as port improvements became further advanced. Antofagasta's trade to and from Bolivia averaged approximately 200,000 tons during the 1960s. Supplementing Antofagasta, the guano port of Mejillones, whose bay remains one of the finest natural deep-water harbours in the world, handles dangerous cargo for Chile and Bolivia, forbidden by the port authorities in Antofagasta. For the most part this consists of ammonium nitrate destined for the dynamite works at Calama, and for Bolivia.

Thus, although Antofagasta's pre-eminence is still retained, it is already being strongly challenged by Matarani, whose search for new business, in combination with the Peruvian Corporation, is aggressive, and whose port handling charges are lower. In the future, however, both Antofagasta and Matarani will be increasingly challenged by the new services at Arica, where the Junta de Adelanto aims to have attracted at least half of Bolivia's total Pacific coast tonnage by the late 1970s. The advantages of any port improvement, however, clearly remain closely allied in the first instance to rail-haulage efficiency to and from the *altiplano*. In line with the probably cheaper, and certainly more flexible, transport alternative offered by highways, feasibility studies for an Arica–La Paz, an Arica–Huachacalla–Oruro, and an Iquique–Oruro road have been undertaken, although the future realisation of some projects, in the light of heavy investment already committed to the improvement of existing rail links, must remain uncertain. Nevertheless, the desirability of making new highway connexion to the Pacific through Chile (accompanied by the necessary agreement on right of transit by road) has been stressed at various times by both Chile and Bolivia. Iquique, for example, has spare port capacity which could be made available to Bolivia, given the new highway linkage to Oruro due to be constructed in the early 1970s.

Whatever the outcome, it still seems likely that, despite continuing competition, Arica will reassert its original supremacy as Bolivia's major port. For the present, however, it is perhaps worth reflecting that for little short of a century, by far the most important line of movement between Bolivia and the sea has been established and maintained through the country's old, inconvenient desert panhandle. It is ironical that, after all, the Antofagasta railway has for so many years provided the overwhelming advantage to an outlet long disregarded in the struggle to obtain a Pacific 'window' farther north at Arica.

12. BOLIVIA'S BOUNDARY WITH CHILE: RESIDUAL PROBLEMS AND CONTINUING PROTEST

Bolivia's constant agitation, and tireless sponsoring of schemes for new or improved links between the *altiplano* and the Pacific still tend to dominate its political exchanges with Chile and Peru. At this practical level, La Paz discovers that the competition for Bolivian traffic between these two States is not without its advantages and is, besides, more productive than the fruitless, though continued call for the adjustment of the 'Pacific boundary'. This boundary line has continued, however, to provide a perpetual source of diplomatic friction between Bolivia and Chile, not only in its age-old context of Bolivia's desire for a Pacific port, but also more specifically with regard to its actual location within the Western Cordillera.

Decisions taken in Chile regarding the promotion of new industrial growth in Arica, and the electrification of the Arica–La Paz railway, have led to the installation of new hydro-electric plant in the Andes to supply the rising demand for power. This in turn has directed fresh attention to the relationship between the *divortia aquarum* and the line of highest peaks in the Andean Western Cordillera. When the Bolivia–Chile boundary was delimited in 1904, it was placed for much of its length in the most easterly of the three chains which here comprise the Cordillera Occidental. The principal watershed in this section, however, is formed by the central chain (Fig. 3). In particular, the Lauca, in common with certain other neighbouring rivers, gathers its headstreams within Chilean territory before flowing into Bolivia, where its course continues across the lightly populated edge of the *altiplano* for another ninety-five miles to end in the Coipasa salt lake. The idea of reversing part of the eastward-flowing Lauca near its source, in order to water the desert behind Arica, was first proposed by Peru (together with other diversions), more than a century ago, before its loss of the region during the War of the Pacific.[1] Chile is now combining the original scheme with a power project to supply the future demands of industrial, railway and urban development in the Department of Arica, northernmost district of the Province of Tarapacá.

Strong protests were lodged by Bolivia in April 1962 when sluice gates on the Chilean section of the river were opened for the first time to begin the westward diversion of part of the Lauca's flow. Bitter and emotional demonstrations took place in La Paz, and Chile sent about one hundred armed police to the border, with orders to prevent any attempt by Bolivians to sabotage dams and other installations in the Cotacotani–Parinacota area. The Bolivian Government requested a meeting of Foreign Ministers of the member countries of the Organisation of American States under the terms of the 1947 Inter-American Treaty of Reciprocal Assistance, which provides machinery for the peaceful settlement of disputes between member countries of the organisation. Bolivia proceeded to break off diplomatic relations with Chile, since it claimed (following the Seventh Pan-American Conference's 1933 Montevideo Resolution on International Rivers) that the formal agreement of both countries was required for such a diversion to be sanctioned.

[1] See above, pp. 77–8.

Chile countered with the point that no official objection had been raised and sustained by Bolivia in either 1949 or 1960, when engineers from both countries, together in the field, examined first the proposals and later the nearly completed works. Following the second Mixed Commission investigation, work had proceeded rapidly, but the Lauca river diversion issue was soon to become inflamed by a resurgence of the much older grievance associated with the Chile–Bolivia boundary, namely, the loss of the independent outlet to the Pacific – landlocked Bolivia's *salida al mar*.[1]

Overt hostility to Chile characterised all major political exchanges by Bolivia after 1962 although in November 1970, with the inauguration of the Allende administration, attitudes became somewhat less strained. Even so, renewed emphasis upon Bolivia's 'mediterránidad' has been made an inevitable subject for reference in every widely reported political speech, both national and international, during recent years. Official recognition again marks such anniversaries as 23 March, 'La dia del Mar' when, in 1879, Cabrera and Abaroa led the defence of the town of Calama, in the Litoral, against successful Chilean invasion. The centenary of the founding of Antofagasta by President Melgarejo on 22 October 1868 was 'celebrated' in 1968 by demonstrations in La Paz in which crowds burned the Chilean flag; indeed, for many years, national posters in several Bolivian towns have displayed the nostalgic cry 'Antofagasta es y sera Boliviana'.

A variety of commercial bodies and educational institutions adopt the name 'Litoral', be it a school or college, a 'bus company or a scout troop. Maps showing, or purporting to show, the boundaries of the Audiencia of Charcas in 1810, together with colourful maritime views, are exhibited in public buildings. A wide selection of posters, advertisements, badges, postage stamps, books, stationery, and other items – to be found all over Bolivia – periodically draw attention to the call 'Hacia el Mar!':

[1] Documents (including maps and plates) relating to the Lauca dispute include *Visita efectuada por los Excmos. señores Representantes Diplomáticos de: Argentina, Brasil, Colombia, Costa Rica, República Dominicana, Ecuador, Estados Unidos, Guatemala, Haití, Honduras, México, Nicaragua, Panamá, Paraguay, Perú, El Salvador, Uruguay y Venezuela, a las obras de captación de una parte de las aguas del río Lauca en su naciente en las ciénagas de Parinacota y su aprovechamiento en el valle de Azapa*, Chile, Ministerio de Relaciones Exteriores, Santiago, August 1962; *La Cuestión del Río Lauca*, Chile, Ministerio de Relaciones Exteriores, Santiago, 1963; A. Salazar Soriano, *Los Derechos de Bolivia sobre el Río Lauca*, Cochabamba, 1961; *La Desviación del Río Lauca*, Bolivia, Ministerio de Relaciones Exteriores y Culto, La Paz, 1962; *Rumbo al Mar*, Bolivia, Ministerio de Relaciones Exteriores y Culto, La Paz, 1963. See also J. V. Fifer, 'Arica: a desert frontier in transition', pp. 516–18; R. D. Tomasek, 'The Chilean–Bolivian Lauca River Dispute and the O.A.S.', *Journ. of Inter-American Studies*, vol. IX, 1967, pp. 351–66.

'El supremo anhelo de Bolivia – su retorno al mar.' (Plate x)

'No importa cuando sera – lo que importa es que un dia Bolivia tendrá un puerto sobre el Pacifico.'

'Bolivia demanda su derecho de salida al mar.'

'Sin mar! Bolivia enclaustrada.'

'Bolivianos hacia el mar! La Patria jamas esta perdida cuando su juventad no renuncia al combate. Nuestro deber es la reconquista territorial. En esta hora no midamos el sacrificio.' (Federación Universitaria local de La Paz)

'Quiero un mar, un mar azul para Bolivia.' (Schoolchildren's rhyme)

Santiago's response to anti-Chilean demonstrations has been to regret the gravity and frequency of their incidence, and to draw attention to the terms, first, of the 1904 treaty, when Chile's absolute and perpetual dominion over the Litoral was accepted by Bolivia, however unwillingly; and secondly, to those associated with Chilean and Peruvian acceptance of the 1929 arbitration settlement of the Tacna–Arica question.

Although contact at the consular level has since been restored, diplomatic relations between Bolivia and Chile remain severed as a direct result of the Lauca dispute. But while the controversy, in the short term, springs from the results of the discrepancy between boundary line and principal watershed within the Western Cordillera, the dispute was neither initiated nor contained by a localised competition for the waters of the river Lauca – significant though this is in terms of power and irrigation for Chile, and of irrigated llama pastures belonging to scattered Indian communities in Bolivia. In the long term, and it is a very long term, the diplomatic rupture represents yet another gesture by Bolivia against congenital problems of location, both real and assumed; another expression of Bolivia's disappointment and perennial discontent at its complete and protracted failure to retain or redeem even a small portion of South America's 5000-mile Pacific coastline.

CHAPTER 3

THE NORTHERN SECTOR: ROUTES TO THE ATLANTIC *via* THE AMAZON

BOLIVIA'S RELATIONS WITH BRAZIL AND PERU

From the summits of the Andean Cordillera Real, Bolivia's northern boundary plunges northwards and north-eastwards into the rain forests of the interior. Formed first by the remainder of the country's boundary with Peru and continued by the greater part of its boundary with Brazil, this vast northern frontier sweeps through more than 1800 miles of central South America to comprise almost half the total Bolivian perimeter.

Within the upper Amazon basin, the rugged nature of the Andes' East Cordilleran slope seriously obstructs east–west communication, and separates highland and lowland circulation. The scale and complexity of the gorge dissection is particularly marked in Peru and Bolivia, where the headwaters of the Ucayali–Urubamba, Javari, Juruá, Purus, Madre de Dios, Beni and Madeira–Mamoré have carved deep ravines in the *montaña* zone of the Yungas. The descent from Cordilleran peaks of over 20,000 feet into the plains of the Norte and Oriente, less than 600 feet above sea level, is extraordinarily abrupt, and beyond the steep foothills, gorges suddenly open on to the almost featureless alluvial spreads covering many thousands of square miles in the continental interior (Fig. 1). Over Bolivia's eastern frontier sprawl the jungles surrounding the Guaporé (Spanish Itenes) and Verde rivers which, together with the Abuná, Madre de Dios and Beni systems, carry the drainage of much of northern Bolivia into the cataracts of the Madeira–Mamoré. Storm surges from the Andean headstreams, heavy local precipitation, and only slight relief result in widespread flooding over much of lowland Bolivia between February and May when, at their peak, rivers may have risen as much as thirty or forty feet.

North and north-east Bolivia lie on the fringe of the world's most extensive region of high rainfall. Moist, unstable air streams rise toward the Andean front, while continuous evaporation and transpiration from leaf, river and swamp surfaces combine with the rainfall in maintaining a high level of relative humidity (frequently 85 per cent or more, even during the drier low-sun season). High humidity and a persistent cloud cover result in remarkably small monthly mean temperature variation, and this contributes to the overwhelming monotony of climate characterising much of the inner Amazon basin.[1]

In many respects, therefore, the Bolivian ultramontane region is one of great physical difficulty – the quintessence of emptiness and isolation. Enclosed between the towering Andean divide and vast stretches of *selva* and swamp, the environment offers striking contrasts with the more densely populated western highlands. Parts of this wilderness, however, witnessed a prolonged series of boundary disputes which again underlined Bolivia's problems of internal organisation and continental location, particularly in relation to the Amazon–Atlantic routeway.

I. THE COLONIAL FRONTIER

Early efforts at penetration into this most landlocked of all South American regions were, in the overall view, slight. They were, nevertheless, characterised by amazing feats of individual enterprise, tenacity and endurance. The Tordesillas line of 1494, even as an approximate demarcation between Spain's and Portugal's rival spheres, had been rendered quite unrealistic by the steady advance of Portuguese trading and mission settlements into the Amazon and Paraná basins. After an initial delay, free-ranging Portuguese penetration of the interior had established a large measure of control over the Amazon, Madeira, Guaporé and Paraguay river routes during the colonial period.

[1] *Rainfall* (inches) monthly average:

Jan.	Feb.	Mar.	Apr.	May	June	July	Aug.	Sept.	Oct.	Nov.	Dec.	*Total*
					San Antonio (Madeira river)							
16	11	14.5	11	6	2.5	0.3	1	2	6	11.3	10	*91.6″* (*2327 mm.*)
					Riberalta (Beni river)							
12	8.7	8.6	5.2	3	0.5	0.5	0.6	4.4	5	6.6	9.7	*64.8″* (*1646 mm.*)

Farther south in the Oriente, annual rainfall totals are usually between 50″ and 60″ (1270 mm. and 1524 mm.), again with a pronounced dry season April–September.

Temperature °F (°C) monthly average:

Jan.	Feb.	Mar.	Apr.	May	June	July	Aug.	Sept.	Oct.	Nov.	Dec.
				San Antonio (Madeira river)							
79	78	78	78	78	77	79	80	80	80	79	80
(26)	(25.5)	(25.5)	(25.5)	(25.5)	(25)	(26)	(26.5)	(26.5)	(26.5)	(26)	(26.5)

Farther south in the Oriente, where the dry season is more pronounced, and the cloud cover less constant, a greater annual range is experienced.

In Spanish America, the Catholic mission rather than the itinerant trader provided the most frequent spearhead of empire. Subsidised and protected by the Crown, Jesuits and Franciscans from Paraguay, as well as from Lima, La Paz, Chuquisaca, and Santa Cruz de la Sierra, had pushed into the eastern plains of the Audiencia of Charcas, and established nearly thirty missions among the Mojo and Chiquito Indians. Spanish penetration of the wilderness along the Mamoré, Grande, Beni, Madeira (Spanish Madera) and other rivers, however, had encountered Portuguese missionaries and Portuguese adventurers in what was technically Spanish territory. In fact, Portuguese westward expansion in Amazonia, especially by the Jesuits, had been particularly marked during the sixty years of the Spanish–Portuguese Union between 1580 and 1640. Subsequently, the extent of Portuguese expansion was recorded, for example, by a contemporary map of the Spanish–Portuguese frontier about 1749, which represented numerous Portuguese Jesuit establishments on the upper right bank of the Madeira, and along the right bank of the Amazon from the mouth of the Madeira to that of the Tapajós. Carmelites were shown to be occupying the west bank of the Negro, as well as areas along the right bank of the Amazon between the confluences of the Purus and the Javari.[1]

Farther south, *bandeirantes* from São Paulo had blazed their trails northwestwards across the Brazilian plateau during the seventeenth century, broadly following the line of the Tietê, the Paranapanema and the upper Paraguay. Extending their range still further, Paulista *bandeiras* had entered the Amazon routeway by way of the Guaporé and Madeira rivers. Portuguese merchants had followed this and other routes from the Río de la Plata into Upper Peru during the late sixteenth and seventeenth centuries. Indeed the degree of penetration into Spanish territory achieved by these Brazilian smugglers and slave-traders was revealed by their designation – *peruleiros*.

By the Treaty of Madrid in 1750, Spain and Portugal attempted to recognise the existing claims of the two nations, but such dissatisfaction followed, particularly among the Jesuits, that it was annulled in 1761 and no further demarcation was attempted after a large white marble obelisk had been brought out from Lisbon in 1750 and erected on the river bank in 1754 at the confluence of the Jaurú (Jaura) and the Paraguay. Set near the major drainage divide between the Amazon and Paraguay river systems, it can still be found marking the boundary of the former empires of Portugal and Spain.

---

[1] J. F. Rippy and J. T. Nelson, *Crusaders of the Jungle*, University of North Carolina Press, 1936; ch. xiv, 'The Missions of the Charcas Frontier'; ch. xv, 'The Portuguese Menace'. This reference pp. 236–7.

The Treaty of San Ildefonso in 1777 once more attempted to halt further Portuguese penetration by recognising the *status quo*. The boundary between Spanish and Portuguese territory in central South America was to follow (Articles IX, X, XI) the river Paraguay to Lake Xarayes, cross the lake to the mouth of the Jaurú, and thence continue in a straight line to the south bank of the Guaporé (Itenes), opposite the mouth of the Sararé, or other more convenient river discovered in the vicinity. The boundary was to follow the Guaporé, Mamoré and Madeira rivers as far as a point equidistant between the Mamoré–Madeira confluence and the Madeira–Amazon confluence. This halfway point was not located in the treaty but was calculated by Portuguese astronomers to be 8° 4′ S, a latitude considerably in their own favour.[1] From this point the boundary traced an east–west line along the parallel to the east bank of the Javari and thence down the Javari to its confluence with the Amazon (Fig. 7a).

In such *terra incognita*, the San Ildefonso decision in this section relied heavily upon the astronomical line, and upon the source and course of the river Javari which were in fact virtually unknown. Settlement was still too sparse to dispel the almost complete ignorance of the interior, an additional confusion arising from the multiplicity of river names. Nevertheless, in 1777 Portugal gained legal title to an area more than twice the size confirmed to it by the Treaty of Tordesillas. Already the Madeira–Guaporé river route to the Mato Grosso had been strengthened by a line of frontier posts established in the mid-eighteenth century: Villa Bella 1752, São José 1756, Bôa Viagem 1758, Conceição 1760, Balsemão 1768 and Principe da Beira 1776.[2] The last-named fort was a major defensive site,

[1] There was considerable divergence of opinion as to which parallel should carry the boundary between Portuguese and Spanish interests westward from the Madeira river, in accordance with the San Ildefonso treaty of 1777. Portugal claimed 8° 4′ S, at the confluence of the river Jiparaná with the Madeira, and had placed a small frontier post at Roscenia de Crato on the Madeira a little farther north at 7° 25′ S although, more realistically, Portugal's frontiers at any time were where its traders were active. After independence, both Bolivia and Peru were concerned with the correct legal interpretation of the equidistant point along the Madeira. Maps record conflicting opinions and an absence of definitive record, e.g. Arrowsmith's maps of Peru and Bolivia, London, 1834 and 1842, show the boundary between these countries and Brazil running along latitude 9° 30′ S in this section. Lieut. Herndon's map of the Valley of the Amazon accompanying his report in 1854 (see p. 98, n. 1) draws a boundary line along 10° S. Peru itself claimed 6° 52′ S as the only correct choice. With the source of the Madeira river at 10° 20′ S and its confluence with the Amazon at 3° 20′ S, 6° 52′ S becomes a more accurate estimate than most of the other claims.
[2] For a note on Portuguese penetration along the Madeira, Mamoré and Beni rivers see J. Gonsalves da Fonseca, 1749, 'Voyage made from the City of the Gran Pará to the mouth of the river Madeira by the expedition which ascended this river to the mines of Matto Grosso, by special order of His Faithful Majesty in the year 1749,' *Royal Academy of Sciences*, Lisbon, 1826.

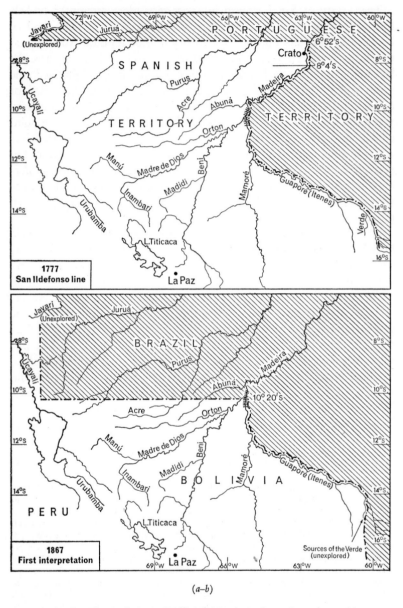

$(a–b)$

7 $(a–d)$ The evolution of Bolivia's Northern Sector boundary with
Brazil: 1777–1958

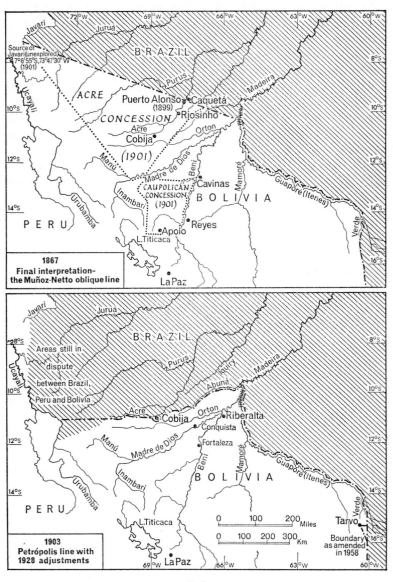

(c-d)

and together with the other centres it protected the Portuguese line of movement which the forts themselves proclaimed.[1] In 1798 Portugal issued a book of rules for navigation on the Madeira river, maintaining its dominance along those sections of waterway theoretically shared between the two Iberian States.

The San Ildefonso boundary had clearly illustrated the pressures exerted upon the Spanish missions by the advance of the commercial and mission frontier in colonial Brazil, and this relentless probing of the Portuguese was to continue, rendering once again the 1777 treaty delimitation quite unrealistic as a *de facto* division of settlement and land ownership. The inheritance of the relevant portion of the San Ildefonso line by the successor States of Brazil, Bolivia and Peru merely transferred old problems to new governments; far from all centralised authority, Brazilian settlement was to remain the decisive factor in determining ownership of the Amazon–Madeira routeway.[2]

2. EARLY EXPLORATION OF BOLIVIA'S NORTHERN FRONTIER

In striking contrast to the westward infiltration of enterprising Brazilians, exploration by the Bolivians and Peruvians into the savanna and rain forest regions of their *oriente* made little impact. A few expeditions were organised to the Beni and Mamoré country, but the majority ended in failure. There

[1] Principe da Beira was visited in 1852 by Lieut. Lardner Gibbon, United States Navy, who with Lieut. W. L. Herndon had been commissioned by the U.S. Government to explore the Amazon and its headwaters with a view to opening up the region for U.S. trade. Herndon followed the main Amazon route from Peru, while Gibbon travelled through Bolivia *via* La Paz, Cochabamba, the Chapare, Mamoré and Madeira rivers to reach the Amazon. Their reports, published as *Exploration of the Valley of the Amazon* in two volumes, Washington, D.C. (vol. I Lieut. W. L. Herndon, 1853 and 1854; vol. II Lieut. L. Gibbon, 1854), were eagerly awaited, the U.S. Senate ordering 10,000 extra copies. Both reports were the product of resourcefulness, courage and detailed observation and have remained classics of their type and period. In a description of his visit to the isolated Brazilian garrison stationed at 'this grim old Portuguese fort' (pp. 272–7), Gibbon recorded: 'As the men forced the canoe through the narrow rapid channel, they shouted the news that Forté do Principe da Beira was in sight. We could see the flagpole and the upper bastions. Its situation was commanding. As we rose upon the forty-feet bank there stood the fort, pierced for fifty-six heavy guns, pointing in all directions towards a perfect wilderness. . . The immense walls of the fort are built of local stone, in the shape of a hollow square encircling over an acre of land, with diamond corners 35 feet deep. In walking round the ramparts I only saw two heavy iron guns mounted, which pointed down the river towards the territory of Bolivia. The date over the main entrance of the fort was nearly erased by the weather. We could with difficulty make out "Joseph I, June 20, 1776".' Today, the great empty fort still stands solidly on the Brazilian bank of the Guaporé.

[2] Brazil, as a general rule, refused to accept the San Ildefonso line as a definitive basis for later boundary settlement, supporting only the principle of *uti possidetis de facto*.

was much rumour concerning the dangers on the northern frontier: 'Along the shores of these rivers [the lower Mamoré, Beni and Madeira] it is believed that many barbarous nations reside, of whom as yet little can be said with any certainty.'[1] The bewildering complexity of the headwater network of the Ucayali, Javari, Juruá, Purus, Acre, Madre de Dios, Beni and Mamoré added to the intense confusion, and the uncertainty of these inaccurately mapped river routes discouraged the Andean plateau- and valley-dwellers in their penetration of the Norte and the Oriente for which, in any case, they had little affection. The Brazilians in contrast, probing upstream, made better progress.

In 1842, the former Jesuit Mission-Reserve Province of Mojos formed the basis for the creation of the new Department of Beni, and in 1844 the Bolivian Government instructed its Prefect, José Agustín Palacios, to explore the river Beni, and the falls on the Madeira–Mamoré. Palacios travelled up the Beni only as far as its lowest fall, but he returned a detailed report on the eighteen sets of falls and rapids on the Madeira–Mamoré, and prepared a carefully annotated map.[2] He exhorted the Government to 'throw open the portals of Bolivia to foreign commerce and the Atlantic...It seems as if Nature strove to hide her richest treasures in those unfortunately pent-up regions...Our statesmen, instead of deliberating over Arica or Cobija, should direct all their energies and attention to the navigation of the Madera.'

Bolivia resolved to promote its first major foreign concession for the development of the northern sector. Negotiations had begun with The Company of French Guiana which led to the establishment of The Franco-Bolivian Company of the Mamoré in 1844. The company was organised in Brussels on 6 February, and in Cochabamba on 26 May of that year,[3] with the purpose of introducing Belgian immigrants into an extensive area virtually coincident with the Beni Department. This 'Comunidad Boliviana' – agricultural, industrial and mercantile – was to establish regular steam navigation upon the rivers within its concession, and on the Amazon beyond, in order to foster trade links with Europe. The settlement of fifty families a year was proposed, with generous tax allowances and bonus payments from the Bolivian Government to every new colonist who was capable of teaching a trade, and extra bonus payments to any master operative capable of establishing and managing a community

---

[1] F. Herrara, 'An Official Report (1827) on the river Beni, and the countries through which it flows', *Journ. Roy. Geog. Soc.*, vol. v, 1835, pp. 99–101.

[2] J. A. Palacios, *Exploración de los Ríos y Lagos del Departamento del Beni, y en especial el Madera, practicada de orden del Supremo Gobierno de Bolivia*, La Paz, 1852.

[3] *F.O. 126/13.*

workshop. The theoretical details incorporated in this charter contrast strikingly with its complete failure to achieve anything at all in practice. None of the long and carefully documented concessionary articles was ever implemented since, apart from the many obvious local difficulties, the Amazon was closed to foreign navigation. Brazil's final comment was that the entire enterprise appeared suspiciously like an attempt to make the Amazon waterway the southern boundary of French Guiana.

After the failure of this grandiose scheme, no further attempts were ventured to promote foreign colonization within any part of the northern sector as long as the Amazon route was sealed. The ultramontane region remained largely inaccessible, a wilderness into which political exiles, however, would occasionally be consigned: 'The Beni is now the Siberia of Bolivia', the British Chargé d'Affaires, J. A. Lloyd, observed in 1853.

In general, after independence, the northern forests probably attracted more exploratory expeditions than did the Beni plains, but even so, reliable knowledge came extremely slowly. Sir Clements Markham's travels in the 1850s provided splendid examples of individual resourcefulness and enquiry,[1] although many other investigations ended in tragedy. The Peruvian explorer Maldonado lost his life on the Madeira cataracts (at Caldeirão do Inferno) in 1861, and la Torre's expedition from Cuzco in 1873 was wiped out by Indian attack along the Madre de Dios. Isolated Jesuit and Franciscan missions were still in existence in small numbers amid the forest wilderness, and of these the most important in Bolivia were at Apolo, Cavinas, Reyes and at Ysiama, near the old, presumed Inca road from Cuzco to the Beni river. Yet in all, no more than a tiny trickle of settlement spilled through the mountain wall into the Bolivian tropical forests, while exploration into the more distant frontiers of Bolivia and Peru, from any direction, remained localised and uncoordinated.

3. THE NORTHERN FRONTIER AFTER INDEPENDENCE.
BOLIVIA AND BRAZIL: *UTI POSSIDETIS DE FACTO*

In March 1867 Brazil and Bolivia concluded a Treaty of Amity, Limits Navigation and Commerce.[2] Again, as in the colonial period, adjustment

---

[1] C. R. Markham, (i) 'On the supposed Sources of the River Purus', *Journ. Roy. Geog. Soc.*, vol. xxv, 1855, pp. 151–8; (ii) *Peru*, London, 1880; (iii) 'The Basins of the Amaru-mayu and the Beni', *Proc. Roy. Geog. Soc.* (New Series), vol. v, 1883, pp. 313–27 (Amaru-mayu is an alternative name for the river Madre de Dios).

[2] L. Markbreit to Secretary of State Hamilton Fish, Cochabamba, 6 February 1870 (enclosure), Diplomatic Despatches from Bolivia, *General Records of the Dept. of State, Record Group 59*, Washington, D.C.; and *Col. Trat. Vig. Bol.*, vol. IV, pp. 175–93.

was dictated by effective settlement. The east–west line was consequently moved south in Brazil's favour from 6° 52′ S[1] to 10° 20′ S, i.e. to the source of the Madeira, which is formed by the confluence of the rivers Mamoré and Beni (Article II). The boundary was to follow this parallel westward until the Javari river was reached. If this in fact proved impossible, and the Javari was found to rise north of 10° 20′ S, then a straight line was to be drawn from the parallel (precise point of departure not specified) to the Javari's principal headstream (Fig. 7b). By the end of 1867, the proposal for a right-angled line had been abandoned in favour of an oblique line, drawn from the Mamoré–Beni confluence (taken as 10° 20′ S) to the source of the Javari (wherever that might be, for its exact position was unknown, Fig. 7c).

Peru and Bolivia, as the two successor States to this part of the Spanish empire, also shared the problems of determining the position of the east–west line of the San Ildefonso treaty of 1777 between the Madeira and Javari. Peru in particular had made extravagant claims as far east as the Madeira river[2] but it remained in the position of a protesting by-stander while Brazil and Bolivia apportioned the area between themselves.

Considerable criticism, however, greeted the 1867 pronouncement in Brazil. The introduction of an oblique line was untraditional, and proved unpopular. Large areas settled and exploited by Brazil were left on the Bolivian side of the boundary, while Peru continued to complain vigorously that some of the territory thus apportioned was still in dispute between Peru and Bolivia. That the oblique line did not contain the limits of Brazilian pioneer penetration in the upper Juruá, Purus, Acre and Mamoré river region was generally acknowledged, although at the time the Brazilian Foreign Minister had remarked to the British Minister in Rio that the principle of *uti possidetis* had served as the basis of the treaty negotiations (*de facto* presumably). Brazil, however, was at war with Paraguay (the War of the Triple Alliance, 1865–70) during the negotiating period with Bolivia, and apparently had sought to avoid antagonising foreign opinion by driving too hard a bargain with yet another weak neighbour.

For nearly forty years attempts were made to locate an essential

---

[1] Or 8° 4′ S (see p. 95 n. 1). Peru complained that this adjustment involved territory apportioned to Peru by its treaty with Brazil in 1851. This complaint was groundless, but based partly on ignorance of the river Javari's source.

[2] The boundaries of three Departments (Loreto, Cuzco and Puno) had been extended on the maps in Lima as far as the Madre de Dios and Madeira rivers in order to substantiate these claims, but the sub-division of the Departments into Provinces had extended no farther east than the Andean Cordillera Real, which thus formed the limit of internal political organisation and effective settlement in Peru. It was on the exploration led by Faustino Maldonado along the Madre de Dios and upper Madeira rivers that Peru based its claims after 1861.

point on the boundary – the source of the Javari – which was variously fixed at:

lat. 6° 59′ 29.5″ S   long. 74° 06′ 26.67″ W (1874)
      7° 01′ 17″   S   74° 08′ 27″   W (1877)
      7° 11′ 48″   S   73° 47′ 44″   W (1895) point Cunha–Gomez

and after exploration in 1899 at

      7° 06′ 55″   S   73° 47′ 30″   W (1901)

No official demarcation of the oblique Muñoz–Netto line (so called from the names of the two signatories of the 1867 treaty) was made at the time except for the erection of two boundary monuments at each end of it, one of which was periodically shifted as progressive exploration demanded. Guillaume's map of 1888 shows the position of these pillars as the line was then located.[1]

4. THE PROBLEM OF BOLIVIA'S OUTLET TO THE AMAZON. AN EARLY RAILWAY FIASCO: 1868–1879

'If Bolivia ever matures into a steady and regular government, it is to the *east* that her wealth and population must progress, and to the Atlantic that her trade must flow.'[2]

The greatest barrier to the opening of the Bolivian Norte and Oriente to the Atlantic was traditionally considered to be the eighteen sets of rapids and falls on the Madeira and Mamoré rivers between San Antonio, an old Jesuit mission centre founded in 1737, and Guayaramerin. This obstacle was indeed a severe one. Between the smooth navigable lower waters of the Madeira and an estimated 3000-mile network of navigable water above the highest fall, lie 230 miles of cataract-broken river, plunging 272 feet in all over the resistant edge of the Brazilian Shield (Plate XI). At this time the thirteen lower sets of rapids lay entirely in Brazilian territory, while the five above Villa Bella were shared between Brazil and Bolivia. Together, they interrupted part of the world's greatest inland waterway system, and effectively terminated navigation out of northern Bolivia, south of the Acre. The result was an almost total inability to reach the extensive navigable waters of the Amazon with either ease or safety, and a

---

[1] H. Guillaume, *The Amazon Provinces of Peru as a field for European Emigration*, London, 1888.

[2] A. K. McClung to Secretary of State Daniel Webster, Chuquisaca, 24 August 1850, Diplomatic Despatches from Bolivia, *General Records of the Dept. of State, Record Group 59*, Washington, D.C.

very real increase in the already oppressive isolation of the region stranded behind the cataracts.

Events in 1866 and 1867 exacerbated this situation, for by a decree on 7 December 1866 the Emperor of Brazil opened the navigation of the Amazon and its tributaries to merchant shipping of all nations on and after 7 September 1867.[1] Since 1852, a monopoly of steam navigation on the Amazon had been held by the Companhia do Amazonas, a Brazilian corporation which at that date had obtained a twenty-five-year contract under an annual government subsidy of about £80,000. The creation of the Amazon as an international waterway, however, within prescribed limits, represented a major modification of Brazil's previous attitude towards the navigation of its great river, and the news was received enthusiastically in the upper reaches of the Amazon basin. The ceremony itself took place at Pará amid great pomp and festivity on 7 September 1867, and the waterfront was thronged with crowds gathered to watch the comings and goings of admirals, foreign consuls and other dignitaries duly assembled for the occasion. Regrettably, it was reported that no foreign vessels were currently available in port to share in, and add reality to the ceremony of opening the Amazon to international shipping, but, this apart, the celebrations provided a noisy and memorable day.

Thus, after both the 1866 decree and the 1867 oblique-line boundary decision, ideas outlined under Article IX of the Muñoz–Netto treaty for the opening of an Amazon–Madeira–Mamoré routeway into north-eastern Bolivia crystallised, and Bolivia decided to push ahead with the scheme for a railway around the Madeira–Mamoré falls.[2] It seemed essential at this stage to realise quickly the opportunity at last offered by Brazil to share the advantages of free navigation to the Atlantic, now lying tantalisingly beyond the lowest Madeira cataracts. Accordingly, Bolivia sought and secured the services in New York of Colonel George Earl Church, a Massachusetts railway engineer and American Civil War veteran, who was destined to pursue the enterprise with quite fanatical zeal. His earliest work had been on North American railroads but, at the age of twenty-one, his first adventurous expedition to South America fired a passionate and

---

[1] *F.O. 13/450* and *F.O. 13/447*. (The 1867 Muñoz–Netto treaty settlement had been made in the light of Bolivia's future ability to share in the free navigation of the Amazon.)

[2] The idea of a *mule-road* around the falls had been suggested by Lieut. Gibbon, *Exploration of the Valley of the Amazon*, pp. 302 and 313, in 1854. He estimated that if this major interruption to navigation could be avoided by 180 miles of trail opened through Brazilian territory, the time taken to transport goods from Baltimore to La Paz could be cut from 118 days *via* Cape Horn to 59 days *via* the Amazon–Madeira–Mamoré route. (A few years before Gibbon's expedition, Palacios had also considered the possibilities of a canal or a cart-way around the falls.)

absorbing interest in the southern continent, and particularly in Bolivia, which remained with him until his death in 1910.[1]

In 1868, in an atmosphere of great governmental enthusiasm, Church became chief agent of the newly formed National Bolivian Navigation Company. By then it had been estimated that the time taken to reach trade centres in U.S.A. and Europe could be clipped from 180 days to 30 by the new route, and freight charges reduced to a quarter of existing rates. Exports of Peruvian bark, cocoa, coffee, vicuña and alpaca wools, copper, tin, silver and gold would no longer, it was announced, have to be carried by mule and llama over the Andes, to the Pacific and Cape Horn. Moreover, the opening of the Amazon route would stimulate new economic activity and add, it was hoped, cotton, tobacco, sugar, rubber, vanilla, sarsaparilla, balsams, gums, timber and many other products to Bolivia's list of exports. For whatever the political and psychological value of the Atacama corridor to Bolivia may have been, transport from the Norte and Oriente to Cobija, or to Arica for that matter, was prohibitive. The long haul to Cobija, wrote Maury, 'is too rough, too tedious, and too expensive ever to admit of its becoming a commercial exporium'.[2]

It would be almost impossible to exaggerate the favour with which the by-passing of the Madeira–Mamoré falls was regarded at this time. The forecasts of the unlimited prosperity which would follow, both in economic terms and in a greatly increased population, were wildly optimistic:

It is an enterprise which carries so much of the commercial and political destiny of South America. The position of this railway is both commanding and peculiar... three thousand miles of magnificent navigable rivers converge on its southern terminus, so that it has control of the greatest area tributary to any single line of railway in the world, not excepting the Pacific road of the United States... It is the key to

[1] Church eventually settled in London where, as an active member of the Royal Geographical Society, he was elected a Vice-President in 1902. Although always to be associated with the ambitious Madeira–Mamoré Railway project, his most notable work lay in the detailed reports of his travels, which so effectively publicised, in English, some of Latin America's least-known regions. His life-long fascination with Bolivia undoubtedly helped to expand the Royal Geographical Society's valuable collection of material on the country in the late nineteenth and early twentieth centuries.

See (i) Archives and Journals of the Royal Geographical Society, *passim*; (ii) Lewis Hanke, *A Note on the Life and Publications of Colonel George Earl Church*, Institute of Latin American Studies, Columbia University, N.Y., 1965. This biographical summary is followed by bibliographical appendices from other contributors on material relating to Church in Bolivia, Brazil and Washington, D.C.

[2] M. F. Maury, *The Amazon, and the Atlantic Slopes of South America*, Washington, D.C., 1853, p. 25.

400,000 square miles of territory in Matto Grosso, Bolivia and Southern Peru – and to two million people.[1]

Indeed, the momentum of 'railway mania' had already carried Church on to his next scheme – a 'Great Central Railway' for Bolivia, to run from Cochabamba to the head of navigation on the Mamoré river. A program of colonization and new towns was fully worked out on paper, and Church declared that he would launch his new project not later than three months after the completion of the Madeira–Mamoré Railway. So to this he bent his first energies.

Once the Navigation Company and the associated Madeira and Mamoré Railway Company had been established in Bolivia, similar permission and authorisation had to be obtained from Brazil, in whose territory the railway would run. Application was therefore made in Rio de Janeiro for a concession to organise a company and establish a railway round the falls, and an exclusive fifty-year concession was formally granted to Church on 20 April 1870.[2] The New Englander was to be allowed to organise the construction of a line approximately 300 kilometres (about 190 miles), from below the lowest fall of San Antonio to a point above the highest fall at Guajará Mirim. Work was to begin within two years of the date of registration of the company set up for the purpose and be completed, with the railway in regular operation, within seven years (except for contingencies arising from the will of God). Otherwise the concession was to be declared void.

Under Article VII, the Madeira and Mamoré Railway Company was also granted land along the railway or its vicinity in alternate lots, each not exceeding four square leagues, with additional sections at the two termini, and on the bank opposite the mouth of the Beni river to which a branch line might be run. There was additional permission to prospect for minerals up to five leagues from the line. In all, the concession formed a long and detailed document, its twenty-nine articles carefully constructed so as to leave all responsibility in the hands of the organisers; the company was free to work out its own salvation, encouraged to produce results, and tacitly reminded to expect no help from Brazil if it did not do so.

As Church himself admitted later, in a more rational moment, 'the

---

[1] From *The Brazil and River Plate Mail*, London, April 1871. In Bolivia, typical of the many publications was M. M. Salinas' *Navegación de los Ríos de Bolivia confluentes del Madera y Amazonas, y Colonisación*, Cochabamba, 1871. (Published also in La Paz, Lima and Valparaiso.)

[2] *F.O. 13/470.* 'Decree of the Emperor of Brazil, granting to an American Citizen [Colonel Church], the exclusive privilege, for a fixed period, of constructing a railway, to be called the Madeira and Mamoré Railway', Rio de Janeiro, 20 April 1870.

enthusiasm exhibited caused me to look lightly upon the fact that the problem to be solved was unique'.[1] The terrain bordering the falls was imperfectly known, and early ideas of a canal or a road instead of a railway had soon to be abandoned.[2] Finance became an outstanding additional problem; the Franco–Prussian War of 1870 tightened capital abroad, while the overthrow of Bolivia's President Melgarejo in 1871 resulted in foreign investors becoming increasingly wary. Little information was obtainable about any part of Bolivia, so that Church was prompted to observe 'that Bolivia was far less known in Europe in 1870 than any country on the globe having a regular form of government'.[3] Nevertheless, at the outset, despite all these problems and despite the added harassment of sectional interest, the U.S. Minister in Bolivia noted overall buoyancy and enthusiasm: 'None of these difficulties, not even the Franco–Prussian war, the recent revolution in this Republic, Peruvian and Chilean opposition to the loss of Bolivian trade by the Pacific coast, etc., etc., have been able to impede the steady march forward of the National Bolivian Navigation Company.'[4]

[1] G. E. Church, *The Route to Bolivia via the River Amazon. A Report to the Governments of Bolivia and Brazil*, London, 1877, p. 6.

[2] G. E. Church presented seven accounts of earlier exploration and commentary upon the Madeira–Mamoré falls in *Explorations made in the Valley of the River Madeira from 1749–1868*, published by the National Bolivian Navigation Co., London, 1875. These comprised: (i) Report of José and Francisco Keller made to the Imperial Government of Brazil, 1870; (ii) 'Exploration of the rivers and lakes of the Department of Beni, also notes relative to the Department of Mojos', by J. A. Palacios; (iii) 'Bolivian Rivers', Thaddeus Haenke, 1799; (iv) 'Rapids of the River Madeira', Lardner Gibbon, 1854; (v) 'The Madeira and its Headwaters', Q. Quevado, 1861; (vi) 'A new fluvial outlet for Bolivia', Y. Arauz, 1868; (vii) The Portuguese Exploring Expedition of 1749.

[3] G. E. Church, *The Route to Bolivia via the River Amazon*, p. 16.

[4] L. Markbreit to Secretary of State Hamilton Fish, Sucre, 28 August 1871, Diplomatic Despatches from Bolivia, *General Records of the Dept. of State*, Record Group 59, Washington, D.C. Markbreit was less enthusiastic about another scheme sponsored by one of his countrymen in this same period. A. D. Piper had incorporated The California Colonization and Commercial Co. of Bolivia in San Francisco in January 1870, and received concessions in the Beni, and farther north, for the settlement of not less than 5000 families in 25 years. The advance party left New York in June 1870: 'I have never heard from Mr. Piper and know nothing of his plans. Neither have I the slightest idea from what points he intends to bring his colonists. The tract ceded to him is now inhabited mostly by savages', L. Markbreit to Secretary of State Hamilton Fish, Cochabamba, 24 March 1870, *op. cit.*

'You know that the Piper expedition has been a miserable failure. The little miserable sailing craft which reached Pará went no farther, and the Americans of Pará had to pay the passage of the poor deluded emigrants, about a dozen in number, back to New York', G. E. Church to L. Markbreit, London, 1 May 1871, *op. cit.* (A few colonists in fact reached Manaus, but most gave up at that point.)

'I have never had any faith in this [Piper] colonization enterprise. I have always considered it as impracticable to introduce colonists into a country which, owing to the entire absence of railways and steam navigation, is almost inaccessible to the immigrant', L. Markbreit to

The work was sub-contracted to the Public Works Construction Company, incorporated in the City of London with capital of £1,700,000. Two iron steamboats and one steam launch were ordered from the U.S.A., the rails from Belgium, and iron bridges and station equipment from England. In November 1871, clearing of the forest began at San Antonio with a party of about 150, and Church himself ceremoniously turned the first sod. One steamboat, the *Explorador*, was slowly dragged up the rapids with immense labour – it took forty-three days – and was launched on the Mamoré to await completion of the railway. But this soon became progressively more remote.[1] The engineers and surveyors stationed at San Antonio languished, drinking and sleeping their time away, complaining bitterly of the deadly climate and impassable country, neither of which, unfortunately for all concerned, could be classed as 'contingencies arising from the will of God'. One year after the Public Works Construction Company had begun to clear the ground, only 3½ miles of the intended route were surveyed – and that inaccurately. Indeed, it was reported that a company engineer had confirmed the course of the track without ever having travelled over the projected route at all. Suitable labourers were unobtainable locally, and few were imported. The Bolivian Government had to be restrained from automatically sending all condemned prisoners to the railway camp, an unwelcome contribution to the quite inadequate labour force.

The incompetency of the Public Works Construction Company resulted in their repudiating the contract. Costs had increased to as much as £12,000 per mile of track, double the original estimate. But no part of the railway had been built and its total length now seemed to be at least fifty miles longer than the Company's original estimate. Of the two further vessels designed to complement the railway at each terminus, one, the *Mamoré*, lay grounded and beyond repair at San Antonio, while the other, the *Silver Spray*, was still in sections aboard her, the crews of both decimated by yellow fever. Piles of rails and rolling stock lay unused and unprotected at San Antonio, and labourers drawn from Cochabamba and Santa Cruz were discharged without wage. Two travellers in the region in 1876 pro-

Hamilton Fish, La Paz, 22 and 24 May 1872, *op. cit.* (Markbreit was busy organising a search for Piper and his wife, reported killed or captured by Indians.)

Markbreit's support for G. E. Church was based on the rail and navigational facilities his scheme would provide, rather than its associated colonization clause.

[1] L. Markbreit to Secretary of State Hamilton Fish, La Paz, 18 April 1872 and 31 July 1872, Diplomatic Despatches from Bolivia, *General Records of the Dept. of State, Record Group 59*. These and other reports during 1872 record information received at the U.S. Legation from the Department of Beni, and from G. E. Church himself.

vided an epitaph to the ill-fated enterprise: 'There is now nothing to show but a slight scratch in the ground – representing the first cutting – a house, a few rough sheds, some cleared land, two wrecks in San Antonio harbour and several great heaps of the cases of tinned meats and broken bottles.'[1]

Church was sued in 1874 in his capacity as Chairman of the Madeira and Mamoré Railway Company and as President and Agent of the National Bolivian Navigation Company, by the Public Works Construction Company, and the Bondholders and Trustees from whom capital had been raised. Church cross-petitioned for breach of contract. After much acrimony on both sides, all suits were dismissed with costs which were, however, considerable, and litigation concerned with these continued well into the twentieth century.[2] The whole project was abandoned after yet another contractor, P. and T. Collins of Philadelphia, had similarly failed to make any real progress.[3]

The image of the cornucopian wealth of the upper Madeira and its tributaries remained untarnished, however. Neither distance and inaccessibility, nor the intrinsic difficulties of the physical environment could shake the conviction of Church, and other occasional travellers through northern Bolivia, that the tremendous potential of this upper Amazon country must soon be developed. That the dream should remain unrealised was unthinkable, for this was Church's 'savage Arcadia, where fertility of soil, hill, dale, mountain slope, rich savanna, lake and river are delightfully mingled, the beautiful and seductive region teeming with varied animal life and abounding in such gifts as nature lavishly confers only when in her most prodigal and generous mood'. But for a while the railway dream was laid aside.

5. 1870–1880: THE DECLINE OF THE TRADE IN PERUVIAN BARK AND THE BEGINNING OF THE BOLIVIAN RUBBER BOOM

Systematic exploration of northern Bolivia, where it had occurred at all for economic reasons, had tended to be marginal to the core area and concen-

---

[1] C. Barrington Brown and W. Lidstone, *Fifteen Thousand Miles on the Amazon and its 'Tributaries*, London, 1878, p. 344.

[2] 'Data regarding the Church Loan', *F.O. 371/5532* (for the years 1917–21). Also, *Council of Foreign Bondholders (Bolivia)*, Press Cuttings Books, 7 vols., Guildhall Library, London.

[3] The firm of Philip and Thomas Collins undertook the commission in 1877 after two further contractors had abandoned the project. But only just over two miles of permanent track were laid before they too declared themselves beaten and bankrupt in 1878–9. It is with this second phase of the enterprise that Neville B. Craig, *Recollections of an Ill-Fated Expedition to the Headwaters of the Madeira River in Brazil*, Philadelphia and London, 1907, is chiefly concerned.

trated, therefore, within the higher, tropical valleys of the Yungas which deeply etch the eastern Andean slopes. From Ecuador to Bolivia, the forests were periodically exploited for Peruvian bark. Many species and varieties of *Cinchona* had long been known, but exploitation had been significant only in Ecuador and Peru until *C. calisaya* attracted attention in the 1820s and 1830s, and transferred the boom southwards into Bolivia.[1]

By the 1850s and 1860s, with the depletion of Peruvian supplies, the Caupolicán–Cochabamba zone of Bolivia dominated all others, and Cochabamba itself became an important subsidiary market on the already well-established La Paz–Arica trade route. For many years, much of the produce from the Peruvian *montañas* had followed convenient trails back through Bolivia to La Paz, which became the eventual assembly point for all mule and llama trains converging for the descent to Tacna and Arica.[2] Smaller quantities moved to the Pacific *via* Arequipa and Islay, but La Paz remained the chief market for foreign buyers. Here, merchants continued to complain of wasteful methods of collection – that as much as one-third of the marketable bark was left behind on the trunks and branches as they fell to the ground.

In 1869–70, about $470,000-worth of bark was sold in La Paz, where the American Consul-General recorded a price fluctuating between $62 and $81 per 150 lb. bundle, two of which formed a mule-burden.[3] These prices may usefully be compared with those supplied for the year 1849 by U.S. Consul Ringgold (p. 49 n. 4), which serve to emphasise the subsequent decline in the Peruvian bark trade. But even at its height, unlike other examples of intensive economic exploitation within Bolivia's borderlands, the Peruvian bark industry sparked off no boundary conflict and no territorial readjustment between Bolivia and Peru. The suggested cession of territory in Caupolicán (Apolobamba) in part-exchange for Arica, which was made by President Sucre in 1826, never materialised

[1] An account of the bark trade in Bolivia is recorded in H. A. Weddell, *Voyage dans le Nord de la Bolivie*. Background material on the rise and fall of the Peruvian bark industry in South America as a whole is provided by Clements Markham, *Travels in Peru and India*, London, 1862, and *Peruvian Bark*, London, 1880. Markham was responsible, at the request of the India Office, for taking seeds and seedlings of *Cinchona* (*Chinchona*) trees from Peru to the Nilgiri Hills in south India in 1859, thereby laying the foundation of cheap quinine production in S.E. Asia. A few years later prices for quinine in England had been slashed from 13s. to 1s. 6d. an ounce.
[2] An interesting sidelight on the significance of Arica as the port for Peruvian bark, and on the extent of its hinterland, is provided by J. J. von Tschudi, *Travels in Peru 1838–1842*, London, 1847. On p. 400 he notes that the extract of bark from the *montañas* of Urubamba was known as *Cusconin* (after Cuzco) or as *Aricin* (after Arica, its port of shipment).
[3] Charles Rand to Secretary of State Hamilton Fish, 30 September 1870, Consular Despatches from La Paz, *General Records of the Dept. of State, Record Group 59*, Washington, D.C.

and was, in any case, made before this region experienced its boom in bark production. The Yungas lay comparatively close to Bolivia's main centres of population, the total penetration remained small, and thus *Cinchona* exploitation in Bolivia did not trace the patterns so often reproduced elsewhere. The rubber regions, on the other hand, were more remote and were to witness a completely different scale of enterprise and development.

At least until 1880, rubber exploitation in Bolivia remained extremely limited. In addition, it was located in two distinctly separated areas of activity. The first of these was in the lower Mamoré–Itenes region, where a small number of Bolivian workers had congregated after the 1867 boundary decision with Brazil had forced them to abandon their *barracas* along the Madeira river, and withdraw southward into territory which had been confirmed as Bolivian. The second area lay, by water transport, about four hundred miles away to the south-west, on the middle reaches of the Beni between Reyes and Cavinas. The old mission post of Reyes had become an important collecting centre for Peruvian bark during the mid-nineteenth century, but as that trade had withered many bark collectors had turned increasingly to other forest products, including rubber, to supplement their cargoes to the Pacific ports. As the bark traffic declined, the export of rubber to some extent reversed this line of movement, for rubber outlets were dominated by Brazil and the Amazon routeway.

Specimens of rubber from the middle Beni had been collected in the forests close to the Cavinas Jesuit mission in 1869, and sent to Europe for examination. Once the quality was found to be good, very small quantities of rubber began to be dispatched into Brazil *via* the Madeira-Amazon system. But the direct route into the Madeira down the Beni river was not employed, for the lower Beni remained virtually unexplored and unknown – or at least forgotten – and surrounded by rumour as to its dangers and the hostility of its Indian population. Instead, therefore, rubber destined for Brazil was rowed *upstream* from Cavinas, and carted overland though Reyes, to the Yacuma, Mamoré and Madeira rivers, a hopelessly time-consuming and roundabout journey of nearly seven hundred miles. Under these circumstances, little rubber exploitation was worth such enormous efforts of transport, and all further progress was delayed until an alternative route could be found.

In 1880, the alternative was dramatically provided by the exploration of the lower Beni by a North American doctor, Edwin Heath. He had been employed as medical officer by the firm of P. & T. Collins during their unsuccessful Madeira–Mamoré railway project of 1878–9. When the company disbanded, instead of returning to the U.S.A. with the main party,

Heath had travelled into Bolivia in 1879 to try and complete a voyage
of exploration on the Beni river which had previously been attempted
by his brother Ivon and the American naturalist, James Orton, in 1876–7.

At the end of 1880, Heath at last achieved his aim of removing the uncertainties shrouding the Beni by travelling from Reyes right down the river
to its confluence with the Mamoré, exploring and mapping as he went.[1]
The commercial effect of this journey was staggering. Before, probably
no more than two hundred were employed in exploiting rubber in the
neighbourhood of the Cavinas mission; a few months later, between
one and two thousand were estimated to be working along the river.
The deeply rooted fear and ignorance of this notorious region had at last
been dispelled.

Heath's exploration of the Lower Beni in 1880 proved a landmark in the
subsequent development of northern and north-eastern Bolivia, for it
triggered a wave of penetration along the lower reaches of the rivers, well
beyond their steeper, *montaña* sections. Moreover, as former *Cinchona*
bark workers quickly set up new *barracas*[2] at strategic points in the lower
Beni, Madre de Dios and Orton districts between 1881 and 1884, the two
formerly separate areas of Bolivian rubber production were linked and
mutually strengthened. Synchronised, therefore, with Brazilian penetration upstream in Amazonia, with increasing world demand and soaring
prices, Heath's exploration of the lower Beni marked the sudden beginning of the Bolivian rubber boom.

By the time Bolivia entered the list of South American producers,
Brazil had long been established as the main source of world crude rubber,
important after Charles Goodyear's discovery of vulcanisation in 1839.[3]

[1] E. R. Heath, 'Exploration of the River Beni in 1880–81', *Proc. Roy. Geog. Soc.* (New Series),
vol. V, 1883, pp. 327–41; *Journ. Am. Geog. Soc. of New York*, vol. XIV, 1882, pp. 117–
65. Edwin Heath sent his diary, map and original surveys made during the voyage down the
Beni river to the Royal Geographical Society, London, in 1883. In Bolivia, the diary was
later translated and annotated by M. V. Ballivián, *La Exploración del Río Beni, revista
histórica por el doctor Edwin R. Heath*, La Paz, 1896. See also the same author's brief summary,
Apuntes para la biografía de Mr. Edwin R. Heath, La Paz, 1897.
[2] *Barraca* (Span. & Port.) usually signifies the dwelling of a rubber gatherer (Port. *seringueiro*
here used throughout) from which a number of *estradas* are worked (these are winding
pathways through the forest, each enclosing 150–200 rubber trees). *Barraca*, however, can
also describe a major collecting and supply centre for rubber workers based at smaller
centros (in Bolivia *centro gomero y agrícola*).
[3] Thomas Hancock worked simultaneously on the problems of vulcanisation in England and
is frequently credited jointly with Goodyear for its discovery and development. An alternative term for rubber used at this time was *caoutchouc*, a French adaptation of the local Indians'
term *cahuchu* meaning 'weeping tree'. C. M. de la Condamine, the French explorer, had
voyaged down the Amazon from Quito, made the first map of the river based on accurate
observations, and brought rubber, long used by the Indians, to Europe by 1743. Fresneau

The wave of exploitation had moved steadily up the Amazon during the second half of the nineteenth century as new areas, rich in the high quality *Hevea brasiliensis*, were feverishly sought. By the end of the 1870s the Madeira and Purus regions were being regularly tapped, and Pará (Belém do Pará) found itself rivalled by Manaus (Manaos),[1] which doubled its rubber trade between 1887 and 1889 as the rubber frontier penetrated more deeply into South America.

The richest rubber districts lay along the south-bank, rather than the north-bank tributaries of the Amazon, and in the two million square miles of rain forest, the 'river roads' inevitably formed the arteries of movement. As the Madeira, Beni, Acre and Purus regions increased in importance, the time-consuming obstacles to easy movement became increasingly irksome. Railways were projected, without success, between Manaus and Paramaribo in Guiana, and west over the Andes. Canals or railways to link the Purus and Beni, and the Madre de Dios and Ucayali basins were mooted. Meantime, the bulk of the rubber moved out from Bolivia *via* the difficult cataract-broken Madeira route, although a small proportion was carried in sealed boxes on the backs of Indian porters and mules to the *altiplano*, and by llama and mule train down again to Mollendo on the Pacific, an incredibly slow and laborious journey.[2]

6. THE CLIMAX OF THE BOLIVIAN RUBBER BOOM AND THE CONTROLLING FACTORS OF LOCATION, ACCESSIBILITY AND OUTLET

Despite the almost overwhelming difficulties of location, Bolivian rubber became increasingly important in the 1890s, the decade of astonishingly rapid development in the upper Amazon basin.[3] Only then was the rubber

made similar discoveries of *caoutchouc* in French Guiana in 1745. The first European, however, known to have completed a voyage down the Amazon from Quito was the Spanish *conquistador* Francisco de Orellana, who performed this extraordinary feat as early as 1542, two centuries before the French expedition.

[1] Following an Orthographic Agreement between Portugal and Brazil, signed in December 1943, the spelling of Manaos was officially changed to Manaus in 1946.

[2] Mollendo remained virtually the only Pacific port to handle Bolivian rubber. Arica did not share in this trade to any appreciable extent.

[3] One of the best sources of information and anecdote on the changing fortunes of the South American rubber boom at this period is to be found in the trade journal *The India Rubber World and Electrical Trades Review*, New York, a monthly publication which appeared first in October 1889, and which was continued after October 1899 as *The India Rubber World*. In addition, *The India-Rubber and Gutta-Percha and Electrical Trades Journal*, London, a monthly publication which began in August 1884, provides a useful supplement to the American publication.

boom getting fully into its stride in this most landlocked of South American regions, and yet a traveller to Bolivia at this period had still to admit disconsolately 'though all the banks of the streams are lined with rubber trees, they are as useless for all the purposes of commerce, except in a few localities, as if they had never sprouted from the ground', so insuperable were the obstacles to navigation, and so great the distances involved.

Wrestling once more with the perennial problem of the Madeira–Mamoré cataracts, Bolivia offered in 1894 to pay 6 per cent interest on the capital needed for canal construction, in an effort to attract foreign investment. It was not successful, however, and no such improvement to navigation was ever introduced. In terms of economic concession, new laws were passed in 1896–7 permitting an individual to work up to 500 *estradas* (1000 *estradas* for incorporated companies), upon the nominal payment of one boliviano per *estrada* per annum for 15 years, after which full ownership could be claimed if a small title fee was paid. Facilities were offered for an outright payment of 15 bolivianos per *estrada* to be made instead if desired. Printed conditions of employment, the condemning of imprisonment and flogging, and the advocating of payment in cash as well as in kind, and medical services, were all stipulated. Lacking financial and manpower resources of its own on the scale required, Bolivia wooed foreign enterprise, and as a result, exploitation intensified in an atmosphere of unbounded enthusiasm. Settlements clustered along the banks of the Madeira, Mamoré, Beni, Madre de Dios, Orton, Acre and Purus, including several large estates, some employing well over a thousand collectors. Steam launches plied along the upper navigable reaches of the rivers, and hundreds of miles of good cart road were built,[1] including 112 miles of trackway around the Madeira falls, still the most serious obstacle to the export of rubber out of the region. This track was never completed, however, owing to the perennial shortage of labour. Other schemes for canal links between the Beni and Purus were revived once more, but again abandoned.

The Bolivian Noroeste and Nordeste were, in company with the adjoining Peruvian and Brazilian regions, proving extraordinarily rich in wild rubber – *Hevea brasiliensis* and *Hevea lutea* – though tapping pro-

---

[1] A. Vaca Diez, *Vías de Comunicación en el Noroeste de la República*, La Paz, 1893. In 1890, Bolivia had created National Delegations in the Purus and Madre de Dios regions, and these were combined into the *Noroeste* by Congressional decree in 1893. The northern districts were known as Territorio de Colonias, and were originally administered from Riberalta which, because it was sited on the right bank of the Beni river boundary, lay in the Department of that name. The Territorio de Colonias, with minor adjustments, became the Department of Pando in 1938.

ceeded for only three or four months out of every twelve. Latex was also obtained from the Caucho tree (*Castilloa*), although in this case continual tapping was replaced by felling. The trunk was drained of its sap by slits made along its entire length, and from these between three and six pints of latex would usually be gathered. After such drastic measures, however, production ceased unless a coppice growth sprang from the stump. Bolivian rubber, entering foreign markets as 'Up-river fine', or as 'Pará' or 'Mollendo' according more with its exit point than with its source, was of the very highest quality. Activity at the close of the nineteenth century intensified and, as the twentieth century began, this section of the upper Amazon basin was acknowledged indisputably as the most important rubber region in the world. Its pre-eminence was maintained in spite of economic penetration venturing no more than a mile in most localities from the waterway. Settlement remained riparian; millions of acres lay untouched, sometimes registered but unexplored.

All the routes out of northern Bolivia were despairingly difficult. North-eastwards, the 230 interrupted miles of navigation along the Madeira–Mamoré still maintained their stranglehold upon rubber movement, although the Madeira, greatest tributary of the Amazon, nevertheless continued to provide the main outlet for the landlocked northern sector. Rubber moved this way, not because it was an easy route, but because the others were even more arduous. Below San Antonio, the Madeira formed a long but comparatively easy highway for ocean-going steamers to and from the Amazon. But above San Antonio, the river still poured uncontrollably over the series of falls George Earl Church had campaigned so vigorously to avoid by railway a generation earlier. Special fleets of wooden boats (*batelões*, Spanish *batelones*), each about 30 feet long, were employed to negotiate the falls when the water level was fairly high, their crews shooting the rapids, either complete with load, or empty while the load was portaged.[1] At the larger falls both boat and load had to be 'overlanded', sometimes for nearly a thousand yards; here, narrow-gauge corduroy tracks were laid, over which the *batelões* were laboriously dragged. It was a slow, prostrating task, performed by gangs stationed at key points along the falls section and, as a general rule, only three trips a year could be made. In the low-water season, maintenance work was carried out: boulders of manageable size were hauled from the river bed and the corduroy roads repaired. The constant breaking of the journey,

[1] H. C. Pearson, *The Rubber Country of the Amazon*, New York, 1911, pp. 119–21. This study, one of many recording information collected during travels through the rubber regions, includes photographs of the Madeira–Mamoré falls and the *batelão* fleets. (Pearson was founder and editor of *The India Rubber World*.)

portaging, and manhandling involved in these 230 miles consumed at least three weeks on the downward journey, and nearly nine weeks on the return against the current, a feat which necessitated twenty-five exhausting portages.

Loss of time was matched by loss of men and of cargo. Each *batelão* carried a crew of sixteen men and up to ten tons of rubber in *pella* (*bolacha*) or slab form. The temptation to take a chance on shooting the rapids, rather than accept the delaying and wearying alternative of hauling overland, frequently proved too strong. On average, between 10 per cent and 15 per cent of the rubber was lost annually as *batelões* overturned in the seething, deafening surge of water. Rubber was prized but life was cheap, and redeeming the cargo assumed considerably greater importance than rescue of the crew. The mortality rate was appallingly high, and crowds of rough wooden crosses formed a forbidding series of markers along this dreaded stretch of the Madeira. Below each fall it was usual to find an individual whose sole means of livelihood consisted of salvaging floating rubber and either claiming the 25 per cent-of-value salvage fee from the owners, or cutting out the brand and substituting his own mark in its place.

Below San Antonio, once the hazardous cataract section had been left behind, the course was set for Manaus, the great 'rubber river' port and entrepôt for the backlands of Bolivia, Colombia and Peru. In smoother waters, cargoes moved eight hundred miles down the Madeira, a magnificent river three miles wide at its confluence with the Amazon. A little to the west, and twelve miles up the dark waters of the Negro, Manaus commanded the rubber trade of virtually the entire central and upper Amazon basin, dominating the second phase of the rubber boom when the tide of exploitation had reached the continental interior. To it came the products not only of north and north-east Bolivia but also of the lower Purus, Juruá, Javari, Ucayali and the Putumayo.

Manaus has earned a unique place in the ranks of South American 'boom-towns'. Countless travellers have since been fascinated by the remains of its past glories, stranded incongruously by the rubber boom's retreating tide. Founded in 1669 by the Portuguese on the left bank of the river Negro, Manaus avoided the difficult swirling waters at the confluence of the Negro and the Amazon, and was sited originally as a fort built to protect Portuguese slave-hunting expeditions among the Indians (the most warlike of whom were the Manaos). Named São José da Barra do Rio Negro, Barra gradually developed as a local regional centre during the early nineteenth century, trading mainly in Brazil nuts, fish and sarsaparilla.[1] A few warehouses had been built and, early in 1850, Wallace estimated the population to be between 5000 and 6000. Later that year, however, Bates noted a population of little more than 3000 and even this figure appeared to be declining. The fort was ruined and the whole settlement 'is now in a most wretched plight'.[2]

It was given the name of Manaos in 1852, when Brazil inaugurated its own regular steam navigation service on the Amazon, simultaneously designating the port as the capital of the new province of Amazonas. Travellers from Europe and North America, however, continued to comment upon its mean appearance. The Agassiz dismissed it lightly in 1865 with: 'There is little to be said of the town of Manaos. It consists of a small collection of houses, half of which seem going to decay, and indeed one can hardly help smiling at the tumbledown edifices, dignified by the name of public buildings, the treasury, the legislative hall, the post office, the custom-house, the President's mansion...',[3] while Keller observed: 'In spite of its pompous title, São José da Barra do Rio Negro, capital of the province of Amazonas, Manaos is but an insignificant little town of about 3,000 inhabitants... [with] unpaved and badly levelled streets, low houses and cottages of most primitive construction.'[4]

Nevertheless, Manaus' coming period of glory was perceived by at least one traveller as early as the 1840s: 'Seringa trees abound upon the Amazon, probably to its headwaters. The demand for the gum has not yet been felt at Barra, where it is only used for medicinal purposes...but when it is wanted, enough can be forthcoming to coat the civilised world.'[5] Certainly, after the regular steamer service between Pará and Manaus had been introduced in 1852, the settlement had begun to grow slowly, and this growth increased modestly once the effects of the opening of the Amazon in 1867 began to be felt. During the 1880s a considerable number of French and German traders had filtered through to Manaus, establishing themselves

[1] A. R. Wallace, *A Narrative of Travels on the Amazon and Río Negro*, London, 1853, pp. 112–14.

[2] H. W. Bates, *The Naturalist on the River Amazons*, in 2 vols, London, 1863, vol. I, p. 338.

[3] L. J. R. and E. C. Agassiz, *A Journey in Brazil*, Boston, 1868, pp. 190–1.

[4] F. Keller (Keller–Leuzinger), *The Amazon and Madeira Rivers*, London, 1874, p. 34. Two German engineers, Josef and Franz Keller, father and son, were commissioned by Brazil in 1867, after the Muñoz–Netto treaty, to survey the Madeira–Mamoré falls, and to examine the feasibility of a railway around them. Franz Keller's study subsequently included sixty-eight fine woodcuts made from his sketches recording the expedition (see, for example, Plate XI), which were frequently reproduced in later studies of the region.

[5] W. H. Edwards, *A Voyage up the River Amazon, including a residence at Pará*, New York, 1847, p. 195. H. W. Bates too had observed (*The Naturalist on the River Amazons*), p. 338, even while recording Manaus' mean appearance, that 'the imagination becomes excited when one reflects on the possible future of this place'.

in the four or five hotels along the waterfront, but by 1892 the population figure had risen dramatically to 20,000. Several three- and four-storey business blocks now added considerable substance to the prospect of the town along the Negro; thirteen exporting firms were represented in Manaus, four Brazilian, four Portuguese, three English and two German.

The astonishing growth continued, the population increasing to between 30,000 and 40,000 in the late 1890s. Elegant villas, parks, libraries and hospitals flourished in this urban anomaly set down in the middle of nowhere. Metalled thoroughfares, dissecting the town, ended abruptly at the edge of the built-up area, for they had no destination in the rain forest surrounding Manaus on three sides. Its lifeblood flowed only from the river, and from those rubber regions which the river alone could make accessible. A daily newspaper, electric light, an enviably efficient electric street-car system, a telephone exchange, waterworks and modern drainage, and a wide variety of shopping and professional services, ordinary in themselves but extraordinary in their location, all contributed to the welfare and comfort of the population. But, in the eyes of the world, the zenith of this booming prosperity was surely represented by the Teatro Amazonas – the splendid opera house and theatre prefabricated in Europe, and erected in 1896 to the order of the provincial Governor Eduardo Ribeiro and the Manaus rubber barons. Its dome, ablaze with thousands of blue, green and gold tiles, Brazil's national colours, shone out across the miles of surrounding rain forest. In the theatre forecourt lay an elaborate mosaic; within the walls of white Italian marble, an interior rivalling any in the world. The finest tapestries, sculpture, carpets, upholsteries, porcelains and chandeliers had been transported to this showpiece of the jungle metropolis. Amid such splendour, the delegates to the Rubber Congress would assemble and fashionable society watch a performance of the latest play or opera from Paris, London or New York. Truly, Manaus was 'not so much a Brazilian city as a city in Brazil', for its closest affinities were undoubtedly with Europe rather than with Rio de Janeiro, whose inferior appearance and standards of living were held in contemptuous regard by the proud citizens of Brazil's northern capital.

7. TERRITORIAL IDENTIFICATION IN THE NORTHERN SECTOR: THE ROLE OF NICOLÁS SUÁREZ[1]

Bonanzas create their own aristocracy and Bolivia produced only one major claimant. Despite the fact that Bolivian nationals were greatly outnumbered in the rubber forests, Nicolás Suárez still ranks among the most remarkable figures ever to emerge during the South American rubber boom – a man whom North Americans felt at the turn of the century had deservedly earned the title of 'the Rockefeller of the rubber trade'. One of six brothers, Suárez was born at Santa Cruz in 1851 and brought up in Trindad in the Beni, where the family ran a small ranch. About 1872, however, Nicolás followed several other *cruceños* and *benianos* to Reyes, at a time when Peruvian bark was still the staple barter in this entire region. He was apparently fearless in his penetration of the forest, trekking alone into unexplored regions where few dared follow, to find first the quinine bark and subsequently the more lucrative rubber. His role as merchant and carrier for other collectors resulted in his obtaining additional *barracas* and *estradas* from those who defaulted on payment for goods imported from Europe and North America; indeed, it was Nicolás Suárez' preoccupation with the transport and communication aspects of northern Bolivia's economic boom that always distinguished the strength and success of the Suárez organisation.[2]

In twenty years, the four surviving Suárez brothers had built an empire which, at the turn of the century, accounted for more than 60 per cent of Bolivia's rubber production. Each directed a vital part of their widely scattered commercial interests. In 1871 the eldest brother, Francisco, had visited London (where sections of the company Suárez Hermanos were subsequently registered), in order to establish his own business, manage the overseas affairs of the company, and purchase supplies. Francisco also assumed responsibility for enrolling Swiss, German and English administrators and technicians for the Suárez offices and agencies in Bolivia and

---

[1] This section provides a short summary of Suárez' activities. Detail and background material on Bolivia's role in the South American rubber boom, on the establishment of the principal rubber houses, and on the varied aspects of the great Suárez enterprise may be found in J. V. Fifer, 'The Empire Builders: A History of the Bolivian Rubber Boom and the Rise of the House of Suárez', *Journal of Latin American Studies*, vol. II, 1970, pp. 113–146.

[2] Other notable Bolivian rubber *patrones* in the early boom period included several former Peruvian bark traders such as Salinas, Vázquez, Salvatierra and Roca. Another *cruceño*, Dr Antonio Vaca Diez, who might well have remained second only to Suárez in the scale of his organisation, drowned in 1897 while on an expedition in Peru. His newly formed company, The Orton (Bolivia) Rubber Co. Ltd, registered in London in 1897, was subsequently taken over by Suárez Hermanos.

Brazil. He settled permanently in London in 1877, and was later re-appointed as Bolivian Consul-General. Rómulo Suárez supervised the setting up of the Brazilian agencies at San Antonio, Manaus and Pará in the 1880s, and later moved south to a new Suárez headquarters near Trinidad, Loma Suárez, from which the extensive ranching and river navigation branch of Casa Suárez' activity in the Beni and Santa Cruz Departments was controlled. Gregorio Suárez, the third brother, was stationed at the Madeira–Mamoré falls section, to maintain the smooth flow of rubber and supplies in this difficult stretch – not only for Suárez Hermanos but also for other companies anxious to avail themselves of the facilities offered there by the Suárez fleet, and the Suárez gangs of Indian porters. Gregorio was eventually ambushed and murdered by a group of Caripúnas along the Madeira.

Nicolás Suárez himself, youngest of the brothers, provided the initiative and driving force of the entire enterprise. He controlled production from his headquarters at Cachuela Esperanza on the Beni river, a site he had personally selected and cleared in 1881 after becoming one of the first Bolivians to repeat Edwin Heath's historic voyage of exploration downstream to confirm the Beni's confluence with the Mamoré. Cachuela Esperanza contained villas and dormitory blocks, an hotel, restaurant, cinema, theatre, club, library, school, playing fields and hospital, as well as shops, offices, warehouses, superb workshops and repair sheds, and a short stretch of railway around the Esperanza falls. The town accommodated over two thousand employees, largely dependent upon the provisions and amenities imported up-river from western Europe and the U.S.A., and engaged in the distribution of supplies among the thousands of *seringueiros* thinly scattered throughout the sixteen million acres of rubber forest registered by the House of Suárez.

Because of the constant demand for labour, and for regular deliveries of beef, rice and sugar, Suárez' influence remained equally important farther south, across the savannas of Beni and Santa Cruz, where others served, and were sustained by, the rubber regions of the north. At the height of its power, Casa Suárez controlled nearly 70,000 square miles of central and northern Bolivia. Within the organisation, delegation of authority, even among the three other brothers, had little real meaning in the shadow of such an extraordinarily dominant personality, and after the death of the last surviving brother in 1908 Nicolás' control was absolute.

Labour conditions, while not in general displaying the excesses of the notorious Putumayo region farther north, provided no exception to the widespread harshness of existence for which this period will be for ever condemned. The transport system of almost the entire Bolivian Oriente was regulated by the company. Hundreds of Indians, for example, were employed to do nothing but portage rubber and *batelões* around the Madeira falls, where Suárez continued to control much of the movement. Upstream, a fleet of eight large and many smaller craft patrolled the great river network above the falls, easing the circulation within the rubber and ranching empire.

Riberalta, Villa Bella, Guayeramerin, Cobija, Porvenir, and many other centres were all Suárez company towns, founded or largely sustained by the organisation. Hundreds of miles of roadway were cut and maintained. In 1925, for example, a United States representative investigating the condition of South American rubber production could still describe the Suárez road between Cobija and Porvenir as 'one of the best highways in the Amazon valley'. In the age of the individual empire builder, Nicolás Suárez became a legend in his own lifetime, a powerful and wealthy figure until his death in January 1940, aged eighty-eight, despite the vicissitudes of the South American rubber trade.

Travelling within the Departments of Pando and Beni today, one is quently reminded of his former presence and influence (Plates XII, XIII, XIV). The faded photographs of this tough, stocky man still hang throughout his former empire, whether on the walls of the Prefectura in Cobija overlooking the river Acre, in his old office at the half-deserted Cachuela Esperanza, or in some smaller isolated dwelling – portraits hung sometimes fifty or sixty years ago and subsequently scarcely disturbed. Elsewhere, former company buildings of brick and stone, distinguished often by two storeys, still display the Suárez Hermanos monogram entwined above gateway and porch, whilst beside the rivers one can occasionally find, similarly identified, a crumbling warehouse or derelict pierhead. All evoke the past in a peculiarly compelling manner; all linger on as symbols of one aspect of the Bolivian rubber boom – a degree of organisation never achieved in this region before or since. They are reminders also of that rare phenomenon in a remote Bolivian borderland, a powerful and enterprising Bolivian entrepreneur whose scale of operation provided a vital and unique form of national territorial identification.

8. 'GOVERNMENT? WHAT IS THAT? WE KNOW NO GOVERNMENT HERE!' THE ACRE BOUNDARY CONTROVERSY: 1899–1903

It had become increasingly clear for some years that events had weakened support for the 1867 oblique (Muñoz–Netto) boundary line. Indeed, as a contributor to *The India Rubber World* had observed tartly in 1894, 'There need be no reason for wonder at the lack of definitive information concerning the extent of the rubber production of Bolivia, when it is considered that even the extent in area of that Republic is in doubt.' The search for rubber had drawn settlement, particularly Brazilian settlement, into the vast forest wilderness, and by the late 1880s this wave of enterprising, acquisitive migration surging along the 'rubber rivers' was assuming disquieting proportions. Penetration had accelerated after 1879–80, when severe drought and crop failure in Ceará province in north-eastern Brazil brought labourers streaming up the Amazon in their thousands, standing shoulder to shoulder on the decks of any vessel plying up-river into the headwater regions. Thousands of squatters and their families had later been aided in their migrations up-river by the Brazilian Federal Government, and many, seeking to avoid the falls on the Madeira and Mamoré, had settled along the banks of the Acre river and its tributaries in the extreme north of Bolivia.

Colonel (later President) José Pando of Bolivia, disturbed by the inadequate knowledge of the country behind the Cordillera Real, and particularly by the scale of Brazilian infiltration there, had personally explored the northern frontier area between 1892 and 1898, producing a new map of the region as a result.[1] Pando was a veteran of the War of the Pacific, and memories of Bolivia's loss of the Pacific littoral to Chile only a few years previously had scarcely faded. Yet events appeared to be set on a similar course as the spur for deeper penetration into the Amazonian forest steadily increased, and the demand for rubber became insatiable. Its use for bicycle tyres (John Dunlop patented his pneumatic tyre in 1888), and later for motor car tyres (introduced in France in 1895 and by Goodrich in Cleveland, Ohio in 1896) boosted production and price to unprecedented levels. Rubber, it appeared, could be used for anything and everything, and an unending stream of the most ingenious patented articles appeared on the North American and European markets at the beginning of the twentieth century.[2]

[1] 'A Map of Northern Bolivia', as corrected by Col. José M. Pando from explorations 1892–8, *Geog. Journ.*, vol. XVIII, 1901, p. 248. Interest had been concentrated in the Brazilian section of the frontier; much of the Peruvian portion was even more remote from Bolivia's core, at least in terms of accessibility, and its rubber forests still remained virtually uninhabited. Nevertheless, Pando explored the upper Madre de Dios and Ucayali–Urubamba regions between 1892 and 1894. See also (i) J. M. Pando, *Viaje a la Región de la Goma Elástica (Noroeste de Bolivia)*, La Plata, 1894; and (ii) *Expedición del Coronel Don José Manuel Pando al Inambary*, La Paz, 1898.

[2] See the regular monthly issues of *The India Rubber World* and other trade advertisements over this period. In 1911 the U.S.A. recorded its millionth rubber patent.

The very nature of wild rubber's growth aggravated the problems of drawing a boundary line. Demarcated at first only at its extremities, the oblique line's exact location at any other point along its course was largely unknown. Rivers formed the only continuously discernible boundaries in country such as this. The *Hevea* and Caucho trees were widely scattered, the narrow *estradas* winding through the forest in a random search. To divide the region now between Bolivia and Brazil meant, in practice, to divide the individual rubber *estradas* between Bolivia and Brazil, and called for the most exacting type of visible demarcation along the entire boundary.

By 1900 there were probably more than 60,000 Brazilians in the Acre region, and all south of the oblique line which frock-coated gentlemen in foreign offices were trying to make the northerly limit of Bolivian jurisdiction. One third of these Brazilian rubber hunters were in the upper Acre region to the south of Caquetá. The Brazilian pioneers seemed to have no respect for the Bolivian boundary when they could see a rubber tree on the other side, and it is doubtful that they always knew where the line was.[1]

By now, the Acre was the richest rubber region in the world. Without this all-important realisation, no sense can be made of subsequent events in the political exchanges which followed.

In January 1899 Bolivia built a custom house at Puerto Alonso on the left bank of the river, just on the Bolivian side of the oblique line.[2] Seven miles downstream was the Brazilian custom post at Caquetá. The luckless Bolivian customs officers, very much in the minority in a region settled almost exclusively by Brazilians, soon fell foul of a population contacting Bolivian Government authority for the first time. For until the 1896 demarcation of the boundary took effect, particularly on the Acre river, ignorance of the precise limits of territorial ownership could justifiably be pleaded, and ignorance could at least be claimed over a very much greater area of the Brazil–Bolivia border country crossed by the 'rubber rivers'. The Brazilian settlers there, as the majority population, had enjoyed a free-booting existence – tax-free and duty-free as far as Bolivia was concerned, and without the enforcement of external law or restraint of any kind.

[1] F. W. Ganzert, 'The Boundary Controversy in the Upper Amazon between Brazil, Bolivia and Peru, 1903–1909', *Hisp. Am. Hist. Rev.*, vol. XIV, 1934, pp. 427–49, this reference p. 434. Ganzert quotes in part here from an earlier commentary by George Earl Church, 'Acre Territory and the Caoutchouc Region of South-Western Amazonia', *Geog. Journ.*, vol. XXIII, 1904, pp. 596–613, map p. 704.

[2] At the end of 1896 a Brazil–Bolivia Boundary Commission had adopted the 1895 (Cunha-Gomez) position of the Javari river source, in order to determine the 1867 oblique-line boundary (the Muñoz–Netto line). Boundary pillars were accordingly erected jointly at places on the river banks where the 1867 oblique line boundary was assumed to cross the Purus, Yaco and Acre rivers.

News of the erection of boundary pillars *downstream* of thousands of Brazilian *barracas* had spread like wildfire and, predictably, there was immediate angry reaction. Then, in January 1899, as the richness of the region continued to surpass even the optimists' wildest dreams, Bolivia levied a 30 per cent export tax at the new Puerto Alonso custom house on all rubber moving down the Acre. Apart from its immediate local effects, this tax deprived the Brazilian state of Amazonas of a gratifying injection of revenue, and over the next three years other taxes and restrictions were imposed at the Bolivian custom house which inflamed tempers, and generally aggravated a situation which was already set on a collision course.

These later developments concerned an extraordinarily tempting land concession which, in desperation, Bolivia had offered on the markets of London and New York in July 1900, and which the American Minister in La Paz urged his government to consider favourably if the opportunity arose: 'Extensive grants in the Acre are first being offered to England... the grants are within the Bolivian boundary line [i.e. the oblique line] as recently endorsed by Brazil and are of *great value*.'[1] Because of the enormous extent of the area offered, approximately 75,000 square miles (Fig. 7c), Bridgman was given authority to approach the Bolivian Government with the request that the concession be divided between England and the United States. As a result, Bolivia granted the concession in December 1901 to an Anglo-American company registered as the Bolivian Syndicate of New York. The whole concession was known as the Acre Concession, or the Acre District, although the Acre river and its feeders flowed through only a small section of it.[2] Nevertheless it was on the basis of the known wealth in this region, and on the anticipation of more wealth farther north and west, that the contracts were exchanged. But from many points of view, the Acre Concession delegated a totally unacceptable or unworkable degree of autonomy into Anglo-American hands. The Syndicate obtained:

   (i) the right for 5 years to purchase any land within the district not already taken up, for only 10 centavos per hectare, a purely nominal sum;
   (ii) all mineral and navigation rights;

[1] G. H. Bridgman to Secretary of State John Hay, La Paz, 23 July 1900, Diplomatic Despatches from Bolivia, *General Records of the Dept. of State, Record Group 59*, Washington, D.C.
[2] Earlier attempts to colonize the upper Acre and Purus region under concession had failed. A. D. Piper, for example, had explored the region south of the oblique line in the late 1860s and early 1870s and established The Colonization and Commercial Co. of Bolivia in California in 1870. Very few settlers ever penetrated beyond Manaus, however, and the enterprise was abandoned (see above p. 106 n. 4).

(iii) an annual net profit tax-free for 60 years, although after the third year the Bolivian Government became entitled to 10 per cent of the net profits.

(iv) The Syndicate was to act as the fiscal trustee for Bolivia, collecting national rents from the other concerns in the designated area, and retaining as much as 40 per cent of the dues collected for this service.

(v) General maintenance, law enforcement and policing of the area were also placed in the hands of the Syndicate (a clause to which Brazil took great exception).

As soon as the details became generally available, Brazil declared itself uncommitted to any of the terms stated or implied in the concession, considering that it opposed Brazilian rights and interests. Henceforth, Brazil announced that it would consider territory south of the Muñoz–Netto (Cunha–Gomez) oblique line litigious.[1] Bolivia at once protested on this last point, since the concession was delimited on the north-east by the oblique line, and lay within territory which, under existing treaty terms, was indisputably Bolivian as far as Brazil was concerned.

A smaller concession farther south, the Caupolicán Concession of approximately 15,000 square miles, was granted to Sir Martin Conway, who was already involved in the Bolivian Syndicate. This allowed the annual net profit from the area to tax exemption for fifty years, but the district was considerably less developed than the Acre.[2] 'Caupolicán is a perfect paradise,' Colonel G. E. Church observed, 'but it is almost as inaccessible as the Paradise which we all seek.' Such relinquishing of national responsibility in the Acre region, however, continued to evoke angry protest from Brazil, whose citizens in this area were now, at least on paper, to be virtually under the complete control of Anglo-American interests. From the beginning of 1902 the Brazilian customs authorities in Manaus declared that they would consider none of the territory within the Acre Concession as Bolivian, and that, as a result, no rubber leaving the

---

[1] Circular from Ministry of Foreign Affairs to Bolivian Government, Rio de Janeiro, 14 April 1902. Replies from Bolivian Minister in Rio (Petrópolis), 14 May, 29 May, 3 June, 17 June 1902, *F.O. 11/39.*

In his note of 14 May 1902, the Bolivian Minister invited Brazil to participate in the Acre contractual lease. Brazil declined on the grounds (1) that the area was now under litigation, (2) that policing had been delegated to outside authorities and (3) that the 1867 agreement to open up the Amazon to commercial flags for all friendly nations had excluded the river Purus. The Purus and Acre rivers were accessible, therefore, only to Brazilian ships. (Reported by W. B. Sorsby to Secretary of State John Hay, La Paz, 16 September, 1902, Diplomatic Despatches from Bolivia, *General Records of the Dept. of State, Record Group 59,* Washington, D.C.)

[2] For a description of part of this largely unknown region, see Sir Martin Conway, *The Bolivian Andes, a record of Climbing and Exploration in the Cordillera Real in the years 1898 and 1900,* London and New York, 1901. Also J. W. Evans, 'Expedition to Caupolicán, Bolivia, 1901–1902', *Geog. Journ.,* vol. XXII, 1903, pp. 601–46. The concession lapsed in 1909.

concessionary area would be classed as 'in transit'. Instead, all would be required to pay Brazilian export dues.

The folly of Bolivia's action was indisputable, but it had been provoked by the need for a last desperate attempt to control the Brazilian colonists. Only four months after the Bolivian custom house had been erected at Puerto Alonso in January 1899 it had been attacked. Flushed with success, one of the colonists, a Spaniard named Luis Gálvez Rodriguez, had taken matters considerably further. On 14 July 1899 he proclaimed himself to be President of a newly created independent State of Acre and hoisted the flag of revolution – a yellow and green diagonal with red star, bearing also the cap of Liberty, shield and laurel wreath entwined with the date 14 de Julho 1899. Occupying the tiny custom house of Puerto Alonso (Pôrto Acre), Gálvez proceeded to lay out a main plaza and a small gridiron of streets in the surrounding jungle. His Rua Ceará and Rua Brasil led to Palácio de Gálvez, a crumbling *barraca* defiantly displaying his flag and coat of arms. Maps purporting to show the limits of the new State included in its boundaries sections of the Juruá, Purus, Acre and Beni rivers, and Gálvez busied himself with appointing a cabinet from amongst his neighbouring *seringueiros*, and with drafting a number of laws, particularly those for the collection of revenue.[1] Distance from both Bolivian and Brazilian authority had bolstered the conviction among some of the hotheaded elements that this new addition to the political map in the depth of the forest might prove to be a viable unit, although given the location of the Acre District, few of their more rational compatriots agreed with them. Friction between Gálvez and some of the other colonists, however, enabled Bolivia to restore some sort of order and re-establish the custom post. Military expeditions from Cochabamba defeated the revolutionaries at Riosinho and Puerto Alonso in April 1901, and the bodies of the less fortunate were ordered to be floated down the Acre river to act as a warning to Brazilians downstream. The Brazilian Government decided for the moment not to intervene, for it had recognised Bolivia's right to erect the custom house at Puerto Alonso in January 1899. Besides, Brazil, like Bolivia, was only too aware of the truth of the correspondent's report in 1899 to the editor of *The India Rubber World* that 'the population [i.e. of the Acre District] will settle for itself a question which diplomacy has up to now been incompetent to adjust'.

[1] Figures for the first 4 months of 1899 show that 1350 metric tons (2,976,628 lb.) of rubber passed through the Puerto Alonso custom house before it was attacked by the rebels. Output such as this indicates the importance of the region to Bolivia, which had derived nearly half the value of its total annual exports from rubber immediately before the Acre crisis.

The concession of December 1901 to the Anglo-American Syndicate, upheld with the hope that foreign interests, generously wooed, would probably succeed where the Bolivian Government was certain to fail, merely precipitated disaster. Protest notes from Brazil stressed the point that the U.S.A. would hold a part of South American territory as a result of Bolivia's action and, acknowledging this, the Bolivian Minister in Washington requested that the State Department should 'strongly support' the Syndicate, and regard the threatened closure of the Amazon as an act of aggression against the U.S.A.[1] The following month, however, August 1902, Brazil withdrew its consul from Puerto Alonso, and sealed off the entire area by closing the Amazon to Bolivian commerce. The dependence of this landlocked region upon the Amazon outlet, and its vulnerability to controls applied in the middle and lower sections of the basin were of course absolute. Although Bolivia condemned the closure of the Amazon as 'an abuse of its topographical position', the fact remained that La Paz was nearly four months away from Bolivia's Acre border country, and could in no way provide an alternative supply base.

The Anglo-American Syndicate was trapped by the very circumstances its creation had helped to expose. Stores, ammunition and supplies dispatched from Pará were delayed by Brazil on the grounds that it did not recognise the concession; Bolivia's hopes that the U.S.A. would intervene to protect American interests in the upper Amazon were quickly dispelled. Two representatives of the Syndicate, W. J. Lee and H. Hastings Horne, of the firm of Cary and Whitridge, had protested to the U.S. Consul at Pará upon their arrival there from New York *en route* for the Acre, but Brazilian authorities remained disinclined to allow them to proceed farther up river. Support for Brazil's adoption of a strong line against the Anglo-American Syndicate came from Argentina where, for example, *El Tiempo* of Buenos Aires observed: 'American capitalists are about to monopolise the territory of the Acre. First come the claims of the business men, and then the soldiers arrive.' Indeed the Latin American States in general were highly sympathetic to Brazil's firm refusal to support the Syndicate. In London, however, a widely quoted, though unnamed, correspondent (it was possibly Sir Martin Conway) campaigned bitterly against Brazil's closure of the Amazon: 'It is hardly to be tolerated by great capitalist countries such as the United Kingdom and the United States, that the legitimate efforts of their sons to open up the trade

---

[1] Note from the Bolivian Legation, Washington, D.C., to the Department of State, 10 July 1902, Notes from Foreign Legations, *General Records of the Department of State, Record Group 59*, Washington, D.C.

and resources of a comparatively small country, not indeed populous. . .
should be thwarted by the mere jealousy and short-sighted selfishness of
Brazil.'[1]

Meanwhile, two thousand miles up river, the closing of the Amazon
had been made the signal for a number of Brazilians in the Acre
District to rise for a second time and, under a new leader, Plácido de
Castro, who had originally migrated into the rubber regions from Rio
Grande do Sul, they declared their independence, in August 1902, of
both Bolivia and the Anglo-American Syndicate. Soon the whole region
was in the hands of the revolutionaries, except the Puerto Alonso custom
house, where the Bolivian garrison resisted a six months' siege before
capitulating.

Both Bolivia and Brazil decided to dispatch army units to the Acre, so
that from January 1903 the revolution took on a new aspect with all the
ingredients of a local war between these two States and the possible
inclusion of Peru into the bargain. President Pando of Bolivia, his earlier
anxieties over his country's ignorance of the Noroeste and Oriente now
unhappily realised, ordered seven hundred Indian troops from the *altiplano*
and the Yungas to be joined by two hundred from Cochabamba and
Sucre, and two hundred more from Santa Cruz. Just before the President
departed from La Paz, however, Brazil made a determined effort to get the
expedition abandoned by suggesting that Bolivia sell the Acre District, or
exchange it (or part of it) for other territory in the Villa Murtinho–Abuná–
San Antonio region. Brazil agreed to indemnify the Bolivian Syndicate,
and proposed the building of a railway from opposite Villa Bella to a
navigable point on the Madeira. Bolivia responded by requesting Brazil to
withdraw its support for the Acre rebels under de Castro, and to consider
an exchange of territory, not within the rubber forests but farther south,
along the Paraguay river, from which Bolivia had withdrawn in its 1867
treaty with Brazil. The negotiations were deadlocked; Brazil declined
both proposals: 'As the Acre is disputed territory, claimed by both Brazil
and Peru, from the parallel 10° 20' S as far as the line drawn between the
source of the Javary and the source of the Madeira, and as all its inhabitants
are Brazilians, we could not consent to Bolivian troops and authorities
entering therein.'[2]

[1] *The India-Rubber and Gutta-Percha and Electrical Trades Journal*, September 1902.
[2] From the Brazilian Ultimatum enclosed in W. B. Sorsby's dispatch to Secretary of State
John Hay, La Paz, 10 February 1903, Diplomatic Despatches from Bolivia, *General Records
of the Dept. of State, Record Group 59*. Brazil refers here to the two lines – the right-angled line
and the oblique line – which were both put forward in the 1867 treaty negotiations (see
p. 101) and of which the oblique line was selected. Although Peru had never accepted the

With the failure of all attempts to avert further armed conflict in the rubber frontier, the Bolivian President led his troops on an appallingly rapid forced march of 800 miles over the mountains and down into the Acre's *inferno verde* by March 1903, an exhausting journey on which few of the 1100-man expedition ever reached their destination. Local resistance against the Brazilians was organised and led by Nicolás Suárez, whose large rubber warehouses on the Acre river had been early targets for attack by the revolutionaries. In October 1902 Nicolás had founded his famous *Columna Porvenir* at a strategic point on the Tahuamanu river. This was a private army of 250 *seringueiros*, equipped with Winchester rifles, with which Suárez campaigned vigorously for several weeks in an effort to protect his rubber empire and Bolivian sovereignty at the same time. But President Pando's force, or the remnants of it, arrived too late, and in January 1903 the Bolivian resistance was crushed with the help of further military and naval contingents from Brazil, which had actively supported the so-called 'independent' Acreans and whose claims Brazil immediately annexed.[1]

The embargo on free movement along the Amazon, except for munitions of war, was lifted on 20 February 1903,[2] an embargo which, though highly effective in cutting Suárez' line of supply and thereby quickly subduing his resistance, had been very adversely commented upon abroad. In January 1903, for example, the U.S. Consul-General in Petrópolis, Eugene Seeger, had pointedly drawn Brazil's attention to American in-

oblique-line decision, Brazil had no basis for describing the area south of the oblique line as disputed territory except on the pragmatic grounds that it had later been populated with Brazilians. Rio-Branco stressed this last point again in April 1903: 'The Acre is at least three months march from Bolivia's seat of government. Bolivia would have to keep a garrison there of not less than 2000 men to maintain order among a population 99 of whom out of every 100 are Brazilians.'

[1] Colonel Plácido de Castro, the revolutionaries' leader, was thereupon made Governor of the Federal Territory of Acre, proving himself an enlightened administrator. Shortly after his meeting with P. H. Fawcett (p. 131 n. 1) in 1906, however, de Castro was assassinated by an unknown assailant while out on the trail. During the Acre uprising he had reduced casualties among his men by ordering uniforms of green, giving them a most significant advantage over the *Columna Porvenir* and the Bolivian army units who wore *white* uniforms made of coarse Cochabamba cloth.

A vivid account of the Acre campaign from the viewpoint of a Bolivian soldier is provided by J. Aguirre Achá, *De los Andes al Amazonas: Recuerdos de la Campaña del Acre*, La Paz, extended edition 1927; and by E. Sagárnaga, *Recuerdos de la Campaña del Acre de 1903: mis notas de viaje*, La Paz, 1909. See also N. Suárez, *Anotaciones y Documentos sobre la Campaña del Alto Acre, 1902–1903*, Barcelona, 1928; and M. J. von Vacano and H. Mattis, *Bolivien in Wort und Bild*, Berlin, 1906, pp. 63–87. The Brazilian case is recorded by Baron do Rio-Branco, Brazilian Foreign Minister 1902–12: *Obras do Barão do Rio-Branco. Questões de Limites*, 9 vols., Ministerio das Relações Exteriores, Rio de Janeiro, 1945–8. See vol. v, pp. 1–41.
[2] *F.O. 13/836.*

terests in that portion of Bolivia (i.e. the Acre District) whose only outlet is the Amazon river. Rebuking Rio-Branco for the injury done to the U.S.A. by the August 1902 closure decree 'issued without a moment's warning', Seeger warned that its continuance would deal 'a death blow to our vast interests in Eastern Bolivia'. Brazil decided, therefore, having made its point upon what was considered to be an unwarranted and intolerable delegation of authority to foreign interests near its own borders, to yield to European and North American pressure.[1] Besides, the representatives of the Syndicate had returned to Pará in high dudgeon early in February 1903 and were preparing to sue heavily for damages, for neither Lee nor Horne had ever been allowed nearer to their vast Bolivian concession than a few miles beyond Manaus. Negotiations were quickly undertaken in Rio de Janeiro and New York, and the whole abortive enterprise was finally concluded with Brazil's payment of a £110,000 cash indemnity which bought out and dissolved the Syndicate.

A *modus vivendi* was negotiated between Brazil and Bolivia in March 1903. Brazilian troops were to occupy the Acre river, Bolivian the Orton and sections of the Abuná river. The export duties on rubber were, for the time being, to be collected by Brazil but divided equally with Bolivia.

The outcome was agreed upon eight months later in the Treaty of Petrópolis, November 1903,[2] when the entire Bolivia–Brazil boundary was reviewed. In the extreme north, Bolivia yielded a considerable area, even south of 10° 20′ S, to which its title had never been questioned – in all about 73,726 square miles (191,000 square kilometres) (Fig. 7d).[3] The

---

[1] Complaints about the interference caused to trade with Bolivia by Brazil's closure of the Amazon had been registered by Britain, France, Germany, Switzerland and the United States.

[2] *F.O. 13/834*; also enclosed in W. B. Sorsby's dispatch to Secretary of State John Hay, La Paz, 7 March 1904, Diplomatic Despatches from Bolivia, *General Records of the Dept. of State, Record Group 59*, Washington, D.C.; *Col. Trat. Vig. Bol.*, vol. IV, pp. 198–208. Protocols making a series of minor adjustments and including the Ina–Chipamanu drainage divide as part of the boundary were signed in September 1925, the Chipamanu river was later substituted and incorporated in the treaty of December 1928, *F.O. 371/10609* and *F.O. 371/12744*; *Col. Trat. Vig. Bol.*, vol. IV, pp. 265–76.
   It should be noted here that many maps printed in Bolivia since 1925 continue to record the proposals made in the protocol agreements of that year. Land between the Ina and Chipamanu rivers is shown as undemarcated (and occasionally as undetermined), although it definitely lies within Brazil, and agreement has long been effective between the two States.

[3] Even so, it was generally acknowledged that without the positive and vigorously defended *Bolivian* national identification provided by Suárez in so much of the northern rubber forest, still more territory would have been forfeited to Brazil. Cobija and Porvenir, however, and the Orton-Abuna area were retained, and the Suárez empire remained virtually intact.

territorial loss of the Acre rubber country was the largest single land cession by Bolivia in the whole troubled history of its boundary changes with
five neighbour nations. Yet it was consistent with an earlier colonial frontier movement – the contraction, under Portuguese pressure, of Spanish
claims to Amazonia. From the Brazilian point of view, it marked the
successful political expansion of a river-basin State. Given the lack of
articulation between mountain and plain, Brazilian territorial gains in the
Amazon headwater region represented a further stage in the political
integration of a drainage network, an extension through familiar terrain
at the expense, in this case, of Bolivia. The loss of the Acre District,
however, despite its size, excited little interest among the majority of
Bolivians, particularly those in La Paz and the mining regions. Few had
been directly involved or were even aware of what had occurred. The
loss left no widespread sense of grievance nor long-standing impairment
of Brazilian and Bolivian relations, rather the reverse. In this respect,
therefore, when compared with losses in Atacama and, later, in the
Chaco, the Acre settlement is unique among Bolivia's major territorial
disputes.

By Article 1, Section 5, the new boundary was delimited as far as
possible by river courses. It followed the Madeira to the Abuná confluence,
before doubling back up the Abuná as far as 10° 20′ S, tracing this parallel
west to the Rapirrán, and continuing along this river to its principal source.
The latitude of the Rapirrán's source was then to be followed as far as the
Iquiry river, whence the boundary would again follow the river to its
source. A link to the Bahía river source was to be made either by a straight
line, or by a line joining the most pronounced physical features (to be
decided during demarcation) (Section 6). Subsequent field investigation
revealed ignorance of many details in the drainage pattern of this section.
Wherever possible, demarcation reduced the reliance on lines of latitude
as links between river sections of the boundary, substituting when necessary straight-line linkages from the source of one river to the mouth or
source of another.

From the source of the Bahía (Section 7), the boundary was to continue
downstream to the Acre confluence (Plate xv), and then follow the Acre
to its source (if not west of 69° W). It was then to follow the meridian of
that source to 11° S, proceeding westwards along that parallel to the
Peruvian frontier. If, west of 69° W, the Acre was found to flow south
of 11° S, then the boundary should follow the meridian to its intersection
with 11° S, before continuing along this parallel to the Peruvian frontier.
In fact, as the Acre flowed variously north and south of 11°S, the boundary

continued along the river to 70° 32′ W, the Acre source, before taking up the line of 11° S.[1]

South of the rubber-producing region, yet still within Bolivia's northern sector orientated towards the Amazon outlet, the 1903 Bolivia–Brazil boundary delimitation scarcely modified the 1867 changes made to the old Spanish–Portuguese Ildefonso line. For much of its length, this remains one of the most durable of South America's boundaries. It follows the Guaporé (Itenes) river as it skirts the Brazilian Shield, and then runs upstream with this same river over the Shield's low swamp-forest and into the sierras farther south, seeking one of the sources of the river Verde. 'The unknown sources [*sic*] of the Verde', selected in Article II of the 1867 treaty as apparently convenient points on which to peg the middle section of the Bolivia–Brazil boundary, continued to give rise to difficulty over the next century, and it was not until 1958 that a provisional delimitation was made through this region, clarifying Article III of the 1928 treaty.[2]

The Verde country was quite unexplored in 1867, and an expedition ten years later to find the sources (by then interpreted as the principal source) of the Verde, found instead two streams about fifty miles to the south-west which united to form the river Tarvo. Here, in November 1877, the members placed a large pillar, assuming they had demarcated the Verde source. In 1908–9, as a result of the 1903 Petrópolis treaty, Colonel Fawcett explored the Verde and established its source at 14° 37′ S, 60° 14′ W (point Fawcett–Guillobel). In 1945, further exploration through this green desolation revealed that Fawcett's point was not in fact the principal source

[1] At the request of the Royal Geographical Society, London, the new boundary was surveyed on Bolivia's behalf in 1906–7 by Col. Percy Harrison Fawcett. His experiences along the rivers and in the rubber settlements are vividly recorded in *Exploration Fawcett*, edit. Brian Fawcett, London, 1953. (In New York the book was published under the title *Lost Trails, Lost Cities*.) A later survey, 1908–9, to discover the source of the river Verde, on which the south-eastern section of the boundary was pegged, is also described. See also P. H. Fawcett, 'Explorations in Bolivia', *Geog. Journ.*, vol. XXXV, 1910, pp. 513–32, and 'Bolivian Exploration 1913–14', *Geog. Journ.*, vol. XLV, 1915, pp. 219–28.

Additional information on this frontier is contained in H. A. Edwards, 'Frontier work on the Bolivia–Brazil boundary, 1911–1912', *Geog. Journ.*, vol. XLII, 1913, pp. 113–28. Edwards' party explored and mapped more accurately the Rapirrán and the Iquiry, finding the latter's source different from Fawcett's location. Iron posts were driven in to demarcate mouths and sources of the relevant rivers. It was along the Acre that a rubber collector remarked to Edwards, 'Government? What it that? We know no government here!' Completion of the frontier survey and primary demarcation is recorded in H. A. Edwards, 'Further frontier work on the Bolivia–Brazil northern boundary', *Geog. Journ.*, vol. XLV, 1915, pp. 384–405.

The final erection of pyramidal concrete posts at river mouths and sources, and across the two straight-line connexions between them, was completed in 1962.

[2] *Acta de la Entrevista en Corumbá y Roboré de los Cancilleres de Bolivia y del Brasil*, 29 March 1958, Foreign Ministry files, La Paz.

of the Verde, but it remains the only one that Bolivia has been prepared to accept in recent negotiations. In addition, the final boundary proposed in 1958 incorporates the old 1877 Tarvo post as an established, albeit mistaken, point (Fig. 7*d*). Brazil, however, has so far refused to ratify the 1958 draft and appears less inclined to do so as the number of Brazilian cattle ranchers steadily increases in the Mato Grosso area.

In the northern rubber forests, in exchange for the estimated 73,726 square miles (191,000 square kilometres) ceded to Brazil in 1903, Bolivia had received a triangle of about 2000 square miles (5200 square kilometres) between the Madeira and the Abuná.[1] This provided Bolivia with easier access to the Madeira navigation, although Rio-Branco's explanation of this particular cession was that it was populated largely by Bolivians, rather than by Brazilians. On the basis, therefore, of *uti possidetis de facto*, the very much larger Acre tract was acquired by Brazil, not strictly as a cession, Rio-Branco stated, but as a reciprocal exchange: an exchange determined by majority settlement, and described (wrongly) as 'our first territorial acquisition since we became an independent nation'. Nevertheless, under Article III, recognising 'the inequality of the territory exchanged', Brazil also agreed to pay an indemnity of £2 million to Bolivia, to be used mainly for the construction of railways or other works calculated to improve communications and develop commerce between the two countries. In his report to the President of Brazil, on 27 December 1903, however, Rio-Branco stressed the relatively small price paid for such a rich area: 'The revenue of the annexed territory is more than a sufficient guaranty for the sacrifice of the Treasury, and will even permit us in a short time to extinguish the entire outlay.'[2]

Finally, Article VII of the 1903 Petrópolis treaty revived once again the old dream of the Madeira–Mamoré Railway which, despite past failures, had never been completely abandoned as the key factor in easing Bolivia's Amazon outlet. Brazil undertook to build a railway within four years from San Antonio to Guajará Mirim, with a branch through Villa Murtinho to Villa Bella. Both countries were to enjoy equal rights on this railway, the need of which was felt more keenly than ever during the early 1900s. Bolivia was to be allowed to maintain customs agents at Manaus and

---

[1] In 1903 this triangle of land between the Madeira and the Abuná was estimated at only 886 sq. miles (2296 sq. kms), owing to errors in the delineation of the Abuná's course.

[2] With rubber prices approaching their peak, Brazil took considerably more than £2 million out of the Acre region in less than three years after its cession by Bolivia. H. C. Pearson noted in 1911 that, surprisingly, Bolivian money was still the basis of all exchange in the Acre even eight years after its transfer to Brazil. In fact, much of the territory remained unexplored and beyond effective national control by either Brazil or Bolivia.

Pará, and Brazil at Villa Bella. Rubber prices were high; the success and ultimate vindication of the whole railway enterprise seemed assured at last.

An ambiguity arises in Article VII of the 1903 Petrópolis treaty when the original Spanish and Portuguese versions are compared. Although the railway around the Madeira–Mamoré falls was clearly to be contructed in Brazilian territory, the Portuguese version states that it shall run as far as Guajará Mirim, whereas the Spanish version states that it shall run as far as Guayaramerin. As these are in fact twin towns at each side of the Mamoré (both names mean 'little falls'), a railway terminating at Guayaramerin (Bolivia) would have involved the construction of a bridge to carry the line over the river, instead of leaving the railhead on the Brazilian side. Bolivia's stated intention was to continue the railway from Guayaramerin westwards to Riberalta (and even at one stage on to La Paz), in which case the Mamoré bridge would have eliminated any break of load. Neither the Guajará Mirim–Guayaramerin bridge, nor the promised branch line between Villa Murtinho, or some other more suitable intermediate station in Brazil, and Villa Bella (Bolivia) was ever constructed. The treaty of 25 December 1928 substituted any further branch construction by Brazil which remained outstanding with an additional £1 million, to be made available by Brazil for railway extensions elsewhere in Bolivia. A railway from Cochabamba to Santa Cruz, and then beyond to some port on the river Paraguay was considered (Article V).

As for the railway extension from Guayaramerin to Riberalta, for which Bolivia had granted a concession in 1903, the collapse of the rubber boom put an end to the project, although the track through the jungle had already been partly cleared, and can still be seen today in Riberalta as the broad Avenida Beni–Mamoré, along which the railway was destined to run to a new terminal station (Plates XVI and XVII). It is said, however, that Nicolás Suárez was strongly opposed to the extension of the railway from Guayaramerin to Riberalta, since this would have diverted the rubber trade of the Beni, Madre de Dios and Orton rivers away from Suárez' headquarters at Cachuela Esperanza. Considerable dues were collected here by Nicolás, as cargo had to be unloaded and taken round the Esperanza falls by eight hundred metres of railway built and owned by the Suárez brothers. This revenue would have been lost if the entire rubber output of this rich region had been tapped and railed to Guayaramerin from a point farther upstream, and it is highly unlikely that Suárez would have allowed this to happen, even if the collapse of the rubber boom had not forestalled his intentions. In fact a protocol in November 1910 had suggested, while not eliminating the Guayaramerin–Riberalta extension, that the Villa Murtinho–Villa Bella branch (always of doubtful value), might be replaced by a line between Cachuela Pão Grande and Cachuela Esperanza.

9. 1912: THE CONSTRUCTION OF THE MADEIRA–MAMORÉ RAILWAY, AND THE COLLAPSE OF THE RUBBER BOOM

What little remained of previous efforts to build this railway served only to emphasise how transient is man's mark upon this forest. Just over two miles of permanent, and two miles of temporary track had actually been laid thirty years earlier in 1878–9, although this could only be traced with difficulty. An abandoned locomotive, the *Colonel Church*, lay buried in jungle with a tree growing strongly through its smoke stack. Old rails had been used as lamp standards in San Antonio, and during the new enterprise were to form telephone posts and provide corduroy road-surfacing across the mud. The American firm of Percival Farquhar was commissioned by the Brazilian Government in 1908 and the following year work commenced, not at San Antonio but at Pôrto Velho, with its better site and safer navigation, and with the total length of track newly estimated at 210 miles.

Large-scale organisation and speed were to be the key-notes.[1] Between 4000 and 5000 men were employed at any one time, about 400 of these North American. Fresh beef was slaughtered at Pôrto Velho, fresh eggs and vegetables were supplied daily from land cleared for the express purpose of providing a sustaining diet for the gangs of labourers. An ice plant, a well-equipped hospital, even a movie-house and a local newspaper were established. Discipline was strict and alcohol officially prohibited. The usual contract was for two years, followed by a three-month vacation, but despite the efforts made to alleviate hardship, the toll on life and health was heavy.

It is a memorable experience to meet and talk at length with one of the very few survivors of this railway construction, and to hear an old man

---

[1] One of the most vivid accounts of the conditions at Pôrto Velho, and of the whole atmosphere of this bizarre enterprise is given by H. M. Tomlinson, *The Sea and the Jungle*, London, 1912. Tomlinson joined the crew of a small Welsh cargo boat taking supplies to Pôrto Velho 1909–10, where he recorded with considerable amazement: 'At every point of the compass from here there's at least a thousand miles of wilderness. Excepting at this place it wouldn't matter to anybody whether a thing were done tonight, or next week, or not at all. But here, they are on piece-work and overtime, where there's nothing but trees, alligators, tigers and savages.' References to the Madeira–Mamoré Railway are found pp. 172–300 *passim*.

recall most vividly and movingly the frantic activity during the building period, when Chinese, Japanese, Hindus, North Americans, Brazilians, West Indians, Spaniards, Greeks, English and Germans were all toiling to push the track through unyielding jungle and swamp. Wages were good, the hospital well organised, but hundreds died from malaria and other fevers, and from beri-beri, while the cemeteries spread with sickening rapidity around the workers' camps. Blinded by an accident during the construction, this particular Barbadian survivor of the jungle railway lived on in the Brazilian–Bolivian border country for another fifty years. Then at the age of eighty he set off down the Acre river for the last time in 1964, bound for Manaus, Pará and Barbados: 'to hear the sound of the sea again before I die'. The author has traced ten other survivors who helped to build the railway, five in Guajará Mirim (three Greeks and two Brazilians) and five in Pôrto Velho.

Although the numbers of casualties have sometimes been exaggerated, the building of the Madeira–Mamoré Railway takes its place in history as one of the costliest enterprises of its kind in human life, as well as in capital investment. In October 1910, 94 miles of track were formally opened amid great ceremony.[1] Starting at Pôrto Velho, an American locomotive slowly hauled two first-class coaches, a third-class coach, and a buffet-car out of the station. The short train was decorated overall with the colours of Brazil and Bolivia, together with the Stars and Stripes, 'its silken folds fluttering proudly as though the far-away Republic was rejoicing that in the building of the Madeira–Mamoré Railway she had been given the privilege of thus helping to draw closer together her two sister Republics of the south'.

This stretch of railway reduced by over two weeks the *batelão* voyage. Rubber loaded at the railhead in the morning reached Pôrto Velho that afternoon. Removal of the old losses each year from wreck and loss of rubber would go a long way, it was estimated, towards building costs. In addition, deaths due to dragging boats overland which had claimed almost as many lives as the rapids, would be eliminated. Efforts were spurred by the all-time record rubber quotation of 3 dollars per lb. in 1910. As one American newspaper-man observed dryly, it looked as if motorists would have to sell their cars to buy their tyres. In July 1912 the 228-mile railway was completed as far as Guajará Mirim, but without any of the proposed extensions (Fig. 8). The formal opening was in September 1912, with a scheduled three trains a week in each direction. At long last, the rubber railway dream had become a reality.

[1] Progress reports on each phase of the railway's extension appear in *The India Rubber World* between 1910 and 1913.

Subsequent events could not have taken a more ironical turn. The year 1912 marked the end of the South American rubber boom. The bubble burst. Exploitation of the upper Amazon had been economic only when world prices were high, high enough to combat distance from market and

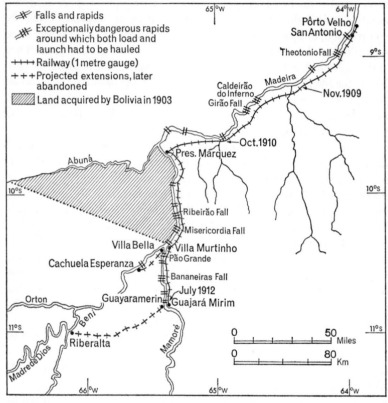

8 The Madeira–Mamoré Railway: 1909–12

difficulties of production. The Madeira–Mamoré Railway, no less than the Opera House at Manaus, symbolised abandoned hopes and a retreating commercial frontier. Since 1911, lower grades of rubber were being increasingly used in manufacture for which the high quality of Bolivian 'Up-river Fine' was unnecessary. Quality of product had always been Bolivia's (and the allied regions') trump card. Buyers had also favoured the 'Up-river' product because the long journey allowed the rubber to dry

out over a considerable period, and the resulting loss of weight gave merchants downstream greater value for money. But the competition of the
Far East was at last asserting itself. H. A. Wickham's work at Santarém
and in the Tapajós plateau in the 1870s, whereby *Hevea* seeds were transferred from Brazil to Kew Gardens and thence to Ceylon, had provided a
later parallel to the story of quinine. Indeed it was an odd turn of fate,
resulting from Brazil's opening of the Amazon in 1867, that allowed
Wickham to commandeer the vessel inaugurating the direct Liverpool–
upper Amazon run in 1876, to carry his precious cargo of seeds back to
England. While it is true to say that no law existed forbidding the export
of these seeds from Brazil, it is certain that the quantity involved would
have moved the customs officials in Pará to seek further guidance from
Rio de Janeiro. Whatever the decision, the delay would have proved fatal
to the seeds. As it was, no eye-catching transfer of cargo was necessary at
Pará, no thorough search was made of the hold, and so the baskets of about
70,000 seeds left the port undetected. Plantations were laid out in the Far
East in 1898, although it was another ten years before any considerable
quantity of plantation rubber came on to the market. When it did it was
cheaper by 18 pence or 36 cents per lb. to produce.[1]

Traffic on the Madeira–Mamoré Railway slumped from three trains a
week in July 1912 to only one a week in November 1913. The large
firms like Suárez, Barber and Braillard held back their rubber shipments,
unable to accept the prices being offered – only 73 cents a lb. and less,
a catastrophic change from the 3 dollars a lb. of 1910.[2] Government

[1] Rubber production (in tons) during the critical early years of the twentieth century (Statistical Division of the International Rubber Study Group):

	Amazon basin	Far East
1900	44,000	50
1910	45,000	11,000
1912	42,000	32,000
1913	36,000	53,000
1930	14,000	800,000

Six or seven rubber trees per acre was about the maximum ever found in the wild rubber
regions. Frequently only one or two per acre were discovered, i.e. one *Hevea* for every
seventy or eighty non-rubber trees. Plantations in the Amazon region at this time were only
to be found in the vicinity of Santarém, where they had been laid out by a group of Tennessee
and South Carolina Confederates who settled there after the Civil War. (The last member
of this original contingent, D. B. Riker, born in Charleston, S.C., in 1861, died at Santarém
in 1953.)

[2] It should be remembered that it was the extraordinarily high *prices* being paid for rubber on
the world market, not high *output*, which had been responsible for northern Bolivia's
booming economy. Official production figures of Bolivian rubber (in tons) for the 1890–

employees here received no salary from other sources; the entire region was dependent on the rubber revenues, and unable to survive in a low market.

Few rubber manufacturers in Europe and North America ever realised the extent to which the crude product was handled before loading on to ocean-going ships, how much weight was lost by drying out (a loss which growers felt progressively the further they were from the Atlantic ports), and the amount of customs duties paid: export duty from Bolivia, import and export duty in Brazil. Many collectors were now near starvation level. Nearly all suffered from disease, the commonest complaints being malaria (tertian fever), blackwater and other fevers, tuberculosis, pneumonia and beri-beri. In addition, the whole structure of rubber exploitation rested upon a precarious credit system, *seringueiros* receiving supplies in kind from the owner or his agent in return for rubber. Most remained perpetually in debt, a state of affairs which had become a subtle form of slavery.[1] Few could work out the costs of production in the Amazon for comparison with the Far East, as little money circulated.

1921 period emphasise that output was always relatively small (up to and including 1902, the Acre production is accredited to Bolivia):

1890	289	*1897*	1644	*1904*	1543	*1911*	3696	*1918*	4288
1891	339	*1898*	3100	*1905*	1661	*1912*	4080	*1919*	5347
1892	357	*1899*	2102	*1906*	1895	*1913*	5143	*1920*	3759
1893	388	*1900*	3434	*1907*	1798	*1914*	4485	*1921*	2844
1894	622	*1901*	3404	*1908*	1786	*1915*	5055		
1895	806	*1902*	1870	*1909*	2998	*1916*	4917		
1896	1121	*1903*	1297	*1910*	2486	*1917*	5842		

Thus although output actually *increased* after 1912, particularly during the First World War, the Bolivian rubber boom, as such, was over.

[1] About this time, the atrocities committed against Indian labourers along the Putumayo river were described both by N. Thomson, *Putumayo Red Book*, London, 2nd edit. 1914, and by Sir Roger Casement's *Blue Book*, presented in 1912. These, and other House of Commons Select Committee Reports, 1913, disclosed many of the worst aspects of the South American rubber boom. Reports to the Foreign Office on the activities of the Peruvian Amazon Company in the Putumayo, articles in *Truth* magazine which first made these activities public, and records of Casement's investigations may be studied in *F.O. 371/722*; *F.O. 371/967*; *F.O. 371/968*; *F.O. 371/1301*; and in *Miscellaneous Parliamentary Papers*, No. 8 (1912), [Cd. 6266], London, 1912.

See also (i) 'Report on a Journey on the Amazon, Madeira and Mamoré rivers and through the rubber districts of Bolivia', C. Gosling, La Paz, 22 December 1913, *F.O. 371/1914*. Gosling was appointed British Resident Minister to Bolivia in 1910 and he subsequently visited Pôrto Velho to watch work on the Madeira–Mamoré Railway. He also inspected the Suárez Hermanos headquarters at Cachuela Esperanza, although he was refused permission to tour the Suárez estates. Enclosed are some details of the local working conditions. Gosling added: 'It is true that this is contrary to Bolivian law, but law does not obtain where the "gold tree" flourishes.' (ii) 'Labour Conditions in Northern Bolivia', in J. V. Fifer, 'The Empire Builders: a History of the Bolivian Rubber Room and the Rise of the House of Suárez', *Journal of Latin American Studies*, vol. II, 1970, pp. 113–46. This reference pp. 137–41.

A stream of conflicting reports appeared in the trade journals – the statement that all was lost, countered in turn by various plans for cheapening Bolivian production. These included more railways, new land grants, the encouragement of Indians from the *altiplano* and Cochabamba to work in the forest (assisted by imported Chinese and Japanese labour), new plantations, fresh instruction in tapping, and a reduction in export tax.[1] Pará improved its port facilities by the addition of electric and steam cranes, dry docks, and considerable extension of quays and warehouse facilities. Twelve new 1000-ton steamers connected Pará with the Madeira, Purus and Juruá, and fourteen small light-draught vessels were introduced to carry merchandise and passengers along the smaller tributaries. But the great new warehouses of Pará stood nearly empty, many steamers loading and unloading in mid-stream to save port charges. The labour force of the Madeira–Mamoré Railway was cut down because of the prohibitive expense of full maintenance for only one train each way per week. *Seringueiros* clamoured so desperately for work that the *batelões* were repaired and shooting the rapids resumed.

By 1915, plantations in the East had cut production costs to less than 25 cents per lb. compared with about 60 cents per lb. for Bolivian 'Up-river Fine'. Nor were the problems restricted to methods of production at this period. The difficulties of outlet from such a continental backwater, and its unavoidable dependence upon the Amazon routeway, were once again re-emphasised by Brazil's foreign policy in 1917. Having declared

[1] J. F. Woodroffe and H. H. Smith, *The Rubber Industry of the Amazon, and how its supremacy can be maintained*, London, 1915. This is a typical example of contemporary literature which surveyed the conditions leading to the Amazon's decline, attacking the attitude that Asia's prosperity could only be 'a flash in the pan', but nevertheless sustaining an outlook of qualified optimism, with positive suggestions for improvement in the Amazon basin. Some difficulties were indeed weathered, and by 1925 production costs in the *most readily accessible* Amazon regions had been reduced to about half those of 1915–16, with small profits being made.

Despite a limited immigration from overseas, however, Brazilian nationals continued to form the dominant element in the population within the northern frontier of Bolivia. Estimates for the 1918–20 period, in the Territorio de Colonias and Vaca Diez province, were as follows: Total population along Acre–Rapirrán–Abuná rivers, and Manuripi–Orton–Beni rivers: 8–10,000. Brazilians 35 per cent, Bolivians 25 per cent, Peruvians 10 per cent, Syrians 8 per cent, Europeans 5 per cent, Japanese 2 per cent, miscellaneous 15 per cent. (W. L. Schurz, 'The Distribution of Population in the Amazon Valley', *Geog. Rev.*, vol. xv, 1925, pp. 206–25. This reference p. 216.) Recording the considerable amount of Brazilian penetration into Bolivia *via* the Acre and Abuná, Schurz noted (p. 224): 'In this connexion I recall an incident that took place while crossing from Cobija on the Acre to the Suárez rubber post of Porvenir on the Tahuamanu. On observing some persons engaged in the preparation of manioc flour, we inquired whether it was "yuca" or "mandioca" (respectively the Bolivian and Brazilian words for manioc), and received the reply: "E mandioca, e somos cearenses".'

war on Germany, Brazil regarded all German trading houses in the upper Amazon, and elsewhere, as belligerents whose supplies in transit were therefore liable to confiscation. German merchants were numerous and highly active in northern and eastern Bolivia – most of the managers and accountants employed by the rubber houses, for example, were German or German-Swiss – and for the last months of World War I they found much of their rubber, provisions and correspondence immobilised along two thousand miles of the Amazon network between the Bolivia– Brazil boundary and Pará. Bolivia's own rupture of diplomatic relations with Germany in April 1917 had not involved it in any reprisals against German nationals, whether in La Paz or Riberalta, but Brazil's action had perforce to be borne without official comment.

10. THE COMPLETION OF THE NORTHERN SECTOR BOUNDARY BETWEEN BOLIVIA AND PERU

As something of a tail-piece to the drama of Bolivia's 'rubber river' boundaries with Brazil, even as the twentieth century dawned, Bolivia's ultramontane boundary with Peru remained undelimited. Indeed it remained virtually unknown, although nearly four hundred miles, at a conservative estimate, had still to be determined, explored and apportioned in that boundary-makers' nightmare region, the Amazon rain forest.

The zone of *selva* and *montaña* left in dispute between Bolivia and Peru lay south of the rich Acre district, beyond the main wave of insatiably acquisitive Brazilian rubber collectors. It is drained principally by the river Madre de Dios (also known as Manutata or Amaru-Mayu), whose headwater network includes the Manú, Inambari, Tambopata and Heath. The river Orton's principal affluents are the Tahuamanu and Manuripi, while farther south, the Peru–Bolivia frontier is drained by the headwaters of the Madidi, Tuichi, and other left-bank tributaries of the Beni river. Although much of the region lies within the rubber forest, between 12° S and 14° S the scattered *Hevea* and Caucho trees are more sparse, so that the southern rivers were never regarded as the liquid gold which lured *seringueiros* along the Acre, Abuná, Orton, and the lower Madre de Dios and Beni waterways farther north. In addition, exploration, knowledge and settlement of the whole region from the Ucayali to the Madidi were so meagre that it might justifiably be regarded as untouched in the Spanish colonial period and equally unchanged by anything that had followed it.

Farther north, small trouble spots had arisen during the rubber boom.

The Madeira falls remained a severe obstacle to the transport of rubber towards the Amazon, and one which had become increasingly restrictive as the rubber boom moved towards its climax. The effect was to stimulate exploration into the Bolivia–Peru frontier region during the early 1890s, partly because of the need to exploit virgin areas of rubber forest, but also because of the desirability of opening new lines of approach into the Amazon. Bolivia, therefore, contended that claims based upon *uti possidetis de jure 1810* had been strengthened by the explorations of Colonel Pando in northern Bolivia, and in the Peru–Bolivia frontier region between 1892 and 1894. Pando's expeditions found the Madre de Dios, explored earlier by the Peruvian Maldonado in 1861, to be a broad, navigable, island-studded river traversing 'one of the richest regions in the world' for coffee, cacao, quinine, gold and rubber. The Inambari, also rich in gold and quinine bark, the Tambopata, and the Madidi regions were further explored, while the Gibbon and Heath rivers were discovered and named. Farther west, parts of the Ucayali–Urubamba systems were investigated by Pando, and a short cross-route surveyed which needed, so his team proposed, only a three-mile canal-cut to link the Ucayali and Madre de Dios basins. A Colonel Muños continued the work in 1893–6, pushing overland from the Madre de Dios to the Acre, and suggesting the construction of a narrow-gauge railway to link the two rivers.

Peru had made vigorous counter-claims to the Ucayali–Urubamba and Madre de Dios basins on similar grounds. Peruvian explorers and rubber *patrones*, notably Carlos Fermín Fitscarrald, had followed possible route-ways between the Urubamba and the Manú–Madre de Dios. Reconnaissance of three relatively easy portages across the watershed in 1893–5, and the projected construction of an eight-mile railway to replace one of them, had led to this portion of the drainage divide becoming known in Peru as the Fitscarrald isthmus. As competition between the rubber *patrones* had increased, particularly between the Peruvian Fitscarrald and the Bolivians Suárez and Vaca Diez, there had been separate negotiations over possible merging of interests, or at least the delimitation of rival spheres of rubber exploitation. During one such discussion, however, Fitscarrald and Vaca Diez both drowned on the Urubamba in July 1897 when their launch capsized, and Suárez subsequently dominated much of the region.[1] Bolivia established custom posts on the Madre de Dios river at Puerto Heath, and at the Manú–Madre de Dios confluence in 1897, to collect revenue from regions claimed by Peru.

[1] J. V. Fifer, 'The Empire Builders: a History of the Bolivian Rubber Boom and the Rise of the House of Suárez'. This reference pp. 130–3.

Protest was vigorously renewed by Peru in 1901, when it was discovered that the immense tracts of forest conceded to Anglo-American interests by Bolivia as the Acre District included thousands of square miles claimed on the maps in Lima. But the Madre de Dios headwater region lay on the fringe of the most productive rubber forests. The quinine bark industry farther south was virtually dead, and throughout this portion of the frontier between Bolivia and Peru the population remained very sparse. Beyond the limits of significant Brazilian infiltration, there was no repetition here of the conditions which combined to produce the transitory independent State of Acre less than two hundred miles away to the northeast.

It was decided to submit the whole northern section of the Bolivia–Peru boundary to arbitration by Argentina in December 1902, with the request that the old boundaries of the Viceroyalties of Peru and the Río de la Plata, and the extent of the Audiencias of Lima, Cuzco, and Charcas be sought and defined as the solution. It is quite astonishing to find these ancient limits still seriously being revived by the two litigants at the beginning of the twentieth century. In October 1902, for example, the President of the Royal Geographical Society had received an official complaint, made on behalf of Bolivia, that the current issue of the *Geographical Journal* failed to acknowledge Bolivian claims to the region disputed with Peru. The writer, the Bolivian Minister in London, continued:

the boundary line which divides Bolivia from Peru is two degrees and a half to the west [of the river Tambopata], on the Cordillera of Vilcanota, in accordance to the Royal Cédula of August 8, 1776, which incorporated Alto Peru to the Viceroyalty of Buenos Ayres, – with the Royal Ordinance of January 28, 1782, which determined the line of division, and the maps and surveys published afterwards by order of the Spanish Crown.[1]

In the absence of any effective organisation and development by either State in this remote frontier, both mutually acknowledged a century of stagnation in unknown territory.[2]

In July 1909 the Argentine President made known his award at Buenos Aires.[3] For nearly seven years a Commission had studied maps and documents, diplomatic acts relating to frontier demarcation, Royal Orders, Governors' Ordinances, Letters Patent and the Laws of the Indies. In

---

[1] F. Avelino Aramayo to Sir Clements Markham, London, 18 October 1902, Royal Geographical Society Archives.
[2] Baron Erland Nordenskïold, 'Travels on the boundaries of Bolivia and Peru', *Geog. Journ.*, vol. XXVIII, 1905, pp. 105–27. This paper refers to a part of the disputed boundary country, although its interest is largely anthropological.　　　　　　　[3] *F.O. 371/721.*

addition, both Bolivia and Peru had submitted their own arguments and claims for consideration. Each grasped the opportunity to extend its boundaries into disputed territory, some of which was acquired by Brazil from Bolivia in 1903 during the arbitration period. The western limit claimed by Bolivia in the period before the arbitration had coincided with the western limit of the great Acre Concession of 1901. A claim based largely on river courses in the *selva* and Andean *montaña* had been substituted, however, to express and support the desired boundary in more geographical terms, and in the north-west it approximated to the Urubamba–Ucayali line.[1] Peru's extreme eastern claim followed sections of the Madre de Dios, Madidi and Mamoré rivers.[2]

The Arbitrator elaborated on the perplexities of his task. Neither of the two most recent claims forwarded by Bolivia and Peru won his support, an observation which can hardly have surprised either country. The President continued:

As appears from the numerous maps of the colonial period and subsequent periods, the disputed zone was unexplored in 1810 and up to a recent period...In these long proceedings which have continued for more than three centuries, it is frequently noticed that the dispositions of the Spanish crown have been contradictory, some of them being vague and many in disagreement with the situation or the topographical features of the places. This latter was due to the want of geographical knowledge, and an equitable interpretation, according to the respective ideas of the period, is therefore necessary for appreciating the true significance and scope of the said dispositions.

Abandoning the impossible and pointless task of determining the border details of the Audiencia of Charcas (Viceroyalty of the Río de la Plata) and the Viceroyalty of Peru in 1810, the Arbitrator in his final pronouncement strove to select an equitable line, a compromise between the extreme claims of both parties (Fig. 9). In Bolivia, the 1909 award was received with great disappointment, and there were repeated mob attacks in the July on the Argentine legation in La Paz. Bolivia refused to accept the

---

[1] Bolivia considered that, in addition to support from colonial records, basis for this extended claim lay, as noted earlier, in Pando's exploration and mapping of some of the disputed areas in the early 1890s. See: (i) Sir Clements Markham, 'Recent Discoveries in the Basin in the River Madre de Dios (Bolivia and Peru)', *Geog. Journ.*, vol. VII, 1896, pp. 187–90; (ii) George Earl Church, 'Northern Bolivia and President Pando's new map', *ibid.* vol. XVIII, 1901, pp. 144–53; (iii) Pando's own reports, *Viaje a la Región de la Goma Elástica*; and *Expedición del Coronel Don José Manuel Pando al Inambary*.

[2] Peru's newly formed *Junta de Vías Fluviales* published a number of reports and maps to support its claims in the arbitration period, following renewed exploration of the Ucayali–Madre de Dios region: (i) *Vías del Pacífico al Madre de Dios*, Lima, 1902; (ii) *El Istmo de Fitscarrald* (Fiscarrald, Fizcarrald), Lima, 1903, 1904; (iii) *Nuevas Exploraciones en la Hoya del Madre de Dios*, Lima, 1904; (iv) *Ultimas Exploraciones ordenadas por la Junta de Vías Fluviales a los ríos Ucayali, Madre de Dios, Paucartambo y Urubamba*, 2 vols., Lima, 1907.

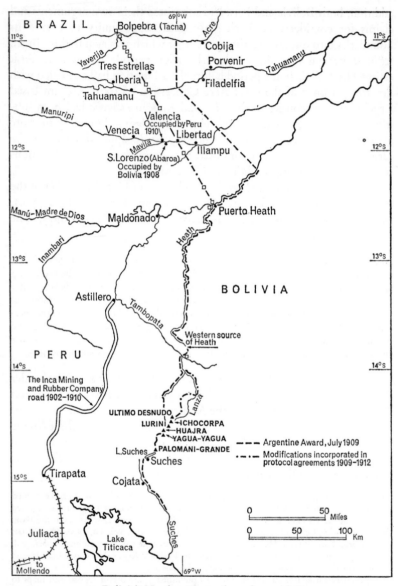

9 Bolivia's Northern Sector boundary with Peru

VIII Casani, a small Bolivian border settlement in Copacabana.

IX The international boundary between Bolivia and Peru follows long-established cultural features and intricate patterns of land ownership across the peninsula. Set within a property boundary, the south arch of the wayside chapel at Casani forms 'boundary post' No. 21.

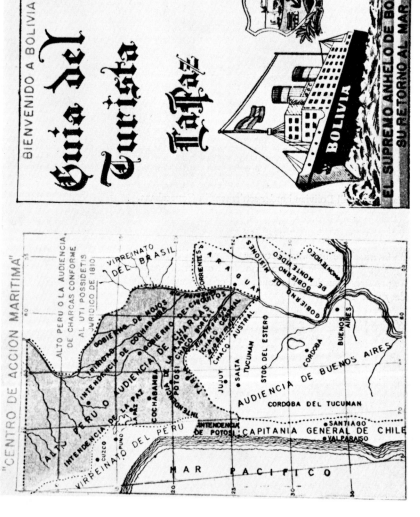

x   *Salida al Mar.* The cover of a street map currently on sale in La Paz records colonial antecedents and expresses present aspirations.

arbitration decision and diplomatic relations were broken between Bolivia and Argentina until December 1910. In the tract of jungle between the Acre and the Madre de Dios, a number of Bolivian-owned (mostly Suárez) rubber stations had undoubtedly been awarded to Peru, and there were fears that if Peru moved forward to occupy these as soon as news of the arbitration announcement reached the area, trouble would flare yet again on the 'rubber rivers'.

At this time the prices for 'Up-river Fine' were still soaring, and with the boom conditions of 1909 a new 'rubber war' was not unlikely. Brazil took the initiative, and in a circular dated 24 July 1909[1] made a confidential request to both the British and United States Governments. Both were invited to suggest to Argentina that it advise Peru to agree to a modification. Although both Britain and the U.S.A. declined to interfere officially unless requested to do so by both Peru and Bolivia, adjustments were agreed to, and Figure 9 shows the modifications resulting from the protocols of 15 and 17 September 1909.[2] These adjustments moved the boundary in Bolivia's favour approximately 30 miles west, for about 125 miles, between the Madre de Dios and Acre rivers.

The most serious practical problems facing the Arbitrator had resulted from the alignment of drainage and watershed features within certain critical portions of the disputed territory. Whereas in 1903 others had found it possible to delimit almost the whole of the new Bolivia–Brazil boundary in relation to river courses, it was apparent that in the case of the Bolivia–Peru line, however it was drawn, the drainage would run across the international boundary for some considerable distance. In a forested region of this nature, straight lines and low inconspicuous watersheds are two of the most difficult features to establish and demarcate in the field. A river's course, pushing aside the bewilderment of forest tangle between its banks, is a godsend to the boundary maker as a permanent stretch of natural demarcation.[3] Beyond the high snowy peaks of the Palomani-Yagua-Yagua–Lurini watershed line, the partly explored river Heath became the kingpin of the new boundary line. Predictably, however, the maps from which the selectors had worked proved to be extremely inaccurate. Indeed in order to illustrate this particular point, the surveyors

[1] *F.O. 371/721.*
[2] *F.O. 177/343* (File 26351/09) and *F.O. 177/350* (File 3021/10); *Col. Trat. Vig. Bol.*, vol. v, pp. 428–32.
[3] Not to be confused with the meaningless, and sometimes mischievous term 'natural boundary'. The selection of a physical feature to carry a political boundary does not establish that feature as a 'natural' boundary. Indeed, a 'natural' boundary may be no more than 'that particular natural feature somewhere beyond a State's present political boundary to which its leaders would like to expand'.

later prepared in colour a 'Sketch Map to illustrate the uncertainty in the knowledge of the river systems at the epoch of the arbitration'.[1] This superimposes three discrepant drainage maps: the rivers according to the map annexed to the memorandum presented to the National Congress by the Peruvian Minister of Foreign Affairs, 1903; the rivers according to a sketch map published to illustrate the Arbitration Award of 1909; and the rivers as surveyed by the Peru–Bolivia Boundary Commission 1911–13. Added to this complication, the surveyors had been forced to contend with a most confusing multiplicity of names.[2]

The river Heath, named after the North American doctor who in 1880 had opened up the lower Beni, appeared at least to be of suitable length (over 130 miles), roughly in a suitable place and to provide a most convenient north–south line. It was duly incorporated.[3] North of the Madre de Dios, in the absence of any major river offering a vehicle for the conveyance of the boundary northward, the straight line was adopted. So often a sign of geographical ignorance, the line crossed the major streams and low, indiscernible interfluves obliquely or at right angles. This was to prove the most difficult and unsatisfactory stretch of the boundary, in demarcation, effectiveness and maintenance.

The Peruvian Government requested the Royal Geographical Society in London to nominate, on its behalf, officers for survey and demarcation of the new boundary. It was decided that any dispute between the Peruvian and Bolivian Commissions was to be submitted to the President of the Society.[4] The field survey and preliminary demarcation were carried out between 1911 and 1913, each of the highly contrasted sections presenting particular problems. The first section consisted of open, moraine-strewn country along the Suches valley. Here, at around 13,000 feet, the llama and

---

[1] *Geog. Journ.*, vol. XLVII, 1916, p. 160.

[2] See the Table of alternative names for rivers of this region, prepared by Major H. S. Toppin, *ibid.* pp. 86–7.

[3] Colonel Fawcett, however, as he wrestled with the bewildering complexities of the Heath in 1910 grumbled that, far from possessing any intrinsic merit as a vehicle for the boundary, the river Heath owed its selection entirely 'to its imaginary course on a small-scale plan'. But Fawcett's erroneous published statement that the river Heath was named after 'an English explorer killed here by the savages...' prompted Dr Edwin Heath (then aged seventy-one) to write personally to the Royal Geographical Society from Kansas City, Mo. in April 1911, protesting that he was alive, American, and had never visited the river which bears his name. 'After my exploration [along the Beni river in 1880]', wrote Heath, 'Colonel Pando was authorized to explore the Madre de Dios river. Finding a stream coming from the south, which he ascended and mapped, he named it river Heath in my honor.'

[4] Although no longer President of the Royal Geographical Society in 1909, the long association of Sir Clements Markham with Peru and the R.G.S. until his death in 1916 was largely responsible for the continuing connexion. Markham had explored much of this frontier, discovering the upper Tambopata river in 1860.

alpaca pastures (comparatively rich even in the dry season because of snow-fed mountain torrents) were jealously guarded by the owners of the large stock holdings and their Indian herdsmen. Numerous property boundary cairns were already in existence; some of the others erected by the Peruvian Commission regularly disappeared.[1]

Beyond the great snow peaks of the Palomani–Yagua-Yagua–Ultimo Desnudo group, rising to nearly 18,000 feet, the boundary continued to follow the watershed line except for a short stretch of astronomical line towards the river Lanza. The discovery in the field that the Lanza–Tambopata confluence lay south instead of north of 14° S necessitated a rewording of the 1909 protocol and a new agreement was sanctioned in May 1912, although Bolivia has refused to accept the modification of the protocol proposed by the Mixed Commission in the parallel 14° S sector. Between them, the Lanza and Tambopata rivers carried the boundary for a further 34 miles before it broke away to seek the western source of the river Heath by a high peaks-watershed approximation.[2] Thus, apart from an isolated pillar at the mouth of the river Colorado, the new Bolivia–Peru boundary was not artificially demarcated in any way between the Ichocorpa peak and the mouth of the river Heath, a distance of just over 300 miles (Fig. 9). Aside from the rivers' natural demarcation, the rugged relief and impenetrable, virtually uninhabited forest (outside the rubber regions) led to an agreement that, in this section, delimitation by a definitive map was all that would ever be required.

But at the confluence of the Heath and the Madre de Dios rivers, the boundary entered the rubber forests. Precision and continuous recognition were now the rule. Through the complex maze of scattered *Heveas* and

1 'The Bolivian Indians amused themselves by putting down our cairns as fast as we put them up, the allegation being that we were erecting boundary marks on Bolivian territory!...I imagine it must be the first time in the history of boundary delimitation that the marks put up by one Commission [i.e. the Peruvian] have been destroyed at least with the connivance of the other' [i.e. the Bolivian Commission]. Letter from Col. A. J. Woodroffe reporting from Lima to Col. C. F. Close, Director-General of the Ordnance Survey, England, 12 February 1912, Roy. Geog. Soc. Archives.

The Peruvian Commission was headed by Col. Woodroffe, Major Toppin, Capt. Nanson and Lieut. Moores; the Bolivian Commission supported by Col. Fawcett, Capt. Edwards and Mr Wilson. Woodroffe's letter to Col. Close described the high Andean frontier between Yagua-Yagua and Ultimo Desnudo as: 'a barren, inhospitable land of beetling crags, impossible quebradas, vertical rock faces and deserted peaks towering amidst the driving mist and sleet, unvisited save for the lightning which plays around their rugged summits. A country where three miles as the condor flies may mean an arduous day's march with danger to life and limb, and which holds no magic call to the weary traveller to stay.'

2 The Heath had been explored to its source for the first time by Col. Fawcett in 1910. P. H. Fawcett, 'Further Explorations in Bolivia – the river Heath', *Geog. Journ.*, vol. XXXVII, 1911, pp. 377–98.

the *estradas* which connected them, a straight swath had to be cut so that every collector might know the boundary when he saw it. Here, where drainage ran *across*, instead of *with*, the boundary, the same problem which had occurred along the old oblique-line boundary between Bolivia and Brazil was repeated. As Sir Thomas Holdich observed:[1]

Boundary-making in the forests of the upper Amazon may be described as quite beyond the experiences of most boundary makers...the complexity and density of these rubber forests of the upper Amazon have been the theme of more than one writer, and the cutting out of an efficient boundary through them, where that boundary could no longer follow the sinuous course of a river, is almost a unique experience in boundary making. The conditions were certainly peculiar. Under ordinary circumstances the great waste places of the world want but little in the way of actual demarcation denoted by fixed lines. It may often be (and generally is) enough to set up the outward and visible signs of partition – pillars, mounds and the like – at points where men and traffic may have passed, or possibly will pass in the future, and to leave impassable tracts between such points to take care of themselves. But here, although we are dealing with all the tangled and impenetrable wilderness of sub-tropical South American forest, we have to remember that it is a rubber forest, and the chief justification for the expense of a boundary demarcation is the protection of rubber interests. Consequently it was considered necessary to cut out an actual boundary track through many miles of forest, and to clear a line from river to river, such as no man could cross without knowing that he was traversing a boundary. It involved slow and strenuous work; and it may be added that it will involve most expensive work in future years to keep that line clear.

Between the Madre de Dios and Acre rivers rival interests had already clashed and armed hostilities broken out between Nicolás Suárez of Bolivia and Rodriguez of Peru. Troops and *seringueiros*, taking advantage of the general confusion before final settlement, had sniped at each other along the Manuripi in 1910, and the situation looked ugly. Pending demarcation, a truce was called in March 1911.[2] Peruvian troops withdrew towards the Mavila ravine, Bolivian troops towards Illampu (Fig. 9), leaving the boundary cutters and clearers to sort their way laboriously through the no-man's-land between.

[1] *The Peru–Bolivia Boundary Commission 1911–1913. Reports of the British officers of the Peruvian Commission*, edit. at the Roy. Geog. Soc., London, 1918. An introduction was written by Holdich, a Vice-President of the Society, in the absence of the surveying officers on active service. Major Toppin and Lieut. Moores were killed very early in World War I, soon after completing the boundary demarcation. Frequent references to current problems and progress had appeared in the *Geog. Journ.*, notably vols. XXXVII and XXXVIII (1911); vols. XXXIX and XL (1912); vols. XLI and XLII (1913); vols. XLVII and XLVIII (1916). Vol. LVIII (1921) pp. 417–43, contains an article by A. R. Hinks on the techniques of boundary delimitation which makes brief reference to the Bolivia–Peru boundary, pp. 431–2. The Archives of the Roy. Geog. Soc. contain useful field survey notebooks and personal letters from the surveyors which yield further information about the making of the boundary.
[2] *Col. Trat. Vig. Bol.*, vol. v, pp. 433–6.

Illampu had been the subject of Bolivian anxiety ever since the original Argentine award had left it on Peru's side of the line. Bolivia claimed both the tiny settlement of Illampu which contained a small garrison post, and the concession of the same name, granted to Suárez in 1897 and extending along both banks of the Manuripi as far as Venecia. In addition, Bolivia claimed that it had built the rubber-collecting station at San Lorenzo (Abaroa) in 1908 (this was during the Arbitration period), two years before Peruvian troops had been stationed at Valencia. As the wording of Article II of the 1909 protocol was still ambiguous, stating merely that the property of the *barraca* of Illampu should remain on the Bolivian side, delegates of both countries visited the trouble-spot.[1] A generally satisfactory decision was reached in 1912, and the boundary on the right bank of the Manuripi was placed equidistant from the principal house in Illampu (Bolivia) and the principal house in San Lorenzo (Peru). Thus the final delimitation comprised two geodetic lines, 123 miles (197 kilometres) in all, radiating from the Manuripi, with the northern arm utilising the last 5 kilometres of the Yaverija river to its confluence with the Acre. Here at Tacna (Bolpebra) the triple point between Bolivia, Peru and Brazil was erected.

The problem of keeping 123 miles of cut-and-cleared boundary effectively open was one about which the surveyors had no illusions. The forest closed its wound fast. In 1912 two pillars had been set on the banks of the Manuripi. Each consisted of forty short trunks bound firmly to enclose a tall central trunk. Each had taken eight men two days to erect. The surrounding forest had been trimmed back cleanly. Both were as good as lost by the following year. The forest had grown to nearly twenty feet and covered one; the other was half swept away by the seasonal flood. 'Unless we had ourselves erected the boundary marks, it would have been impossible to find them', wrote Toppin, in charge of the work. Posts would have to be of iron, examined and maintained at least twice a year.

But while the arduous clearing proceeded, the very industry which made it necessary was in decline. Abandoned *barracas* were everywhere evident. There seemed little hope that the boundary path would ever be used as a

---

[1] Protocols respecting this and other decisions made during the course of demarcation are found in *F.O. 371/970*, *F.O. 371/3166*, and in *Col. Trat. Vig. Bol.*, vol. v, pp. 428–32, pp. 437–43, 444–5, 449–51.

By *barraca*, Peru declared that only the house was to be considered. A letter from the Bolivian Consul in London, dated 9 December 1910, to the Royal Geographical Society requested the Society to note the true geographical interpretation of the term *barraca*. This, it was stated, always included both a house and a given number of rubber *estradas* (of which Illampu had 200, each enclosing about 150 rubber trees). Tax was payable on the *barraca* as a complete unit of land holding, Roy. Geog. Soc. Archives.

track for portaging rubber between the rivers, and thereby kept open. The various rubber houses controlled the entire organisation within the forest. Their roads and trails were already established, and would not be diverted in order to keep open the boundary path. Even the official surveyors were entirely dependent on the labour, canoes, mules and provisions supplied by these rubber empires whose local control remained paramount, but whose organisations were soon to contract or, in some instances, to wither away.

II. THE DECLINE OF THE NORTHERN SECTOR

The last fifty years have witnessed the futility of the effort expended on clearing the 123-mile track through the jungle from the Madre de Dios to the Yaverija–Acre rivers. Indeed, with the contraction of the rubber frontier, the open swath no longer retained any significance and was quickly invaded by the forest. While the whole of the northern boundary between Bolivia and Peru, north that is of the Andean Cordillera Real, remains very lightly peopled or completely uninhabited, demarcation has been obliterated only in this far northern section, where it was attempted artificially. Although the iron boundary posts still exist, they can be found only with difficulty, hemmed in by jungle which gives no indication of the direction in which the boundary strikes. There is more population, in both Bolivia and Peru, between the Manuripi and the triple point of Bolpebra, where *Hevea* is more plentiful, than in the even more negative zone between the Manuripi and the Madre de Dios. But in all it is still only a population of a few hundreds, neither Bolivians nor Peruvians usually knowing for certain exactly where the boundary is located except where it crosses the river banks.

In recent years Bolivian army patrols have noted limited Peruvian infiltration into the Bolivian forest to collect rubber and Brazil nuts. This has been most marked around the Tahuamanu river, which appears to have replaced the Manuripi as a potential trouble-spot along this frontier, penetration being concentrated between the Tahuamanu and Tres Estrellas, a small *barraca* centred in a particularly rubber-rich zone. Although infiltration also characterises the Bolivia–Brazil boundary, especially when rubber prices are high, there are few places where it can be considered accidental, for there the rivers throw an almost complete cordon around Bolivia's north and east perimeter. Thus, while still awaiting a Joint Commission to re-examine the condition of the Bolivia–Peru boundary, Bolivia decided in the 1950s that a visible indication of the frontier, if not the boundary, was urgently required through certain sections of the rubber forest. Although the rubber industry is very small indeed, it still remains, with Brazil nuts, the chief means of livelihood in the extreme north-west, and this prompted the Bolivian Foreign Ministry (Department of Boundaries) in 1961 to authorise the reopening of part of the forest as quickly as possible. A path 4 metres wide, 100 metres *inside* Bolivia, but parallel to the actual boundary in selected sections, was completed by the end of 1965. Both Bolivians (and Peruvians straying over the hitherto invisible boundary) expressed surprise at finding themselves so near to the divide, while others became convinced that the pathway being cut well within Bolivian territory must be the boundary itself. While this section is due for fresh demarcation by a Joint Commission, with the erection of large new metal tripod posts on circular concrete platforms, the proximity of the boundary was announced at least for a limited period by the new Bolivian track, which prevented unwitting, though not deliberate, infringement by either Bolivia or Peru of the other's territory.

At present, the very small quantities of Bolivian rubber and nuts from this extreme north-west corner of Bolivia move away from the region almost entirely *via* Brazil. No significant export through Peru has been seriously attempted since the last days of the great rubber boom, when certain individuals holding concessions from Peru combined their efforts to improve the overland routes to the Pacific, and reduce the long delays experienced in moving rubber eastward by the Amazon. The Inca Mining Company and Inca Rubber Company, an American corporation with headquarters in Pennsylvania, allied themselves with a group of competitors to bring down costs and deflect rubber export to the south-west, *via* Arequipa and Mollendo. A 270-mile mule-road was built though appallingly difficult country between Astillero and Tirapata in nine years (1902–10) (Fig. 9). With railway connexions to the coast from Tirapata, a considerable rubber area was brought within a week of Mollendo if weather conditions were good. Thousands of mules were brought in. The company also hired five hundred Japanese to collect rubber, grow rice and raise cattle along the Tambopata and Madre de Dios rivers.[1] Whether

---

[1] All together, a few hundred Japanese immigrants, entering by the Mollendo–Arequipa–Puno route, were employed in the rubber forests of Peru and Bolivia. They were engaged chiefly by North American firms such as The Inca Rubber Co. and The American Rubber Co., although Suárez Hermanos and others employed a few. One can still find isolated *barracas*, with names such as Mukden, Yokohama and Tokio. In the early 1960s the author met a number of descendants of this small core of Japanese immigrants in the rubber region, including one at Cobija who was then holding the senior political appointment in northern Bolivia – the Prefect of the Department of Pando. A summary of Japanese immigration into Peru and Bolivia (1900–15) may be found on pp. 207–11 of J. L. Tigner, 'The Ryukyuans in Bolivia', *Hisp. Am. Hist. Rev.*, vol. XLIII, 1963, pp. 206–29.

the line of movement south-westwards from the Bolivian Department of Pando to the Pacific will ever again become a reality is uncertain, although any extension of the road south from Porvenir to Puerto Heath might encourage it.[1] But at present, and for the foreseeable future, in profound contrast to the relatively densely populated southern section of the Bolivia–Peru boundary through the Titicaca basin, which is orientated to the Pacific ports, the northern section still winds through hundreds of desolate miles before approaching the slightly less desolate rubber forests in its final section. With the perpetual lack of any adequate land transport to link this zone to the major western centres of population, the extreme north-west corner of Bolivia still finds its outlets inevitably controlled by the Amazon network. In consequence, it continues to lie on the most inaccessible fringe of a notoriously inaccessible area, the remote and isolated western periphery of Bolivia's northern sector.

Farther east, within the great triangular wedge of Pando and northern Beni which juts into Brazil between the Abuná and the Madeira–Mamoré, the rivers are 'rubber rivers' still. But while the old patterns of activity are essentially the same, their scale and intensity have once again progressively declined. Indeed, the very persistence of these traditional activities, weakened as they are, serves to emphasise the general stagnation and lack of flexibility in the economy of the Norte. It is a region which, doubtful of a future, dreams of its past.

Although output of rubber from the Departments of Beni and Pando was increased to about 4000 tons annually during the minor boom of World War II, it is only about 1400 tons a year today. The biggest single Bolivian producer is now the House of Seiler at Riberalta, the Swiss successor of the original French House of Braillard, which moved from Peru to Reyes during the heyday of the Peruvian bark trade, and subsequently descended the Beni river shortly after Edwin Heath's exploration there in 1880, clearing a new site on the Beni's high right bank opposite the confluence of the Madre de Dios in 1884. Riberalta was officially founded there on 3 February 1894, with two hundred and fifty-two inhabitants. Today Seiler's headquarters still occupies the same site overlooking the Beni river as did the original Braillard *barraca* at the very beginning of the Bolivian rubber boom.

Braillard/Seiler thus experienced both the boom and its aftermath. Discussion of the problems afflicting rubber producers in this region reveals that the high costs of transportation remain the most severe

[1] See below, p. 159.

limiting factor on present and future development. The selling price per lb. of rubber in northern Bolivia has fluctuated as follows:

1908–10	$ U.S. 1.20–$ U.S. 3
1913	73 cents
World War I	55 cents
Between the wars	a record low of 5 cents
World War II	48.5 cents
1955	35 cents
1963	15 cents
1968	23 cents[1]

Seiler is producing about 1000 tons annually, 150 tons of high quality and high elasticity, which goes to the U.S.A. market, and around 800 tons for Brazil. Brazil's demand, however, is soon likely to disappear with the increase of its own synthetic rubber industry, where production is cheap and close to consumer centres. Seiler's first shipment of rubber *upstream* to the new tyre factory at Cochabamba began in July 1968, when a small cargo of 50 tons left Guayaramerin in three river launches; it remains to be seen whether or not this internal market can stimulate any significant reversal of traditional rubber trade movement.

A tentative start was made in the Bolivian north and north-eastern forests in the 1950s to promote a plantation industry, with selected plant material distributed to growers from the Riberalta Tropical Crops Experimental Station. This station is a mile outside Riberalta and was originally run by the Servicio Agricola Interamericano (S.A.I.) in co-operation with U.S. advisers. Work is proceeding slowly, hampered now by shortage of funds, on the control of South American leaf blight, a severe fungus disease, on the development of successful hybrid strains, and on the promotion of inter-cropping in the plantation nurseries. Twenty local growers agreed to cooperate in the scheme to plant *Hevea* in specially prepared ground, covering between them just over 750 acres (300 hectares). Seiler laid out the largest planted area: two nurseries at Conquista on the Madre de Dios, and one at Fortaleza on the Beni covering 500 acres (200 hectares), but none is regarded as being particularly success-ful. This is partly because grafts were not always of local *Hevea* varieties, and largely because the constant maintenance and attention demanded by plantation cultivation have not been applied, given the perennial problems of labour shortage, and the lack of a sufficiently secure and ex-panding market. Visits to isolated *barracas* in Pando and Beni reveal little change in the old-established methods of collecting and treatment of the

---

[1] The decline in the value of the dollar makes this fall in price even greater than these figures indicate. 1900 = 100 cts; 1910 = 80 cts; 1925 = 53 cts; 1940 = 70 cts; 1960 = 30 cts; 1970 = 26 cts;

latex. The *seringueiro* exchanges perhaps four or five *bolachas* (each between 120–220 lb.) of smoked rubber a year for supplies and, just occasionally, for cash from the merchant's warehouses, situated at assembly points like Riberalta on the Beni river, Guayaramerin on the Mamoré, and Cobija on the Acre.

After rubber, Brazil nuts (*castañas* or *almendras*) provide the second principal export from northern Bolivia, a position they have occupied since the early 1930s when Nicolás Suárez introduced the first cracking machine from England into Cachuela Esperanza. They are sought by the *seringueiro* in order to provide him with an additional cash crop (Plate xvi), and are exchanged through rubber houses such as Seiler's, which until the mid-1960s sent about 800 tons (in shell) to England, and 600 tons (shelled, dried and bagged for the retailer) to the U.S.A., the entire consignment going down the Amazon. It appears that *castañas* will not lend themselves to plantation cultivation. Germination is difficult, and anything from twelve to twenty years are required before the tree comes into commercial production. Nuts from the extreme north of the region around Cobija similarly move progressively down-river to the Amazon, although very small quantities of shelled and dried nuts are flown to La Paz, and taken by rail to Arica or Matarani for shipment to the U.S.A. Penetration road-building programs in Brazil, however, since the mid-1960s, have discovered, and at the same time made accessible, vast new areas of virgin forest particularly rich in nuts. These discoveries have effectively crippled the Bolivian trade, creating slump conditions in which Bolivia's inevitably higher transport costs cannot be recovered. The time factor also still aggravates and increases the isolation of the Bolivian Norte; even today no rubber or *castaña* producer there can confidently and reliably guarantee arrival of his down-river cargo at Pará in less than three months.

The Madeira–Mamoré Railway, that relict feature of the South American rubber boom, a railway 'beginning nowhere and ending in the same place', survived until 1970–1, when it was finally replaced by a highway. Thus it passed into history after a turbulent century of persistent failure, brief triumph, and fitful decline.[1] Its traffic in the 1950s and 1960s con-

---

[1] As the Madeira–Mamoré Railway was specifically designed in the 1903 Petrópolis treaty to provide a strategic and economic link between Bolivia and Brazil, decisions as to its future had to be mutually agreed. Decline in traffic, delays, and problems concerned with track and rolling-stock maintenance (much of this dating from the construction period) led to the signing by Bolivia and Brazil of an Additional Protocol on 27 October 1966 which agreed to replace the railway with a highway between Guajará Mirim and Pôrto Velho. The latter is now linked by a new, all-weather road to Rio de Janeiro *via* Cuiabá and Brasília.

Local feeling about the closure of the Madeira–Mamoré Railway is mixed, and hope was

sisted of two passenger trains, and two or three freight trains per week run in each direction between the Brazilian ports of Guajará Mirim and Pôrto Velho (Plate XIX). In 1967, only 5034 passengers and 8596 tons of freight went down to Pôrto Velho to continue the journey by river along the Madeira and Amazon route, a figure which included 2681 tons of rubber, 576 tons of nuts, and 21 tons of alligator, jaguar and pig skins. Although these figures represented a small overall increase of traffic during the preceding decade, they would nevertheless have appeared unbelievably low to those nineteenth- and early twentieth-century optimists who saw only the obstacle of the Madeira–Mamoré cataracts and ignored, in their desire to by-pass them, the time and distance which still lie between this remote bottleneck and the ocean trading routes of the Atlantic.

Guayaramerin (Puerto Sucre) on the Bolivian side (Plate XVIII), and Guajará Mirim on the Brazilian bank, face each other across the Mamoré. Guajará Mirim, at the old railhead, is the larger of the two settlements with a population of about 14,000; Guayaramerin, with 8500 people, is linked by ferry to the rail (road) terminal, and is heavily dependent on supplies from Brazil rather than from Bolivia, although this frontier town is in regular contact with the larger Bolivian centres by air. The cost of living, however, remains high on goods which must be flown in, often four times as much as in La Paz, and the Guajará Mirim terminal forms the principal local supply market for coffee, sugar, nearly all tinned goods, flour, tobacco and other consumer articles which are brought freely back across the river into Bolivia from the town's many general stores. Approximately 4000 Bolivians live in Guajará Mirim, and several hundred more cross the Mamoré river daily from Bolivia to work in the Brazilian town. In contrast, very few Brazilians live in Guayaramerin or its immediate vicinity although, both up and downstream, many are known to live permanently on the Bolivian side of the Abuná, Madeira (Madera) and Guaporé (Itenes), working rubber, nuts and ipecacuanha root.

The river forms the only boundary demarcation here, as it does for so much of the Bolivia–Brazil frontier. One remaining portion to be finally settled in this locality is the Isla Suárez, a large island in the Mamoré

expressed earlier that it might continue to run in addition to the highway. Meanwhile, Brazilian army engineers have already extended a road from Pôrto Velho to Rio Branco, capital of the state of Acre, and the target is to reach the Peruvian border, *via* the town of Cruzeiro do Sul, before the end of 1971. This Atlantic–Pacific (Rio de Janeiro–Lima) highway is stimulating prospecting and development in western Amazonia, particularly in Brazil's Federal Territory of Rondônia. Exploration for alluvial tin and other deposits, for example, has begun in both Brazil and Bolivia. It remains to be seen, however, what further effects these new Brazilian penetration roads will have on the economy of northern Bolivia and what population movements they may encourage within the Brazil–Bolivia borderland.

between Guayaramerin and Guajará Mirim. Although a boundary coin-
ciding with the principal navigable channel is claimed by Bolivia to leave
this island on the Bolivian side, the median line of the river divides it
between the two countries and in the absence of more specific treaty terms,
the Isla Suárez is at present undetermined.[1] Each State regards it as part of
its own territory and until the early 1950s the small population was predominantly Bolivian. Since then, however, increases in Brazilian settlers
have revised this state of affairs but, even so, not more than about thirty
families are involved, and no particular interest is evinced by the majority
of the local people as to which country Isla Suárez officially belongs. The
individual families concerned clearly regard themselves as either Bolivian
or Brazilian by origin, background and language, and place their respective
land holdings accordingly in one or other of the two States.

Apart from the regular flight connexions to La Paz and Cochabamba,
Guayaramerin has a daily air link to Riberalta, as well as to other centres
in the Department such as Trinidad, Santa Ana, Magdalena and San
Joaquin. Flying is now commonplace or, rather, the daily exchange of news
and happenings in the main centres along the way is routine. Air communication had undoubtedly been of prime importance in identifying
these distant frontier zones with the main national foci, but in terms of
trade and supplies the Bolivian Nordeste is still extremely isolated from
the Andean centres, and must of necessity rely on Brazilian goods which
are brought up by river and railway (or by the road which now replaces
it). The new all-weather sixty-mile dirt road from Guayaramerin to
Riberalta, completed at the end of 1968, shortens the latter's connexion to
the Madeira–Mamoré terminal, and avoids the long tortuous trip down the
Beni river, and round the Esperanza falls, to the Villa Murtinho rail
junction.

Before the completion of the Guayaramerin–Riberalta road, the latter
remained isolated not only from the Andean centres but also from easy
contact with Brazilian supplies, far more so than its proximity to the
boundary would suggest. Only with this road's construction, more than
fifty years after the proposed railway along the same route was abandoned

Article II of the 1928 treaty apportioned thirteen islands in the Madeira (Madera) as follows:
to Bolivia, the islands of Bolívar, Sucre, Seis de Agosto, Riberón, Amistad and Colombo;
to Brazil, the islands of Dos Ammus or Confluencia, Marinha, Quince de Noviembre,
Misericordia, Siete de Septiembre, Periquitos and Araras. It was clearly stated that in the
Madeira river between the Beni–Mamoré confluence and the mouth of the Abuná, the
boundary is a line equidistant from the banks, and the islands were divided accordingly.
But no mention was made of the islands in the Mamoré. In 1958 the question of Isla Suárez
(the Brazilians, perhaps significantly, call it Ilha de Guajará Mirim) was raised 'for consideration at some early date', and there the matter still rests.

with the collapse of the rubber boom, did any direct land communication between Riberalta and the railhead become practical. If the ferry between Guayaramerin and Guajará Mirim was made suitable for loaded trucks, a through-route between Riberalta and the new road to Pôrto Velho would be established. As a result of existing conditions, however, while the cost of living in Guayaramerin is about four times as much as in La Paz, costs in Riberalta have been eight or ten times those on the *altiplano*. For not only has Guayaramerin gained economically from its contact with the Madeira–Mamoré railhead; the modest amount of river traffic which has officially been developed on the navigable waterways of the Oriente, to exchange products between highland and lowland Bolivia, is concentrated on the Mamoré. Although cargo amounts remain small, the 1968 figures of 4500 tons carried downstream and 1500 tons carried upstream between Guayaramerin and the small headwater ports linked with Cochabamba by road represent in each case approaching double the tonnage carried in the early 1960s.[1] Guayaramerin's population increase in this period (1960–8) from about 3000 to over 8000 inhabitants, contrasts with a gradual decline in that of Riberalta – from about 9500 to 8500 over the same period.

To the north-west, the small river port of Cobija remains the principal settlement on Bolivia's far northern boundary. The name Cobija, applied originally to a group of *barracas* known as Bahía to the Brazilians in the area, simply signifies a shelter or haven (as does the small port of the same name on Bolivia's former Pacific seaboard). Built high on a bluff above the river Acre, which flowed so strongly through every page of the history of Bolivia's rubber boom, this little town still echoes the former activity along the 'rubber rivers'. In order to establish Bolivian authority more visibly on this section of the boundary with Brazil, Cobija was selected to be the capital of the new Department of Pando created in 1938, and its status was confirmed in 1945. Thus, although Cobija's population is only 2800, it contains the administrative centre (the Prefectura), and a fairly large army garrison. Considerable dissatisfaction was expressed in Riberalta (Department of Beni) when the insignificant settlement of Cobija secured this political plum in 1938, and grievances over the drawing of the internal political boundaries in 1900 were once again aired.[2]

At the beginning of the century it had been suggested that a new Department of Vaca Diez be formed in the northern rubber forests, which was to include Riberalta, Cachuela Esperanza, Villa Bella and Guayara-

[1] J. V. Fifer, 'Bolivia's Pioneer Fringe', *Geog. Rev.*, vol. LVII, 1967, pp. 1–23. This reference pp. 8–11.

[2] Oswaldo Vaca Diez, *Creación de Nuevo Departamento*, Riberalta, 1938.

merin. All of these were felt, rightly, to be too distant from Trindad to maintain easy contact with that town, the administrative centre of the Department of Beni, which had been created from the old Province of Mojos in 1842. The new Department of Vaca Diez was not established, however, and President Pando failed to detach even the province of Vaca Diez from the Department of Beni in 1903 and transfer it to the northern Territorio de Colonias, so great was the howl of protest from Trinidad at the prospect of losing its revenue-rich northern province. The resultant loss of income and prestige by Riberalta, which with reason had always regarded itself as the regional capital of northern Bolivia, was a severe blow, and has contributed in some respects to its sense of frustration, and progressive stagnation in a region where government office provides the major single urban source of employment. Thus, even before the desirability of establishing the departmental capital on the Acre boundary became the paramount consideration, and despite the abandonment of the Federalist policy at the turn of the century, there is evidence to suggest that the principle of 'divide-and-rule' motivated later decisions made in La Paz over the selection of the northern internal administrative boundaries. Certainly, whatever locational advantages Cobija may have been thought to possess in strategic terms, it is not well placed in comparison with Riberalta to organise and administer the Pando, which has always been orientated to the Beni–Mamoré–Madeira routeway, not to the Acre.

Cobija is thus the assembly point for the rubber, nuts, timber and skins extracted from the Puerto Rico, Filadelfia, Porvenir and Cobija region of the extreme western Pando. A glance at the drainage pattern of the region reveals that the Acre quickly draws traffic *away* from Bolivia downstream of Cobija, for unlike all the other major rivers of northern Bolivia, the Acre does not form part of the Madeira system but flows instead into the Amazon by way of the Purus. Since the beginning of the twentieth century, the trade of the Tahuamanu river has been drawn to Cobija by a 23-mile dirt road from Porvenir, negotiable except for two months at the height of the rains. This was another of the trackways originally cut by Nicolás Suárez, already noted as having been responsible for most of the existing rudimentary road pattern in the Pando, as well as much of the Beni. To replace Suárez' old road between Porvenir and Cobija, important during the Acre War for the movement of his private army of *seringueiros* (the *Columna Porvenir*), the Bolivian army constructed a new all-weather dirt road in the mid-1960s, 20 miles long and mostly on the line of the old track, to link the two settlements and the Tahuamanu and Acre rivers.

The region remains dependent on the Brazilian outlet, and on the prices in the Brazilian market, for all Bolivian rubber and nuts move downstream as the produce of Brazil. About 90 per cent of the population along Bolivia's Pando frontier, west and east of Cobija, is Brazilian, and penetration increases whenever rubber and *castaña* prices are high. The Prefectura in Cobija is well aware of this state of affairs, and keeps it under surveillance as far as possible, but the character of the terrain and sparse settlement throughout the entire area render further measures impracticable, and probably unnecessary, given depressed economic conditions. The virtually exclusive dependence upon the Brazilian outlet in this region might eventually be challenged by the extension of the road southward beyond Porvenir to Puerto Heath (Fig. 9), the Bolivian frontier settlement on the river Madre de Dios; indeed this section forms part of the projected and ambitiously conceived 'Edge-of-the-Selva Highway', initially designed to run through the cordilleran foothill zone from Colombia to Bolivia. From Puerto Heath, it is envisaged that river boats at some future date could carry rubber, *castañas* and other products upstream to Maldonado in Peru, a river journey which at present is made from Porvenir to Iberia, and continued thence by air. Maldonado is already linked by dirt road to Arequipa, on the railway to the Pacific port of Matarani. But in present, rather than in future terms, such new roads as have been constructed in the 1960s confirm the orientation of this frontier to Brazil. The small town of Brasilea on the Acre, opposite Cobija, is now the terminus of a road north-eastward to Rio Branco which is, in consequence, becoming increasingly important as an alternative centre of employment for Bolivians in this region.

Efforts to maintain a measure of cohesion within such sparsely populated territory place heavy demands upon the administrative authorities. In this context, it is interesting to observe the traditional and continuing role of the mission (Roman Catholic and Protestant), both in the regular connexions it establishes along the extensive river network, and in the schools and medical facilities provided at Cobija, Riberalta and Guayaramerin. The political identification of the northern frontier is also aided by the albeit modest activities of Bolivia's Fuerza Naval. This small force repairs quays and stairways, maintains a hospital vessel for some of the more isolated settlements, and lends 'coastguard' support to Bolivian custom posts engaged in the well-nigh impossible task of effectively controlling smuggling across the river boundaries (Fig. 15). In addition, the Fuerza Naval attempts to locate and control any disturbing increase of Brazilian squatters upon Bolivian territory.

Inevitably, however, in the overall view, the physical isolation of the northern frontier and its inaccessibility by surface transport modes remain daunting. The entire northern sector, including the northern part of the La Paz Department, together with the whole of the Pando and the Beni, still averages a population density of less than two persons per square mile. Small riparian settlements lie scattered and separated by thousands of square miles of empty forest, much of which, even today, has never yet been effectively penetrated. Farther south, the seasonally flooded surface of the Llanos de Mojos occasionally reveals traces of old raised-field and settlement patterns constructed by indigenous Indian tribes, and long since abandoned – patterns of an environmental adjustment more delicate and more precise than any obtained, or even attempted, in subsequent periods. While regular flight paths over mountain, forest and savanna, therefore, now leave little territory completely unseen, so often this serves to emphasise how much of the land is still unknown.

XI The Theotonio Fall, on the Madeira (700 metres from shore to shore, 10 metres height of cataract). Woodcut from Keller, *The Amazon and Madeira Rivers*, 1874.

XII The one formal monument to Nicolás Suárez, erected at Cachuela Esperanza shortly after his death there in 1940.

XIII The 60-year-old hulk of a Suárez river boat found abandoned near Guayaramerin, and photographed in 1963. It has since been salvaged by Bolivia's Fuerza Naval and, as the *Nicolás Suárez*, now patrols the Mamoré and Itenes rivers. Brazil owns the farther bank.

XIV Esperanza falls, the only interruption to navigation on the middle and lower Beni river. The site was selected by Suárez in 1881 as his major control point on an extensive system of inland waterways in lowland Bolivia. The Italian marble tomb, its column symbolically broken, was erected by Nicolás Suárez to mark his grief at the death of Constanza Roca, companion of his early years at Cachuela Esperanza.

XV The Acre river at Cobija, northern Bolivia, scene of bitter fighting in the 'rubber war' of 1903. Both banks of the Acre below this bend were subsequently ceded to Brazil, part of whose left-bank settlement of Brasilea is shown. (Boundary posts stand near the mouth of the Bahía tributary, right.) The Acre, seen at low water, flows into the Amazon *via* the Purus, thus avoiding the Madeira–Mamoré falls.

XVI Avenida Beni-Mamoré, Riberalta. It was cut originally in 1903 to carry an extension of the Madeira–Mamoré Railway from Brazil into Bolivia to reach this rubber boom-town. The railway was never completed. (Foreground, Brazil nut kernels drying before export *via* Amazon routeway.)

XVII The proposed railway track was partially cleared, but never finally levelled before the collapse of the rubber boom. Abandoned, it became instead Riberalta's widest street, running back into the jungle.

XVIII The Bolivian river port of Guayaramerin. *Bolachas* of wild rubber await ferrying across the Mamoré to the Brazilian railhead on the opposite bank. The highest of the Madeira–Mamoré falls, obstructing navigation to the Amazon for 230 miles, can be observed downstream.

XIX One of the original wood-burning locomotives on the Madeira–Mamoré Railway at Guajará Mirim, Brazil. Built by Baldwin's of Philadelphia in 1913, it is seen here in 1968, hauling mahogany and bound for Pôrto Velho. The son of one of the original railway construction workers from Grenada stands by. The railway was closed progressively in 1970–1 and replaced by a highway to Pôrto Velho under agreement with Bolivia.

xx   Puerto Suárez, Bolivian 'ghost' port on Lake Cáceres, river Paraguay. The pier, built in 1910, stands in the shallow Tamengo Channel which winds round the edge of the lake (here covered by a raft of vegetation) to reach the Paraguay river at Corumbá.

xxi   Looking across the international boundary between Bolivia and Brazil along the only road to link them on a 2000-mile border. It runs between Puerto Suárez and Corumbá, and here at Arroyo Concepción two concrete pyramids demarcate the boundary. Brazil maintains a small military post, Bolivia the checkpoint seen in the distance.

CHAPTER 4

THE SOUTHERN SECTOR:
ROUTES TO THE ATLANTIC
via THE PARAGUAY–PARANÁ–PLATA

BOLIVIA'S RELATIONS WITH ARGENTINA, BRAZIL
AND PARAGUAY

We looked out across the rolling leagues of the Gran Chaco. It was a brilliant day and we could see for a hundred miles...mile upon mile of silent, motionless green tapestry, it stretched away to the horizon that was slightly blurred by the heat. To the southward the silver snake of the Río Pilcomayo uncurled itself in the sunlight, only to be lost in the marshes beyond. There are five such horizons, he said, between us and the Río Paraguay.[1]

Almost one-third of the 850,000 or so square miles claimed by Bolivia at independence lay within the Paraguay basin (Figs. 1 and 2). The old 1777 Ildefonso line between the Spanish and Portuguese empires had followed the Paraguay river's sluggish course southward from its confluence with the Jaurú; nearly five hundred miles away to the west, the Bermejo flows south-eastwards from the sierras surrounding Tarija. Between them, and beyond, sprawls the huge, featureless, swamp-ridden plain of the Gran Chaco.[2] Whilst this great wedge of land forms the northern section of the vast central South American lowland known farther south as the Pampas, the Chaco differs from that virtually treeless grassland in the stands of fan palm (*palmar*) and *quebracho* which locally stud its savannas. *Quebracho* (*quebrar hacha*, lit. break-axe), is one of the hardest woods known, and forms the chief building material and metal substitute in the stoneless Chaco,[3] as well as an important source of tannin. The great Quaternary

[1] J. Duguid, *Green Hell*, London, 1931, p. 334.
[2] The name 'Chaco' appears to have developed as the Spanish form of 'chacu', a Quechua term for hunting or chase. Great hunting expeditions were organised by the Incas along the western fringe of the Chaco, rich in game, using thousands of Indians as drivers. The Chaco Boreal lies between the Paraguay and the Pilcomayo; the Chaco Central between the Pilcomayo and the Bermejo (Teuco); the Chaco Austral south of the Bermejo. Bolivia claimed the Chaco Boreal and Chaco Central.
[3] Travellers have commented on the very fine alluvial cover of the Chaco. Rafael Karsten's *Indian Tribes of the Argentine and Bolivian Chaco*, Helsingfors, 1932, records, for example, that the author did not see even the smallest stone in hundreds of square miles.

silt plain, almost everywhere less than 1000 feet, slopes imperceptibly towards the south-east, often falling less than one foot per mile. The summer rainstorms quickly result in widespread inundation of the landscape and, as the floods slowly recede, much of the Chaco retains a swampy character until the dry season is well advanced, and activity becomes entirely controlled by the need for water at dwindling streams and brackish wells.[1] This tormenting annual rhythm of flood, storm and hot north wind, alternating with increasingly devastating drought and cooler southerly air-streams, is the controlling factor upon survival in the Chaco, for it is an annual rhythm with which all life and movement must be synchronised.

Approximately four hundred desolate miles beyond the last Andean sierra the river Paraguay marked the boundary, first between Spanish and Portuguese claims, and subsequently between those of Bolivia, Brazil and Paraguay. To the west of the great Paraguay river, no major permanent stream crosses the Chaco Boreal or Chaco Central, and flood waters retreat to no well-defined channels. Even the river Pilcomayo is useless as a continuous line of movement, for its barely navigable upper and lower reaches are severed by the great oozing swamps of Esteros de Patiño into which the southern arm spreads at 23° 50′ S, to emerge again as the river Misterioso, Riache Porteño, Brazo Norte and Brazo Sud. The shallower northern arm of the Pilcomayo, the Confuso, winds independently into the Paraguay. Throughout, as many of the names suggest, the constant braiding, shallowing and tortuous meandering of the rivers forced their abandonment as reliable lines of movement.[2] Although the apparent certainty of their delineation upon maps, even late in the nineteenth century, actively encouraged attempts at navigation, in the event the rivers served only to increase the problems of penetration into the region by the dislocation and confusion they imposed.

Within the mountains, west of the Chaco's fringe, the frontier between

---

[1] No reliable climatic statistics are available for this region. Annual rainfall is usually 40–50″ (1016–1270 mm.), with a pronounced summer maximum, followed by severe drought between April and September. Summer temperatures average more than 80° F (26.5° C); the winter (dry) season about 60° F (15.5° C), although a cool south wind (the *surazo*) may lower temperatures temporarily to as little as 35–45° F (2–7.5° C).

[2] In John Graham Kerr's record of expeditions in the Pilcomayo region between 1889 and 1891 (published as part of *A Naturalist in the Gran Chaco*, Cambridge, 1950), the author describes the lower reaches of the Pilcomayo as frequently less than 20 yards wide, with meanders sweeping almost 360°. He records the excessive shrinkage of the river after April, and the efforts to construct a series of small dams in order to gain the few vital inches of depth to stay afloat. This frequently meant a week's wait while water accumulated slowly behind each earth and brushwood dam. Further description by the same author of abandoned vessels along the Bermejo river may be found in 'The Gran Chaco', *Scott. Geog. Mag.*, vol. VIII, 1892, pp. 73–87.

Bolivia and Argentina straddled the complexities of the high Cordilleras, and was characteristically varied. Below the lofty 20,000-foot Andean chains, with their plateaux and intermontane basins, the border country included longitudinal, sharp-crested ridges rising to 6000 feet, and narrow valleys enclosed between them, in the series of rugged corrugations which form the central foothill zone. Beyond the last hogsback ridge, the frontier descended abruptly into the Chaco, but within the central region, dissection by the Bermejo, Tarija and Pilcomayo headstreams revealed some of the most attractive and agriculturally diversified valleys in the entire continent. The Tarija basin had formed an early paradise for a handful of Pizarro's followers, although the town was officially founded by order of the Viceroy of Peru in 1574 as la Villa de San Bernardo de la Frontera. Secluded within this fertile but remote valley, irrigated maize, sugar, tobacco, olives, vines, flax and wool were only some of the varied products to be exchanged with other less-favoured regions. Thus the geographical characteristics of Bolivia's southern-sector frontier once again exhibited a pronounced physical dichotomy, a contrast of landscape between mountain and Chaco, which has always impressed the traveller as one of the most striking in the continent: 'After nine days' riding from Sucre, the capital,...a sudden bend in the track brought me within sight of the plains...that immense sea, for such indeed appeared the dark blue forest, stretching out, apparently unbroken...I seemed indeed to stand on the dividing line between two worlds.'[1]

I. EARLY EXPLORATION OF BOLIVIA'S SOUTHERN FRONTIER

The dominance of the Portuguese along much of the Paraguay river routeway had led to the establishment of their forts and trading settlements on both banks of that river, despite Spanish riparian claims. Although these forts were well separated, they confirmed the upper Paraguay, as did those on the Guaporé and Madeira farther north, as a line of movement on which the Portuguese retained the initiative.

Spanish exploration of the frontier had penetrated this varied region of mountain and plain from two opposing directions. The Andean valleys and intermontane basins had been discovered by *conquistadores* roaming

[1] J. B. Minchin, 'Eastern Bolivia and the Gran Chaco', *Proc. Roy. Geog. Soc.* (New Series), vol. III, 1881, pp. 401–20. This reference p. 404. (Also in translation, *Bol. Soc. Geog. Sucre*, vol. XXVIII, pp. 116–37.) Minchin, engineer to the Bolivian Government, was appointed in 1874 as Richard Reader Harris' assistant on several railway projects sponsored under concession in various parts of Bolivia. He also worked on the Bolivia–Brazil boundary survey, 1877–8 (see above, p. 131).

southward and south-eastward from their primary bases in Lower Peru. As a result, the settlements founded within the southern sierras in Upper Peru had tended to remain orientated towards the north, particularly towards Potosí and Chuquisaca. The Chaco, however, had been approached primarily from Asunción, founded in 1537 as the small river fort of Nuestra Señora de la Asunción, and later to become the principal base for Spanish colonising expeditions in the whole of south-eastern South America. The directive from Spain to seek alternative routes into Upper Peru impelled Spanish explorers to strike north-westwards towards the mountains. Among these men was Ñuflo de Chávez, who ascended the Paraguay river to Gaíba, and then proceeded to skirt the edge of the Chaco, establishing a string of settlements of which Santa Cruz de la Sierra (1560) became the most important.

Santa Cruz was not, however, founded at its present site, but nearly two hundred miles farther east, close to San José de Chiquitos in the northern sierras which fringe the Chaco. Its ruins may still be found. Ñuflo de Chávez' city was abandoned in 1590 as a result of repeated Indian attack, and re-established one hundred and fifty miles farther west on the bank of the Grande, with the apt title of San Lorenzo de la Frontera. But this site proved an unhealthy one, and shortly afterwards the remnants of the population moved west again to the city's present location near the banks of the river Piray where, on its third successive site, the original name of Santa Cruz de la Sierra was revived. Closer to the Andean foothills, but still very definitely a town of the plains, it remained the regional capital of lowland Bolivia, and the source of most of the small groups of colonists who spread themselves across the Bolivian Oriente.

Most explorers of the Chaco were doomed to perish either from thirst, or from Toba and Chiriguano Indian attacks, which had resulted in the massacre of several Spanish military contingents approaching both from Asunción and from Peru. The Jesuits and Franciscans were similarly unsuccessful in their efforts at systematic penetration beyond the missions established around the Chaco fringe among the Chiquitos. Only along the extreme south-west edge of the Chaco was exploration from Peru at all significant; by order of the Viceroy in Lima, a Spanish officer, Captain Andrés Manso, had founded a number of small settlements between the Parapetí and Bermejo rivers. These early sites around the periphery of hostile, untamed country were incorporated into the Audiencia of Charcas in 1563, confirmed in 1743, and inherited, therefore, along with a portion of the Chaco by Bolivia at independence.

The frontier between Bolivia and Argentina was crossed by two long-established colonial lines of movement. The older was the road between Potosí and Buenos Aires, through La Quiaca, the Humahuaca Pass, Jujuy, Salta, Tucumán and Córdoba – a route which notably increased its traffic after the transfer of Upper Peru's administration from Lima to Buenos Aires in 1776.[1] In 1777–8, what might be called a restricted free trade was permitted in the new age of Bourbon reform. Buenos Aires' trade with other Spanish possessions was sanctioned at certain specially registered ports, although trade, apart from slave trade, with non-Spanish territories was always to remain illegal. The recognition of the port of Buenos Aires and the creation of the new Viceroyalty of the Río de la Plata had been part of the disruption and weakening of Peru's economic monopoly in South America. Upper Peru was officially turned about to augment the territory and revenues of the new Viceroyalty where, in the south-east, a politically and economically powerful focus of population was to emerge around the Plata estuary, to stiffen the Spanish flank against the inroads of the Portuguese.

The second line of movement across the frontier between Argentina and Bolivia branched north-east from Salta to follow the sierra foothill–Chaco junction zone through Tartagal, Yacuiba, Villa Montes, Charagua and Cuevo to Santa Cruz de la Sierra. An ox-cart trail connected these settlements, most of which were later in origin than those on the road to and from Potosí. Bolivia had scarcely advanced even to the fringe of the Chaco before the second half of the nineteenth century. Then the nucleus of settlements such as Charagua, Cuevo and Tarairí had been the Franciscan mission, where irrigated gardens produced maize, sugar, rice and vines. At other centres, ranching provided the only form of livelihood. Along the trail, small streams breaking through the bounding ridges spread easily over the levels, and fording usually presented no difficulty to the large-wheeled wagons. But the major rivers could rarely be negotiated in this way, and Indians clustered at the banks to unload and ferry the cargoes in crude flat-bottomed boats, or on rafts while the animals were coerced into swimming. During the rains, the rapid rise in water level of streams flowing from the high sierras in spate made all movement along this foot-hill trail extremely hazardous, for the current swept rafts and animals anything between half a mile and a mile downstream before the opposite

[1] Pre-Columbian links had already been established between the Andes and the Pampas. The Río de la Plata was originally discovered by Juan de Solís in 1516, but was named the Silver River a few years later by Sebastian Cabot. This choice of name appears to have been derived from the numerous silver ornaments worn by the Indians of the region. The silver, however, came not from the surrounding area but from the mountains of what was to become Upper Peru.

bank could be gained. Dangers and delays caused by the unpredictable behaviour of the rivers inevitably characterised the difficult trail southward from Santa Cruz, and the problems of their negotiation figure prominently in travellers' journal records.[1]

Salta and Jujuy were true frontier settlements, serving and served by a wide range of country in Argentina, Bolivia and Chile (Fig. 10). Their function continued long after new political boundaries had been superimposed on the traditional economic life of this region, although both centres were affected by the general decline in Bolivia's trade with Buenos Aires and the central *pampas* immediately after independence. In the year 1826, for example, J. B. Pentland had reported that as few as two thousand mules and horses had been imported into Bolivia from the Argentine provinces and Paraguay, while all other trade had fallen away. The import of live animals from the *pampas*, however, was soon revived, and some of the earlier regional exchange patterns were re-established. Both Salta and Jujuy had been founded as strategic settlements along the old road between Potosí, the *altiplano* and the *pampas*. Post-houses and regular stages for the supply of fresh mules, horses, oxen and wagons had been maintained along the route. In addition, forts were manned to protect the supply line from constant harassment by Indians, particularly the Chiriguanos in the foothill zone, and the dreaded Tobas and Matacos in the Chaco fringe, which the road was forced to skirt south of Salta. Salta was founded in 1582, Jujuy rebuilt for the third time ten years later, after repeated Indian attack. Both provided an outer line of defence for the larger centre of Tucumán. Other attempts by Spain to establish towns on the rim of the Chaco ended in massacre.

Salta held the key position in the frontier, for there the ox-drawn wagons which were used on the plains were exchanged for mules to continue the journey into the mountains.[2] Apart from the transport of general supplies, Salta played a significant role in the mass movement of mules, horses and cattle across the continent to satisfy the demands of the colonial mining centres. Stock raised on the *pampas* was slowly transferred north in three stages. The first ended at Córdoba, where a slightly higher rainfall

[1] E.g. (i) 'Report on a journey through Bolivia', C. Gosling, Santiago, 1 February 1910, F.O. *177/350*, F.O. *371/969*; (ii) H. M. Grey, *The Land of Tomorrow – a mule-back trek through the swamps and forests of eastern Bolivia*, London, 1927, pp. 202–3 and 207–9; (iii) J. Duguid, *Green Hell*, pp. 313–15 and 321–5. These early twentieth-century descriptions of the trail stress how little conditions had changed in more than three hundred years.

[2] G. M. Wrigley, 'Salta, an early commercial centre of Argentina', *Geog. Rev.* vol. II, 1916, pp. 116–33. Impressions of this frontier were also recorded by Isaiah Bowman, *Desert Trails of Atacama*, pp. 191–201.

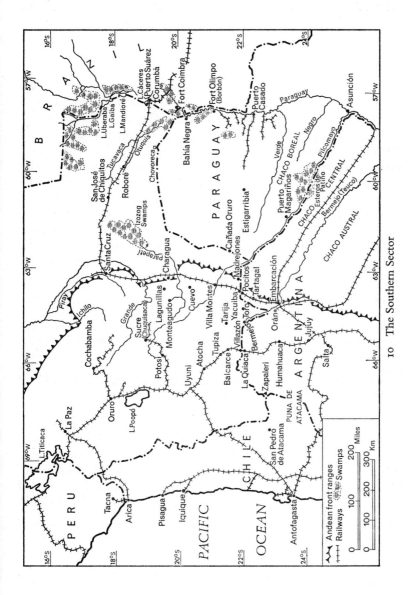

10 The Southern Sector

167

provided sufficient pasture to rest and recondition the animals for some months.[1] The stock, in herds of 1300 to 1400 head, resumed the trail after the floods of the rainy season began to subside in April in order to reach the pastures of Salta in June, before the drought stopped all large-scale movement of animals.

The great fair at Salta took place in February and March, when an estimated sixty thousand animals changed hands. Both before and after independence, once the trade had revived, the Salta fair was an annual Mecca for stockmen from Peru, Bolivia, northern Chile, the Chaco and the Argentine *pampas*. Mules dominated the market, and tens of thousands of them were moved every year into Bolivia and Peru, where they proved themselves sure-footed, faster and tougher than llamas, as well as tolerant of extremes of temperature and altitude. After the Salta fair the *pamperos* turned for home, while the muleteers turned northward, to drive herds of up to two thousand at a time into the mountains by way of the intermontane basins. This accustomed the animals more gradually to the altitude, as well as to wind exposure and sudden lowering of temperatures at night. These high pastures have always proved invaluable to life in the frontier country, as Bowman observed again in the early 1920s:

The difficulties of the way oblige the dealers to drive their cattle slowly and rest them frequently in favourable spots. Every year a stream of mules, asses, llamas, sheep and cattle go north from the Poma valley (over 9000 feet), over high passes to Bolivia where they are sold to the mines, or to the railroads where construction is in progress, or are held for the great annual fair at Huari, Bolivia. At this celebrated fair there gather every year an immense number of merchants from northern Argentina, Bolivia and Peru. They trade in all manner of products of mine, forest, field and garden. It is one of the principal bartering places of Hispanic America.[2]

2. TARIJA 1825–1826: 'BASTIÓN DE LA BOLIVIANIDAD'

After the independence declaration of 1825, few changes occurred within this region with one small but notable exception. The political future of Tarija remained undecided, for although its economic orientation had always been to Potosí and Chuquisaca, the province lay outside the limits

[1] C. E. Akers, *A History of South America, 1854–1904*, London, 1904, p. 11. Largely because of the extensive local pastures, a custom house was set up at Córdoba in 1623 where a 50 per cent transit duty was supposed to be collected on all commodities passing between Peru and the River Plate provinces.

[2] Isaiah Bowman, *Desert Trails of Atacama*, pp. 214–15. The famous fairs of the central Andes, like those of medieval Europe, were (and still are) a powerful factor in binding together economically dissimilar regions, transcending and thereby to some extent subduing political boundaries. See also G. M. Wrigley, 'Fairs of the Central Andes', *Geog. Rev.*, vol. VII, 1919, pp. 65–80.

which Bolivia could legitimately inherit if the *uti possidetis de jure 1810* ruling was to be strictly applied to the new boundaries. By a royal cédula of 17 February 1807, Tarija had been removed from the Intendancy of Potosí and, despite strong local protest, placed under the jurisdiction of Salta. Tarija itself, however, showed considerable determination in its desire to be linked with Upper Peru, rather than with the Argentine plains country south of the Humahuaca Pass, and in July 1825 deputations were sent both to Marshal Sucre and to the Governor of Salta to apprise them of this fact. Sucre was sympathetic, and dispatched Burdett O'Connor to Tarija with a small contingent of troops.

In October 1825 the guidance of Bolívar, then in Potosí, was requested and, predictably, the Liberator reminded *tarijeños* that in 1810 Tarija had been under the sovereignty of the United Provinces of the Río de la Plata. Nevertheless, later the same month, Sucre publicly upheld the principle of self-determination for Tarija, stressing also the strategic (and agricultural) importance of the region's continuing association with Potosí and Chuquisaca. Argentina, meanwhile, refused to recognise Bolivian independence because of the violation of the principle of *uti possidetis de jure 1810*, and also because Bolivia was still occupied by Colombian troops and its new President was a foreigner.[1] It would appear, however, that the refusal was based more specifically on the case of Tarija than on any other. For once independence from Spain was a certainty, Buenos Aires never displayed any real intention of resisting Bolivia's desire for a separate existence. Since Upper Peru could not be effectively retained nor controlled from Buenos Aires, two thousand miles distant, the creation of the independent buffer State of Bolivia appeared propitious. If Upper Peru had prevented Argentina from reaching and controlling Lima, it had similarly baulked Peru from penetrating southward, with any success, into the cattle plains and on towards Buenos Aires.

Continued agitation from Tarija found Argentina insufficiently disposed, therefore, to take serious action to retain this far northern frontier province. In a letter from Chuquisaca on 12 September 1826, Sucre informed Bolívar:[2] 'More news reached us on the 6th of this month. Tarija, which has always resisted union with Buenos Aires, rose in rebellion on 26th August, deposed the Governor... and announced its reincorporation with Bolivia.' The impassioned Manifesto Tarijeño of 1826

---

[1] Argentina's refusal to recognise Bolivian independence at this time contributed to the decline in traffic between the two States. In 1826 the Bolivian Congress imposed a 40 per cent duty (which was to operate from 1 January 1827) on all merchandise entering Bolivia from countries in South America which had not formally acknowledged Bolivian independence.

[2] D. F. O'Leary, edit., *Cartas de Sucre al Libertador*, vol. II, p. 103.

declared, 'Tarija ser boliviana. Su voluntad es pertenecer a Bolivia, y sin Bolivia no quiera existir en el mapa geográfico', and so it was decided.[1]

3. 1832–1846: PRELIMINARY EFFORTS BY BOLIVIA TO NAVIGATE THE PARAGUAY AND PILCOMAYO RIVERS

Despite the distance between Chuquisaca and Bolivia's south-eastern frontier, and despite the fact that the harsh nature of the Chaco discouraged encroachment by Brazil, Paraguay or Bolivia, the attention of all three countries was nevertheless directed into that region because of the significance of the Paraguay river routeway. Effort was concentrated upon establishing successful claims along its banks, and on securing control of its navigation; this in turn involved questions of ownership in the intervening Chaco territory.

Just seven years after independence had been declared, on 5 November 1832, the Bolivian Congress authorised a concession of land on the fringe of the Chaco, adjoining the Paraguay river and intersected by the Tucavaca and Otuquis, to a Manuel Luis de Oliden as repayment for 'heavy pecuniary losses incurred by him in the wars of independence'. It comprised a circular tract, fifty leagues in diameter, in the southern part of Chiquitos province, and was designed to attract colonists to engage in the production of cotton, coffee, sugar cane, and medicinal and dye woods, as well as cattle ranching and iron mining. The new capital and port of this territory, Ciudad de Oliden, was to accommodate vessels of up to two hundred and fifty tons, requiring about thirty days to sail upstream from Buenos Aires, and half that time to return. A new, direct mule road to Chuquisaca, avoiding Santa Cruz de la Sierra was proposed, for the Otuquis territory was expressly granted for the purposes 'of facilitating foreign trade into Bolivia and of opening a new entrance for its admission'.

The implementation of this concession, however, quite apart from the practical problems it raised inside Bolivia, soon ran into trouble with Paraguay and Brazil. The severely isolationist policy decreed by Francia in Paraguay until 1840 effectively imposed the same negative controls on countries lying farther up-river. In 1836 Oliden's son, José León de Oliden, launched a small canoe into the river Cuiabá, Mato Grosso, and proceeded downstream into the Paraguay, passing the old Portuguese fort of Coimbra (built in 1775) without incident. Travelling south, and unaware that

---

[1] Communications and decrees relating to Tarija's desire for inclusion within Bolivia may be studied in the Archives of San Andrés University, La Paz (document nos. 297–337), as well as in the National Archives at Sucre. (Also in personal letters of Burdett O'Connor held by Eduardo Trigo O'Connor d'Arlach, of Tarija.) Tarija was granted Department status in 1831.

the Otuquis river in fact disappeared into swamps one hundred miles before reaching the Paraguay, Oliden anxiously searched the western bank. Once the mouth of the river on which the new port was to be founded came into view, his plan was to follow the Otuquis upstream to a suitable navigation head. But nearly two hundred miles on his way south from Coimbra, Oliden was still vainly scanning the Paraguay's right bank as he approached Fort Borbón, the old Spanish colonial fortress originally built in 1792 by orders of the Viceroy in Buenos Aires to impede the advances of the Portuguese (Fig. 11 *a*). It was then Paraguay's most northerly outpost on the river, and warning shots from some of the twelve pieces of iron cannon still mounted strategically in defence of the Paraguay river route brought Oliden to a halt. All progress southward was denied:

> Mr Oliden, finding his requests fruitless; that the gates of Paraguay were shut in his face;...that the trade of Chiquitos and all of Bolivia was blocked by this passage... took leave and returned to his canoe to await a passport giving him permission to *retrace* his steps. The logs of wood that floated by on the stream of the river excited envy...they were free and he was chained;...had he dared to push his canoe off, and let her float quietly down by the sides of the logs with the current, there were one hundred soldiers ready to take arms against him and insultingly turn him back.[1]

It was not until 1840–2, after the reopening of navigation on the Paraguay, that Oliden made any further attempts to take up his concessionary rights. By then, however, it was an attempt to dispose of them, in particular to an English company, based in Rio de Janeiro, for the sum of £40,000. But once again it was an abortive attempt, owing to the unequivocal attitude adopted by Brazil. In Bolivia, the British Vice-Consul reported that the failure of the company in Rio to follow the negotiations through should be attributed

> to the Brazilian Government's refusal to allow the British, or any foreign flag whatever, to navigate the river Paraguay, or to suffer any European colony to establish itself in the vicinity of the boundary line of its empire – a determination which effectually alarmed the British speculators...With the support of Argentina, Brazil will avoid the appearance of any but South American flags in the interior waters. Thus the plans of Bolivia to colonise its territory are sure to be embarrassed for some time, if not rendered totally nugatory.[2]

[1] Lardner Gibbon, *Exploration of the Valley of the Amazon*, vol. II, p. 171. Gibbon recorded an account of the 1836 exploration provided for him by Manuel Luis de Oliden.

[2] C. Masterton to J. Bidwell, Chuquisaca, 13 February 1842, 20 April 1842, 30 October 1842, 17 January 1843, *F.O. 126/11*; 8 January 1843, *F.O. 11/1*.

    U.S. Minister J. Appleton, reporting from Chuquisaca, 1 May 1849, considered Argentine opposition to be the most significant cause of failure.

    See also (i) Mauricio Bach, *Descripción de la Nueva Provincia de Otuquis en Bolivia*, Buenos Aires, 1843, *F.O. 11/10*; (ii) 'Map of the Headwaters of the river Paraguay as far as Fort Borbón', José León de Oliden, 1836.

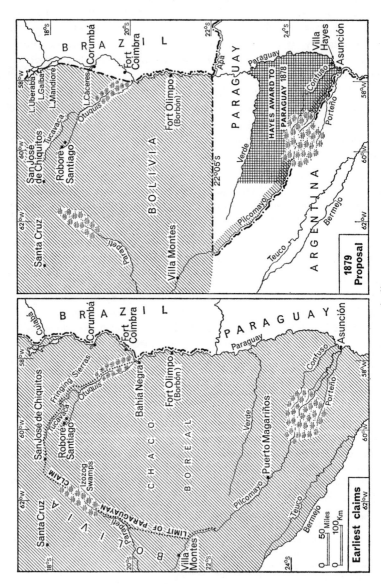

Earliest claims

1879 Proposal

(a–b)

172

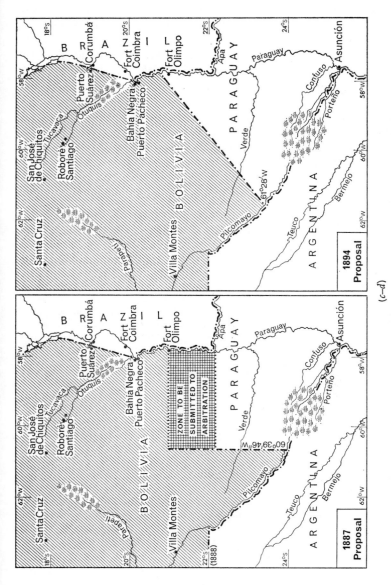

(c–d)

11 (a–d) Bolivia and Paraguay – earliest claims and nineteenth-century proposals for access to the middle Paraguay river, and for ownership of the Chaco Boreal

Problems beset the furthering of the project at every turn, and long before those of the swampy terrain and unnavigable Tucavaca and Otuquis were even considered, the unwillingness of Brazil, Paraguay and Argentina to see a foreign flag displayed on the river Paraguay was decisive. This involved also an unwillingness to see the Bolivian flag displayed on that country's behalf by European colonists. In any event, Brazilian settlement was already a notable feature of the right as well as the left bank of the Paraguay river, and Brazilian penetration for several miles into Bolivian territory, as claimed, was by then so well established as to be marked as such on maps of the period.[1] Nor was it a new feature, for early Portuguese/Brazilian advances in this section had been one of the reasons raised by Bolívar in 1825 to explain his lack of confidence in the future of an independent Upper Peru.[2]

Thus, in referring to land west of the Paraguay river awaiting determination between Paraguay and Bolivia, the former British Minister in Peru observed that: 'to no portion of such territories has Brazil any right, or does she lay claim. On the other hand...Brazil has peopled all the banks of the rivers on the east side of the Paraguay which flow into that river until within a short distance of Asunción.'[3] With reference to Brazilian settlement on the *west* side of the river, Masterton had already

[1] E.g. 'Map of the Province of Matto Grosso in Brazil, of the Provinces of Chiquitos, and of the Cordillera of the Department of Santa Cruz, of the Province of Otuquis and of the Department of Tarija in Bolivia; with the navigation of the rivers of Cuiabá, Paraguay, Jaurú, Otuquis and Pilcomayo', Mauricio Bach and Augusto Severger, Cuiabá, December 1843, *P.R.O. Map Collection MPK 42*. On this manuscript map, between approximately 16° S and 20° S, a line drawn to delimit territory claimed by the Brazilians is placed 40–100 miles *west* of the Paraguay and the 1777 San Ildefonso line, i.e. *inside* Bolivian territory as claimed at independence.

[2] 'It appears that the Brazilian commander...with between three or four hundred men... has possession of Chiquitos...General Bolívar is greatly incensed', U. Passmore, British Consul in Arequipa, to J. Planta, 7 June 1825, *F.O. 61/5*.

[3] B. H. Wilson to the Earl of Malmesbury, London, 1 June 1852, *F.O. 11/10*. Wilson had received a letter from Andrés Santa Cruz, Paris, 29 April 1852: 'Up to the present moment, the question of right to the whole of the territory has been received with indifference [in Bolivia], on account of its being so far from our principal towns, therefore nobody has been at the trouble to enter upon a serious investigation of its Geography with a view to determining the boundaries.'

In 1837, in contrast to the more frequent complaints about Brazilian encroachment into Bolivia, Brazil had complained that Bolivian authorities in Chiquitos were reported to have apportioned lands in the Province of Matto Grosso, supposing them to be Bolivian territory. Assuming that Chiquitos officials had acted without government approval, the Brazilian Foreign Minister instructed his Chargé d'Affaires in Bolivia to request that injunctions be issued, preserving the 1777 Ildefonso treaty boundaries until a new treaty could be concluded. (From the Brazilian Foreign Minister's Annual Report to the Legislative Assembly, forwarded by Hamilton Hamilton to Lord Palmerston, Rio de Janeiro, 24 May 1837, *F.O. 13/134*.)

noted in Chuquisaca that 'though the Brazilians are not entitled to such occupation, they will not be easily induced to abandon it'. For did Brazilian ranchers in this region not say that Brazil would claim as far as Brazilian cattle roamed?

The failure of the Otuquis concession was immediately followed in Bolivia by an investigation into a possible alternative route to the Paraguay *via* the Pilcomayo river. To this end, the construction of three small boats was completed in the Department of Tarija in 1843. English carpenters had been specially recruited for the work in Chile and, upon completion, the boats were carried in sections down to Magariños on the Pilcomayo. At this point the expedition to Asunción was scheduled to begin. 'The lack of sailors in a country essentially unmaritime leaves the men, and their command (adventurers, not scientific persons), all under the "landlubber" category', was Masterton's laconic comment. In January and February 1844 the flotilla had managed to proceed only ten leagues downstream in thirty-seven days, before running aground in sixteen inches of water. Depths of as little as four inches lay ahead, but even while reconnaissance work was being undertaken, sudden floods surged down the river and all three vessels were completely wrecked.[1] Carrying their wounded, for the crews had been continually harassed by Toba Indian attack, the survivors limped back on foot.

The news that the Pilcomayo diminished into a trickle and then vanished into a swamp was received with widespread gloom and dismay in central and south-eastern Bolivia. Considerable hope had been pinned to the Pilcomayo as a navigable outlet to the Paraguay, particularly as a journey upstream from Asunción to the Pilcomayo's Cahiza Falls (in the Andean foothills) by a Jesuit Padre Gabriel Patiño was supposed to have formed a precedent for the trip more than a century earlier. Indeed Patiño's journal of the voyage was still in print and contained no mention of the severity of the swamps interrupting the Pilcomayo, swamps which were now bitterly to be dubbed Esteros de Patiño. Although five hundred troops were soon dispatched to construct a road south-eastwards from Tarija to the Paraguay through the Chaco Central, it was of little avail. No commercial penetration was tempted beyond the Chaco fringe, while parts of the Chaco itself occasionally assumed for Bolivia the characteristics of a military frontier. Troops were periodically directed to patrol the upper

[1] 'Abridged Account of the Capabilities of the river Pilcomayo for navigation, being the results of the observations of the flotilla of discovery wrecked in that river on its way from Port Magariños to Paraguay', encl. by C. Masterton to J. Bidwell, Chuquisaca, 17 June 1844, *F.O. 11/2*; also note, 24 August 1843, *F.O. 126/11*.

Paraguay river. In July 1846, for example, three hundred men were armed in Santa Cruz and dispatched to take Fort Coimbra (significantly, on the west bank of the Paraguay) by assault, and 'drive back the Brazilians to the limits assigned to them in 1777'.

4. RIVAL NINETEENTH-CENTURY CLAIMS TO THE MIDDLE PARAGUAY

During the years which followed Bolivia's first unsuccessful attempts to navigate both the Paraguay and the Pilcomayo, the country could keep no more than a watching brief upon the movements of others whose frontiers also lay somewhere in the unknown wastes of the Chaco. The courses of rivers, real or imagined, inevitably supported the framework of the early treaties, for all rivers were evaluated first in terms of their location, and the access they could provide to the main stem of the region's communication system – the Paraguay river itself.

Among the first tentative claims after independence involving Chaco territory were those of July 1852, when a treaty of Limits, Commerce and Navigation between Argentina and Paraguay stated (in Article IV) that the Paraguay river, south of Brazilian claims (unspecified) and as far as its confluence with the Paraná, belonged from bank to bank to Paraguay.[1] This was quickly countered by an official protest from Bolivia on 22 August 1852, in which Bolivia's right as a riverine State on the west bank of the Paraguay river, at least as far south as 22° S, were reiterated.[2] Argentina's reply was non-committal, which Bolivia chose to interpret favourably. Bolivia ignored also the implication of Article V, which stated that navigation of the Bermejo was common to Argentina and Paraguay (an agreement repeated in their treaty of 1856), and of Article XII which permitted Paraguay, whenever invited to do so by Argentina, to open and garrison a port on the river Pilcomayo at the highest navigable point. From this port it was observed that commerce might be encouraged by a road through Paraguayan territory to the frontier of Bolivia.

Brazil also made known its reservations upon the terms of the 1852 Argentine–Paraguay treaty, the first to break official silence upon national claims to navigable rivers in this region. A note from Brazil's Minister in Buenos Aires to the Argentine Foreign Minister on 26 August 1852[3] recorded disapproval that the term 'Brazilian possessions' had been included without Brazil having been party to the treaty; also that, lately in receipt of Bolivia's note stressing its claims to the Paraguay's west bank,

[1] F.O. 59/2.   [2] *Ibid.*   [3] F.O. 59/3.

Brazil took the opportunity of declaring that it was not prepared to accept Bolivia's status as riverine between 20° S and 22° S unless Brazil, in subsequent negotiations, ceded Bolivia such a tract.

Not surprisingly, Bolivia was continually on the defensive in such diplomatic sparring, and decided to attempt at least a verbal initiative by the publication of a new and determinedly optimistic decree on 27 January 1853.[1] This declared the rivers of Bolivia to be free and open to world commerce:

> The Eastern and Southern parts of the Republic embrace vast territories of prodigious fertility, intersected by navigable rivers which, running into the Amazon and the Plata, present the most natural vehicles for the trade, settlement and civilisation of these districts...By the law of nature and of nations, confirmed by modern European conventions, and applied in the New World to the navigation of the Mississippi, Bolivia as possessor of the Pilcomayo, its tributaries, and the upper part of the Madeira; of the left bank of the Itenes, from its junction with the Sararé, as far as where it mingles with the Mamoré; of the western bank of the Paraguay from the Marco del Jaurú [i.e. the marble obelisk, see p. 94] as far as 26° 34′ S; and of the upper part and left bank of the Bermejo – has a right to navigate these rivers, from the point where such navigation is practicable in her own territory, as far as where they enter the sea, without any power being at liberty to arrogate an exclusive sovereignty over the Amazon and the Plata.

A large number of river settlements within Bolivia were declared free ports, including the Bahía Negra and Borbón Point on the Paraguay river, and Magariños on the Pilcomayo (although Magariños was quite inaccessible to navigation from the Plata–Paraná–Paraguay waterway as it lay on the northern side of the great Pilcomayo swamps). In extending 'the unquestionable rights possessed by Bolivia to navigate these rivers to the Atlantic', land grants were also promised, from one league to twelve leagues square, to companies or individuals who approached any of the free ports from the Atlantic, intending to establish agricultural or commercial enterprises there. Moreover, a prize of U.S. $10,000 was offered to the first steam vessel making the trip to any one of the free ports *via* the Amazon or the Plate.

A letter addressed to the Prefects of the various Departments within Bolivia accompanied the Decree:

> Unable ourselves to carry out this navigation on account of the depopulated nature of the country, its want of resources and industrial means, the Government has deemed it more proper to leave this stupendous enterprise to the efforts and

---

[1] Submitted by A. Alvarez, on behalf of R. Bustillo, to Secretary of State Edward Everett, 20 February 1853, Notes from the Bolivian Legation in the United States to the Department of State, *General Records of the Dept. of State, Record Group 59*.

emulation of the mercantile nations of the world...for a vast portion of Bolivian territories towards the eastern frontiers of the Republic have been for a long time usurped, which frontiers had been so clearly defined by the treaties of 1750 and 1777.

The January 1853 Decree should be considered first in the light of the two major attempts already made, unsuccessfully, to grant land concessions to foreign colonists in eastern Bolivia – colonists who were inevitably to have been entirely dependent upon freedom of navigation through Brazil, Argentina or Paraguay. The earlier concession had been that to Oliden in 1832, relying upon the Paraguay–Paraná–Plata routeway; the second to The Franco–Bolivian Company of the Mamoré in 1844, dependent upon the Amazon routeway for its success (see pp. 99–100). Whatever criticisms could be levelled at these two ambitious projects, both had failed to survive even the planning stages because of the concerted opposition raised to the principle of free navigation.

Nevertheless, such action by Bolivia in the attempted promotion of settlement within, and of navigation beyond its eastern lands on the Amazon and Plata systems must also be viewed in the wider context. There was growing interest, and increasing pressure, particularly by the U.S.A., Britain and France, for the securing of freedom of navigation on the major rivers of South America. Indeed, both the United States' and Britain's recognition of Paraguay, for example, were made conditional upon the securing of free navigation on the Paraguay–Paraná network, and were thus delayed until 1852.[1] Only then, with the successful outcome of specially accredited missions, did the United States, Britain and France recognise the independence of Paraguay and agree to diplomatic representation in Asunción.[2]

In July 1866 Bolivia once again found cause to express its anxiety over terms agreed by foreign powers concerning territorial claims along the Paraguay.[3] The case in point formed Article XVI of the Treaty of Offensive

[1] F.O. 59/1.
[2] Following the agreement to open the Paraguay–Paraná, in 1853 the United States sent a naval frigate under the command of Lieut. T. J. Page, to explore the river and its principal tributaries. In 1859, on a second expedition, Page extended his investigations above Corumbá and reached Lake Uberaba, Bolivia, on the upper Paraguay. Lewis Joel, U.S. Consul at Cobija, 'supposing that any news of Capt Page's movements would be acceptable to the Department', reported receipt of a notice from Chuquisaca. In it, the Corregidor of San Matías recorded Page's visit to Lake Oberaba (*sic*) in September 1859: 'He has left his ship at the entrance of the lake in the river Paraguay...Tommorrow we return to Salinas (from Santo Corazón), being very sorry for not having visited the Otuquis from this side, the road being shut up and nobody could be got to show him the entrance of this river into "Bahia-negra"...According to probability we will soon have a port [on Lake Uberaba], at least so Mr Page promises.' But nothing more was heard of this.
[3] F.O. 13/446.

and Defensive Alliance signed by Argentina, Brazil and Uruguay in May 1865[1] as a result of Paraguay's declaration of war, an article which confirmed that with the successful completion of hostilities the Gran Chaco and the entire west bank of the Paraguay river as far north as Bahía Negra would belong exclusively to Argentina. In the event, however, Bolivia was not to be faced, at least at this stage, with the problem of maintaining a foothold *de jure* on the west bank of the Paraguay:

> Although the Argentine Government appear to claim the right bank of the river Paraguay as far up as the Brazilian frontier [Bahía Negra], they are willing to acknowledge that Bolivia has a right to an intervening space from the Brazilian frontier to the river Pilcomayo, and they would even consent upon certain conditions to cede to Bolivia as far down as the river Bermejo; but both the Brazilian and Argentine Governments think it very desirable that Paraguay should at no point have dominion over both banks of the river of that name.[2]

Even so, Bolivia itself remained uncertain of Argentina's intentions at a time when the country's boundary negotiations had already reached crisis proportions simultaneously with both Chile and Brazil. The 1866 treaty with Chile had yielded the Atacama panhandle and Pacific shoreline as far north as 24° S, and accepted further economic penetration by Chile as far north as 23° S. The 1867 (Muñoz–Netto) treaty with Brazil had subsequently yielded enormous areas in the northern rubber forests, in return for free navigational facilities through Brazilian territory to the sea. But not only had Bolivia withdrawn behind the Madeira cataracts with the pegging of the oblique-line boundary to 10° 20′ S; it had also signed away its claims to the right bank of the river Paraguay as far south as 20° 10′ S (Bahía Negra),[3] a major withdrawal from a line of movement hitherto shared (*de jure*) with Brazil. The new boundary touched only the shallow lakes of Cáceres, Mandioré, Gaíba and Uberaba, leaving both banks of the intervening Paraguay within Brazilian territory. Thus it is not surprising that Bolivia continued to express the gravest anxiety over the terms of the 1865 Treaty of Triple Alliance, which supported Argentina's future possession of the right bank of the Paraguay as far north as Bahía Negra, since its ratification would effectively sever Bolivia from the Paraguay waterway.

Bolivian pressure after 1865 for clarification of Article XVI resulted in the

---

[1] F.O. 6/256.

[2] Confidential report of a personal interview with the Argentine Foreign Minister by E. Thornton to Earl Russell, Buenos Aires, 11 May 1865, *ibid.*

[3] The confluence of the small river Negro with the Paraguay, taken as 20° 10′ S, was often referred to as Bahía Negra. A little farther south, the small port of Bahía Negra lay at 20° 13′ S.

conclusion of a treaty with Argentina in July 1868.[1] But the phrasing respecting boundaries was still vague and Bolivia immediately sought a more precise arrangement, fearing that Argentina might well implement its claims, recorded in the Triple Alliance Treaty, while mobilised for the war with Paraguay. It was decided, therefore, by a protocol in February 1869[2] to suspend further discussion until after the war (in which Bolivia was involved), with the added proposal that difficulties which might arise should be settled by arbitration.

Inevitably, Paraguay was defeated by the combined efforts of Argentina, Brazil and Uruguay in 1870. But nothing positive resulted from Bolivia's request for a boundary settlement. Argentina meanwhile, whatever its intentions concerning Bolivia may have been, found itself thwarted in the claim for the whole of the Gran Chaco and the west bank portion of the Paraguay river largely through the opposition of Brazil, which bolstered the claims of the defeated Paraguay. Brazil's determination to preserve the latter as a buffer State against Argentine expansion prevented the complete pinching out of Paraguay from the political map after this disastrous war. By the terms of the Peace Treaty of 1876, and the Hayes Award of 1878, the Pilcomayo river was confirmed as the boundary between Argentina and Paraguay, and Argentina relinquished its claims to the Chaco Boreal.

The Hayes Award represented the final boundary settlement between Argentina and Paraguay after the War of the Triple Alliance. Land between the Verde and the main arm of the Pilcomayo had been submitted for arbitration to the U.S.A. in 1876, and was awarded by President Hayes in 1878 to Paraguay (Fig. 11 *b*), The whole section, of course, lay within the great wedge of Chaco territory claimed by Bolivia at independence, but no reference was made to this point, considered only an academic one, by the U.S. arbitration. The award represented the first official distribution elsewhere of Bolivia's Chaco claims, although to claim as far south as the mouth of the Bermejo had generally been considered extreme, even by Bolivians, who were by this time more concerned with holding their claims on the Paraguay river between 20° S and 22° S.

Thus in 1878 the Pilcomayo emerged undeservedly unscathed as the apparent *sine qua non* of boundary delimitation in the Chaco. It was estab-

---

[1] L. Markbreit to Secretary of State Hamilton Fish, Cochabamba, 6 February 1870 (enclosure), Diplomatic Despatches from Bolivia, *General Records of the Dept. of State, Record Group 59*; *Col. Trat. Vig. Bol.*, vol. IV, pp. 35–46. A lack of precision in Article xx caused the Bolivian Assembly to reject the treaty until this article was modified. Article xII was of extreme importance, however, as it guaranteed Bolivia free navigation on the river Plate and its affluents. [2] *Ibid* pp. 52–5.

lished by Hayes as the new boundary between Argentina and Paraguay, without any additional qualification, and Paraguay's ownership of that part of the Chaco Boreal lying between the Verde, the Paraguay and the Pilcomayo was confirmed. So also was its possession of the river port of Villa Occidental, called Nueva Bordeos by French colonists in 1855, and now gratefully renamed Villa Hayes. Argentina was contained south of the Pilcomayo in the Chaco Central and Chaco Austral. Inevitably the river was to prove a most unsatisfactory choice as an international boundary. Nothing appeared to be known (or recalled) in the U.S. State Department's records of the confusingly compound nature of the lower Pilcomayo. Not until attention was directed away from the few inaccurate maps available in Washington on which the river was still drawn as a continuous line, to detailed survey in the field, was the exasperating unreliability of the Pilcomayo's course again revealed – and an interminably wearying series of disputes initiated.

Bolivia remained unreconciled to the Hayes Award, and hard on its heels in 1879 came the first of a series of boundary delimitations in the Chaco Boreal between Bolivia and Paraguay which was to stretch inconclusively over the next fifty years and end, almost unbelievably, in war. Throughout this period, the protracted negotiations have been frequently dismissed merely as the antic performance of two weak nations – the time-consuming, flag-waving apportionment between themselves of a waste land. Yet the ready appraisal of the Chaco question as a diversionary, almost ludicrous display of filibustering by two territory- and prestige-conscious minor States is incomplete. Relevant though these attitudes were in part, diplomatic exchanges were motivated by the desire for, or denial of, access to the Paraguay river. As possible sites on the Paraguay and Pilcomayo rivers between which a boundary line might be slung were tentatively suggested, so huge slabs of the intervening Chaco Boreal automatically fell, on paper at least, to Bolivia or Paraguay. But the changing geometry of ownership in the Chaco merely reflected the only important issue – the balance of power poised upon the river Paraguay. For it was not until the closing phases of the boundary negotiations that the essential problem of accessibility became complicated by other considerations of a possible intrinsic merit in the Chaco territory itself.

In October 1879 representatives Quijarro of Bolivia and Decoud of Paraguay, meeting in Asunción, suggested the parallel of latitude 22° 05′ S between the rivers Pilcomayo and Paraguay, as a possible line of demarcation (Fig. 11 b). This would have provided Bolivia with about two hundred miles of the Paraguay's west bank, as far as the Apa mouth (although this is at 22° 6′ 45″ S). In addition, however, Bolivia claimed sufficient territory on the east bank of the Pilcomayo, *below the great swamps,* to establish at least one port. As this involved land which Paraguay considered well within the area acquired by the Hayes Award, the treaty remained unratified.

Exploitation, even penetration of the Chaco by Bolivia remained negligible, although occasional concessions were made along the west bank of the Paraguay which provided test cases of intent and foreign reaction. In March 1879 a Francisco J. Brabo had requested a concession in the Oriente from the Bolivian Government in order to colonize portions of the Chaco, Chiquitos and Beni. The following month he approached Uruguay, to explore the possibilities of securing sufficient land on the coast near Nueva Palmira to establish a transit port from Bolivia, and this appears to have been favourably received in Montevideo. Details of the plan, in the southern sector, for a steamboat service on the Paraguay and railways from this river to the towns of Santa Cruz, Lagunillas and Higuerones (as surveyed by J. B. Minchin), were published in London on 18 November 1879. The proposed company, however, failed to raise the required capital, and the concession lapsed.[1]

In 1880, another project was launched. Bolivian developer, Miguel Suárez Arana, was granted permission to construct two roads across the Oriente: one between Santa Cruz and Lake Cáceres and the other from Lagunillas to Santiago de Chiquitos. On Lake Cáceres, Suárez was granted a sufficiently large area on the Bolivian shore to establish a port, and here he proceeded to erect a few dwellings and the nucleus of Puerto Suárez.[2] But the terms of the 1867 treaty with Brazil had left the western shores of lakes Cáceres, Mandioré, Gaíba and Uberaba without any direct access on to the Paraguay river. North of 20° 10′ S, all Bolivian port construction in relation to the upper Paraguay was quite meaningless, for the 1867 treaty terms had nullified all Paraguay-orientated concessions along the Brazilian boundary.

In consequence, Suárez Arana turned his attention southward, to a point below Bahía Negra where direct access on to the middle Paraguay could

[1] Memorandum from Ministry of Finance and Industry to President of National Chamber of Deputies, La Paz, 15 July 1880; F. J. Brabo to President of National Chamber of Deputies, La Paz, 1 August 1880 (encl. by Charles Adams to Secretary of State William M. Evarts, La Paz, 14 August 1880, Diplomatic Despatches from Bolivia, *General Records of the Dept. of State, Record Group 59*).

[2] It is sometimes wrongly assumed that Puerto Suárez was established by Nicolás Suárez, as part of the Suárez Hermanos organisation which later dominated Beni and Pando. The Suárez brothers, however, had no connexion with the Lake Cáceres concession.

still be attempted. It was to be nearly another twenty years before Bolivia regained access to the river Paraguay at a few points above Bahía Negra by treaty settlement with Brazil in 1903, although the reality of access was, even then, to prove somewhat illusory. No port worth the name was ever to be maintained along these west-bank swamp sections of the river Paraguay. In the 1880s, however, a site south of Bahía Negra was still feasible and attention, therefore, was focused to that end. Just below Bahía Negra, on the west bank of the Paraguay, Suárez Arana exercised a new concession, and in July 1885 founded a small trading station there named Puerto Pacheco in honour of the Bolivian President, Gregorio Pacheco, who had supported the enterprise with great enthusiasm. The possibility of a wagon road, even a railway, was mooted between Puerto Pacheco and La Paz, but at the end of 1887 the tiny port was attacked and captured by a Paraguayan gunboat. Paraguay declared the entire west bank as far as Bahía Negra to be a military zone, controlled by the garrison at Fort Olimpo (formerly known as Fort Borbón), seventy miles downstream.

Diplomatic relations between Bolivia and Paraguay were broken, and remained so for the following eighteen months. Earlier, in February 1887, suggestions had been made for a triple division of the Chaco Boreal by the Tamayo–Aceval lines, with a central zone to be submitted to arbitration by the King of the Belgians (Fig. 11*c*). But this treaty also remained unratified while both States collected evidence to support their claims to the whole Chaco Boreal. Adherence to legal processes and historical records, however, revived the age-old problem – both parties could justifiably claim the same area on the basis of colonial grants since these had frequently overlapped, or been inaccurately drawn. In 1894 a new approach to the problem was the institution of the oblique line, the Ichaso–Benítez line, which was to run from a point on the river Paraguay three leagues north of Fort Olimpo, south-westwards to the Pilcomayo at 61° 28′ W (Fig. 11*d*). Like its predecessors, this straight line got no further than the conference table, although Goblet has called it the least absurd proposal.[1]

In the closing years of the nineteenth century, discussions grew more protracted. Unlike the circumstances associated with boundary disputes along other sections of the Bolivian frontier, nothing that could be regarded as large-scale exploitation added point to the arguments of either

[1] Y. M. Goblet, *Le Crépuscule des Traités*, Paris, 1934; English edition, *The Twilight of Treaties*, London, 1936, p. 186. The oblique line had the advantage of greater simplicity, although it continued to confine Bolivia north of, i.e. on the wrong side of, the great Pilcomayo swamps. Paraguay's resolve to exclude Bolivia from the Paraguay river was intensifying, so that refusal to ratify was not unexpected.

State. Of the two, however, Paraguay had begun to permit some vicarious penetration into the Chaco by Argentine, American and English companies to exploit the *quebracho* forests for timber and tannin, and the more open range for beef.[1] The Paraguayan Government, crippled by debt and anxious to encourage speculators, had begun to concede belts of country to foreign investors: strips which ran back into the Chaco for twenty or thirty miles at one-league intervals along the river Paraguay's west bank. No systematic survey was made as the great plain, with its creeks, swamps, *palmar* and *quebracho*, was divided arbitrarily in Asunción into huge paddocks. Lawsuits proliferated, particularly when land grants fenced off the all-important dry-season water supply, or denied access to 'islands' of slightly higher ground without which cattle frequently drowned or starved during the floods. Trails and, in a few cases, railways ran back into the interior from the small river ports which grew along the west bank of the Paraguay at the end of the nineteenth and beginning of the twentieth century:

> Some of the prospective landowners acquired huge tracts of land...but, in most cases, they didn't know what they were buying...At one place an ill-defined track meanders out to a mission; at another a narrow *decauville* line pokes out a skinny finger in the interests of a *quebracho* company;[2] at a third a cattle-breeder fences in a further slab of land for his increasing herds. But for the most part the back-blocks remain unknown, virgin, genuinely unexplored.[3]

With the continuing failure of Bolivia in the nineteenth century to establish a foothold anywhere at all on the right bank of the Paraguay, penetration

[1] Mission settlement also could be noted, although it was very localised at this period. The Church of England's South American Missionary Society had begun work in the region in 1889 and this is described by W. Barbrooke Grubb in *A Church in the Wilds*, London, 1914.

[2] A narrow-gauge railway, from *Chemin de fer Decauville*. The French manufacturer Paul Decauville (1846–1922) developed an easily assembled narrow-gauge track composed of prefabricated sections (metal rails and sleepers riveted together) which could be laid quickly and cheaply. It was widely used in overseas territories for hauling agricultural produce.

[3] M. H. Gibson, *Gran Chaco Calling*, London, 1934, p. 35. This record of travel and adventure contains useful incidental information on various aspects of foreign exploitation in the 'Paraguayan' Chaco begun at the turn of the century. Later, World War I was to stimulate the demand for low-grade beef, and packing plants increased along the Paraguay river banks. The American International Products Company, which controlled the *quebracho* mill at Puerto Pinasco and the Pinasco Railroad, were important meat packers. The type of frontier settlement sponsored by Paraguay at this period is usefully recorded by a prismatic-compass traverse of the Chaco along latitude 23° 31′ S, approximately between 57° W and 61° W (C. N. Blood *et al.*, Oct. 1921–Jan. 1922, *Roy. Geog. Soc. map collection*). The traverse notes *palmar*, *quebracho*, much swamp and stagnant water, and the position of waterholes vital in the dry season. In addition the grazing lands of the Paraguay Land and Cattle Co., occasional mission centres, and Indian settlements are also plotted on this representative cross-section of the Chaco Boreal.

into the Chaco remained minimal, and what little settlement there was clung mainly to the western periphery, close to the junction of mountain and plain. About twenty Franciscan missions had been established south of Santa Cruz between 1850 and 1890. In addition, a thin line of trading settlements extended southward along the Andean foothill zone from Santa Cruz, through Charagua, Cuevo, Boyuibe and Camatindi to Villa Montes on the Pilcomayo, and beyond again to Yacuiba and Tartagal.

These small Chaco-fringe settlements survived, therefore, as mission centres, way-stations or ranching towns, trailing cattle periodically southward into Argentina, whence they in turn received their supplies. Even then, despite shortages, Chaco beef was generally of poor quality and difficult to sell to the Argentine *frigoríficos*. More often than not, it was disposed of as jerked beef and, as such, was never in greater demand than during the years at the turn of the century, when the rubber boom in the northern forests led to a meat boom in the central and southern plains. For about three decades this northern market provided an alternative outlet for ranchers, as well as for rice and sugar planters, in the south-east. The tempo and scale of activity in the rubber regions were far-reaching in their effects, particularly before the construction of the Madeira–Mamoré Railway, which eased communication with the Amazon routeway and, to some extent, increased the import of cheaper foreign foodstuffs into the northern territories, at the expense of lowland Bolivia's own products. But once the rubber boom had collapsed, the orientation of Bolivia's few Chaco-fringe settlements was again almost exclusively southward into Argentina, particularly as new railway links between the *altiplano* and the Pacific were similarly facilitating the import of foreign foodstuffs into the more densely populated western highlands, and thereby increasing the oppressive isolation of the Oriente.

5. BOLIVIA'S SOUTHERN FRONTIER: TRAIL AND RAIL INTO ARGENTINA

While the unsuccessful attempts to acquire and retain a frontage on the river Paraguay, or even on the lower Pilcomayo, traced an ever-more complicated series of lines across maps of the Chaco Boreal during the nineteenth century, some attention had also to be given to the territories farther west. In this portion of Bolivia's 'southern lands', treaty settlement with Argentina, rather than with Brazil and Paraguay, was required after the long period of silence which had followed the transfer of Tarija in 1826. Little effort had subsequently been made to delimit the boundary with Argentina for almost forty years, and even then it was in the form of an agitated complaint from Bolivia over Argentina's claim in 1865 to the west bank of the Paraguay, south of Bahía Negra.

A further period of twenty-three years passed by as desultory discussion, and occasionally quite bitter dispute ensued between Buenos Aires and Chuquisaca over the former limits of the Viceroyalty of the Río de la Plata, and their relationship with those of Upper Peru. If, as Argentina claimed, that region was strictly interpreted as the four provinces (Intendancies, Presidency) of La Paz, Cochabamba (which included the city and bishopric of Santa Cruz de la Sierra), Chuquisaca (La Plata or Charcas), and Potosí, then the bulk of lowland Bolivia lying within the extensive mission provinces of Mojos and Chiquitos was excluded.[1] Instead of being part of an Upper Peru which had declared its independence from both Lima and Buenos Aires on 6 August 1825, Argentina contended that the separation of these provinces from the bishopric of Santa Cruz in 1777 had placed Mojos and Chiquitos legally under the administration of Buenos Aires when the new Viceroyalty of the Río de la Plata had been created. As a result, therefore, quite apart from the early friction over Tarija, by then old history, Argentina disputed a Bolivian boundary on the Bermejo river on the ground of *uti possidetis de jure 1810*, although it was clearly not going to be feasible for Argentina to press its claim to a northern boundary on the Guaporé–Mamoré–Beni river triangle within the rubber forests! In fact, because of their frontier location, the provinces of Mojos and Chiquitos had been subject to a distinctive form of joint colonial administration from both Buenos Aires and Chuquisaca.

Together with Montevideo and the *pueblos de misiones*, the provinces of Mojos and Chiquitos also continued as military governments outside the intendant system and immediately subordinate to the viceroy. *All four were significant exceptions to the régime because they were distant frontier regions where contiguity with Portuguese territory demanded a specialized government* . . . The governors of Mojos and Chiquitos were subordinate in exchequer matters to the superintendent and in economic affairs – industry, agriculture and commerce – to the *audiencia* of Charcas.[2]

In June 1888 the parallel of 22° S, as far as its intersection with the Pilcomayo, was made the provisional boundary between Bolivia and Argentina in the little-known Chaco. Farther west, no detailed delimitation was recorded and it was understood that neither country was to advance beyond its actual possessions. Such vagueness was partially remedied in

[1] *F.O. 11/4.*
[2] J. Lynch, *Spanish Colonial Administration, 1782–1810*, p. 68 (my italics).

May 1889[1] when a boundary through the mountain and foothill country was outlined, but Argentina was still not satisfied, demanding in 1891[2] that the line in the high Andes section should be shifted from the eastern branch of the Cordillera to the line of the highest peaks. In this region these ran through the western branch of the Cordillera, and in 1892–3 Bolivia agreed to yield to Argentina the corner of the high windswept inter-montane plateau known as Puna de Atacama.[3]

Considerable confusion arose when the 1889 and 1891 delimitations were surveyed in the field. For both the Argentine and Bolivian com-missioners had studied inaccurate maps of the frontier (including that of Martin de Moussy, Paris, 1866), and had selected a series of physical features to carry the boundary which were found to be quite differently located when demarcation was attempted. In general, the position of the boundary was influenced by the distribution of predominantly Argentine or predominantly Bolivian settlement, with mountain peaks and selected sections of river courses included, where appropriate, to aid definition and recognition of the line. It was not an easy task, for in addition to the in-accuracy of the available maps, the boundary was transverse to the Andean ridges and, running against the 'grain' of the country, was inevitably composed of a series of relatively short and varied sections which increased the margin of error.

Exploration revealed ignorance of the positions of Zapalegui (Zapaleri) peak at the western end of the boundary, the Quiaca ravine, Porongal peak and the Porongal river, and in fact almost all the relative positions of the settlements and streams which had been included in the 1889 and 1891 delimitations. One of the more serious errors discovered by Bolivia was that the settlements of Yacuiba and Tartagal lay on the wrong side of the boundary line running between the Itaú and Pilcomayo rivers, i.e. south of latitude 22° S. Yacuiba in particular, capital of the Gran Chaco province, was regarded as an important Bolivian frontier station. At 22° 1′ S, however, it was found to lie one and a half miles inside Argentina, which resulted in renewed discussions at the conference table, and the signing of

---

[1] *F.O. 11/32; Col. Trat. Vig. Bol.*, vol. IV, pp. 70–6.   [2] *F.O. 11/32.*

[3] The main section of the Puna de Atacama remained politically unsettled. After Bolivia had lost the Litoral Department to Chile during the War of the Pacific, and withdrawn behind the 1884 mountain truce line, Chile and Argentina had still to determine how they would arrange their boundaries in a part of the country vacated by Bolivia and beyond. Part of the high Puna passed to Chile in 1884, but in 1899 a portion was ceded to Argentina, as a result of an arbitration award by the United States, to become the territory of Los Andes. (This finalised the boundary between Zapalegui (Zapaleri) peak and 26° 52′ 45″ S, while south of this again the Argentina–Chile boundary was the subject of King Edward VII's award in 1902.)

an additional protocol on 26 January 1904 to rectify the anomaly. Argentina agreed to cede Yacuiba to Bolivia, and with it a sixty-square-mile triangular piece of land adjoining the Pocitos gully, in order that the town and its immediate surroundings should remain under Bolivian ownership. Before this protocol was ratified, however, relations between the two countries suffered a sharp setback over Argentina's 1909 Arbitration Award on the northern section of the Bolivia–Peru boundary (see pp. 143–5). Widespread rioting and demonstrations against Argentina had followed. Bolivia broke off diplomatic relations and, despite mediation by Mexico, refused to attend the Pan-American Congress in Buenos Aires. Argentina, in turn, refused to ratify the 1904 Yacuiba protocol,[1] although its opposition was later withdrawn, and diplomatic relations between Bolivia and Argentina were restored on 14 December 1910.[2]

Although the population of Tartagal, forty miles beyond Yacuiba, was also dominated by Bolivians at this period, Argentina was not prepared to waive its authority thus far south. When the final boundary settlement was at last achieved in July 1925, it was agreed that adjustment be made to include the Yacuiba triangle officially within Bolivian territory.[3] Argentina subsequently established a consulate in Yacuiba, but no custom house was encountered until the traveller had penetrated several miles into Argentine territory. Nevertheless, a journey along the foothill country between Villa Montes and Tartagal revealed the position of the frontier in other ways:

The contrast between the modern homes and thrifty appearance of the northern Argentine towns and *haciendas* on the one hand, and the squalid huts and vast vacant spaces of eastern Bolivia on the other, is an object lesson which cannot but direct attention toward the possibilities of the more northern area. The frontier of civilization is creeping northward along the mountain front; in the next few years one may confidently expect great changes in this pioneer land.[4]

[1] L. J. Jerome to Sir Edward Grey, La Paz, 5 September 1910, *F.O. 177/350*. It was subsequently rumoured that Argentina would retain Yacuiba and instead offer Bolivia some additional point on the river Pilcomayo, *F.O. 371/1050* and *F.O. 371/1914*.

[2] *F.O. 371/1050* and *F.O. 371/970*.

[3] *F.O. 371/21416*; *Col. Trat. Vig. Bol.*, vol. IV, pp. 99–106. Ratification of the July 1925 settlement was delayed, however. See below p. 211 and p. 218 n. 2. This treaty delimited the boundary as far as the Pilcomayo river but excluded any definitive statement on the location of the triple point with Paraguay, for the division of the Chaco Boreal between Bolivia and Paraguay was not finalised until 1938. Demarcation of the Bolivia–Argentine boundary by metal tripod posts was completed in 1953, since when minor adjustments to the position of certain boundary markers have been amicably concluded by Mixed Commissions.

[4] K. F. Mather, 'Along the Andean front in south-eastern Bolivia', *Geog. Rev.*, vol. XII, 1922, pp. 358–74. This reference p. 374.

The two long-established lines of movement crossing Bolivia's southern frontier were both primarily stock trails. Trade returns for the Salta–Tupiza route regularly recorded thousands of live animals imported annually into Bolivia, a movement dominated by mule herds until the end of the nineteenth century. By then the demand for pack mules was dwindling as more of the mining centres became linked by rail network; in 1895, for example, the mule trade had noticeably declined and out of the 35,762 live animals imported into Bolivia from Argentina,[1] almost two-thirds were sheep and cattle moving slowly up to the Andean centres. Animal imports on the hoof, nearly half of which were sheep, supplemented domestic supplies of wool and meat, and so modified the former emphasis on the mule transport trade.

Little else, under normal conditions, moved in significant quantities across this frontier between the principal Argentine and Bolivian towns, although local exchanges within a relatively restricted zone were not uncommon. Only when the Chilean blockade of the Pacific ports diverted Bolivian trade elsewhere in the 1879–82 period, and the exigencies of the 'Nitrate War' in general disrupted communications across the western desert, did the route southward to and from Buenos Aires briefly revive. The diversion of Bolivian silver, tin, and bismuth exports to Buenos Aires was recorded there in the 1883 official returns,[2] while the report from a former British Vice-Consul at Santiago, submitted after completing a journey through Argentina in 1883–4, made a similar observation.[3] It was noted that a high proportion of Bolivia's silver (£3,247,433-worth in 1883), was leaving *via* the Plata route, and that much of the in-coming cargo destined for Bolivia, mostly British, German and French manufactured goods, was moving up-river from Buenos Aires to Rosario de Sante Fe. Thence it was carried northward by train as far as Tucumán (though the railway had been extended north of the town), beyond which it continued the tediously long journey into the sierras by cart and pack-mule. As many as 25,000 mules had to be found for the sudden increase in traffic, for it is doubtful whether this old trail had been as busy since the days of the Viceroyalty.

After the War of the Pacific, a vigorous trans-Andean traffic in both *peón* labour and mules developed between Salta and the nitrate and copper centres in the Atacama. In this traffic San Pedro de Atacama complemented Salta on the western side of the Andes, acting as a gathering ground and distributing centre for the needs of the desert. Fresh meat supplies were

[1] *Op. cit.* p. 70 n. 2.   [2] *Op. cit.* p. 70 n. 1.
[3] James Seccombe to Earl Granville, London, 29 January 1885, *F.O. 11/31.*

no less important. *Criollo* cattle destined for the harsh journey across the Puna de Atacama came usually from the edge of the Chaco, for they were fast disappearing from the Argentine *pampas* farther south, where accelerated programs of selective breeding from imported stock and seeded pasture were being carried through, following the demands of the overseas export market. Chaco cattle remained large, bony, long-horned beasts, similar to those of Mexico and Texas and, like them, able to keep themselves alive under the most rigorous of conditions. The movement of meat on the hoof into Chile thus formed a second, east–west axis of trade passing through Salta and the border country.[1] At its established crossing places, therefore, although the scale of activity fluctuated considerably, this frontier had become a recognisable economic unit encompassing the edge of the Chaco, the mountain foothills and southern basins, the high Puna, and the desert fringe.

After 1890 the northward extensions of the Argentine rail network began a new phase in the life of this frontier country. In what amounted to a 'rail-for-trail' construction period, the new lines were to reinforce old patterns of movement, and direct them rather more consciously south-ward into Argentina. Between Salta and Jujuy, therefore, the Belgrano railway branched to follow the two traditional trails into Bolivia. To the north-west, it advanced through Humahuaca as far as La Quiaca at the Argentina–Bolivia boundary, over twelve hundred miles from Buenos Aires, and placed a perfect replica of a small English country railway station on the windswept plateau at well over 11,000 feet. Extension north-ward from La Quiaca into Bolivia, however, was long delayed, despite a series of rail conventions. Anxiety mounted as a gap of nearly one hundred miles between Villazón and Atocha remained open, and the French contractor's promised completion date of September 1918 passed by.[2] Other firms became increasingly disinclined to take over the work. It was widely rumoured that the Antofagasta(Chili) and Bolivia Railway Co. was obstructing the completion of the through-rail route to Buenos Aires 'behind the scenes', in order to retain their virtual monopoly *via* the Pacific outlet. Although this was not proved, freight rates through Chile and

---

[1] This east–west trade axis flourished between 1883 and 1918 during the nitrate boom in the Atacama. The line of movement has been revived since 1948 by the construction of a 559-mile railway between Salta and Antofagasta, which climbs to 14,680 ft as it crosses the Chorrillos Pass. It carries small (though increasing) quantities of the traditional exchange products, particularly live cattle, vegetables and dairy produce into Chile, but inevitably fails to pay its way. Little cargo between Chile and Bolivia ever moves along this rail route *via* Salta unless the Antofagasta–Ollagüe–Uyuni line is blocked with snow.

[2] The extension of the line from La Quiaca–Villazón to Tupiza, begun in 1912, was not com-pleted until 1924.

Peru were very high, and Bolivia made no secret of its need to promote competition, nor of its desire to forge some additional rail link to the ocean by way of Argentina (Fig. 4).

Eventually, in 1922, the Ulen Corporation of New York agreed to take over the contract, and this company completed the 124-mile line between Atocha, Tupiza and Villazón three years later, in time for Bolivia's centenary celebrations. On 26 July 1925 President Saavedra of Bolivia travelled to a point just south of Atocha to witness the driving in of the final spike. Much was made of the fact that the *second* transcontinental rail link had been completed between Argentina and Chile – first the famous Buenos Aires–Valparaiso line, and now the Buenos Aires–Antofagasta route, *via* Uyuni in Bolivia. La Paz, in addition, was only three or four days from the Río de la Plata. The section was subsequently operated by Dates and Hunt, an Argentine company, but indifferent administration and small freight volume quickly resulted in heavy financial loss, and the firm cancelled their contract. The Bolivian Government requested the Bolivia Railway Co. to take over the line, a company which was already running other lines in Bolivia under concession, and which had first begun construction of the Oruro–Viacha rail section in 1906. But it had then run into difficulties and become a subsidiary of the Antofagasta (Chili) and Bolivia Co. in 1908. Although the two were run as separate companies, one in New York and one in London, their boards of directors were almost identical and the distinction between them a technical one.

During the early 1920s particularly, amid the rash of proposed rail extensions into the Yungas and Andean basin towns, the idea of a branch line to Tarija had been revived and placed on the list of proposed works. It never materialised, however, and even in the 1920–30 period when 'railway fever' still ran high, the suggested construction of a Tarija railway was privately dismissed as a sop thrown to dissatisfied elements in the town. Certainly, the persistent failure to attract a railway increased the already oppressive isolation of this small 'garden-city', for Tarija has remained the only Departmental capital in highland Bolivia to be without rail transport.

The second rail extension from Argentina, the north-eastward branch of the line from Salta, followed the trail through the Andean foothills and the Chaco fringe. Embarcación was reached in 1912, and thereafter this temporary railhead became the terminus for the long cattle drives from the Bolivian Department of Santa Cruz and, not infrequently, from the Beni. Slowly the railway was extended to Tartagal, and on 6 January 1922

Bolivia signed an agreement with Argentina which proposed the extension of the line first to Yacuiba, and then northward again for approximately four hundred miles to Santa Cruz.[1] In 1922 K. F. Mather reported that the preliminary survey had in fact already been made, but that the Bolivian Government was opposing its construction until the projected railway between Santa Cruz and Cochabamba should be completed: 'because of the fear of increasing the already close coordination of eastern Bolivia with Argentina before the contacts of eastern Bolivia with western Bolivia are perfected. Both these railroad projects, however, will probably be consummated within ten or fifteen years.'[2]

This forecast proved to be highly optimistic. The long-cherished dream of a railway between Cochabamba and Santa Cruz has still to be realised. Yet the fears over the consequences of facilitating contact between the city of Santa Cruz and Argentina were not without foundation at that time. Economic and social ties, where they existed, were often closer with Argentina than with many parts of highland Bolivia, and in the 1920s the citizens of Santa Cruz were recorded as having sung the Argentine anthem for more than half a century, instead of the Bolivian national song.[3]

The Argentine railway extension into Bolivia as far as Santa Cruz was the subject of further conventions and protocols in 1929, 1937, 1938,[4] 1940 and 1941,[5] when it was agreed that Argentina would advance funds both for the construction of the railway, and for the sinking of oil wells in the Sanandita–Madrejones area inside the Bolivian border. Pipelines were to be run from this field and from the Bermejo district, and Bolivian oil would flow into Argentina as return payment.

6. 1903: THE REVIVAL OF INTEREST IN THE PARAGUAY ROUTEWAY

In 1903, as a result of the Treaty of Petrópolis boundary settlement with Brazil, Bolivia gained a series of four small 'windows' on to, or towards the river Paraguay. Three years earlier, in 1900, the Bolivian Government had looked again at the site possibilities afforded by the western shores of the lakes lying behind the western bank of the upper Paraguay. Only on

---

[1] Argentina was to operate the trunk line, and such branch lines as might be constructed later, e.g. Boyuibe–Sucre, and El Palmar–Tarija–Balcarce, until handed over to Bolivian ownership.
[2] K. F. Mather, 'Along the Andean front in south-eastern Bolivia', p. 374.
[3] Jaime Mendoza, *El Factor Geográfico en la Nacionalidad Boliviana*, Sucre, 1925, p. 76.
[4] F.O. 371/21412, F.O. 371/21416, F.O. 371/21419; *Col. Trat. Vig. Bol.*, vol. IV, pp. 107–14 and 121–5.
[5] F.O. A.2162/2162/2; *Col. Trat. Vig. Bol.*, vol. IV, pp. 131–4. Additional protocols were announced as the work on the railway proceeded.

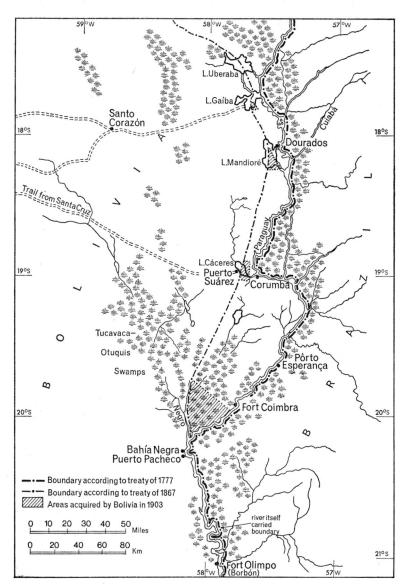

12 Bolivia and Brazil – access to the upper Paraguay river:
1777 (colonial period), 1867 and 1903

Lake Cáceres, at Suárez Arana's tiny port of Puerto Suárez, had any marked attention been given to these shallow water bodies since the primary demarcation of the 1867 Muñoz–Netto line by a Mixed Boundary Commission in the late 1870s. The suggested construction of a small port, Tamarinero, closer to Corumbá at the end of the Tamengo Channel, in order to provide a low-water season alternative to Puerto Suárez, had never been implemented. Among other occasional investigations farther upstream, however, an English Captain, Henry Bolland, was commissioned in 1900 to examine Lake Gaíba and, if possible, to establish a port on the west bank. For it was to Lake Gaíba that a few of the sixteenth-century explorers from Asunción, including Cabeza de Vaca and Ñuflo de Chávez, had penetrated and disembarked. Accordingly, on 21 November 1900, having ascended the Paraguay, Bolland selected the site of a new port, Puerto Quijarro, on the west bank of Lake Gaíba, where he reported finding a minimum depth of six feet. Possible road and rail routes west to Santo Corazón and Santa Cruz were delineated and other reconnaissance work in the Uberaba–Gaíba and Corumbá–Gaíba reaches recorded.[1]

In 1903, therefore, in the light of renewed interest by Bolivia in navigation along the upper Paraguay, adjustments were made to the southern section of the 1867 Muñoz–Netto line which involved a total Bolivian acquisition of approximately 330 square miles (868 square kilometres),[2] and included a small riparian zone along the Paraguay river itself above Bahía Negra (Fig. 12). These minor adjustments on the Cáceres, Mandioré and Gaíba lake shores in practice, however, merely extended Bolivian ownership around the flood relief basins along the Paraguay, without yielding direct access on to the river itself. Yet despite the fact that even with the fourth area at Bahía Negra, none provided Bolivia with satisfactory port facilities, the 1903 concession by Brazil incurred extreme displeasure in Paraguay. Once again the old Puerto Pacheco irritation of 1885–7 was revived.

In the early years of the twentieth century, therefore, while investigating the future possibilities of these small 'windows' on to the Paraguay river, Bolivia began at the same time to probe south-eastwards down the

---

[1] Enrique Bolland, *Exploraciones practicadas en el Alto Paraguay y en La Laguna Gaíba*, Buenos Aires, 1901. Maps: (i) Lake Gaíba, scale 1:25,000, depths in feet; (ii) Paraná–Paraguay route from Buenos Aires to Puerto Quijarro; (iii) plan of new port, scale 1:5000; (iv) map of Paraguay route from Corumbá to Lake Gaíba.

Also correspondence, Henry Bolland to Sir Clements Markham, Buenos Aires, 1 October 1901, *Roy. Geog. Soc. Archives*.

[2] 723 sq. km. on Paraguay river bank: 116 sq. km. on Lake Cáceres; 20.3 sq. km. on Lake Mandioré; 8.2 sq. km. on Lake Gaíba. The possibility of such an adjustment between Bolivia and Brazil had been the subject of discussion in a March 1896 protocol.

Pilcomayo. Small forts appeared on the east bank at Guachalla and Ballivián in 1906, as part of a conscious effort to establish visible control around more of the Chaco Boreal's fringe. In 1907, a fresh attempt was made at settlement by a protocol signed at Buenos Aires by representatives Pinilla

13   Types of frontier demarcation in the Chaco Boreal: 1922–32

and Soler, which agreed to submit the zone between 20° 30′ S and the northern line claimed by Paraguay, and the zone between 61° 30′ W and 62° W to arbitration by the President of Argentina (Fig. 13). Both agreed to observe a *status quo* regarding penetration, and to refrain from extending their possessions during arbitration. This 1907 protocol was never ratified.

Discussion continued in 1913, when the two States agreed once more to abide by the *status quo* of 1907, and to negotiate a final boundary treaty within two years, or submit the issue to arbitration. But at the end of the two-year period both parties appeared disinclined to take definitive action, and discussion dragged wearily through a series of postponed decisions in 1915, 1916, 1917, 1918 and 1923, during which time the line of Bolivian forts crept farther down the east bank of the Pilcomayo. The establishment of forts[1] was particularly active in 1922 and 1923, during a period of civil war in Paraguay. Muñoz and Saavedra were completed in 1923, Muñoz becoming the principal fort in a line running right back to Villa Montes. Nearly all supplies for the Bolivian garrisons, however, had to be obtained from Argentina across the Pilcomayo river.

Meanwhile, Bolivia had attempted to open negotiations once more for Puerto Pacheco,[2] this time with the support of Brazil. It was mooted in 1917 that such support might take the form of partially reducing Paraguay's debt with Brazil, in return for the cession of this small port to Bolivia. Paraguay, however, stood firm, observing that as Puerto Pacheco lacked either trail or rail westwards towards Bolivia's centre of population, the port would probably become exclusively Brazilian in character, and be supplied exclusively from that country. In 1916 the British Chargé d'Affaires in Paraguay had reported that the Government there was by then decidedly averse to the possession by Bolivia of *any* port on the river Paraguay. The Paraguayan War Minister was said to have stated that the security of Paraguayan territory would be seriously threatened if such a port were to be established, and linked by rail to Bolivia's core area. Bolivia, it was thought, would place war vessels on the river – 'strategic considerations outweigh any commercial advantages'.[3]

Bolivia, however, continued to stress the superior site-qualities of Puerto Pacheco: its direct access on to the Paraguay, and its position upon a slight knoll, largely free from the river's annual flood. Puerto Suárez by comparison lay on a backwater, completely dependent upon the depth of water in the Tamengo Channel which linked the pier-head to the Paraguay river at Corumbá. Between November and January, not only was the channel almost dry, but sometimes the lake also, so that during drought a wagon could be driven straight across the lake bed towards the Brazilian port. One of the less pleasant tasks of the local army garrison was to remove

---

[1] Although the term *fortín* was applied to these and other stations which multiplied so rapidly in the Chaco Boreal at this time, most were simply a collection of huts, sometimes surrounded by trenches and housing a comparatively small armed garrison.

[2] The name Puerto Pacheco was by now often used synonymously with that of Bahía Negra.

[3] F. A. Oliver to Sir Reginald Tower, Asunción, 23 August 1916, *F.O. 371/2718.*

the thousands of dead fish left stranded and rotting in the mud by the dwindling Tamengo Channel.

While the diplomatic haggling continued in a vain attempt to secure Puerto Pacheco, Puerto Suárez, about 170 miles up-river, achieved a modest development. A pier was built in 1910 which could unload small vessels running a local shuttle service for about six months of the year to and from the major navigation head at Corumbá. A number of German trading houses had established offices in Puerto Suárez to handle the import of European manufactured goods arriving *via* Buenos Aires and Montevideo, and regular wagon trains left this small Bolivian port bound for Santa Cruz along the trail through Roboré and San José. The control of commercial activity in the Oriente by German houses was a marked feature of the 1910–30 period. It was not of course confined to the Oriente, but was particularly significant there, as large numbers of German merchants sought to avoid confiscation of their property by Brazil during the First World War. New wagon trails were cut from Puerto Suárez to San Ignacio, Concepción and Trinidad until a skeletal, but nevertheless well-established network of German-controlled import houses could be found from the Chaco-edge to the rubber forests: 'There are practically unlimited resources and commercial opportunities ready and waiting to fall into any British hands, containing sufficient means with which to enter into serious competition with the thoroughly detested Teutonic firms. They trade here practically without serious competition and on their own terms.'[1] Despite the official 'black-listing' of German firms after Bolivia's gesture of support for the Allies in April 1917, American and British businessmen declared the powerful German monopoly of trading in eastern Bolivia to be 'unassailable'. Certainly, Brazil appears to have been less successful in closing, or attempting to close, the Paraguay river routeway during the First World War than that of the Amazon. But as the tempo of activity within the Oriente, largely sustained by the rubber and ranching boom, gradually slowed, movement along the rivers and trails in the distant southern sector similarly began to decline. The volume of trade officially recorded at Puerto Suárez had always been small. In 1911, for example, imports of 1340 tons were recorded, while exports during the last years of the rubber boom averaged only about 200 tons annually – mostly rubber, sugar and coffee. Although Puerto Suárez was declared a free port for a four-year period in 1924, it

[1] G. Haggard to Lord Curzon, La Paz, January 1920, quoting a report made by the British Vice-Consul, in Concepción, Department of Santa Cruz, to the British Embassy, La Paz, *F.O. 371/4428.*

did little to stem the exodus of population, particularly to the Brazilian port of Corumbá. The suggested creation of a new Department of Chiquitos, with Puerto Suárez as its capital, never materialised.[1]

Desultory attempts were made, meanwhile, to encourage land speculators to take an interest in the other 'outlets' on to the Paraguay gained (or regained) by Bolivia from Brazil in 1903. Two British engineers, for example, Radley and Brown, who had been employed by the firm of Sir John Jackson on the construction of the Arica–La Paz railway, decided to explore the possibilities of the Lake Gaíba area. In 1912 they rode the trail right across Bolivia to Puerto Suárez. Turning north, however, both were attacked and killed somewhere in the wilderness between Mandioré and Gaíba, although the exact circumstances of their deaths could never be discovered. But at all events, there followed a new phase in land speculation in Bolivia's eastern lands.

7. 'PIONEERING IN WILDEST BOLIVIA': COLONIZATION PROJECTS IN THE SOUTH-EASTERN SECTOR, 1919–1929

In the decade after the First World War, two ambitious projects were launched to introduce North American and European colonists into the empty lands of eastern Bolivia. Both were based, from the Bolivian point of view, on the desirability of strengthening *de facto* the claims of possession to the Chaco on its south-western and north-eastern fringes, and at the same time on the need to test the efficacy of the routes from Buenos Aires on which the colonists would depend.

The first of these two major concessions was made in 1919 to a former U.S. Congressman, William H. Murray of Oklahoma. It initially comprised a grant of 300,000 hectares of free land, extending in a strip eastward across the Chaco from a base on the Argentine boundary (which still awaited final settlement), between Yacuiba and Sanandita. The first wave of immigrants was intended to settle not less than two hundred and fifty white North American colonists within a three-year period. The U.S. State Department immediately declined any responsibility for what, it emphasised, was a private contract. In replying to an individual enquiry about the scheme, the Secretary of State recommended careful consideration of the risks involved: 'The Department believes you should know

[1] In January 1911 the Territory or Delegación of the Oriente had been created in the eastern part of the Department of Santa Cruz, and was administered from Puerto Suárez. It was the last of the three colonial Territories (Delegaciones) created in lowland Bolivia. These were (i) the Purus/Acre/Madre de Dios regions (i.e. the Noroeste) in 1890–3; (ii) the Gran Chaco in 1905; (iii) the Oriente in 1911.

that in the past some difficulty had arisen in the execution of a similar project in Eastern Bolivia owing to the unsettled boundary situation and the conflicting claims of Bolivia and Paraguay in the land covered by the concession.'[1]

Nevertheless, Murray ('Alfalfa Bill' Murray), pushed forward with promotion material, and his *Prospectus for the Murray Colony of Bolivia*[2] was widely circulated in the Great Plains and the Mid-West in 1920. It stressed the need for farmers and stockmen in south-east Bolivia, and with its detailed lists of laws and rules of conduct, and its offer to sell land for sixty cents an acre, it appealed strongly to the old pioneering spirit of the West. Faint-hearts, ready to give up at the first sign of hardship, were sturdily rejected by Murray. But he nevertheless painted a glowing picture of the opportunities which lay ahead:

The country I've selected is located in Eastern Bolivia not far from navigable water, with outlet to the world through the Paraguay and Paraná rivers, and the La Plata to the Atlantic Ocean. These rivers are world highways...

In my opinion, when God made the country between Santa Cruz down to Lagunillas, and east five hundred miles to the Rio Paraguay, together with north-east Argentina, and west Brazil, and north Paraguay as a farm and stock country, He threw the molds away, having no desire to duplicate its achievement...

My opinion is that in fifteen years all of East Bolivia and West Brazil will be settled like most of Argentina. Now is the time to lay the sill of this settlement of Americans ...left alone Italians, Germans or English will settle it.

The planned departure in 1921 was delayed, however, and in 1922 Murray went out again to explore his concession (by then reduced to 17,000 hectares) between Yacuiba, and the old mission settlements of Aguayrenda and Itaú (Fig. 13). A record of this trip was incorporated as 'My Trip on a Mule', August 1922, in Murray's second *Prospectus for the Murray Colonies of Central South Bolivia*, published in July 1923.

It is significant to note that, as a result of the 1922 visit, Murray began to stress the importance to the colonists of the proposed *railway* extension north from Argentina to Yacuiba and Santa Cruz; no further emphasis was laid on the Paraguay river routeway. Not surprisingly, Murray was excited by the increased activity along the foothill zone. The wagon-road north from the railhead, which by then was twenty-four miles beyond Embarcación, was busy with convoys of heavy carts slowly hauling oil-boring and pipeline equipment towards Lagunillas. Petroleum deposits

---

[1] Secretary of State Robert Lansing, Washington, D.C., 21 October 1919.
[2] Published at Tishomingo, Oklahoma, 1919–20.

had long been known to exist in the Andean foothill zone, indeed one of the first oil strikes in South America had been made in Bolivia in 1875.[1] At Santa Cruz, in 1909, Cecil Gosling had recorded that 'there are evidences of the existence of a large deposit of petroleum in this district, but no attempt has yet been made to exploit it.[2] Serious study of Bolivia's oil potential may be said to date from 1920, when the Standard Oil Company of New Jersey acquired a concession for exploration and exploitation of resources in the Departments of Chuquisaca, Tarija and Santa Cruz. Rumours of a possible oil pipeline to link the Bolivian oilfields to the Paraguay river were current, and had been heightened in 1922 by the unloading at the Argentine railhead of large consignments of pipes to connect up a trans-Chaco oil pipeline. It was these that Murray had observed, and although the trans-Chaco pipeline project was soon abandoned as impracticable by Standard Oil's wholly owned subsidiary, the Standard Oil Company of Bolivia, the year 1922 was one of bustle and anticipation in the south-east foothills. The future looked rosy. North American oil-men and water-borers were regularly encountered – planning ahead suddenly appeared feasible. Had not K. F. Mather only recently observed: 'It is plainly evident that this is a land of rich promise'?[3]

Nearly fifty colonists, mostly Oklahomans, left for Antofagasta in 1923, to take the 'sidewinder' rail route towards their concession, *via* Uyuni, Jujuy and Embarcación. Unfortunately, no advance warning of their arrival had been given to the Ulen Company's representatives at Atocha, where the last section of the line between Buenos Aires and La Paz still lay unfinished. While temporary accommodation was hastily erected on the wretchedly exposed *altiplano*, and conveyances found to carry the colonists and their belongings across the gap to the southern rail section, much physical distress was experienced from the cold and the altitude. Less than six months later, a number of this same contingent were sadly retracing their steps, and the American Consul-General in Valparaiso[4] reported their departure

[1] A reference to exploration for oil in 1886 is made by Baron Erland Nordenskiöld, 'Travels on the boundaries of Bolivia and Argentina', *Geog. Journ.*, vol. XXI, 1903, pp. 510–25, in a paper largely of anthropological interest.

[2] 'Report on a Journey through Bolivia', C. Gosling, Santiago, 1 February 1910, F.O. *177/350* and F.O. *371/969.*

[3] K. F. Mather, 'Along the Andean front in south-eastern Bolivia', p. 374. Elsewhere, Mather added, 'The same frontier life which fifty years ago appealed to the red-blooded American makes its appeal from this southern land today. America has the first opportunity; if she fails, some other country will step in.'

[4] C. F. Deichman to Secretary of State Charles E. Hughes, Valparaiso, 25 July 1924, Records of the Department of State relating to the Internal Affairs of Bolivia, *Record Group 59*, Washington, D.C.

The Southern Sector

after losing the greater part of their savings, and witnessing the vanishment of their dreams of wealth which they had hoped to extract from the wilds of south-eastern Bolivia...It was discovered that the valley in which the concession lay was broken up in its entirety by small patches of cultivated ground from five to fifteen acres and occupied by Indians and Catholic priests...who presented themselves to the new title-holders showing them their titles and deeds for the same ground granted them by the local representative of the Bolivian government. They were forced to accept such land as remained untilled and unclaimed...

It is respectfully suggested that the Department of State take steps if possible to prevent the migration of more American families to settle upon the farm lands of Bolivia.[1]

The State Department's file on the Murray colony grew heavy with a mounting correspondence from insurance companies, contractors, and American Ministers in Bolivia and Chile. Letters of enquiry continued to arrive also from would-be colonists, anxious to escape from their own depressed farming conditions at home, for Murray's Prospectus had been read avidly by his fellow stockmen and farmers in the problem areas of the American Great Plains. But although a few additional families did sell up and emigrate, they served only to swell the numbers who eventually departed, plagued by isolation, drought, inferior homestead lots and, an old familiar enemy, grasshopper swarms. Early in 1925, no more than thirty colonists remained in the Palmar region, and most of these were members of Murray's own family. The State Department in Washington meanwhile opened an emergency fund 'For the Relief of Colonists in Bolivia', and requested the manager of the Standard Oil team working farther north to make enquiries as to the welfare of the remaining colonists.[2]

Murray himself stoutly defended the enterprise, ascribing all the setbacks to crass ignorance of farming methods among the colonists, to the slowness of the railway's extension northward from Embarcación (it had reached Tartagal), and to the general adverse attitude displayed by Argentina to the North American settlers whose supplies, Murray alleged,

[1] Apart from further colonists bound for Murray's concession, this refers also to another colonization scheme for the Charagua area which was then being organised in Portland, Oregon: 'The Bolivia Colonization Association', R. V. Jones, Portland Chamber of Commerce, 1923. Land was to be sold at U.S. $1 per acre, but nothing came of it, and it was generally regarded as fraudulent.

[2] Correspondence relating to some of the colonists' experiences may be studied in the Records of the Department of State relating to the Internal Affairs of Bolivia, *Record Group 59*, Washington, D.C. E.g., (i) Warren Gates (colonist) to C. O. Gates in Oklahoma, Tartagal, Argentina, 22 December 1924; (ii) Robert Gallentine (colonist) to J. Cottrell, U.S. Minister in La Paz, El Palmar, Tarija, 9 January 1925; (iii) Leland Harrison to W. Roswell Barker of the American Legation in La Paz, Washington, D.C., 13 March 1925.

201

were delayed unnecessarily in transit. Several of the colonists in fact migrated southwards into Argentina.

Meanwhile, in London also an ambitious scheme was being launched to colonize a tract in eastern Bolivia adjacent to the Brazilian and Paraguayan boundary. It lay five hundred miles north and east of the Murray concessionary area in the Yacuiba foothills, but registered in July 1922 as the Bolivian Oil and Land Syndicate, it derived much of its initial momentum from the interest Standard Oil was showing in south-east Bolivia, and from the speculation in 1922 over the trans-Chaco pipeline which, it was assumed, would highlight the Paraguay river routeway.

The new company, the Bolivian Oil and Land Syndicate (Bolivia Concessions Ltd) was founded by a Norwegian consultant engineer, Christian Lilloe-Fangan, who had acquired British citizenship and worked for several years in Buenos Aires. Considerable confidence and prestige were gained when the names of Sir Martin Conway and Henry Mond were added to the Board of Directors, and the immense size of the concession – thirty million acres (over twelve million hectares) – attracted widespread attention. Details of the new port to be constructed on Lake Gaíba, the new railway to be run from it westwards through Santo Corazón, San Juan and San José to Santa Cruz, and the size and type of the homestead plots available received extensive publicity. Reference to the map which accompanied the concession revealed that all the land between the Pilcomayo and Paraguay rivers had been shaded as Bolivian territory. Indeed the concessionary area was shown comfortably wedged between navigable waterways on both sides, and the implications of the map immediately brought a stiffly worded note of displeasure to the Foreign Office from the Paraguayan Legation in London.

In order to prepare the colonists ('public schoolboys we believe will probably be more suitable as settlers than the real working class') two 'training farms' were established in Cambridgeshire. In addition, however, central and southern Europeans were to be encouraged, for it was hoped that the Emigration Cooperatives already established on the continent to assist the flow of emigrants to the U.S.A. could be tapped instead for the Bolivian project, since U.S. quota restrictions had cut the steady flow of immigration into North America. In September 1925 the 600-ton steamship *President Saavedra*, flying the Bolivian flag, left Dunkirk with thirty colonists on board, bound for what was virtually an unknown destination.

There had certainly been little official encouragement in Britain for the enterprise. The Foreign Office declared itself to be 'anxious' and 'uneasy' about the suitability of the area for European settlement; the revelation that even the highest points in the main area of the concession were barely above swamp level prompted the observation that any proposed European settlement in the tropics below 3000 feet was likely to be a risky venture and better left alone. Moreover, Conway was considered to be 'a poor businessman', and peremptorily cautioned 'to get his facts right'. The Royal Geographical Society, asked for its opinion by the Foreign Office, pronounced the region to be unhealthy and the scheme to be ill-judged. In Bolivia itself, the British Minister was frankly pessimistic: 'No young men should be encouraged to come out here. If they do so they will most certainly be stranded...My opinion is that it should be "choked off", and if our young men desire to colonise, let them go to our colonies where they have to deal with white men who speak the same lingo.'[1] It was an observation curiously reminiscent in part of Masterton's sentiments expressed more than eighty years earlier upon the folly of encouraging emigration to Bolivia.

The company was obviously unprepared for the volume and weight of criticism the scheme had called forth, and not a little alarmed privately at the negative official attitude adopted against all concerned with its promotion. In the U.S.A., opinions in general were similarly adverse, and occasionally tinged with a thinly veiled note of reproof:

It would seem strange that in the enormous expanse of the British Empire, now covering over thirteen million square miles, or one-fourth of the earth's surface, British promoters cannot find room enough for their enterprising activities...Bolivia is one of the most backward countries of South America, mainly for the reason that it has no port of its own in the Pacific.[2]

As the first group of colonists reached Buenos Aires to begin the two-thousand-mile journey by river into the centre of the continent, work began to clear the ground for the first section of the railway between Lake Gaíba and Santo Corazón (Fig. 12). With the scarcity of Bolivian population in the region, workers had to be recruited in Brazil, and a small party of labourers was eventually gathered from the Mato Grosso. For a while, nothing more was heard. Occasional magazine articles described the project in 1927 and 1928,[3] basing their copy on vivid imagination, and

---

[1] R. C. Michell to Sir Edward Crowe, La Paz, 29 June 1926, *F.O. 371/11114.*
[2] *Los Angeles Daily Times*, 23 February 1926. Unfavourable reports on the project were also returned by A. Nutting to Secretary of State Frank B. Kellogg, London, 15 February 1926; G. L. Kreeck to Secretary of State Frank B. Kellogg, Asunción, 29 February 1928, Records of the Department of State relating to the Internal Affairs of Bolivia, *Record Group 59*, Washington, D.C.
[3] E.g. 'Blazing the trail in South America – Port built 6000 miles from the sea – the story of British Pioneers', January 1928; and 'Pioneering in Wildest Bolivia', August 1928, in *Wide World Magazine*, London.

on the company's booklet, which had been widely distributed to keep interest alive in the absence of reliable information. This booklet was quite fraudulent in its omissions and implications; several of the photographs of the Paraguay river and 'the environs of Lake Gaíba' were obviously taken many miles downstream, and give a totally misleading impression of the country they purport to represent.

By the middle of 1928, reports of misery and failure were filtering back to London. The railway had not been laid, nor the road which had been suggested as an alternative to the railway earlier that year. In July 1928 one of the colonists, a Mrs Constance Cline, addressed her complaints directly to the Prince of Wales,[1] and in a long letter presented a harrowing tale of life at Gaíba, where no decent habitations and no marketable crops had been produced at all since her arrival there in March 1926. Financial assistance was requested to enable the colonists to return home, and authority for their repatriation was eventually sanctioned by an exasperated Foreign Office in October 1928. At the end of the year the remaining British colonists struggled back to London and witnessed the official liquidation of Bolivia Concessions Ltd, in January 1931.

The entire episode has since been virtually forgotten, although it created considerable diplomatic tension between Britain, Paraguay and Bolivia in the mid-1920s, and certainly more political unease than its eventual results warranted. For, as an effort to consolidate Bolivia's position in the south-eastern sector, the Gaíba concession was a dismal failure.

The individual to profit most from the enterprise, indirectly, was possibly the British freelance journalist Julian Duguid, who accepted an invitation from Mamerto Urriolagoitia (then Bolivian Consul-General in London, and later President of the Republic), to join him on an expedition to eastern Bolivia. It declared purpose was to investigate the Gaíba region and the progress of the colonization scheme there on behalf of the Bolivian Government, and to explore the feasibility of the Chaco-edge route from Gaíba to Santa Cruz. Duguid travelled as the self-styled correspondent of both *The Daily Telegraph* and the *Financial Times* – also, the Foreign Office observed dryly, as the self-appointed Foreign Office investigator into the welfare of the British colonists. There was little happening in the concessionary area and no sign of activity along the proposed rail or road route to Santo Corazón. But the hazardous journey westward from Lake Gaíba along the narrow mule trail to San José de Chiquitos and Santa Cruz subsequently became the subject of Duguid's best-seller, *Green Hell.*

[1] *F.O. 371/12739.*

On the bright blue official map of Eastern Bolivia a little row of dots runs away
into the distance...and would cause a stranger to think that the country is highly
populated. To one such dot we made our entry in the cool of an evening...and the
inhabitants of the boldly marked San Lorenzo turned out to welcome us.

'What do you think of our first town?' asked Urrio.

I stared, uncomprehending, at the single rickety house that stood by a broken-down
cattle corral.

'When do we come to it?'

Urrio laughed.

'You must adjust your scale of values. That shack is San Lorenzo.'

'Good Lord!' said Bee-Mason. 'Your map-makers *have* got nerve.'

'One must fill in the country somehow', said Urrio.

...We told the owner of San Lorenzo that we came from beyond the sea.

'I know the word', he said, 'but what does it mean?'[1]

8. 1919–1932: THE GROWING CRISIS IN THE CHACO BOREAL. MILITARY PREPARATIONS AND EXTERNAL RELATIONS

In January 1911 a German military mission headed by a Major Hans
Kundt of the Berlin General Staff arrived in La Paz on a three-year contract.
Its purpose was to organise and instruct Bolivian army personnel, and
despite local English and French diplomatic misgivings over its 'Prussian
methods', and the reinforcement it provided to the already strong German
influence in Bolivia, there was general approval of its achievements. The
mission in fact did much to advance the status of the Bolivian soldier, for
Kundt had decreed that every illiterate conscript should be taught to read
and write. At a later stage this proved impossible to implement, but the
popularity of service life boomed as the prospects of a better job in
civilian life, following the prescribed period of military service, added their
own powerful incentive to recruitment.

During the First World War Kundt was recalled to Germany. It was his
return to Bolivia, however, in 1919 which was regarded as being more
significant, and questions were immediately raised by foreign observers as
to the nature of Kundt's work in relation to the terms of the Treaty of
Versailles.[2] Kundt accordingly became a naturalised Bolivian subject in
1920, and was at once reappointed, not as Chief of Staff of the Bolivian
army, but initially as Chief of the Office of Mining Survey and Plans.
Kundt was generally regarded as the strong man behind the Saavedra
Administrations (1920–5), although as a professional soldier, bent almost

[1] J. Duguid, *Green Hell*, pp. 142 and 145–6.
[2] Which prohibited the subsequent employment of German officers in the armed forces of
signatory nations.

exclusively upon creating a new, well-disciplined army from a small officer-élite and a groundmass of Indian labourers, his purpose, he declared, was to keep out of politics.

By 1924 the army comprised about ten thousand men, and in that year certain detachments were active in the south and south-east along the Argentine border, and on a broad front between Tarija and Santa Cruz de la Sierra. The Republican Party was generally strongest in the north and west of Bolivia, weakest in the south and east. The Department of Santa Cruz in particular was already strongly hostile to the Saavedra régime and when, in 1922, a number of anti-government activists were deported from La Paz into Santa Cruz, they found there fertile ground for discontent and mounting agitation. For the collapse of the rubber boom was by then causing a severe economic recession in the city, and perennial neglect by La Paz strengthened the demand for secession either to Brazil or to Argentina, particularly the latter. Since the journey by mule trail from Santa Cruz even as far as Cochabamba usually took the best part of two weeks, and frequently longer, the isolation was serious. Santa Cruz could not, after all, be dismissed or ignored with impunity. Although 'tucked away in the heart of nowhere', as Ministers posted to La Paz would describe it, the town was nevertheless a major centre of population, containing even then approximately twenty-five thousand people. Its inaccessibility was, above all, politically dangerous.

Anxiety over the dissension and ultimate vulnerability of the south-eastern sector led to new telegraph lines and new wireless stations being constructed after 1922 in Santa Cruz, Roboré and Puerto Suárez, in order to improve communications between La Paz and the Oriente. It led also, in 1923 and 1924, to the posting of General Kundt to Tarija and Santa Cruz to round up political exiles and to suppress revolution which was flaring all over the south-east. In March and April 1924 rebels were active in the eastern sector of the Department of Tarija – in Gran Chaco province which, like some other remote frontier regions, had formerly been administered as a Delegación. The Yacuiba custom house was seized. In July revolutionaries occupied the public buildings in Santa Cruz, declared the Department to be an independent State, and decided to request annexation by either Brazil or Argentina. About one thousand Bolivian troops marched from Cochabamba, however, and order was restored later that year.[1]

[1] J. Cottrell to Secretary of State Charles E. Hughes, La Paz, March–August 1924, *passim*, Records of the Department of State relating to the Internal Affairs of Bolivia, *Record Group 59*, Washington, D.C.

Meanwhile, Kundt proceeded with his training program and with the major overhaul and refitting of Bolivian cavalry, infantry and artillery units. Contracts for new equipment were put out to tender, and in October and November 1926 one of the largest orders was won by the British firm of Vickers Armstrong to supply just under £2,000,000-worth of war materials.[1] Delivery routes were carefully considered, since the nature, weight and bulk of the cargo were to provide particular problems in transit. For a number of reasons, the route *via* the Panama Canal and any of the Pacific ports was rejected. Instead, the longer rail routes from Santos, and particularly from Buenos Aires (or up-river Santa Fe), *via* Villazón, were selected as more practical alternatives. Indeed, this very large consignment of war materials was to form the first major pay-load carried by the Argentina–Bolivia international railway into La Paz since its completion in 1925.

The British Government, however, declared its unease over the size of the arms order secured by Vickers Armstrong, and was particularly disturbed to learn that the British Minister in La Paz had actually been present at the signing of the contract. In fact, the Minister had strongly backed the British tender, claiming that had he not done so, the contract would have been placed in France. Nevertheless the Foreign Office considered that official support for an arms order of such proportions did little to allay suspicions of Britain's attitudes and intentions in South America. Even at this time, the Foreign Office was already treading warily in its relations with Paraguay over the proposed limits of the Gaíba concession.

Bolivia continued to construct a line of defensive posts down the Pilcomayo river. After 1927 the great swamps were encircled with forts and, well within the zone of the 1907 *status quo*, contact was being made more frequently with Paraguayan forts built, in the first place, to protect concessionary settlement from Indian attack. The line of Bolivian forts turned away to strike north, approximately along meridian 60° W, through the arid heart of the Chaco Boreal and in the general direction of Puerto Suárez, about three hundred miles away on Lake Cáceres. Across this no-man's-land the chain of Bolivian forts was matched by that of Paraguay, a duplication which embodied the growing determination of each State to express visibly its territorial claims (Fig. 13). Each could recall crushing nineteenth-century defeats in which considerable territory had been lost. Events perhaps were now to present an opportunity to

---

[1] Detailed schedules of the Vickers Armstrong contract were dispatched by J. Cottrell to Secretary of State Frank B. Kellogg, La Paz, 27 August 1927, *ibid.*; see also *F.O. 371/11114*. The amount of the Vickers contract was reduced to £1,250,000 in 1928, exclusive of shipping and freight charges.

vindicate past humiliations by the acquisition of the Chaco Boreal. The line of paired forts across this wilderness thus represented a most extreme form of territorial delimitation, while for the first time in its history the frontier of Bolivia, along this tract at least, had become a military frontier, to be demarcated almost continuously by its own armed forces.

By this time Paraguay was vigorously encouraging foreign settlers and investment into the Chaco, particularly groups of Mennonites to whom the isolation of the region held considerable attraction.[1] Under the terms of the *Privilegium* Mennonites were granted self-government, freedom of religion and language, educational autonomy, and military exemption. With generous land and tax concessions, nearly two thousand Mennonites arrived from Canada between 1926 and 1928 to establish the Menno colony about 130 miles west of Puerto Casado. Between 1930 and 1932 a further two thousand, mostly from the U.S.S.R. and Germany, set up the Fernheim colony, and together these immigrants did much to strengthen Paraguay's claim to the Chaco Boreal (Fig. 13). Limited Bolivian efforts, however, to attract Mennonite settlers into the region between 1926 and 1930 were unsuccessful.

While rumour and unrest grew, a period of intense activity developed among the military installations strung out over the plains. Forts on both sides were strengthened and extended, occasionally at the site of an old mission. Detachments of troops formed exploratory parties, building roads and digging wells. Inevitably, the tedium of so isolated and monotonous an existence was occasionally relieved by skirmishing between opposing garrisons, facing each other in a way which reminded observers of the First World War's western front. The incident at Fort Sorpresa, in which a Paraguayan officer was killed when his small group entered the Bolivian fort in February 1927, was the first in a series of minor engagements which caused emotions in La Paz and Asunción to rise to fever pitch. With the suspension of talks, and in the absence of any positive decision, a hardening of attitude at the conference table became more pronounced, as compromise was abandoned and the more extreme early claims were resurrected once again.[2]

[1] A. E. Krause, 'Mennonite Settlement in the Paraguayan Chaco', *Univ. of Chicago Research Paper No. 25*, 1952; also *Geog. Rev.*, vol. LII, 1962, pp. 599–600. (The Newland Mennonite colony was established later, in 1947–8; together there are about 15,000 Mennonites today in Paraguay.) Limited Mennonite settlement in the Bolivian Oriente began only in the 1950s, with colonists from Paraguay, and latterly from Canada and Mexico, moving into the Santa Cruz region.

[2] Bolivia's original Chaco claims consisted of the great wedge thrust between the Paraguay and Bermejo rivers. The Paraguay–Pilcomayo wedge was later sustained as Bolivia's most

Raids across the Chaco continued, despite assertions from both sides that matters could be settled without armed aggression. In September 1928 a recruiting drive in Bolivia enlisted four thousand new troops specifically for the Chaco theatre of operations; Paraguay too, built three new forts in the disputed territory. On 5 December 1928, Paraguayan troops from Fort Galpón attacked and routed fifty Bolivian troops at Fort Vanguardia, the first real incident to capture world attention. Two hundred and fifty miles away to the south-west, Bolivia retaliated by seizing Fort Boquerón later that month, after some fighting. Each successive attack resulted in a wave of triumph or despair in La Paz and Asunción, as national honour became identified with the small, apparently worthless plot of ground which had changed hands in the Chaco. Both States were urged to suspend hostilities by the International Conference of American States on Concilia-tion and Arbitration, meeting at Washington, D.C. Delegates[1] encouraged the re-establishment of diplomatic relations, as well as the restoration of the two forts, and this was at last effected in July 1930. Since the Washing-ton Commission's terms of reference had been confined to an investigation of the circumstances surrounding the December 1928 attacks on the forts, Bolivia expressed a willingness to submit the whole Chaco territorial dispute to a Commission of Enquiry of the Permanent Tribunal at The Hague, but this was not implemented.

Meanwhile, the delivery of war materials ordered by Bolivia was running into difficulties. Two thousand cases of rifles aboard a German steamer, destined for Bolivia, were held at Santa Fe and prevented from proceeding any farther in January 1929, although they were subsequently released. The presence of two Bolivian army officers in Santos purchasing tents and general provisions led to protests from Paraguay, which again denounced the movement of these supplies by rail to Pôrto Esperança, and thence by launch to Corumbá and Puerto Suárez, as unfriendly and prejudicial to Paraguay. The rapid build-up of the Bolivian army garrisons in the Puerto Suárez area, supplied almost exclusively by imports from Brazil, left Paraguay vainly seeking legal loopholes whereby such transit should be disallowed. Chile had already declared that shipment of arms would not be permitted through Chilean territory, and that Chile itself would not sell arms to Bolivia. Peru pondered the dilemma, considering what its own line of action should be in the light of existing transit agreements with

extreme claim in this sector. Paraguay claimed the Chaco Boreal as far as its northern 'natural limits' which were formed, so Paraguay stated, by the Parapetí, Izozog swamps, and fringing sierra–Otuquis arc (Fig. 11 a).

[1] From the U.S.A., Mexico, Colombia, Uruguay and Cuba. Bolivia and Paraguay were also represented.

Bolivia. Advice was sought from the U.S.A., but the State Department declined to comment specifically upon whether or not arms shipments should be allowed through the port of Mollendo.

Bolivia had complained vigorously at being denied access to rightful import of arms, and at the Sixth Pan-American Conference at Havana in February 1928 it was agreed that, provided 'vital interests' of the transit State did not suffer, free transit across neutral territory of arms and ammunition for belligerent States must be permitted when any one of those States had no access to the coast.[1] The article was tentatively approved by the Argentine delegation (although subsequently not ratified by them), partly it was thought because of Argentina's own obligations under the 1868 treaty,[2] partly because Brazil was already implementing the agreement, and also because it was generally known that Paraguay was by then itself receiving arms shipments through Argentina. Neither Bolivia nor Paraguay was a belligerent at the time but, largely because of the Argentine attitude during the remainder of 1928, arms shipments for that year entered Bolivia almost entirely *via* Mollendo. Most of these belonged to the Vickers Armstrong consignment, part of which had been subcontracted to the Skoda works in Czechoslovakia, and to Swedish and French firms. Permission to bring all these war materials through the Panama Canal was sought, and granted by the U.S.A. Although agreeing that such traffic was not prohibited, the State Department was clearly alarmed by its proportions, and declared the hope that Bolivia would do nothing to prejudice peace in South America. American arms companies, however, like those of Europe, were already dispatching orders to both Bolivia and Paraguay. In February 1929 Argentina withdrew its embargo on the transit of arms to Bolivia, and the following month Chile did the same.

While official Argentine circles remained non-committal, in the late 1920s the Argentine Press continually argued that the struggle for petroleum rights, rather than access to the Paraguay river, formed the root cause of the entire Chaco dispute. Bolivia and Paraguay were regarded as pawns in a game played between the Standard Oil Co. of New Jersey on the one hand and the Royal Dutch/Shell Group on the other. Shell was said to be strongly supporting Bolivian interests against all rival oil companies, particularly Standard Oil, and this view was strengthened by the financial guarantees offered by Sir Henri Deterding in London (representing Shell interests), in support of Bolivia's weak credit position with Vickers

[1] Article 22, para. 2, Convention of Maritime Neutrality. Chile signed the Convention, but with reservation on this paragraph.
[2] See above, p. 180 n. 1; below, p. 214 n. 2.

Armstrong. Indeed, Bolivia increased the amount of its commitment with the firm on the strength of Deterding's backing.[1]

Large quantities of arms made their way into Bolivia and Paraguay in the 1929-30 period. In April 1929 the American Minister noted that the release of a shipment of arms detained by Argentina at the port of Rosario had been made conditional upon Bolivia's ratification (on 26 April 1929) of the July 1925 Bolivia–Argentina boundary treaty.[2] Such bargaining was prompted in part by the uncertainty over how far south across the 1925 boundary line the Bolivian oilfields extended, and by the feeling that Bolivia might be encouraged to abrogate the treaty and press for a revision of its terms. During the late 1920s, therefore, the general situation steadily deteriorated. The Chaco question by this time was complicated by several different issues, and aggravated by the presence of an armed military frontier running through the disputed territory. The situation continued to remain highly volatile, while public opinion in both Bolivia and Paraguay reacted violently against any concession which might be mistaken for weakness.

In the south-eastern sector, meanwhile, the separatist unrest which had been so much a feature of the 1923-4 period had become submerged under the bitter antagonism now displayed (and encouraged) towards Paraguay. The region was, for the first time in Bolivia's history, close to the political storm centre rather than on its periphery. Physical contact with the Andean cities had been improved also, in 1925, by the arrival of the first Junker flight from Cochabamba. While it did nothing to relieve the economic isolation of Santa Cruz, politically the air link-up was of considerable importance. The city's communication system, still without rail or even good highway connexions to any of Bolivia's urban centres, had made its first tentative step into the air age. The enormous possibilities of air communication for Bolivia had been practicably demonstrated for the first time by the visits in 1919 of teams of ace French and American aviators, who gave a series of daring exhibition flights over what is still one of the most hazardous of flying areas – the *altiplano*. In 1922, after a number of unorganised efforts had failed, General Kundt re-established the nucleus of a Bolivian Army Air Force. Then, in September 1925, a small group of German businessmen resident in Bolivia founded the civil airline Lloyd

[1] Alanson B. Houghton to Secretary of State Frank B. Kellogg, London, 19 January 1929; G. L. Kreeck to Henry L. Stimson, Asunción, 28 May 1929, Records of the Department of State relating to the Internal Affairs of Bolivia, *Record Group 59*, Washington, D.C.

[2] J. F. Martin, Chargé d'Affaires, to Secretary of State Henry L. Stimson, La Paz, 26 April and 3 May 1929, *ibid.* Argentina did not ratify the July 1925 boundary treaty until after the end of the Chaco War.

Aereo Boliviano. Its first aircraft, a 300 h.p. Junker *El Oriente*, carrying four passengers, inaugurated the Cochabamba–Santa Cruz flight that same year. Soon it was doing the flight in two to three hours, and ever since that momentous day in 1925, the La Paz–Cochabamba–Santa Cruz flight path has remained the principal axis of air communication in Bolivia.

After 1925, therefore, current events combined to divert Santa Cruz' sentiments into more pro-national channels, and when Urriolagoitia's small party eventually completed the trail from Lake Gaíba and entered Santa Cruz in December 1928 they found anger and excitement at fever-pitch over the recent attack on Fort Vanguardia, four hundred miles away. Now the cry was 'Viva Bolivia! Muera el Paraguay!'

Further attacks punctuated a series of negotiations which never seemed to be anything more than delaying tactics. As an editorial in *El Diario*, La Paz, had observed, concerning the position of the boundary on the right bank of the Paraguay: 'In this case there is no hurry about a settlement, and each five years which elapse will mean for us a gain of one degree in the Chaco.'[1] Upon the downfall of the Siles régime in June 1930, Kundt's services were dispensed with, and he withdrew from Bolivia to Berlin during the following month. Towards the end of 1932, however, many were clamouring for his recall and in December 1932 he returned to La Paz in triumph. For in June 1932, after a prolonged period of negotiation at the conference tables, and continual local skirmishing between paired military forts in the field, a raid by Bolivian troops on Fort Pitiantuta had officially signalled the outbreak of war.[2] War in the Chaco seemed at once both inconceivable and inevitable. Both governments were by now committed too far to withdraw without loss of national prestige, and procrastination with the intention of gaining a more favourable settlement had failed to breed any spirit of compromise.

9. THE CHACO WAR: 1932–1935

As the war began, Bolivia appeared to be in a vastly superior position, for the process of modernising and equipping the army had continued since 1911. But this was to prove a struggle in which the location and physical conditions of the Chaco were to combine as the most powerful antagonist.

[1] 24 April 1929.
[2] G. Ireland, *Boundaries, Possessions, and Conflicts in South America*, Harvard Univ. Press, 1938, pp. 66–95. Although this volume went to press before the completion of the Chaco dispute, its current interest and mass of available documentation resulted in an expanded study. The Bolivia–Paraguay Chaco question consequently receives more than twice the coverage allotted to any other South American boundary conflict in Ireland's comprehensive survey.

One of the decisive early engagements was the siege of Fort Boquerón in September 1932.[1] Here, the Bolivians were well dug in within lines of trenches and machine-gun nests perched in the *quebracho* forest. But after repelling many Paraguayan attacks, the garrison eventually yielded; its wells had become contaminated, and some of the horrors of the next three years had been experienced seriously for the first time. Together, both sides suffered about two thousand casualties, which for Bolivia included many of the country's most hardened Chaco troops. It was a powerful psychological victory for Paraguay, particularly as its army, though well equipped on this occasion, was raw and almost untried. Largely as a result of the defeat at Fort Boquerón, popular opinion in Bolivia had demanded the return of Kundt at the end of 1932.

Still greater Bolivian losses, however, were incurred in January and February 1933, after a series of heavy frontal attacks on Paraguayan Fort Nanawa had resulted in appalling carnage. About three thousand men were killed or wounded in an assault which, by its location and timing, had committed most of the troops to fighting waist-deep in flood water. After a final costly and still unsuccessful assault on this fort in July 1933, Kundt's strategy began to be openly questioned. As a veteran of the First World War, and an exponent of the direct offensive, his grasp of the Chaco conditions was slender in the extreme. Critics have described Kundt as incapable of any real appreciation of defensive warfare and guerrilla tactics.[2] Troops were rarely deployed in sufficient numbers, despite the fact that Bolivia fielded many more men than Paraguay. Considerably greater use, it is suggested, could have been made of the small but superior Bolivian Air Force. Major offensives were inevitably launched during the dry season, so that control of the waterholes was decisive. Andean troops, taken in their thousands into an environment totally dissimilar from that of the *altiplano*, suffered severely from the enervating heat, from insects and from epidemics. Many had already marched at least four or five hundred miles, and often much more, from the railhead beyond Cochabamba, to arrive in a state of near or complete exhaustion. Within the confines of swamp and, in certain localities, low jungle, thrown into a series of wasteful frontal attacks against a well-concealed enemy kept remarkably well informed of troop movements, the highland Bolivian Indian was frequently tried

[1] An analysis of the war from the military point of view is given by D. H. Zook Jnr (United States Air Force Academy), *The Conduct of the Chaco War*, New York, 1960.
[2] Surprisingly, however, Kundt himself was reported to have stated that he would fight a defensive war in the Chaco. Perhaps it is worth recalling the British Minister's report upon the German Military Mission in 1911: that there was 'a tendency to criticise the officers as being more theoretical than practical'.

beyond endurance. Paraguayan supply lines were shorter, so that Estigarribia was usually able to harry opposing forces at points of his own
choosing.[1]

The attitudes of the neutral powers were significant. Argentine
neutrality favoured Paraguay, for in May 1933 the navigable portions of the
Pilcomayo were closed to all shipments for Bolivia, before supplies for the
dry season had been brought up, despite the free transit agreement in
1868.[2] Buenos Aires declared that as there was no Bolivian civilian
population in the Chaco Boreal, all cargo was therefore contraband. This
was an extremely serious ruling, as Bolivia had always relied on purchases
in Argentina to supply much of the army in the pre-war period. Bolivian
troops going on leave to La Paz or Cochabamba in the 1920s had usually
travelled home by rail *via* Argentina, even *via* Argentina and Chile before
1925. They found this route not only easier, but actually shorter in time
than the more direct route, by a series of indifferent roads or tracks,
across the central Bolivian sierras. A Bolivian request to Argentina to
reopen Puerto Irigoyen on the Pilcomayo was refused. Bolivian troops
were to be interned. Argentina by this time had considerable capital investment in Paraguay; one of the largest land concessions in the disputed
area was owned by Casado, brother-in-law of the Argentine President.
Popular opinion in highland Bolivia tended to display more animosity
towards Argentina during the Chaco War than it did towards Paraguay.

Chile also, between January and May 1933, once again changed its
policy on the passage of arms shipments through its territory, and refused
to allow the passage of further war materials for Bolivia through Arica.[3]
Chile had consistently claimed since the time of the 1904 treaty that the
commercial transit guaranteed under Article VI did not automatically
extend to munitions of war. For these, a fresh application for transit was
required on each consignment, although it was true to say that such

---

[1] Marshal Estigarribia, trained at St Cyr, emerged as Paraguay's 'Man of Destiny' during the
Chaco War, proving himself a master of strategy and underlining the inadequacies of Kundt.
His own account of the war may be consulted in *The Epic of the Chaco: Marshal Estigarribia's
Memoirs of the Chaco War 1932–1935*, edited and annotated by P. M. Ynsfran, Univ. of
Texas Institute of Latin-American Studies, No. 8, Austin, 1950. Estigarribia was killed in
an air accident in September 1940.

[2] Articles XI (commercial transit) and XII guaranteed Bolivia free navigation on the Plate
river and its tributaries. In 1876, however, Argentina and Paraguay had agreed that while
navigation of the Paraná, Paraguay and Uruguay rivers (not including tributaries) was to
be free to the trade of all nations, and while vessels of war of the riverine States were to
enjoy free passage, those of nations *not* bordering on the rivers might go only as far as each
river State within its own boundaries should permit.

[3] On other counts, however, Chile was charged by Paraguay with displaying pro-Bolivian
sympathies.

applications had been something of a formality until the Chaco dispute had assumed serious proportions. Whilst the Chilean decision particularly affected the Vickers Armstrong deliveries, the Foreign Office in London felt it to be unwise to make any representations to the Chilean Government on Vickers' behalf. In any case, Britain, like others, was still selling arms indiscriminately to both sides, for Imperial Chemical Industries had dispatched large quantities of ammunition to Paraguay. Both Bolivia and Paraguay bought surplus World War I equipment, and tested out latest designs for foreign powers.

Brazil, however, like Peru, declined to impede free transit with either Bolivia or Paraguay, because of existing treaties; ports remained open to both belligerents (Corumbá was used to supply the Bolivian army in the north-east section), and escaped prisoners were not necessarily interned. Nevertheless, the hostility of Argentina was serious in a war fought in the extreme south-east of Bolivia where, by contrast, Paraguay's own supply lines were flexible – Estigarribia himself described the war as a 'war of communications'. The extent to which south-east Bolivia had so completely failed to share in the country's railway construction program now became disastrously apparent. Paraguay, however, used the American-owned Puerto Pinasco Railroad and the Casado Railroad, which ran one hundred miles into the Chaco, as well as the facilities of the port of Buenos Aires and the Argentine railways. Important also were the fresh food supplies made available to the Paraguayan forces by the two Mennonite colonies, so significantly located close to the front lines in the heart of the Chaco Boreal.

Bolivia's lack of supplies and rail communication was paralysing in its effect on mobility, and on the overwhelming increase in fatigue and delay. The plan to establish two Bolivian armies, one on the Pilcomayo and the other on the Paraguay, never developed the classical pincer movement. Disillusionment with Kundt's strategy led to his removal at the end of 1933, but the steady retreat towards the north-west continued. The neutral A.B.C.P. (Argentina, Brazil, Chile and Peru) powers' efforts to bring peace were followed by those of the Chaco Commission, set up in November 1933 by the League of Nations, despite the caution required by the terms of the Monroe Doctrine. Delegates visited various parts of the front, but the resulting truce between 19 and 30 December 1933 brought only temporary respite, neither side prepared to concede demands – instead, using the time to place fresh arms orders abroad. When hostilities were resumed, Bolivia fielded an army of only 7000 men. Since the beginning of the war, over 70,000 Bolivians had been mobilised and sent into the

Chaco. Of these, about 10,000 were prisoners in Paraguay, 32,000 had been evacuated as sick or wounded, 14,000 were dead, 8000 were serving in the communications zone and 6000 had deserted into Argentina.[1]

Relentless pressure from Paraguay continued to push back the Bolivian line, despite a series of visits from military advisers from Spain, Czechoslovakia and Chile to bolster Bolivia's tottering command. By the middle of 1934 there appeared to Paraguay to be a distinct possibility of capturing Villa Montes, severing the road between Santa Cruz and Yacuiba (the main supply line along the Andean foothill zone), and even of reaching the oilfields and refinery at Camiri and Sanandita. There was talk in Asunción of the possible annexation of Santa Cruz, and the creation of an autonomous republic.[2] Certainly, separatist tendencies still survived in the region, to be fanned as the Paraguayans advanced towards the Andean foothills. There was little chance now of successful outside intervention bringing about a suspension of hostilities, for Paraguay was adamant in its refusal to consider Bolivia's continuing condition for a ceasefire: an outlet on to the Paraguay river. The forts at El Carmen, Irindagüe, 27 de Noviembre and Ibibobo fell, and in November 1934 Paraguayan troops entered Ballivián, an important centre of Bolivian resistance.

President Salamanca, touring the front, was seized by a group of his army officers, including Peñaranda, Toro and Busch, in Villa Montes that same month, and forced to resign. He had been an inflexible, almost fanatical, supporter of war, and of the defence of 'national honour' in the Chaco. His presidential message in 1933 had argued: 'It might be asked if the Chaco is worth for Bolivia the pain of this sacrifice of life... but surely there is in this problem something more than a balance of gains and losses; the very existence of Bolivia, her full sovereignty, her dignity as a nation, her honour.' But few, if any, were still convinced by such arguments. Indeed, in lowland Bolivia, distressingly few were left to be convinced by them. As the Bolivians withdrew, their abandoned equipment supplemented the dwindling Paraguayan resources, in fact Paraguay boasted that it could have equipped its army with the material left behind by the retreating Bolivians. Much had been tossed aside as useless when the use of a screwdriver was all that was required.

The League of Nations Commission continued its efforts to promote a settlement, with remarkably little success. The League's embargo on the export of arms to Bolivia and Paraguay was not effective, for ¦both

[1] D. H. Zook, *The Conduct of the Chaco War*, p. 174.
[2] A commentary upon Paraguayan propaganda at this time is given by Plácido Molina M., 'Una nueva república en América: Santa Cruz de la Sierra', *Bol. Soc. Geog. Sucre*, vol. XXXII, 1938, pp. 204–8.

belligerents had agents elsewhere, and foreign consciences were salved by exporting instead to these 'third-party' buyers.[1] In any event, the bulk of the orders had been dispatched from source before the embargo came into effect.[2] Overall, some observers regarded the general ineffectiveness of the League's Chaco Commission to be the result of anxiety on the part of the U.S.A., and certain other South American States, that the distinction of solving the Chaco problem should not fall to the League of Nations.

The war continued, mainly by Estigarribia deploying his comparatively small numbers in harassing the demoralised Bolivians by guerrilla attack. In January 1935 the Paraguayans reached the banks of the Parapetí,[3] Carandaiti and Boyuibe fell, and the vital Santa Cruz–Yacuiba artery was cut. The triumphant drive towards the oilfields, and the cities of Santa Cruz and Tarija, began. But try as they would, the Paraguayans were unable to prolong their offensive. Camatindi and Ingavi (close to Palmar) eventually fell, but the repeated attacks against Villa Montes failed. A large Bolivian force was placed in front of the town, and all assaults were repulsed. No Paraguayan aircraft were available to destroy the single bridge across the Pilcomayo.[4] Bolivia, with the advantage of shorter supply lines at last in its own favour, vigorously defended the oilfields and the road to Santa Cruz with a newly raised army of 25,000 men. Morale among the Bolivian Indian troops improved noticeably as retreat brought them back into the Andean foothills. Wealthy mine-owners, anxious now, poured in fresh funds for the new army.

The war had reached stalemate. A Mediation Committee, comprising representatives from Argentina, Brazil, Chile, Peru, Uruguay and the U.S.A.,[5] met in Buenos Aires on 12 June 1935, to fix a truce line between the final positions held by the opposing forces at the ceasefire, called for noon on 14 June 1935. The truce line thus represented the *uti possidetis de*

---

[1] Some of the methods of 'side-stepping' the embargo were disclosed, for example, in the case brought by Bolivia in 1936–7 against two Britons, Ashton and Webster, charged with the sale of defective weapons during the Chaco War. In an attempt to show that faulty materials had not been passed on, the defendants were compelled to reveal a great deal more about their methods of evading the British embargo. *F.O. 371/20600.*

[2] The U.S.A.'s embargo on the sale of war material to Bolivia and Paraguay, for instance, was not enforced until 28 May 1934 (and lifted by President F. D. Roosevelt on 29 November 1935).

[3] 'The information that my troops had reached the Parapetí [regarded by Paraguay as one of the "natural limits" of the Chaco] filled me with pride and satisfaction. They had accomplished one of the objectives of my military life. After centuries a lost branch was grafted anew upon the old Guaraní trunk.' *Marshal Estigarribia's Memoirs*, p. 192.

[4] Estigarribia comments on the lamentable lack of air support and general shortages afflicting the Paraguayan campaign in the closing stages of the war, *ibid.* pp. 191 and 195–6.

[5] *F.O. 371/18691.*

facto demarcation and as such, it left Paraguay virtually in complete command of the Chaco Boreal.

Post-war suggestions for Bolivia to have a free-port zone at Puerto Casado on the river Paraguay with use of the Casado Railroad were considered, but ownership of the river below the Negro confluence remained firmly in Paraguay's hands, with Bolivia confined as before to the 'windows' it had been granted by Brazil in their 1903 treaty settlement. Down the Pilcomayo river, Bolivia extended its territory only as far as Esmeralda (22° 13′ S). The final Treaty of Peace, Friendship and Boundaries concluded on 21 July 1938,[1] and the Arbitration Award which it involved, resulted in the apportionment shown in Figure 10, with a Paraguayan agreement (Article VII) to allow Bolivia freedom of transit through its territory, and permit the establishment of customs offices and warehouses at Puerto Casado.[2] This outlet to the Paraguay river, however, across more than three hundred miles of the Chaco, has not become a practical reality. In 1963, following a June 1962 joint Highway Convention, Paraguay completed the final section of a 480-mile dirt road (known as the trans-Chaco highway) from Asunción, through some of the Mennonite colonies and Estigarribia to Cañada Oruro (Strongest),[3] on the Bolivian border. It forms part of a projected all-weather Pan-American Highway route designed to link the Brazilian Atlantic port of Paranaguá to La Paz, *via*

---

[1] *F.O. 371/21457; Col. Trat. Vig. Bol.*, vol. V, pp. 329–40. Additional transit agreements were signed in October 1939, November 1943 and December 1956.

[2] The eventual placing of the boundary through the Chaco Boreal was the result of arbitration by Argentina, Brazil, Chile, Peru, Uruguay and the U.S.A., October 1938, *ibid.* pp. 341–5. Boundary demarcation is complete, with the erection of metal tripods 2.2 metres high at the eleven primary points, and subsidiary concrete markers set intervisibly between. Only one problem remains, and that is to confirm the position of Post 8. The 1938 delimitation calls for its erection on the *hill* of Chovoreca, but no such eminence could be found by the Joint Commissioners when they began their survey work in the field. At the moment, therefore, while Chovoreca is fixed on the map according to its coordinates, the absence of a hill at the stated location has so far prevented Paraguay from agreeing to confirm as final the present position of the tripod. There is no settlement in this area.

Once the Chaco War was ended and the approximate final position of the Bolivia–Paraguay boundary became obvious, Argentina at last ratified the 1925 Bolivia–Argentina boundary treaty on 9 September 1938. Additional protocols were signed in March 1939, in February 1941 (when the boundary was extended from parallel 22° S down the river Pilcomayo to Esmeralda, the new triple point with Paraguay), and in August 1963.

The Strongest and *Always Ready* are two La Paz football teams whose names record one of the few British cultural influences ever to penetrate Bolivia. Such influences originated with the small mining and Antofagasta railway community of technicians and administrators who arrived in Bolivia at the turn of the century. When the entire *Strongest* team enlisted during the Chaco War, the fort at Cañada Oruro was named in their honour.

Asunción, but the road in Bolivia from Villa Montes, which runs east to link with the Paraguayan highway, is still very poor. Given the limited development of the entire south-eastern tract beyond the foothill settlements, and the lack of exchange, the trans-Chaco routeway has no significance at present for Bolivia, and no use is made of the 1938 Puerto Casado concession.

The sheer wastefulness of effort and resource in the Chaco dispute gave rise to considerable contemporary and retrospective discussion upon underlying causes. 'As in the case of Tacna–Arica', wrote Schurz in a general commentary,[1] 'the intrinsic value of the area in dispute between Bolivia and Paraguay is not commensurate with the persistence of the controversy or the bitterness of feeling which it has engendered on both sides.' Both were undoubtedly fighting for a principle and a vindication of national honour. Bolivia sought recognition of its demands for an outlet to navigable water, intensifying its activity when hopes for the long-awaited corridor to the Pacific were dashed by the final settlement of the Tacna–Arica question in 1929. This desire for an outlet to the middle Paraguay sharpened when the economic possibilities of petroleum exploitation, and of the trans-Chaco pipeline, became an issue in the 1920s. Because of the oilfields' location, such an export, had it ever been a practical proposition, would have demanded a base on the Paraguay river, well to the south of those 'windows' lying above Bahía Negra. Without such a site, the only feasible outlet for petroleum was into Argentina, for the Bolivian market itself was too limited to encourage any large-scale capital investment on the part of a foreign oil company. Ironically, the Chaco War itself had provided Standard Oil with the only doorstep market for its products that the company ever found.

More than one commentator at the time considered the need for a convenient and economic export route for the products of the Standard Oil Company of New Jersey to be the driving force behind Bolivian determination to secure a port on the river Paraguay:

Petrol is the invisible cause of the Chaco War. Let us stop talking of the Bolivia–Paraguay question being one of frontiers, of an outlet to the sea and other sentimental nonsense given as the explanation of the cause of war. This is a war of despoliation, of brutal conquest which Bolivia has waged against Paraguay thinking, with their German general, that in a few weeks they could possess themselves of an immense territory, one of the richest oil-fields in America.[2]

[1] W. L. Schurz, 'The Chaco Dispute between Bolivia and Paraguay', *Foreign Affairs*, vol. VII, 1928–9, pp. 650–5.

[2] J. W. Lindsay, 'The War over the Chaco', *International Affairs*, vol. XIV, 1935, pp. 231–40. This reference p. 235. Lindsay is quoting here from an Argentine source. Undoubtedly,

Others feel, however, that the significance of oil as a cause of the war has been exaggerated, although the possibility of extending an oil pipe-line across the Chaco has been raised again on several occasions, notably in 1939, 1943, 1956, 1957 and 1969. In this context care should be taken, before dismissing petroleum as a major factor in the Chaco conflict, to dis-tinguish between the direct challenge for ownership of the productive oilfields, and the need to confirm Bolivian ownership of territory involved in future exploration, exploitation and oil export southward or eastward to the Paraguay. Land speculation, and international interest in running oil pipelines across Bolivian territory towards suitable markets had been relevant issues since the 1920s; the possibility of Paraguay's actual annexa-tion of the known Bolivian foothill fields, on the other hand, became a significant factor only in the last phases of the Chaco War. Certainly the future resources of the south-eastern oilfields were greatly exaggerated at the time, but this in retrospect merely strengthens the role they played in moulding opinion during the final stages of the conflict. In the long term, however, access to the Paraguay routeway provided the recurrent theme.

Thus, from being confident of victory, Bolivia was beaten by a smaller nation. Bolivia had the larger army but lost the war. During the three years, Paraguay had mobilised 140,000 men and Bolivia about a quarter of a million.[1] The Chaco War produced the greatest struggle the Western Hemisphere had witnessed since the American Civil War, and the greatest in South America since the wars of independence. For both contestants, mountain and riverine, the loss of manpower was disastrous and the aftermath sadly prolonged. Paraguay in particular had still not recovered from its staggering losses incurred during the nineteenth-century war against Brazil, Argentina and Uruguay, when more than half the total Paraguayan population was killed, and fewer than 30,000 men survived in 1870. Once again, to sustain the Chaco offensive, fresh generations of youths and boys had been sent into battle, and although Paraguay more

prevailing Argentine opinion was that Bolivian oil should be permitted to move out *only* through the Argentine network. Argentina's antagonism to Bolivia is also illustrated by W. L. Schurz, 'The Chaco Dispute between Bolivia and Paraguay', p. 652, when he quotes the comment of an Argentine diplomat, 'We do not want another flag on the Para-guay river.' Before petroleum became an important issue in the Chaco dispute, Bolivia assumed Paraguay's economic interest in the region to be based on the desire to exploit *quebracho* and beef. See *El Derecho de Bolivia sobre El Chaco, desde el punto de vista geográfico*, La Paz, 1930.

[1] Bolivia's losses: 52,397 killed; over 21,000 captured (4264 died in captivity); nearly 10,000 deserters. Paraguay's losses: approx. 36,000 killed. (These figures are those of D. H. Zook, *The Conduct of the Chaco War*, pp. 240–1.)

than doubled its total national area by the acquisition of the Chaco Boreal, only a fraction of this can, even today, be regarded as effective territory.

From the Bolivian standpoint also, the Chaco War was catastrophic. Even more serious than the quashing of territorial claims, and with them the dream or reality of an independent outlet to the middle Paraguay, was the vacuum created in the Oriente. Very severe depopulation of lowland Bolivia resulted from men and boys in the Departments of Santa Cruz and Beni being pressed into service and carried away to the front. As in Paraguay, memories of this period are still comparatively fresh, and there are vivid recollections of successive Bolivian army raids through the towns and outlying ranches, each one, it seemed, taking a younger crop of youths and boys, and bearing them away to the dreaded Chaco. Many consider that this was in fact the most terrible legacy of the Chaco War, for certainly the Oriente could ill-afford the decimation of manpower suffered in defence of this great wasteland. Politically, defeat at the hands of Paraguay constituted a national humiliation, and the growing dissatisfaction among certain sections of the Bolivian population found its eventual expression in the Social Revolution of 1952.

As late as 1919 the President of the Royal Geographical Society could still, with perfect justification, introduce a lecture on the South American Chaco to members of the Society with the words: 'It is one of the remotest regions of the globe, one of the few regions which may be called almost unexplored, and about which I think I may safely say that nine-tenths of the people present know nothing whatsoever.' Yet within a few years, the Chaco had achieved notoriety in the eyes of the world as the scene of one of the most fruitless and bitter territorial disputes in American history, for the finalising of its boundary with Paraguay involved Bolivia in a last futile effort to delimit and sustain the boundaries claimed as those of the 1810 Audiencia of Charcas.

10. THE POST-CHACO WAR PERIOD: NEW 'RAIL-FOR-OIL' AGREEMENTS, AND THE DECLINE OF THE PARAGUAY ROUTEWAY

The insatiable demands for revenue to finance the costs of the Chaco War had underlined the fact in La Paz that the great bulk of Bolivia's taxable interests lay in the hands of foreign companies. Protected as these were by 'most-favoured-nation' agreements in the commercial treaties already exchanged with Britain, Germany and the U.S.A., Bolivia had found it

---

[1] Sir Thomas Holdich, 16 June 1919.

impossible to increase taxation to meet military expenditure without protracted negotiations. Even these were not always successful.

Partly because of this dissatisfaction, and partly, it was said, because of Bolivia's bitterness against the decision by the neutral powers (which included the U.S.A.) to leave Paraguay in virtual possession of the Chaco Boreal, the Standard Oil Company's property was expropriated in 1937. Specific grounds for the confiscation were charges of tax avoidance, and the alleged smuggling of petroleum by the company across the Bermejo into Argentina. Their concessions were cancelled and their equipment taken over to form the nationalised Yacimientos Petrolíferos Fiscales Bolivianos.

Over two hundred seepages have been noted along the eastern foothill belt of the Andes, some of which have since been developed into producing areas where the quantity is good, and transport costs have not proved prohibitive. Close to the Argentine boundary in the south-eastern sector, the three small oilfields of Madrejones, Bermejo and Toro were found to be an extension of the north Argentine Salta field, opened in 1925. Since the first railway agreements in this area were signed in 1922, and augmented progressively in the 1920s, 1930s and 1940s, the export into Argentina of oil from these border fields has been firmly based on the fact that Argentine loans for railway extension northwards into Bolivia are repaid in oil. Accordingly, Bolivian oil has since moved south to join the Campo Durán pipeline for transport to the San Lorenzo refinery on the river Paraná, and negotiations in 1968 and 1969 led to further conventions for the construction of a new gas pipeline to run from the Caranda, Colpa and Rio Grande fields, near Santa Cruz, southward into Argentina.

The continuing sale of Bolivian oil and gas to Argentina, in return for railway (and some highway) construction, resulted in fresh proposals in 1965 to extend the railway even farther northward into Bolivia – beyond Santa Cruz to Santa Rosa, and beyond again to a navigable point on the river Mamoré (Fig. 6 b). As such, the proposal in part recalls that of George Earl Church, made almost exactly a century ago, for Bolivia's 'Great Central Railway'. However, the wisdom of this latest railway extension, at present under way north of Santa Cruz, is highly questionable on economic grounds. Highway construction to the Mamoré navigation-heads dominated planning and investment programs in this region during the 1960s, and the future of such small river ports as Puerto Villarroel and Puerto Grether, on new Andean highway linkages, would appear to have been compromised – at least in part. Railway cargoes of timber, coffee and fruit could almost certainly find a market in northern Argentina, but there is little doubt that the desire to purchase Bolivian oil and gas motivates the decision to renew and extend the 'rail-for-oil' agreements which have now existed between the two States for nearly fifty years. For neither cargo nor passenger traffic figures have ever substantiated the early fears in La Paz that the rail extension would lead to a dangerously large-scale economic penetration of south-eastern Bolivia by Argentina. The substitution of more '*highway*-for-oil' agreements, however, would seem to be considerably more to Bolivia's advantage in terms of interior transport flexibility.

Beyond Tartagal the railway had slowly advanced in the late 1930s towards Pocitos, the Argentine frontier town, south of Yacuiba, and on 9 July 1944, the anniversary of Argentina's declaration of independence, the rails were ceremoniously laid to reach the Argentina–Bolivia boundary, and 'establish a new commercial and cultural link between the two States'. The international route was eventually extended the three hundred and sixty miles to Santa Cruz between 1945 and 1957. Just as the old wagon-trail had been interrupted by rivers spreading uncontrollably from the foot-hill zone across the Chaco plain, so the railway was similarly dislocated. The need to construct numerous bridges increased costs enormously, and temporary bridges over the Pilcomayo, Parapetí and Grande were not replaced until 1965, when for the first time intermediate breaks-of-load were eliminated. In November 1967 the railway was officially transferred to Bolivian ownership, by which period still only 30,000 tons of general cargo were being carried annually to and from Argentina, although this figure was raised to about 50,000 tons annually along certain sections of the line by the end of the 1960s, largely reflecting the movement of new oil-drilling and pipeline equipment northward from Argentina. Should the increase be maintained, and in the light of current rail extension north of Santa Cruz, the railway will probably resist any threat of replacement by highway, at least in the foreseeable future.

Oil and gas production from the most remote south-east border fields, so optimistically forecast in the 1920s when the Yacuiba district was alive with rumour and unrest, has declined. Then, the projected railway – the 'oil-belt railway' – was said to have been strategically sited along the new 'growth zone' in Bolivia's south-eastern foothill sector. But output from the Madrejones oil and gas field has since fallen sharply, and the Bolivian section ceased production in 1966, although it is still tapped in Argentina.[1] At Bermejo, Bolivian prospects appear brighter in the heavier grades than

[1] Argentina possesses the larger portion of this field. No drilling by either State was permitted within 200 metres of the boundary line. In 1969–70, new oil and gas discoveries were made by Argentina in the provinces of Jujuy and Salta. Some of the new strikes in Salta have been relatively close to the Bolivian boundary.

those of Argentina, again working in the same field south of the border. But the main productive regions, both now and probably in the future also as far as Bolivia is concerned, lie considerably farther north at Camiri, Monteagudo and particularly around the city of Santa Cruz. The long-awaited economic boom in oil has failed to stimulate a wave of prosperity in the south-eastern border country, and now it is regretfully recognised that such a boom is unlikely to occur.

Yacuiba, with a population of approximately 7000, is firmly linked by L.A.B. flight to the larger highland Bolivian centres by regular services on four days of the week, although surface connexion remains extremely difficult. The steep, narrow dirt road reaches only as far as Villa Montes, and is continued to Yacuiba by about sixty miles of very poor track. Into this frontier town, and into Pocitos (pop. 2000), a little farther south on the boundary with Argentina, come a number of Argentines to purchase sugar and rice, and a selection of imported foreign manufactured goods (mostly North American, German and Japanese) which, if they compete with Argentine home manufactures, are often considerably cheaper to obtain in Bolivia, where they are not subject to the very high import tariffs applied to many foreign manufactured articles in Argentina. This applies, for example, to such goods as whisky, radios, cameras, high-quality ceramics, cutlery and textiles, cosmetics, and various specialised electrical items which are smuggled from Bolivia into Argentina at this point. Bolivians, in their turn, shop regularly in Pocitos (Argentina), or in Tartagal for soap, cooking oil, wheat flour, apples, wine, fabrics and domestic furniture and utensils, as well as for the wide range of other Argentine manufactured goods brought north by rail. 'Essential articles' for the inhabitants of Pocitos and Yacuiba are permitted to enter Bolivia duty-free.

While probably no more than five per cent of Yacuiba's population is Argentine there are still considerable numbers of Bolivians living south of the border – occasionally as high a proportion as fifty per cent in some centres, at least as far south as Tartagal. There is also a very important seasonal labour movement from southern Bolivia into the Argentine provinces of Jujuy, Salta and Tucumán. This movement consists largely of sugar workers, whose passage southward by rail and road involves an annual migration of about 40,000 labourers from the Departments of Tarija, Potosí, Chuquisaca and Santa Cruz. Many of these Bolivians have remained in north-west Argentina, an average indeed of almost 10,000 each year during the 1960s. In Jujuy province, Bolivians make up nearly the whole of the recorded foreign resident population, and represent over seventeen per cent of the total. In Salta province, Bolivians comprise three-quarters of all the foreigners living there, and approaching nine per cent of the total population.[1]

The exodus of Bolivians has been particularly marked from the central area of the Department of Tarija, and from Tarija itself (still containing only 27,000 people), for the failure to link the regional capital city into highland Bolivia's rail network left this southern portion of the country severely isolated in terms of growth and market. Here, few *tarijeños* will care to draw the line between tranquillity and stagnation. The vitally important L.A.B. flights to Cochabamba and La Paz (increased from four to six per week in the mid-1960s), together with a weekly flight to and from Salta, provide the only modern alternative to the surface transport system, which still involves long, gruelling journeys by mountain road through the wild, desolate beauty of the central Andes. These steep, tortuous ways climb slowly out of the Tarija basin towards their old traditional destinations – the urban foci of Upper Peru. But even today, under the most favourable conditions, the journey along the winding dirt road to Potosí demands twelve hours of continuous concentration from truck drivers carrying Tarija's agricultural produce northward. Grapes and wine, citrus fruits, cereals, sugar and vegetables still provide the exports northward from this old 'garden-city's' agricultural basin, but although the variety of products is prodigious, the volume of traffic is very limited indeed.

In other directions also, routes beyond the Tarija basin remain daunting, despite some efforts at improvement. Steep, circuitous journeys by road of nine or ten hours at best link Tarija to the Bolivian railway towns: south-westwards to Villazón (pop. 10,000), and eastwards or south-eastwards to Villa Montes and Yacuiba. But the smoothest and easiest route in terms of gradient and curve lies southward, and links Tarija in five hours to Bermejo on the Argentine border. Beyond lies Orán, at one of the Argentine railheads, and it is by this economic lifeline that many of Tarija's needs are sustained, particularly in terms of domestic manufactured goods and construction materials. Coca forms the only significant return cargo in what, in any case, is a very modest trade exchange.[2]

[1] Argentina: Censo Nacional, 1960.
[2] Imports from Argentina (by value) recorded by the Bolivian custom houses for 1966 were as follows: Yacuiba U.S. $6,294,690; Villazón U.S. $1,932,185; Bermejo U.S. $11,736. Yacuiba's figure is boosted by the specialised oil-drilling machinery and pipeline equipment, etc. which enter on this route. The Tarija–Bermejo–Orán road was built by a Mixed Argentine–Bolivia Highway Commission, established in February 1942 with the purpose of linking Potosí and Tarija to the Argentine road network. As with the Yacuiba–Santa Cruz railway, Bolivian repayment of funds advanced by Argentina (initially 10 million pesos) was to be in oil exports. The Tarija–Bermejo section of the highway was officially turned over to Bolivia in March 1965.

Thus, within that portion of Bolivia's southern sector which is adjacent to Argentina, difficulties of east–west movement accentuate the north–south orientation of highland and highland fringe. Nevertheless, although two international rail routes have maintained the traditional lines of movement across this old frontier zone, the exchanges even here are limited. The long-established movement of cattle southward to Embarcación withered away after the decimation of the herds during the Chaco War, and the added disaster of the rabies epidemics which followed it. Farther west, the international rail route *via* La Quiaca–Villazón continues, as always, to compete unfavourably with routes to the Pacific ports (Fig. 6b). It attracts considerably less freight than any of the three rail routes to Matarani, Arica and Antofagasta – only about 20,000 tons annually, which consists for the most part of incoming foodstuffs and general cargo. This figure represents as little as one-tenth of the freight traffic handled under normal circumstances by the Antofagasta railway, and even this proportion is declining. In purely economic terms, with air transport competing favourably for long-distance passenger traffic between Buenos Aires and La Paz, receipts on the rail section between Atocha and Villazón (and for several miles south into Argentina) would justify closure. But this must be set against its place in the transcontinental railway system, and the desirability felt of maintaining alternative outlets to the coast by way of the Atlantic ports. Certainly, the zone between Atocha, Tupiza and Villazón generates little local traffic for, unlike the northern section of the Bolivian *altiplano*, the southern portion is very sparsely populated – much in fact is uninhabited. It forms a bleak and desolate platform, a dissected 'scabland' interrupted by salt deposits and stony wastes. Indeed, the landscape contrasts on the Bolivian *altiplano* between the Argentine and the Peruvian (Titicaca) frontiers are very pronounced. Despite the opportunities for movement which this great north–south plateau corridor has traditionally provided, the harsh nature of its southern approaches has consistently repelled settlement, while permitting exchange.

Away to the east, although the 1938 Paraguayan concessions to Bolivia on the middle Paraguay at Puerto Casado, and the accompanying navigation and transit agreements, remain unused, attempts were made by Bolivia and Brazil in the post-Chaco War period to improve communications farther north, between Santa Cruz and the Brazilian upper-Paraguay river port of Corumbá. Under the terms of the December 1928 treaty, which incorporated a series of minor adjustments along the extreme northern rubber forest boundary,[1] preliminary decisions had already been made concerning railway construction to be undertaken in Bolivia by Brazil, specifically, under Article v, a rail link between Cochabamba and Santa Cruz.[2] For the decision not to complete further extensions on the Madeira–Mamoré 'rubber railway', originally sanctioned in 1903, had been discharged by the promise of an additional million-pound sterling payment by Brazil to provide some agreed alternative. This eventually substituted a railway between Corumbá and Santa Cruz, for one between Santa Cruz and Cochabamba, and a new treaty was signed on 25 February 1938.[3]

At the same time, a second treaty was concluded which was to allow Brazil to prospect for petroleum in Bolivia along the Cordillera foothill zone between the Parapetí and Ichilo rivers, with a view to exporting the oil into Brazil by a new pipeline. It was understood that if Brazil spent more than one million pounds on the railway, then the remainder would be repaid by Bolivia in oil (Article iv). Brazil agreed to extend its own existing railway link between Santos–São Paulo and Pôrto Esperança to Corumbá, so that, with other lines to be completed internally by Bolivia, the Corumbá–Santa Cruz railway would become part of a complete transcontinental railway from Santos to Arica – el Ferrocarril Interoceánico – an idea first proposed by Brazil in 1871.

The 403-mile line between Corumbá and Santa Cruz was begun later in 1938 by a Mixed Bolivian–Brazilian Commission, and was eventually opened in 1956, with a temporary bridge (completed in 1964) over the Rio Grande. The railway was officially transferred to Bolivian ownership in October 1964, but although the construction costs far exceeded one million pounds, no petroleum deposits were found in Brazil's concession zone, and the debt has been scheduled for repayment between 1970 and 1990. Once again, the proposed oil pipeline eastwards from the Bolivian foothill fields to the Paraguay river, and beyond, was abandoned.

Instead, the most successful strikes in the foothill zone have, after all, been in the vicinity of Santa Cruz – strikes by Bolivia Gulf Oil, the Pittsburgh-based subsidiary which began prospecting in Bolivia as recently as June 1956. The company's remarkable success over the next decade resulted in new pipeline construction – towards the Pacific, however, rather than the Atlantic. At the end of 1966 Gulf began exporting 25,000

[1] See above, p. 129 n. 2
[2] This railway had also been suggested even earlier under Article iii of the 1904 treaty with Chile, see above, p. 66 n. 4. Three routes were explored and surveyed in 1920–4 by the German engineer, Hans Grether.
[3] *F.O. 371/21428; Col. Trat. Vig. Bol.*, vol. iv, pp. 291–318. Also preliminary protocols, *ibid.* pp. 277–90.

barrels per day westwards along its new pipeline to Sicasica. Here, on the *altiplano*, sixty-five miles south-east of La Paz, Gulf's oil flowed in to the Y.P.F.B. pipeline which runs down to Arica by the side of the railway, and which was completed for test flows in 1961. Rather than seeking possible outlets in Brazil or Paraguay, as trans-Chaco pipeline rumours suggested in the 1920s, oil moved west, to where the insatiable demands of the southern Californian market called the tune. An additional 10,000 barrels per day were sold annually by Gulf to Y.P.F.B. in the late 1960s for export into Argentina under the 'rail-for-oil' agreements. Most of the natural gas is returned for storage underground, however, until the negotiations for the new 360-mile gas pipeline southwards from Santa Cruz into Argentina (estimated cost U.S. $56 million), and its subsequent construction *via* Yacuiba, are completed.

The situation was changed, however, at the end of the 1960s when a new Bolivian Government nationalised the Bolivia Gulf Oil Co., and occupied its installations in October 1969. Negotiations had already been completed between Gulf and Y.P.F.B., and joint application made for a U.S. $23 million loan from the World Bank to finance the projected natural gas pipeline. After several weeks of uncertainty, it was announced that the Bank would honour its commitment; Argentina had offered to replace Gulf as principal guarantor for the loan. This has now been set at over $40 million and is to be provided jointly by the World Bank and the Inter-American Development Bank. The pipeline was to have been operated by Y.A.B.O.G., a company originally formed by Bolivia Gulf Oil and Y.P.F.B., and a contract had been concluded with Argentina for the sale of up to 300 million cubic feet of gas per day in the 1970s. After some delay, this is likely to be implemented, and was re-scheduled to begin in August 1971.

The necessity to seek alternative oil markets to those in southern California led to Bolivia's hope that Argentina, Paraguay or Brazil would import the 25,000–26,000 barrels of crude oil per day formerly sold in the U.S.A. In October 1970, however, oil shipments to the Gulf refinery in California were resumed. Should Brazil elect to compete, it is thought that tankers would still load crude oil at Arica, although the suggestion of a trans-Chaco oil pipeline has once again been tentatively revived. The line would run, in that case, to Corumbá where a refinery could be set up to distribute products to the states of Mato Grosso and west São Paulo. The route westwards to Arica, however, involves no new pipeline construction and is initially considered to be a more feasible proposition, despite the distances involved. Alternative overseas buyers would also be likely to load at Arica. In any event, despite an increased domestic demand which would follow the proposed development of a petrochemical industry at Santa Cruz, the future marketing pattern of Bolivian oil will remain a highly critical factor in the country's economy.

Meanwhile, the Corumbá–Santa Cruz railway's total cargo traffic remains small, only about 24,000 tons annually, of which roughly three-quarters consists of Brazilian manufactured goods. There is a daily, 48-hour rail connexion between São Paulo and Corumbá, but delays (including customs delay) of up to two weeks are commonly experienced in moving goods from Corumbá to Santa Cruz. Occasionally such delays may be doubled or trebled. The track is slow and worn, with thousands of its sleepers burned by cinders dropped from the wood-burning locomotives. Of the twenty-nine wayside stations punctuating the line, only Roboré (pop. about 7250) and San José (about 5000), two of the old mission centres on the trail between the Paraguay and the city of Santa Cruz, have any significantly sized settlement. Thus, very little cargo is added to that being carried between the terminal stations. Operating costs are so high that in the case of *autocarril* passenger fares, the railway barely competes with the aircraft flying overhead, conveniently following the rail track's narrow red gash through the almost continuous jungle lying below.

Constant deficits have led to talk of lifting the track and replacing it with a road into Brazil, where work has begun on the projection of a highway westwards from Uberaba (Minas Gerais) to Corumbá. The costs of conversion to diesel operation, and the need for extensive track repairs to increase the present low running speeds, are estimated at over six million dollars. Thus the future of this line is uncertain, for so far it lacks the backing of the oil and gas sales which have stabilised and extended railway construction northwards into Bolivia from the Argentine baseline. Nevertheless, the longstanding desire of La Paz to link Cochabamba and Santa Cruz by rail (they were linked by a paved highway in 1954), has never been officially abandoned, and in the late 1960s the plan was actively revived once again. Further, it was given top priority by a Government determined at last to effect the link between the country's separate western and eastern rail systems, although construction cannot be justified on present economic forecasts. With enormous effort and expense, the line is at present probing the heart of the cordilleras beyond Cochabamba, Mizque and Aiquile towards Valle Grande, through some of the steepest and most appallingly difficult country in the world. At some as yet unspecified date, it is scheduled to join the final sixty miles of the Yacuiba–Santa Cruz railway at Florida and thus run to its eventual destination. The two terminal stations on the outskirts of the city of Santa Cruz, one built by Argentina, the other by Brazil, were linked in 1967, since when the two lines have together been referred to as the Yacuiba–Santa Cruz–Corumbá railway. It is possible, therefore, even probable if the Bolivian Government continues its interior rail-building program, that the line to Corumbá will survive because of its significance in the wider context of Bolivia's internal and external rail communications.

If it does so, it will continue to emphasise Corumbá's relationship with the Bolivian Oriente as a *railway town* (if not as a highway centre) on the transcontinental route from São Paulo and Rio de Janeiro, rather than as a *river port* on the Paragay route from Buenos Aires and Montevideo. The distinction is a significant one, for it underlines the continuing decline of the Paraguay river routeway's importance to eastern Bolivia's commerce. The peak years in the growth and development of Puerto Suárez, moderate as these were, stretched over three decades between 1903 and the end of the Chaco War. The 1903 Lake Cáceres 'window', however unsatisfactory, was the only one of the four ever to achieve any economic significance. This was sustained by the proximity and stature of the port of Corumbá, and it confirmed the orientation of the region to the Paraguay river. The construction of the Corumbá–Santa Cruz railway, however, banished Puerto Suárez to virtual oblivion, for the railway does not touch the tiny Bolivian port, left stranded, like the creatures in the lake, upon the banks of the Tamengo Channel.[1]

Puerto Suárez' beleaguered position is nowhere better observed than from the air as the weekly L.A.B. flight from Santa Cruz and Roboré circles in above the sinuous Tamengo Channel, and skims over the short grassy main street, the deserted custom house and the ruined jetty – all enclosed by the huge green void of forest, thicket and swamp. Even the lake itself is frequently hidden under the enormous raft of grass and water hyacinth which seasonally covers its surface. As the water level falls, hundreds of cattle wade into the lake to forage on the raft until storms tear it apart and sink the vegetation, or send it floating past Corumbá and down the river Paraguay. Then Lake Cáceres is again revealed, and waves break violently against the shore, which here takes the form of small cliffs about twenty feet high. At night, it is difficult to realise, as one listens, that the

---

[1] The official population figure of 3279 for 1962 (latest estimate) was not supported by field evidence and is almost certainly still too high.

Puerto Suárez is linked to Corumbá by a sixteen-mile dirt road, negotiable except at the height of the rains and following the course of the railway as far as possible. The road is now more frequently used than the Tamengo Channel to reach Corumbá – a final epitaph upon the fate of this tiny ghost port.

ocean is in fact nearly two thousand miles away. The condition of Puerto Suárez emphasises the fact that Bolivia has never yet been able to secure, maintain or improve any good port site on the upper and middle Paraguay (Plates xx and xxi).

At no point on the entire Bolivian perimeter is there a greater contrast between two border settlements, for Corumbá stands high on a 300-foot limestone bluff overlooking the Paraguay at its upper limit of commercial navigation (for vessels of 1200 tons cargo capacity).[1] With its highly cosmopolitan population of approximately 40,000, including many German, Japanese and Middle Eastern merchants and traders, Corumbá also contains more Bolivians, for example, than most of Bolivia's own border settlements in the Oriente put together. Thus, the Corumbá–Santa Cruz railway, i.e. the São Paulo–Santa Cruz railway, has if anything lessened still further the significance of the Cáceres 'window' through which it passes. The port facilities which the 1903 treaty adjustments were designed to provide are completely by-passed, and the principal custom house has been transferred from Puerto Suárez to Paradero (Quijarro) station on the railway line (Fig.14).

Whether serious, sustained attention will ever be given to any of Bolivia's outlets on or close to the Paraguay river remains to be seen. If so, it is likely to be at the most southerly of the four regained in 1903 – that known as Corredor Man Césped, where a thirty-one-mile (fifty-kilometre) frontage directly on to the Paraguay river extends above Bobrapa (the Bolivia–Brazil–Paraguay triple boundary point) at the mouth of the river Negro. It is a low, swampy, riparian strip, very difficult to reach overland, but Bolivia has stated that it intends to build a new port on the Paraguay – Puerto Busch – at the least unfavourable site available within it, and in 1970 took delivery there of a floating dock donated by Argentina.

This plan forms a small part of the highly ambitious international development project for the whole of the Plate river basin which is at present being investigated by Argentina, Brazil, Paraguay, Uruguay and Bolivia. The first Cuenca del Plata conference took place in Buenos Aires in February 1967, and the second at Santa Cruz de la Sierra, Bolivia, in May 1968.[2] The scrutiny and selection of projects, and the instigation of feasibility studies were authorised from among the many wide-ranging improvements to navigation, to port, road, rail and canal facilities, flood

[1] While Corumbá, the chief commercial city of the Mato Grosso, and Brazil's most important Paraguay river port, handles considerable river traffic in live cattle, jerked beef, hides and skins, wheat and other cereals, ipecacuanha, ores and cement (about 100,000 tons annually), *rail* cargoes are more significant in the Bolivian context.
[2] Intentions were formalised in the Acta de Santa Cruz de la Sierra, 20 May 1968.

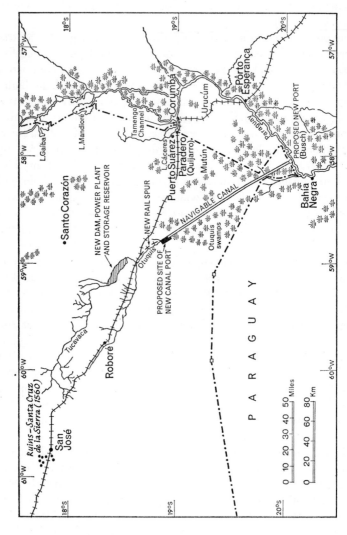

14   The revival of the Otuquis project: a proposed new Bolivian port on the river Paraguay

control and power projects, variously put forward by the member nations. A third conference, at Brasília, culminated in the signing of the River Plate Basin Treaty on 24 April 1969.[1]

While the Cuenca del Plata exercise in international cooperation remains in its preliminary stages, Bolivia's intention (among other suggestions) to locate the new Puerto Busch on the Paraguay is closely linked with the Government's desire to be represented visibly on the waterway, as well as with two other projected developments within the same area. The first of these brings the wheel full circle, for it revives the old 1832 scheme of Manuel Luis de Oliden to develop the Otuquis and Tucavaca swamps.[2] Once more, the agricultural potential claimed for this portion of Bolivia's south-eastern sector has been restated, and the Otuquis Project now aims at reclaiming, draining and then irrigating at least 100,000 hectares from the extensive Otuquis swamps (which cover about 600,000 hectares) for rice, sugar cane and cattle. The flood waters which inundate these vast areas would be regulated by a new storage reservoir, which at the same time could supply a hundred-mile navigation canal to reach the river Paraguay at Puerto Busch. A short branch line to a new inland port at the canal-head would link it to the Corumbá–Santa Cruz railway (Fig. 14). With the additional provision of 10,000 kw. of hydro-electric power, the cost is conservatively estimated at about U.S. $23 million, excluding interest rates. Success would depend, among the many other considerations, upon the promotion of large-scale immigration into this area, which is extremely uncertain. Viewed objectively, there can be no immediate prospect that money will be found for any such projects on this scale, given the almost completely negative character of the region and its persistent failure to attract speculative development.

The second project related in part to the siting of Puerto Busch concerns the Mutún–Urucúm area, and the immensely rich Ordovician iron and manganese deposits which straddle the Bolivia–Brazil boundary south

[1] J. V. Fifer, 'The Plate Basin Project: new proposals for South American Economic Cooperation', *Geography*, vol. LV, 1970, pp. 209–14.

[2] A River Plate Regional Conference at Montevideo in 1941, attended by Argentina, Bolivia, Brazil, Paraguay and Uruguay, had agreed to set up technical committees to investigate improvements to navigation in the Plate basin. The project now presented by the Bolivian delegates is broadly based on the outline study drawn up by Alfonso Balderrama Maldonado, *El Proyecto Otuquis*, La Paz, 1961. It contains the same fundamental proposals as Oliden's scheme, except that it does not make the same initial error of presuming that the Otuquis river is navigable, or that it flows directly into the Paraguay. Farther west, preliminary investigations have also been instituted into the feasibility of draining, cultivating and irrigating another tract of swamp of about 200,000 hectares on the Chaco fringe – that of Abapó-Izozog, between the Grande and Parapetí rivers.

of Corumbá. Already, great wedges have been removed from the hills which rise abruptly to about 1700 feet, above the palm-and-cactus thicket along this north-eastern fringe of the Chaco. There are abundant reserves of haematite (45,000,000,000 tons in Bolivia, and 6,000,000,000 tons in Brazil have been estimated),[1] while in addition rich manganese deposits occur on the Brazilian side which have recently been found to extend also into Bolivia. The port of Corumbá (with Ladario) is already handling about 75,000 tons of processed Brazilian manganese ores annually, both by rail and river, and attention is being turned to the haematite deposits, particularly in the Bolivian section. Mining as such is not necessary, for almost all the ores are readily accessible to open cut, often without the removal of an overburden. It is the costs of transport which are the controlling factor, and future successful exploitation will depend on the securing of large markets for very large tonnages, coupled with new low-cost methods of bulk transport. If Puerto Busch were ever to handle the Bolivian Mutún ores, destined initially for Argentina as well as Brazil, then the construction of a new seventy-mile railway, road, canal, or belt-conveyor would be required. Even with foreign loans made available through the Cuenca del Plata development plan, it is difficult to avoid the conclusion that Corumbá, rather than Puerto Busch, may still in the future provide the most economically viable outlet for the Bolivian ores. Political considerations, however, may well encourage Bolivia to attempt to develop its own alternative.

Meanwhile, as in the case of the existing agreements with Paraguay, Bolivia makes virtually no use of the navigation concession extended by Brazil in the southern sector. Despite the fact that the 12 August 1910 Treaty of Commerce and River Navigation confirmed[2] (Article VIII) Bolivia's right to free transit on the Paraguay river (as well as on the Amazon and Madeira rivers), and (Article XVIII) Bolivia's right to maintain customs agents in Corumbá (as well as in Pará and Manaus) – agreements which were repeated in 1958 – the Paraguay route must at present be totally disregarded as a Bolivian outlet or supply line.[3] With isolated

---

[1] N. H. Fisher, *Geological Report on the Mutún Iron Deposit*, United Nations Technical Assistance Report, La Paz, 1955. The presence of the iron ores was known in colonial times, and noted also by d'Orbigny and Oliden.

[2] *Col. Trat. Vog. Bol.*, vol. IV, pp. 226–39. (Formerly set out in Article VII [1867 treaty], and in Articles V and VI [1903 treaty].)

[3] Free surface and river transit for Bolivian goods through Brazilian territory was reaffirmed by a Free Transit Convention signed on 29 March 1958 (see above, p. 131 n. 2). In addition, free zone privileges and maintenance of customs agents at Corumbá, Pôrto Velho, Manaus and Pará (Belém) were confirmed, and Bolivia was granted a free zone in the port of Santos. This followed an earlier proposal made by Brazil in 1943. Taken together, these concessions emphasise the roles of the *Amazon waterway* (and highway connexions) and the *Santos–São Paulo–Corumbá rail route* (or highway alternatives) in any Bolivian transit trade through Brazil.

exceptions, few sites on the outlets to the upper Paraguay river have been visited at all during the last forty years save by the Boundary Commissioners, toiling between 1957 and 1962 to erect the pyramidal concrete pillars in the swamps along the southern section of the border with Brazil. Through mostly uninhabited wilderness, men were frequently working up to their waists, even to their necks, in water and mud – working to demarcate and check the 1903 boundary around the access points on to the river Paraguay, a line which had long since ceased to have any significance whatever in practical terms.

Farther south, additional transit agreements were concluded with Argentina in 1947, 1954 and 1957, while on 18 August 1963, Argentina announced that Bolivia had been offered a free zone in the Paraná river port of Barranqueras. This was confirmed by the treaty of 19 September 1964, and was followed, on 4 June 1969, by the granting to Bolivia of extra free-port facilities on the Paraná at Rosario. If these, or any similar concessions, were ever to be taken up seriously, it appears that they would tend to be linked more closely to the Villazón or Yacuiba rail routes, or to complementary highway systems, than to increased use of Paraguay river navigation, although the future bulk transport of ores could provide an exception. Thus, as in the case of Corumbá, the value of the Paraguay–Paraná river ports to Bolivia must be judged largely in terms of the greater efficiency of their surface transport connexions.

The various port concession zones once secured (in Argentina, Uruguay or Brazil), still entail journeys *in toto* of up to two thousand miles from the Andean centres to the Atlantic, and the time and distance involved inevitably form strong deterrents. Indeed they emphasise the advantages of developing regional markets closer to Bolivia's own borders. However, in the twentieth century, the official recognition by Brazil, Argentina and Paraguay of Bolivia's freedom of navigation on the Paraguay–Paraná at last removed what the country had long regarded (or chosen to regard) as the major stumbling-block to the successful development of its south-eastern sector. But other considerations apart, the navigational concessions were gained too late to attract and mobilise the necessary manpower, capital and resources necessary for successful development – if indeed this had ever been possible.

Where traditional activities failed to revive after the Chaco War, much of the stagnation, even the prostration, of the south and south-eastern regions remains, and recovery is slow. Many of the sweeping changes following the 1952 Social Revolution and Agrarian Reform have proved unrealistic, or unworkable, in the context of lowland Bolivia. Over much of the Oriente, change is localised, often sharp but elsewhere imperceptible. Tarija (pop. 27,000) and Sucre (pop. 50,000) show only slow growth. More substantial development and immigration are concentrated in the Santa Cruz area which, while it lies on the fringe of the Amazon basin, has always been closely associated with the southern sector. Indeed, it has provided the only major focus for the Bolivian Oriente as a whole. The city of Santa Cruz now contains a population of more than 96,000 (1967 official estimate), while the Santa Cruz region, with such colonization centres as Montero, Portachuelo and Warnes, includes approximately 150,000 people. The construction of the eastern railway system has strengthened Santa Cruz' links within the southern sector during the last twenty years, although the effects of the international rail connexions with both Argentina and Brazil have been balanced by the city's improved highway communication with the major Andean centres of Cochabamba (pop. 138,000) and La Paz (pop. 490,000).

Despite all the effort and sacrifice, however, which have been expended since independence upon securing an outlet to the Paraguay–Paraná–Plata routeway, it is not the river, nor indeed the railway, that now provides the most significant medium of exchange southward. In terms of transport, it is the existing and proposed oil and gas pipelines into Argentina which appear at present to have forged the strongest economic ties of all.

CHAPTER 5

THE WIDER IMPLICATIONS
OF LOCATION

I. BRITAIN, THE UNITED STATES AND BOLIVIA

One December evening in London in 1904, having listened to an account of a recent expedition to Bolivia, the Bolivian Chargé d'Affaires was invited to open the ensuing discussion. He began thus:

> I have listened with great pleasure to the very interesting lecture about Dr. Hoek's travels in Bolivia. I am very pleased indeed that some interest is being taken now in South America. It is not very long ago that I was invited to a country house in England, and when I arrived there I only found the ladies of the house-party. They were all staring at me, and I could not make out what was the reason. But soon I discovered it. One of the ladies of the house-party brought me her album, and asked me to write my name down, and the country from which I came. I did so, and having written 'Bolivia', she asked – 'Something else?' I said, 'Something else?...What?...South America?' 'Yes', she said, 'that is what we want.'
> And then the lady of the house told me they had been discussing at length where Bolivia was; some said it was in South Africa, and some in Bohemia.[1]

His story was capable of much wider application. Bolivia remained *terra incognita* for many, perhaps for the majority, in nineteenth- and twentieth-century Britain, while for the few who had any cause to concern themselves officially with such matters, the facts concerning Bolivia's location and development inspired doubt and pessimism. Unquestionably, on the part of the British Government, this attitude has been shown to have emerged as soon as it became clear, after 1825, that Bolivia was bent upon remaining independent from Peru. Regretting the announcement of the new *República Bolívar*, and anticipating the anxieties of his immediate superior, C. M. Ricketts, the British Vice-Consul in Lima feared that the breakaway of Upper Peru would provide 'an evil precedent, calculated to awake in other parts of this ill-connected territory a spirit directly hostile to that concentration and consolidation of interests and energies, which are so much to be desired in the present crippled and exhausted condition

---

[1] Pedro Suárez (nephew of Nicolás Suárez), 12 December 1904, at the house of the Royal Geographical Society. Col. George Earl Church was in the chair.

237

of the country, and which seem indispensable to ensure its peace and security'.[1]

In a country, indeed in a sub-continent, where independence introduced so little change in the social and economic structure, such negative forecasts were inevitably confirmed by the continual instability characterising the Bolivian political scene. Intrigue, turmoil and threatened secession – whether it be of the Departments of La Paz, Cochabamba and Oruro, or of the Departments of Santa Cruz and Tarija – formed a recurrent theme in diplomatic reporting, where 'convulsed' became one of the most frequently used epithets to describe the internal political situation during the early decades. For the prolonged peripatetic nature of the Bolivian Government, and the necessity to maintain some degree of Cabinet balance between *paceños* and *chuquisaqueños*, were themselves indicative of a long struggle to appease rival factions. Throughout the nineteenth and early twentieth centuries, stores of arms were forbidden to be held in the Departmental capitals for fear of the separatist insurrections they might successfully sustain.

The apparent security forecast by the creation of the Peru–Bolivia Confederation in 1836 had at length encouraged Britain to sanction the promotion of J. B. Pentland as Consul-General to Bolivia in August of that year, and to extend diplomatic recognition to the Confederation with the conclusion of the Treaty of Amity, Commerce and Navigation in June 1837.[2] But Pentland was soon to be recalled, and Lord Palmerston declared in May 1839 (shortly after the collapse of the Confederation) that such a senior post in Bolivia would henceforth be abolished. A renewal of the treaty with the unitary State of Bolivia took place in September 1840,[3] and under Articles II and VIII complete protection and security for British merchants in Bolivia was guaranteed. The stormy advent of the Belzu regime, however (December 1848 to August 1855), began the disastrous thirty-year period of political turmoil and military dictatorship which lasted until President Daza's overthrow in December 1879. In a spurious effort to win popular support, Belzu's antagonism to foreign business enterprises in Bolivia reached exaggerated proportions, until xenophobia characterised domestic policy. On 7 April 1849 all foreign warehouses were forcibly closed for an initial period of one hundred days. With the purpose, it was declared, of boosting Bolivian enterprise, Belzu stipulated that all internal trade was henceforward to be handled exclusively by

[1] P. W. Kelly to George Canning, Lima, 17 September 1825, *F.O. 61/6.*
[2] *F.O. 94/161.*   [3] *F.O. 94/344.* (See above, p. 47 n. 1.)

Bolivian nationals, and that foreign wholesale commercial houses were to be severely restricted. Despite the plea for the exemption of British subjects on the basis of the 1840 treaty, the position was maintained.

Continued harassment of the small number of Britons in Bolivia led to the recall to London in August 1853 of the British Chargé d'Affaires, J. A. Lloyd – 'ill, disgusted and tired of life' – and to Britain's official rupture of diplomatic relations with Bolivia in the October of that year. Although some exchange at consular level was resumed in April 1858, no British diplomatic representation was established again in Bolivia for the next fifty years. Even then, in 1903, it was the British Resident Minister in Lima who was charged with making periodic visits to La Paz, and separate diplomatic representation in Bolivia was not ultimately sanctioned again by London until 1910.

This very long period of relegation by Britain into the diplomatic wilderness is the striking feature of Anglo-Bolivian affairs, both political and commercial, during the nineteenth and early twentieth centuries, particularly in the context of Britain's relations with others of the South American nations over this period. Infrequent requests by British business houses for the reappointment of a Chargé d'Affaires in Chuquisaca or La Paz, on the grounds of the security and status it would provide for their agents, were unwaveringly refused by the Foreign Office. Complaints that Bolivia was the *only* Pacific State without a British diplomatic representative, and that former British business contacts, even as early as the 1850s and 1860s, were passing into the hands of active American agents, left the Foreign Office quite unmoved. Support for the Foreign Office's decision came from the Board of Trade which, in respect of Bolivia, was principally concerned only with proposals for consular representation in the mineral ports of Mejillones and Antofagasta, down in the desert panhandle. Elsewhere, the Board agreed that the volume of trade with Bolivia, actual or potential, did not warrant the appointment of any more minor officials to show the flag while becoming an additional drain on Treasury funds.

Nevertheless, there were occasional claims that the absence of British diplomatic representation was itself responsible for the widespread loss of confidence in Bolivia among British commercial interests. A small group of Britons in Oruro had complained of unjust imprisonment during the violent years of Mariano Melgarejo's régime (December 1864 to January 1871). Accordingly, the Foreign Office was persuaded in 1875 to accredit a special mission to Bolivia, instructing its leader, Spenser St John, to assess the necessity, or desirability, of re-establishing British diplomatic representation. At the end of its investigation, however, the delegation remained unimpressed – trade, and opportunities for trade, appeared minimal. La Paz, the only commercial centre of any significance at all, St John observed, was exhausting, and to be avoided as far as possible; Cochabamba entailed long, arduous journeys by mule along preposterous mountain trails; Sucre was stagnant and overburdened with priests. 'Travelling in Bolivia necessitates not only passing over great distances, but preparation as if to plunge into a deserted country, where little but fuel and water can be obtained.'[1]

Its opinions thus confirmed, the Foreign Office continued to reject all further requests for diplomatic representation in Bolivia. For the remainder of the nineteenth century the British Government was more than content to accept the services of the United States' Resident Minister in La Paz. Thus it was the American diplomatic representative who held a watching brief over British interests, protected personnel, and forwarded to London (by way of the State Department) copies of the more important political documents.

The loss of the Bolivian littoral in 1879 strongly reinforced Britain's negative assessment of the region. Without either a seaboard or a major navigable waterway, the country lay completely beyond the range of sea power. *Pax Britannica* rested upon the Royal Navy's traditional role of the protection of British interests abroad, a role well illustrated, for example, by conditions in Paraguay a few years earlier. There, British residents detained in Asunción during the War of the Triple Alliance in 1867 requested the immediate assistance of a Royal Navy gunboat for their evacuation.[2] This was agreed to by Argentina and Brazil, and the gunboat was permitted to proceed up-river into Paraguay, in accordance with Foreign Office instructions.

But the landlocked nature of Bolivia's location in the South American interior presented unique features, even when compared with Paraguay. When, therefore, early in 1886, the Bolivian Minister in Lima called upon the British Ambassador there to enquire once more about the possibilities of renewing British diplomatic representation in Bolivia, his request was rejected with a classic re-statement of British policy: '*In a country possessing no seaboard*, questions with Great Britain can rarely, if ever, come under discussion, whether as regards political or commercial matters.'[3] Warming

---

[1] 'Account of a Journey through Bolivia in 1875, by Mr. Spenser St. John', 25 January 1876. F.O. 97/442.

[2] F.O. 13/446.

[3] Reported by Col. C. E. Mansfield to Lord Salisbury, Lima, 14 January 1886, F.O. 61/364.

to his theme, the British Minister subsequently explained some of the reasons for this attitude: that, in practice, much of the business handled by British Legations in South America arose from queries and requests connected with sea-going commerce, an area of activity in which Bolivia, alas, could have no concern. Virtually all British business transactions in Bolivia could be more than adequately handled, the Ambassador stressed, by the Consulates at Lima and Arequipa. Whether or not Mansfield was entirely disinterested in the emphasis he laid upon the Peruvian routeway, one must remember that he spoke at a time when the Mollendo–Arequipa–Puno railway had temporarily given Peru a clear twenty-year lead over the Chilean (or Chilean-occupied) ports as Bolivia's principal outlet to the Pacific. Clinching matters, Mansfield added after some further investigation, 'I cannot learn that we should derive any advantage even by the appointment of a Consul at La Paz', an opinion Lord Salisbury was very ready to endorse.

Among other considerations, Britain's continued unwillingness in the nineteenth century to become involved with Bolivia because of its landlocked location, is evidenced by a number of Foreign Office memoranda accompanying its persistent refusals to place a British Minister there:[1]

I do not think it would be advisable to appoint a Diplomatic Representative [to Bolivia]. No influential recommendation in this direction has been made here.

The attraction of British capital [into Bolivia] would mean the flow of British money into the pockets of the authorities for the time being. We should have the usual story of rascality – not wholly it might be on the South American side – with its sequel of complaints and claims, *and as Bolivia has no seaboard, we should have no means, in the last resort, of forcing redress.*

The great difficulty to my mind is that if our Representatives or Consuls are ill-treated, *we have no means of exacting redress.*

I always feel misgivings as to the appointment of Consular officers *in the semi-civilised interior of South America, where we can neither control nor protect them.*

Thus, although Bolivia's landlocked location was certainly not the only factor responsible for Britain's continuing lack of confidence in the country, Bolivia's inaccessibility to sea power and to sea-based trade was undoubtedly a major stumbling-block in any attempts to arouse Britain's

[1] Foreign Office memoranda and correspondence, 1891–9, *F.O. 11/32; F.O. 11/34; F.O. 11/35, passim* (my italics).

interest in the region.[1] Such attitudes also undoubtedly gave colour and credence to the oft-quoted, though apocryphal, tale of attempted gunboat diplomacy by Britain against Bolivia. It was recounted that some alleged discourtesy to the Bolivian President, committed by the British Minister in La Paz in 1880, had resulted in his being run out of the city, seated backwards upon an ass, to the accompanying jeers of an abusive populace. Upon hearing of the indignities suffered by her Minister, Queen Victoria is said to have ordered a gunboat to stand by off the Bolivian coast. The news that Bolivia had no coastline, a most rare geographical phenomenon, prompted the Queen to strike Bolivia's name from the map of South America with great ceremony, and to declare that thereafter its place on English maps would be marked as 'unexplored territory inhabited by savages'.

Bolivia's reaction to such official extinction is unfortunately not recorded. Since Britain had no accredited Minister in Bolivia at this period, authenticity yields to allegory. Yet, while British records contain nothing in its support, an earlier dispatch by the American Minister in La Paz may reveal the origins, accurate or otherwise, of the story.[2] Noting in 1869 the Bolivian Government's receipt of an autographed letter from Queen Victoria, the Minister inferred the apparent revival of more amicable relations between Britain and Bolivia. Some years previously, he recorded, Britain's accredited Minister Floyd (presumably J. A. Lloyd) was said to have brought in very large quantities of English goods, duty-free under diplomatic privilege, for his own use, and then to have proceeded to sell these goods on the open market. Declared *persona non grata* by President Belzu in 1853, Lloyd was summarily dismissed from Bolivia, while harsh words, similar to those attributed to Queen Victoria, were uttered by an outraged Lord Palmerston (who was said to be a relative of Lloyd), in defence of the Minister's protested innocence. But the basis of Lloyd's unacceptability in Bolivia, apart from the general intolerance of Belzu's régime, may well have been the fact that he was suspected of meddling in internal affairs, and of conspiring with the exiled Andrés Santa Cruz in

[1] As a result of Bolivia's loss of coastline in 1879, and of the terms of existing 1884 truce agreements between Chile and Bolivia, Chilean goods were entering Bolivia duty-free. To offset this arrangement, very heavy import duties were periodically laid on various other foreign imports by Bolivia. In a letter to the Foreign Office, 21 June 1898, Peek Frean & Co. Ltd, London, complained, for example, that Bolivian import duties of 75 per cent *ad valorem* on their goods were rendering them wholly uncompetitive with inferior biscuit products imported from Chile, and that the obligation to import Chilean goods duty-free was in general a severe impediment to the development of British trade. (*F.O. 11/35*.)

[2] J. W. Caldwell to Secretary of State Hamilton Fish, La Paz, 1 May 1869, Diplomatic Despatches from Bolivia, *General Records of the Dept. of State, Record Group 59*.

order to aid the latter's return to power. 'To this day', wrote Caldwell, 'Englishmen and English interests have been deprived of the usual aids and safeguards in a foreign land.'

At the close of the nineteenth century, rather more steady pressure was exerted upon the Foreign Office to appoint a British diplomat to Bolivia. Letters appeared in the press; a pamphlet entitled *Bolivia: its position, products and prospects* was printed for private circulation in London in 1901 as a plea for diplomatic representation in Bolivia – the 'Transvaal of South America'. Although its authorship remained anonymous, it is likely to have been written on behalf of the Antofagasta (Chili) and Bolivia Railway Co., whose line had reached Oruro in 1892. The Government was informed that there were now between one hundred and fifty and two hundred Britons in Bolivia, mostly in Oruro and La Paz. While these figures were supposed to persuade the Foreign Office to take some action, they do in fact demonstrate how remarkably few Britons were resident in Bolivia, especially when compared with the large numbers of British expatriates in some of the surrounding States. The Foreign Office remained circumspect, but agreed at length, in 1903, to instruct the British Minister in Lima to extend his administrative duties periodically to La Paz. The turn of the century had witnessed a dramatic increase in Bolivian tin production in response to rising world demand, and consular representatives were placed, also *via* Lima, in Oruro, La Paz and Sucre. But the Foreign Office continued to reject the recommendation made in 1898 to follow the example of so many other European States and place a Vice-Consul in the Bolivian rubber-boom town of Riberalta, declaring roundly, among other points, that it was still not marked in any of their gazetteers.

Increasing emphasis was laid by this time upon the desirability of sending competent representatives into the region: 'the U.S.A. is sending abler and more efficient men to Bolivia', wrote E. R. Moon, M.P., to the Foreign Office on 6 January 1902. Certainly the long period of official disregard of Bolivia by Britain had enabled not only German but American commercial influence also to assume significant, if overall modest, proportions. United States diplomatic representation had been continuous since 1848[1] and consular representation in La Paz since 1869, when it was initiated during the period of remarkably favourable relations and attitudes towards the U.S.A. displayed by President Melgarejo.

America's desire to strengthen commercial ties and open up Bolivia as a

---

[1] America's delay until May 1848 in recognising Bolivia was entirely due, wrote Secretary of State James Buchanan, to the country's location in the South American interior, and that for want of good ports on the Pacific, the U.S.A.'s commercial intercourse with Bolivia had been of a very limited character.

source of raw materials and tropical products for the North American market was inevitably tied to transport development. The pattern of Bolivia's future circulation, successive U.S. Ministers observed, was to be 'steamboats in the east and locomotives in the west' – all preferably of American manufacture. In this context, therefore, the work of Lieuts Lardner Gibbon and Thomas Page, as well as the railroad and navigation schemes of Church, Meiggs, Collins and Farquhar, and the various U.S. colonisation and rubber concession proposals in and around the Acre District, all contributed to the promotion of this policy. Indeed, Gibbon had been somewhat disconcerted during his travels in Bolivia, between 1851 and 1853, by one of the questions put to him by his hostess at a La Paz dinner party: '"And what are you doing here, Señor Gibbon; do you want Bolivia also?" After setting forth the advantages of trade through the rivers of Bolivia…, she approved of the enterprise, and expressed herself friendly to it; but concluded by saying – "I believe the North Americans will some day govern the whole of South America!"'[1]

In 1870, however, the U.S. Consul in La Paz could only report that North American trade with Bolivia was negligible, and quite unable to compete with English goods imported *via* a Pacific coast supply base dominated by English and French steamship companies. The English Pacific Steam Navigation Co. had been initiated by preliminary meetings as early as 1838, and received the Royal Charter incorporating the Company in February 1840. Later that year, it began operations along the west coast of South America and had thus gained an impressive head-start over later rivals. Besides, as far as the United States was concerned, its own settlement frontier was still advancing and consolidating west of the Mississippi, and with the enormous demand for development at home, the U.S.A. was as yet no match for mid-nineteenth-century Victorian Britain in the quantity and range of manufactured goods it could supply to overseas markets. Nevertheless, wrote U.S. Consul Rand in 1871, it was essential to break the trade monopoly in Bolivia held by France, Germany and England, and 'let in the U.S.A.'. In this connexion, the repeated failures in the Oriente of Church's Madeira–Mamoré Railway in the 1870s were frequently referred to as a major blow to American trade prospects, particularly as Lardner Gibbon's favourable report in 1854 regarding the by-passing of the falls had sparked off a projected 'steamboat mania', new dreams of the Amazon as the 'South American Mississippi', and discreet pressure upon Brazil to open its great river to free navigation.

[1] L. Gibbon, *Exploration of the Valley of the Amazon*, pp. 115–16.

Thus, while both the demand and the capacity of the Bolivian market remained insignificant, English manufactured goods contrived in general to dominate the major western urban centres of the country during most of the second half of the nineteenth century, despite the virtual absence of British resident population, and the lack of political and consular support. This state of affairs was wholly related to Bolivia's Pacific orientation, and thus to prevailing conditions in Chile and Peru. There, Britain's dominant role in the regular cargo and mail traffic along the west coast of South America, and its very strong position in the Peruvian and Chilean markets (the latter particularly in the 1880s) were conclusive, although German competition was evident even there before the century closed. External trade preferences, therefore, inevitably shaped the choice of manufactured goods available to the Pacific hinterland State, dependent as it was upon the port agents in Mollendo, Arica and Antofagasta. In contrast, the sources of manufactured goods in eastern Bolivia in the late nineteenth and early twentieth centuries, limited in quantity though they remained, showed more variety. Orientated not to the Pacific and the western rail system, but to the Amazon and Plata river routes, manufactures of German, Swiss, French and English origin were imported in response to the demands of the German trading houses, and to the whims and tastes of the owners of the major rubber and ranching enterprises.

By the 1890s, however, the U.S. Minister to Bolivia was gratified to be able to report that 'goods of *American* manufacture are now to be seen in the show-windows and on the shelves of the shops of La Paz', and, moreover, to pass on with some satisfaction the comment that 'Bolivia is as yet *the only remaining country in South America not in the hands of England*'.[1] When Britain at last turned some official diplomatic attention towards Bolivia in 1903, after virtually half a century's reticence, the visiting British Minister's dispatch to Lima noted some of the effects of the prolonged overall neglect of the country by Britain. Both the Germans and the North Americans were reported to be forging ahead – the Germans in general trade, the Americans in mining and railroads. As the 'railway mania' now gathered momentum, it was observed:

Regarding contracts open to public tender in Bolivia...I am much inclined to think that contracts will be placed with the United States. If English manufacturers wish to do any business, they must be just as alert, and more, than their neighbours and

[1] Private communication received from a visiting fellow-countryman and forwarded by U.S. Minister Thomas Moonlight to Secretary of State Richard Olney, La Paz, 28 June 1896, Diplomatic Despatches from Bolivia, *General Records of the Dept. of State, Record Group 59*, Washington, D.C.

competitors, and I would recommend them to send out representatives without further delay, and not wait until the business is offered them.[1]

The expansion of German and North American trade competition was not, of course, unique to Bolivia, for it had become a marked feature in several of the hitherto traditionally British markets in Latin America towards the close of the nineteenth century, and was to become even more pronounced before the First World War. But while the steady overhauling of Britain as the major single supplier of manufactured goods to much of Latin America could be everywhere increasingly observed, to a greater or lesser degree, in the early twentieth century, Britain was less easily dislodged from her dominant role in those countries where her nineteenth-century trading position had been well consolidated. With one or two notable exceptions, Britain's nineteenth-century disenchantment with Bolivia, in both the political and economic fields, left no substantial reservoir of investment, and no residual trading inertia to cushion the impact of aggressive German and North American competition. Subsequently, the balance of this competition changed yet again and, in the decade after the First World War, the U.S.A. was left in an almost unrivalled position throughout the greater part of Latin America.

In Bolivia, a case in point, U.S. investment in the 1920s was more extensive than that of any other country, as former European rivals endured the consequences of the 1914–18 War. In mining, petroleum, railways and financial loans, the United States pressed home its advantage. The new American-registered tin company, Patiño Mines and Enterprises Consolidated, was incorporated by Simón Patiño in Delaware in 1924, illustrating in part an urgent U.S. desire to secure greater control in the production of a metal notoriously rare in the North American continent. The domestic demand for tin in the United States – in the canning and automobile industries, for example – was reaching unprecedented rates, and Bolivia remained as always the only significant source of the metal in the entire Western Hemisphere. In 1922 the Guggenheim Brothers established the Caracoles Tin Company of Bolivia, and this quickly became second only to the Patiño complex. In addition to these, during the 1920s, six other tin companies were recorded as being owned outright or in part by North American capital, to leave only the Compagnie Aramayo de Mines en Bolivie, a British–Swiss concern, as a major tin-mining company outside American investment interests at this period.[2]

---

[1] G. Harrison to W. N. Beauclerk, La Paz, 17 March 1904, *F.O. 177/322.*

[2] M. A. Marsh, *The Bankers in Bolivia, a study in American Foreign Investment* (Studies in American Imperialism), New York, 1928, pp. 45–9.

Petroleum concessions in south-east Bolivia were dominated by the Standard Oil Co. of New Jersey, which in 1921 had assumed the concessions granted in 1920–1 to the New York company of Richmond Levering, and subsequently those of the Braden Copper Co. also. In what elsewhere was generally regarded as a too-heavily-capitalised and highly risky venture, the Standard Oil Co. of Bolivia successfully resisted other would-be competitors, including Shell, until eventual expropriation in 1937.

Railway construction in Bolivia, however, and its subsequent operation, exposed the rivalry of American and British interests in a somewhat different manner. The main phase of railway building within Bolivia was a very late feature of development when compared with the striking speed and density of railway extension in parts of, say, Brazil, Argentina and Chile between 1850 and 1870. Indeed, while the initial spur to railway construction in western Bolivia was closely related to mineral export requirements, the limited extension eastwards beyond Cochabamba, La Paz and Potosí in the 1920s and 1930s, took place long after the passing of the steam railway's golden age, in Bolivia as elsewhere. One of the most expensive sections of line ever built linked Oruro to Cochabamba in 1917, and was extended to Arani in 1924. Thirty-five miles of the La Paz–Beni railway were also laid by 1924, but not until 1936 did a line reach Sucre from Potosí. This was clearly well within the period when, in many other areas, motor-road transport had already superseded rail, particularly in mountainous terrain. Even so, politics demanded that Cochabamba and Sucre be awarded the status of railway towns, although the cities of Santa Cruz and Tarija, similarly wooed, remained forsaken.

The first major length of railway built in Bolivia represented an extension of English capital investment in the 1880s from a Chilean baseline. Preliminary negotiations in 1887 had involved the Compañía Huanchaca de Bolivia, with its important silver and tin mines near Uyuni, in the purchase of the existing Chilean railway, down in the nitrate fields, from the Compañía de Salitres y Ferrocarril de Antofagasta. The following year the Antofagasta (Chili) and Bolivia Railway Co. was formed and registered in London, purchasing in its turn the Huanchaca Company's railway in Chile, and spearheading its own extension into Bolivia, with Government concessions, as far as Uyuni and Oruro. The ownership of this vitally important Uyuni–Oruro section, controlling movement in the heart of the mining district, was to place the British company in a uniquely strong and competitive position.

The British Minister, assessing the trade situation in 1903–4, had rightly anticipated that new railway contracts (together with loans to supplement

the money received from Brazil for this purpose under the 1903 Petrópolis Treaty terms, and from Chile under the 1904 Santiago Treaty terms),
would fall to North American companies. In 1906, the 'Speyer Contract'
was negotiated between the Bolivian Government and two New York
financial houses – the Speyer Syndicate and the National City Bank – on
notoriously unfavourable terms to Bolivia. A new American company,
the Bolivia Railway Co. was formed and commissioned to build a series
of lines, including northward and southward extensions to the existing
Antofagasta railway between Oruro and Viacha, and Uyuni and Atocha.
But before long, financial and other difficulties had brought progress
almost to a standstill, and the Antofagasta Railway stepped in to complete
the work after 1908; while the Bolivia Railway Co. remained incorporated
in the United States, it thus became a subsidiary of the Antofagasta (Chili)
and Bolivia Railway Co. (see p. 191). Ironically, therefore, although most
of this, and other, railway construction in Bolivia was originally secured by
American contract, in place of the hoped-for competition with 'the
Antofagasta' which the American railroads were intended to provide,
Bolivia found that monopoly control of the most critical sections of its rail
system remained in the hands of the British company.

From the time of this merger…the Antofagasta and Bolivia Railway Company
exercises over Bolivia's railways a control so complete that it reduces materially the
effectiveness of Arica as an outlet for Bolivia. By means of excessive freight rates on
goods exported by way of Arica, which must travel from Oruro to Viacha over a line
operated by the Antofagasta and Bolivia Railway, the big mineral output of the
Oruro district is deflected to the longer route via Antofagasta.[1]

Upon the Atocha–Villazón railroad, recently completed in 1925, and
newly leased to the Argentine firm of Dates and Hunt, Marsh added
a further comment. The Bolivia Railway Co. (i.e. 'the Antofagasta's'
subsidiary) already operated the northern section between Atocha and
Uyuni. 'With the Antofagasta and Bolivia Railway in control of the con-
necting strip of road from Uyuni to Atocha, there seems to be no reason
why it cannot paralyze the Atocha–Villazón Railway in the same way that
it has the Arica route.' Indeed, Dates and Hunt soon ceased their operation
and, as predicted, the Atocha–Villazón section was taken over by the
Bolivia Railway Co. Even the most objective observers at this period were
constrained to comment upon the undesirability for Bolivian interests of
'the Antofagasta's' strong controls.

Extensive and widely criticised additional loans by U.S. banking and

[1] M. A. Marsh, *op. cit.* p. 77.

investment companies in 1922 involved more than fifty-eight per cent of Bolivia's total national income being pledged towards its refund in 1925. Overall investments of United States citizens in Bolivia were estimated at approximately $100,000,000.[1] Not only was this considered to be a highly undesirable and vulnerable position for the United States, it was understandably accompanied by Bolivian charges of exploitation and manipulation, and held to be inconsistent with national sovereignty.

The situation was aggravated during the later 1920s and 1930s (when the level of U.S. investment fell sharply), by relations between the United States and Bolivia on the political plane. Attempted mediation, and a series of boundary arbitrations, had linked the United States, directly or indirectly, with Bolivian affairs and interests over several decades: in the 1878 Hayes Award to Paraguay, in an unsuccessful mediation attempt during the War of the Pacific, in the 1929 settlement of the Tacna–Arica dispute, and as one of the neutral powers in the 1938 boundary delimitation after the Chaco War. Such political involvement had, more often than not, proved a bed of nails for the United States, particularly the furore raised during the late 1920s by the various suggestions put forward to resolve the Tacna–Arica question, including the proposal by Secretary of State Kellogg regarding the possible cession of Arica to Bolivia. Britain viewed the United States' efforts from the sidelines, with caution and some complacency: 'The Americans have burned their fingers...His Majesty's Government ought, I am sure, to keep out of South American politics, whatever the temptation to the contrary may be.'[2]

After the nadir of the thirties, the mutual relationships of Anglo-America and Latin America in the 1940s were dominated first by the emergencies of World War II – at strategic, political and economic levels. Subsequently, relations between the U.S.A. and Bolivia entered a new phase, one characterised by new cooperation, new vision and new tensions. Technical assistance programs in the first stages were followed by an ever-deepening financial involvement after the United States' official support of the 1952 Social Revolution's political structure was confirmed.

[1] M. A. Marsh, *op. cit.* p. 4. In 1919 the official figure of total British capital investment in Bolivia received by the Foreign Office was £9,449,099. More than two-thirds of this was by the Antofagasta railway and its Bolivia Railway Co. subsidiary, together with the small Guaqui-La Paz railway. The ailing Madeira and Mamoré Railway Co., which ran a few steamboats in north-east Bolivia, was legally an American company, registered in Maine, although its shareholders included British, Belgian and French interests, and a Board of Directors sat in London. *F.O. 371/3652.*
[2] R. G. Vansittart to J. C. Sterndale Bennett, London, 15 September 1926, *F.O. 371/11108.*

On the one hand, there were at that time no large American land-owning
or company interests left in Bolivia to influence the U.S.A.'s new commitment; on the other, there were obvious advantages in pledging support
for a non-Communist government which possessed widespread popular
appeal. The strengthening and stabilising of the vulnerable centre of the
South American continent were judged to be desirable from both political
and economic viewpoints. Economic assistance programs and, after 1961,
projects developed as part of the Alliance for Progress, resulted in Bolivia's
receiving $430,000,000 in American aid between 1942 and 1968. With a
population of considerably less than four million people during most of this
period, such a sum, according to U.S. sources, represented the highest *per
capita* injection of American aid anywhere in the world, before it was surpassed in the mid-1960s by the increased demands of the war in Vietnam.

Britain's relations with Bolivia at the political level, on the other hand,
even when viewed only in the South American context, have never
assumed any marked degree of significance. While a number of con-
tributory factors may be discerned to account for this prolonged
indifference, it is true to say that early patterns were shaped very much
by the negative attitudes of a nineteenth-century, imperial sea power
towards a politically unstable, uncomfortably lofty, and wholly landlocked
State which had persistently failed to attract British investment and foreign
immigration. The potential market for British manufactures remained
torpid; there was little or no demand for urban improvement, or for the
installation of public utilities – there were no port and harbour works to
be constructed. The Victorian merchant and investor looked elsewhere.

Subsequently, official policy continued actively (and passively) to
discourage British investment and emigration to Bolivia; at best it
remained lukewarm:

The present state of the laws of Bolivia are such as to hinder rather than advance its
development, for they tend to induce much litigation and give little security of
tenure...[Conditions] embolden me to advise great caution on the part of any
capitalists intending to make a loan to this country.[1]

It is not thought that His Majesty's Government would be justified at the present
stage, in encouraging British firms to endeavour to secure the contract for the construction of the line [i.e. the La Quiaca–Tupiza railway].[2]

Any scheme for the employment of British workmen in Bolivia would be viewed
with mistrust by His Majesty's Government.[3]

[1] L. J. Jerome to Sir Edward Grey, La Paz, 21 May 1910, *F.O. 177/350.*
[2] R. Sperling to G. Haggard, London, 6 January 1920, *F.O. 371/3652.*
[3] Foreign Office Memorandum on possible recruitment of British workers and immigrants
from Manchester area, 3 January 1922, *F.O. 371/5533.*

British built (or operated) railway extensions from both Chile and Peru tended to dominate the slender total investment figure, and progressive nationalisation has more recently reduced this to negligible proportions. Britain's long control of world tin-smelting operations, however, produced the somewhat anomalous trading situation whereby about fifty per cent (and periodically much more than fifty per cent) of Bolivia's tin, tungsten, antimony and other non-ferrous metal exports have made their way to a country whose return flow of cargo and investment has always remained extremely limited. Britain's exports to Bolivia, mostly machinery and even so, frequently less than one-twelfth of the reverse trade by value, have not competed seriously with the vigorous export expansion of the United States, Japan and West Germany. With isolated exceptions, Bolivia has never been actively sought-after in British export trade terms. It has lain increasingly within the North American and Pacific spheres of interest and influence, and consistently outside the prescribed focus of Britain's political vision in South America, at least since since the middle of the nineteenth century.

2. BOLIVIA AND ITS RELATIONSHIPS WITHIN LATIN AMERICA

The conduct of Bolivia's own foreign relations has been persistently clouded, and largely determined by its international boundary problems. Communications and outlets have assumed the dominant role in the affairs of a weak State to which other considerations have always been subordinated. Bolivia might well have been used to lend support to Ritter's suggestion that a high proportion of coastline to land area augured well for a country's more advanced development, and that without it progress would be seriously retarded.[1] Nevertheless, while Bolivia's five neighbouring States have, in varying degrees, trimmed back approximately half of the inherited claims, Bolivia's role as a South American buffer State has been simultaneously confirmed. Its central location, and the consequent reduction of points of direct contact and possible friction it has afforded between the major powers, have helped to ensure its survival. Bolivians have always chosen to express it another way: 'Si Bolivia no

---

[1] Carl Ritter (1779–1859), Professor of Geography in the University of Berlin, argued that an extensive coastline and, more particularly, a coastline lengthened by deep indentations and projecting peninsulas was of great significance in the early development of a State. The increased accessibility thereby accorded to a land interior for trade and immigration, among other advantages, was considered indispensable for advancement, and was among the reasons cited by Ritter for the early and continuing prosperity of Europe.

existiera, seria necesario crearla.' There were other dangers, however: 'Bolivia's position', wrote U.S. Minister Bridgman from La Paz in 1899, 'is geographically such that she in a way holds the balance of power, and neither Chile, Peru nor Argentina would consent to her absorption by any one of the three named adjoining States. The danger is that Bolivia will be divided among the three, Chile controlling by far the more valuable part.' It was of course true, particularly during the late 1890s, that excessive internal regionalism might pave the way for partition – the 'Polandisation of Bolivia' was a recurrent phrase. Revolution in 1898–9 had ended the comparatively long Conservative administration which had followed the War of the Pacific, and placed the Liberal Party, under José Pando, into power. The Liberals, deriving their strongest support from the mine-owners and businessmen of the north and west, were responsible for finally confirming La Paz as the *de facto* capital and permanent seat of government. Their strongest opposition came, inevitably, from the great land-owners and old-established families in the Departments of Chuquisaca, Tarija and Santa Cruz. The Liberals even introduced and for a while maintained a Federalist platform, declaring the unitary system of government to be unworkable in terms of the country's topographical characteristics and its strong regional loyalties. Despite these, however, or rather because of them, Federalism was subsequently dropped as a solution to the ever-present separatist tendencies. The politically fissile nature of the country continued, unassuaged: 'The chief weakness of Bolivia is the want of unity; the ill feeling existing between the inhabitants of the different provinces being very remarkable...Perhaps some serious peril may weld the Bolivian Provinces into a nation',[1] but the observer clearly doubted it.

Put bluntly, Bolivia survived largely upon terms dictated elsewhere; it remained 'a mere collection of small states with nominal allegiance to La Paz' – a gloomy vindication in part of Bolívar's earlier foreboding.

Bolivia's neighbours include the most powerful nations of the Continent, and her natural frontiers have passed into their control, so that she lies, with her diminutive army, practically at their mercy. Yet only in her weakness is her salvation. For so intimately are the territorial interests of her neighbours bound up in Bolivia that an attack by one would almost certainly lead to reprisals from another.

Hence she endeavours to preserve her somewhat precarious immunity by maintaining the *status quo*, bad as it is, for fear of something worse arising, i.e. a mutual agreement among all her neighbours for her partition.[2]

[1] L. J. Jerome to Sir Edward Grey, La Paz, 5 September 1910, *F.O. 177/350.*
[2] G. Haggard to Arthur Balfour, La Paz, 7 December 1917, *F.O. 371/3166.*

But, in the event, it is truer to record that no desire to partition Bolivia has ever been seriously displayed by any of the five surrounding States. Even at independence, Peru showed no reluctance to recognise Bolivia's breakaway, and acknowledged the new State with alacrity – a fact which disconcerted some foreign diplomats. 'Its separation from this part of Peru does not appear to cause any sensation here, which is not a little surprising', the British Vice-Consul informed Canning from Lima in October 1825. Argentina's disapproval was little more than a gesture. Thus, although Bolivia struggled for its independence from Spain, it can scarcely be said to have met much resistance from its former viceregal administrators. The bonds, never taut, quickly fell away.

Rather, Bolivia's size alone, if nothing else, ensured that neighbouring States could pare away towards the bone, under the pressures of economic exploitation and territorial aggrandisement, without weakening the core area in any real sense. The dangers of separatism came always from within – Bolivia boiled and seethed away in comparative isolation. As time progressed, other motives aside, one can discern a growing impatience among the surrounding States with Bolivia's continued resort to *de jure* claims of ownership – an exasperation with a country still unable to do little more than plead the sanctity of colonial boundaries to a modern and unheeding world.

In the wider context, it can be justly argued that Bolivia's interior location was of serious practical disadvantage. Indeed, more specifically, there is little doubt that the vain attempts to retain a readily accessible outlet on to the Pacific seriously retarded the country's development in the nineteenth century, and provoked a situation from which recovery remains very slow. Taking the long view, the failure to incorporate Arica within its own territory at the time of independence must be regarded as Bolivia's greatest single impediment to subsequent progress. Prior ownership of Arica might well have staked a more tenable claim to the Pacific coast, and one which, given the same pattern of Chilean expansion, would probably have again been recognised by an international arbitration award.

This is not to ignore the rail links to selected seaports which Bolivia was later to acquire, nor the country's crucial internal difficulties and dissensions which persistently hindered development. Although observers are quick to demonstrate, rightly, the many other factors responsible for Bolivia's limited achievement, most of these problems have been aggravated (or at least remained unrelieved) by the major cities' continuous political isolation from the nearest good port. Bolivia was to suffer from its non-participation in the fast-growing, but strongly localised, wealth of the South American coast. It lost a share in the Pacific's rich littoral and marine resources; it remained aloof from the successive waves of overseas immigrants which were largely absorbed by the coastal or near-coastal regions. Indeed, Bolivia consistently failed to attract immigrants during the nineteenth and early twentieth centuries, and so failed to experience any significant modification to its essentially colonial population structure.[1] Although immigration did much to diversify certain sections of society in Latin America after independence, the balance and composition of Bolivia's population, for example, changed little. The country's total population, officially estimated in 1967 as 4,294,000,[2] remains predominantly Indian. Whereas Ecuador records 39 per cent of its population as Indian, and Peru 46 per cent, Bolivia registers 70 per cent – by far the highest proportion of the indigenous population remaining within any single State of the Americas.[3]

With few exceptions, therefore, the coastal areas and their most readily accessible hinterlands focused such cultural and technological change as occurred in South America during the nineteenth and twentieth centuries. Seaports continued to dominate the urban hierarchy, for their essential role as the hinge-points upon which the great colonial seaborne empires were swung continued uninterruptedly into the period of independence. In Bolivia, however, the highland centres were not to be matched or surpassed by the growth of their own coastal cities. The contrasted development in Ecuador, for example, of Guayaquil (est. pop. 900,000) and Quito (est. pop. 600,000), could not be duplicated in Bolivia. The port and near-port cities, selectively, remained the thriving growth centres which attracted foreign capital and foreign enterprise in an economy geared essentially to the export of foodstuffs and raw materials. The ocean pro-

[1] Out of a national total of 3,019,031, the 1950 census still recorded only 35,471 people resident in Bolivia (i.e. 1.1 per cent of the total population) who were born abroad, and nearly one-third of these were Peruvians. The major countries of origin were as follows: 10,269 from Peru, 4682 from Brazil (most of whom remain in the Pando), 3964 from Chile, 3278 from Argentina, 3207 from Germany, 1256 from Spain. The exodus of Bolivian nationals into the surrounding States (with the exception of Paraguay) has remained a significant factor, however, and one which shows little change.
[2] Official projections based on the 1950 National Census had previously estimated that Bolivia's total population would reach 3,751,000 in 1966, and 3,801,000 in 1967. A supplementary estimate, however, published by the Dirección General de Estadística y Censos in 1968, raised the total figure for 1967 by nearly half a million. 1970 estimate, 4,900,000.
[3] The remarkable degree of constancy in this proportion is illustrated by J. B. Pentland's report on Bolivia made in 1826–7 (see above, p. 18) when, out of a total population estimated at 1,100,000, approximately 73 per cent (800,000) were recorded as Indian.

vided the only geographical unity in a sub-continent lacking any coherent pattern of land communications, and the most significant orientation remained ultramarine.

To be landlocked in South America under these conditions proved a serious hindrance to growth and development. Bolivia was, and is, no 'South American Switzerland'. Indeed, Switzerland's own preference for its designation as a 'non-coastal', rather than as a 'landlocked' State, is significant here. Bolivia commanded no mountain passes nor well-trodden routeways linking highly developed areas, and its position in a South American heartland remained inconveniently central at a time when the coastal periphery was all-important. Closest to the ocean lies its lofty and most intractable terrain; farthest from marine contact and marine communication, lie its easiest gradients and most varied agricultural regions. The extreme altitude of the *altiplano*, the massive bastions of the Cordillera Occidental and the arid repellent nature of the intervening hundred-odd miles of Atacama have played a major role in dissociating the Titicaca–Poopó basin from the Pacific, reinforcing the political separation of the plateau and the coast. It has never been easy to find many Bolivians who have seen the sea.

Few will dispute that a landlocked position contains a number of inherent disadvantages which will figure prominently in the subsequent body of legislation and diplomatic exchange they promote. Not until the twentieth century was more widespread and specific attention given to this particular aspect of a State's location, with President Woodrow Wilson's statement, and with subsequent Conventions in the post-World War I period. In 1958 the question of free access to the sea by landlocked countries was the subject of a special United Nations study during the Conference on the Law of the Sea held in Geneva.[1] While acknowledging the 'adverse geographica situation' of landlocked States, discussion

[1] United Nations, *Conference on the Law of the Sea*, vol. VII, Fifth Committee, Geneva, 24 February–27 April 1958. For a general commentary see H. Osborne Mance et al., *International Transport and Communications*, 7 vols., Royal Institute of International Affairs, Chatham House, London, 1943–7. In particular, *International River and Canal Transport*, vol. III, 1944, pp. 85–7; *International Sea Transport*, vol. IV, 1945, pp. 22–6; *International Rail Transport*, vol. V, 1946, pp. 117–22; *Frontiers, Peace Treaties, and International Organisation*, vol. VII, 1946, pp. 19–25.

The basic source of international law concerning freedom of transit by civil aircraft is provided by the Chicago Convention of 1944. By this document the contracting parties (now including all the South American States) recognise that every State has complete and exclusive sovereignty over the airspace above its territory. There are no rights of innocent passage and no rights of free transit other than those acquired by international agreement. Bolivia has negotiated rights of transit for non-scheduled commercial air traffic through all neighbouring States; scheduled, through all except Chile but with special concession to Arica.

centred on whether the present principles recognised by international law were sufficient to permit the exercise by all nations of their right to the freedom of the high seas. The right of innocent passage through the territorial sea, the right of landlocked States to fly a maritime flag (Barcelona Declaration 1921), and the right of their ships to be accorded the same treatment as a contracting maritime State's ships while in the territorial sea, or in the ports of the transit State (Geneva 1923), were reiterated. But the transit State's right to protect its own sovereignty and legitimate interests were confirmed also, together with the view that the position of a transit State is not one of unqualified advantage. Rights of transit are not universally accepted in international law – at most this acknowledges an obligation on the part of adjacent States to negotiate transit agreements – and delegates from Afghanistan, Bolivia, Czechoslovakia, Laos and Nepal deplored that landlocked States should be 'humble petitioners' for a fundamental and inalienable right to have access to the high seas. Inevitably, it was concluded that this could only be achieved by the improvement of existing conventions, bilaterally or multilaterally.

Once again, in 1965, the United Nations Conference on Trade and Development examined the problems of transit trade for landlocked States, whose number had almost doubled since the 1958 Conference with the creation, between 1960 and 1964, of ten new African landlocked States.[1] Representatives of Bolivia, Argentina, Chile and Paraguay were present among other delegates from landlocked, transit and interested States. Emphasis was firmly placed on the maintenance of full sovereignty by the transit State. While the right of every landlocked State to have *negotiated transit* to the sea is generally acknowledged, in the last resort the transit State cannot be forced to admit goods which it considers a danger, for example, to its health or security. For absolute freedom of transit inevitably implies the possibility of some conflict with, or infringement of, the transit State's own legitimate interests, and thus, despite bilateral agreements, the coastal State retains an initial advantage in every bargaining situation.

The landlocked State assumes a subordinate role in the decision-making processes which affect its transit trade: in the speed and efficiency of the transport facilities which have been made available, for example, and in the labour costs and conditions operating in the neighbouring State. The additional handling, policing and administrative costs involved

[1] United Nations, *Conference on Trade and Development, Report of the Committee on the Preparation of a Draft Convention relating to Transit Trade of Landlocked Countries*, New York, 1965.

in negotiated transit, as opposed to independent access to the high seas may be reduced and more evenly distributed by favourable treaty terms, but they cannot be completely eliminated. Moreover, in internal national emergencies (whose gravity is determined by the neighbouring State) there remains the right and the initiative on the latter's part to suspend transit operations. In such cases, added to the more obvious immediate difficulties, are the time and expense involved on the part of the landlocked State in mobilising diplomatic machinery, or in invoking the cumbersome and indirect procedures of international law.

In this respect, therefore, the advantages of alternative routes to the sea must be fully exploited, and some of the benefits experienced by the landlocked State set against other undoubted disadvantages. There is relief from the financial burden of port and link-transport improvement and maintenance. In the case of Chile and, since 1948, of Peru also, there is the granting of free storage and warehousing in the ports for one year, although the liberal use made of this concession by Bolivia undoubtedly hampers administration in the port areas, and must be regarded as undesirable and unjustified from all points of view. Alternative concessions, mutually agreed, should certainly be considered. Nevertheless, greater, rather than less, efficiency often characterises the handling and dispatch of goods in transit when compared with conditions inside Bolivia – conditions which, arguably, might also obtain in any territory giving direct access to the Pacific over which Bolivia had jurisdiction. Bolivia has transit agreements with all five of its neighbouring States, although, as has been shown, they were variously delayed in their formulation and guaranteed implementation until the twentieth century. However, a recent investigation upon Bolivia's existing transit conventions records that 'except for Paraguay, Bolivia has greater – and in the case of Chile, substantially greater – rights of transit under existing treaties than would be dictated by general international law'.[1]

Provided that there are, as in Bolivia's case, alternative outlets to ocean transport, a landlocked State is not necessarily completely powerless. It can, within limits, vary that irksome political role of continual suppliance at the bargaining table by playing off one country against another in competition for the transit trade. But this in turn depends upon the economic stature of the landlocked State, and the volume and value of its traffic. Such competition is promoted only from a position of strength, not

[1] J. H. Merryman, 'A Working Paper on the International Agreements of Bolivia as they relate to Transportation', prepared in conjunction with the Bolivia Transport Survey, School of Law, Stanford University, 1968, p. 157.

of weakness. Bolivia has, in terms of its own internal development and external trade, still far to go before fuller exploitation of this particular aspect of location can be realised. Given the limited size of the Bolivian population, however, its very irregular distribution, the high costs of the country's inadequate internal transport system, and the possible dangers of a 'one-port monopoly' in any narrow Pacific access corridor of its own, the 'rail-for-territory' exchange which has ultimately characterised so much of Bolivia's foreign policy should not be regarded as a totally unfortunate substitution.

During the last decade particularly, considerable attention has been given to increasing the country's outlets to the exterior, both in the number of routeways and in the modes of transport, and this widening of the range of options available for international trade is clearly a policy Bolivia is determined to pursue. Once again, however, its success will ultimately depend on the careful selection and realisation of certain internal development programs which must, in the future, provide the only convincing economic rationale for Bolivia's improved external political relationships.

At present, poor interior surface communication inevitably leaves much of the country's periphery within the economic orbit of neighbouring States. Indeed, such dependence is locally acknowledged in the relaxation of customs tariffs on 'essential articles', and on the periodic extension of 'free port' facilities to isolated areas. Cobija, and the whole of the Department of Pando, for example, were declared a free port zone for four years in the mid-1960s. On all Bolivia's international boundaries, contraband traffic becomes a major problem at certain points: particularly across the desolate *salares* of the *altiplano* between Uyuni and the Chilean border; across Lake Titicaca; at the sweeping northern boundary, vulnerably exposed to international air-smuggling routes linking Miami, Panamá, Lima and Leticia, as well as the the free port zone of Manaus; *via* the many small scattered airstrips of the Oriente air-lifting goods from the free port zone of Asunción; and on the Yacuiba–Pocitos and Corumbá border entries. A country which recognises that at least 10 per cent of all imported goods are smuggled faces a formidable task (Fig. 15).

Among the many problems bequeathed or aggravated by location, the loss of the Pacific littoral and the denial of independent access to the sea has had a profound emotional effect upon that small but vociferous section of politically conscious Bolivians. In a country beset with internal problems, considerable mental energy has continually been expended on the obsessive aspirations for a Bolivian Pacific port – aspirations and

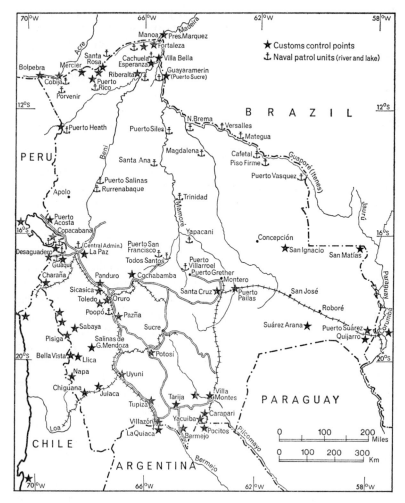

15 Bolivia: Customs control points, and base-stations of the Fuerza Naval.
Sources: Ministerio de Hacienda y Estadística: Aduanas de Bolivia; Administración
de la Fuerza Naval Boliviana; Bolivia Transport Survey; field observation

impassioned demands which have rarely distinguished between the desire
for national vindication and the achievement of practical means to promote greater national development. Moreover, the loss of the Pacific
littoral established a platform of grievance readily communicated to a
population otherwise relatively unmoved by less dramatic issues, and over

an extended period it has provided perhaps the only aspect of foreign policy on which vehement opinions, where expressed at all, have shown a unanimity of outlook. It became one of the most easily projected principles upon which to focus, or attempt to focus, Bolivian nationalism. Negative though such an attitude may be, in the search for national identity and political unity Bolivians derived an element of national and political cohesion from the memory of their misfortunes. 'Bolivia is always *remembering*, never forgetting', observed one nineteenth-century North American diplomat.

Yet caution must be exercised in the tendency to exaggerate the significance of the lost littoral in promoting true national awareness. As outlined earlier (pp. 27–8), Ratzel's theme of the 'State-Idea' – a body of traditions, purposes or aspirations which command *widespread* loyalty, and assist effective State organisation – continued to have limited application to Bolivia. Even respecting the 'Pacific question', opinion was divided as to which port should be claimed, and reflected sharply conflicting regional interests within the country. More critical, however, in the context of the 'State-Idea' was the fact that only a very small minority of the total population took an active part in political life. Literacy and property requirements within the existing structure of rigid cultural and social stratification had confined any direct participation in internal politics to a very restricted electorate. In the late nineteenth century, and the first half of the twentieth century, this comprised a small (if slowly expanding) civil and military urban middle class, and an even smaller land-owning, mine-owning and commercial élite – an exclusive oligarchy whose main purpose was to exercise and retain power. The traditional ruling class drew upon its own persistently limited resources in terms of statesmanship, experience and expertise; the disenfranchised majority stood apart, unaware of the issues in which they were only occasionally involved:

When the creoles...fight the battles of their country, the Indians seat themselves on the brows of the hills around, and quietly witness changes or continuance of administration. They seem to be the philosophers of the country, and to take the world very easy. After the struggle is over, they come down and pursue their daily occupations under the new constitution, laws and powers that be.[1]

It was a comment which, in part, had been applicable for centuries, although the Indian's detachment from the turmoil of Bolivian politics was less easily maintained as the nineteenth- and twentieth-century frontier wars disrupted his existence. As in the struggles for creole indepen-

[1] Lardner Gibbon, *Exploration of the Valley of the Amazon*, vol. II, p. 115.

dence, the Indian followed the leadership and allegiance of his *patrón*. Service obligations determined nationality; when, for example, the political boundary between Bolivia and Peru was eventually drawn through the densely settled Indian communities around Lake Titicaca in the 1930s, it followed the patterns of 'Spanish' land ownership, dividing a virtually homogenous indigenous cultural landscape.

Language barriers have always emphasised the dichotomy still further in political terms, isolating the great majority of the population from the Spanish-speaking administrative class. Indeed, language still represents one of the major barriers to more fundamental political involvement, and to the associated improvements required in educational, agricultural, commercial and general living standards. Out of the total Bolivian population, an estimated 36 per cent speak *only* Quechua, 25 per cent speak *only* Aymara, and 2.5 per cent other Indian tongues.[1] In a country where little bilingualism exists, the problem of integrating more fully some 63 per cent of the population still unable to communicate readily in the 'national' language remains formidable.

A more broadly based State awareness dates from the 1930s with military service in the Chaco War, a frontier conflict which involved a wider spectrum of the population than ever before in Bolivia's history, although in terms of the nation's political structure, the War's most profound immediate effects were undoubtedly on sections of the middle class.[2] Subsequently, however, the land reform program and the introduction of universal suffrage which followed the 1952 Social Revolution have probably achieved more in a single generation in projecting a 'grass-roots' sense of national identity than any previous factor. When news of the 1953 Bolivian Agrarian Reform spread around Lake Titicaca, many Indians from Peru travelled to La Paz to apply for land, unaware or uncertain of the new implications of the international boundary. The increasing mobility and purchasing power of the Bolivian Indian – *campesino* now rather than *indio* – has been noted elsewhere, although progress is inevitably slow

---

[1] Dirección General de Estadística y Censos, Ministerio de Hacienda y Estadística, La Paz, 1955. The last published national census took place in 1950; another is due to be published in the mid-1970s. Periodic provisional estimates since 1955 indicate little marked change in the language distributions. Considerable research has been carried out in the U.S.A., Peru and Bolivia into Quechua, but relatively little work has been done, either in the U.S.A. or Bolivia, on Aymara. The majority of Aymara-speakers, just over one million, live in Bolivia. New research programs into language analysis, and into courses for instructors in Aymara have recently been launched at the University of Florida, and at the Universidad Mayor de San Andrés in La Paz, supplementing courses already established at the Instituto Nacional de Estudios Lingüísticos.

[2] H. S. Klein, *Parties and Political Change in Bolivia, 1880–1952*, pp. 187–9.

and change too easily exaggerated. Much of the new 'mass nationalism' as yet remains superficial, and at a local level.

Linked, however, with the Bolivian Government's current national plans for internal social and economic progress is the declared intention, as always, of acquiring a Pacific corridor and port. This has proved to be the most durable item of foreign policy throughout the country's successive and diverse administrations. But while the persistent call for a Pacific port has thus become dogma, it has in later years appeared more postural. Bolivia failed to exercise the right to fly a maritime flag, despite the fact that Chile ratified the Barcelona Convention. Not until August 1968 did Bolivia demonstrate a clearer intention to establish the nucleus of a merchant fleet, 'Transmarítima Boliviana', operating from a Chilean port. Even now, it could be little more than an expensive luxury. Registered in the capital, however, the first vessel will confirm La Paz in the role it has assumed in practical terms since independence, that of the port of Bolivia.

As a traditional plea, Bolivians in time may well come to regard the required uncompromising attitudes concerning a Pacific port as something of an embarrassment – a political obstacle to attempted economic co-operation. In the late 1960s Bolivia's foreign relations in Latin America tended to stress the country's location as a keystone, emphasising the desire to assist and participate in new proposals for regional economic coopera-tion. In February 1967 Bolivia joined the Latin American Free Trade Association (Asociación Latino-Americana de Libre Comércio), and in August of the same year communicated its desire to join also the sub-regional Andean Group, then comprising Chile, Colombia, Ecuador and Peru, with the possible inclusion of Venezuela. The declared aims of these western L.A.F.T.A. (A.L.A.L.C.) countries, as confirmed by the Carta-gena Agreement of May 1969, are to work towards complete economic integration by 1980–5, with the adoption of a common external tariff after 1975.

In becoming a signatory in 1967 to both the Treaty of Montevideo (L.A.F.T.A.), and the Bogotá Declaration (Andean Group), the Bolivian Foreign Ministry was immediately charged by members of the Opposition parties with having abandoned, or compromised, Bolivia over the 'mari-time question', particularly as Chile had become a strong supporter of the Andean Group. Critics were repeatedly assured that, in an agreement which it was stressed was multilateral, not bilateral, the problem of Bolivia's 'mediterráneidad' would be kept alive. Indeed, in this connexion, the president of Transmarítima Boliviana in 1970 announced his country's intention of joining the recently established organisation for the pooling of the merchant fleets of States within the Andean Group. Bolivia's subsequent participation in yet a third economic development grouping – that of the River Plate Basin, this time in association with Argentina, Brazil, Paraguay and Uruguay – has been viewed, at least in part, as a means and an opportunity of emphasising Bolivia's wish for closer alliance with its southern and eastern neighbours.

Realisation, or part-realisation, of new and experimental plans for regional economic cooperation remains conjectural. Bolivia, burdened by heavy and long-overdue planning commitments at the national level, quite apart from involvement at the international or supranational level, regards such politico-economic groupings with both the caution and the hopefulness of a smaller, weaker State. Even so, while Bolivia as yet makes a minor contribution to regional or subregional development programs, tentative groping towards economic integration on this scale will inevitably demand a reappraisal of certain longstanding political attitudes, not least over the 'Pacific question'. The problems are formidable, but the dilemma will require solution. In the years ahead, it is more likely to be by means of customs unions, by regional cooperation in power and irrigation projects, and by agricultural and mineral exchange, that working relationships at professional, technical and administrative levels will be established, practised, and become more routine – thus creating a climate of cooperation and goodwill in which political collaboration may be fostered and stabilised.

This is particularly true within Bolivia's western sector. Renewed interest in the frequently discarded, but undeniably sound, geographical proposals for regional economic integration between the *altiplano*, the cordilleran watersheds, the desert and the coast, might possibly sponsor the stipulated measure of agreement between Chile, Peru and Bolivia which is required for any new and acceptable political solution to the problems of this area. Future developments, therefore, could well promote some reassessment of the traditional objections to change put forward by the two coastal States; future developments may also, however, encourage the reassessment of some of the traditional demands and objectives of the landlocked State. At political and economic levels, and in all the varied sectors of continental exchange, it remains to be seen whether Bolivia is prepared, or able, at last to come to terms with both the liabilities and the assets of its location.

LIST OF SOURCES

I Principal Sources of Cartographic Material; II Manuscript Collections; III Printed Collections; IV Books and Articles

I PRINCIPAL SOURCES OF CARTOGRAPHIC MATERIAL

British Museum map collection, London.
Public Record Office map collection, London.
Royal Geographical Society, London.
John Bartholomew & Son Ltd, Edinburgh – library collection.
American Geographical Society of New York.
Archivo y Biblioteca Nacional de Bolivia, Sucre.
Consejo Nacional de Caminos, La Paz.
Corporación Boliviana de Fomento, La Paz.
Departamento Nacional de Geología, La Paz.
Dirección de Límites, Ministerio de Relaciones Exteriores y Culto, La Paz.
Instituto Geográfico Militar, La Paz.
Universidad Mayor de San Andrés, La Paz – library collection.

II MANUSCRIPT COLLECTIONS

Board of Trade Archives, Public Record Office, London.
Diplomatic Reports, Consular Reports, Treaty Records and Political Correspondence, *in* Foreign Office Archives, Public Record Office, London.
Foreign Office Archives, Foreign Office Library, London.
London Business House Archives, Guildhall Library, London.
Royal Geographical Society Archives, London.

Diplomatic Despatches, Consular Despatches, Notes from Foreign Legations, and the Records of the Department of State relating to the Internal Affairs of Bolivia, *in* the General Records of the Department of State, National Archives, Washington, D.C.

Archive Collection, Ministerio de Relaciones Exteriores y Culto, La Paz.
Archive Collection, Universidad Mayor de San Andrés, La Paz.
Archive and Library Collections, Sociedad Geográfica e Histórica 'Sucre', and Universidad de San Francisco Xavier de Chuquisaca, Sucre.
National Archive Collection, Archivo y Biblioteca Nacional de Bolivia, Sucre.

III PRINTED COLLECTIONS

(i) Correspondence; diplomatic, consular and general political material

Simón Bolívar, *Selected writings of Bolívar*, compiled by Vicente Lecuna, edit. H. A. Bierck, 2 vols., New York, 1951.
Antonio José de Sucre, *Cartas de Sucre al Libertador*, edit. D. F. O'Leary, 2 vols., Madrid, 1919.

List of Sources

British and Foreign State Papers, Foreign Office, London.

Burr, R. N., and Hussey, R. D., edit., *Documents on Inter-American Cooperation, 1810–1948*, 2 vols., Univ. of Pennsylvania Press, 1955.

Colección de Tratados Vigentes de la República de Bolivia, Ministerio de Relaciones Exteriores, La Paz.

A Compilation of the Messages and Papers of the Presidents of the United States, 20 vols., Bureau of National Literature, New York, 1897–1927.

Cuestiones de Límites con el Paraguay, con el Brasil, con el Perú, con Argentina, y con Chile, in the Julio A. Gutierrez Collection, Universidad Autónoma 'Gabriel René-Moreno' Santa Cruz de la Sierra, Bolivia.

Davenport, F. G., edit., *European Treaties bearing on the History of the United States and its Dependencies*, 4 vols., Washington, D.C. 1917–37.

Humphreys, R. A., edit., *British Consular Reports on the Trade and Politics of Latin America, 1824–1826*, Royal Historical Society, London, 1940.

Manning, W. R., edit., *Arbitration Treaties among the American Nations to the close of the year 1910*, Washington, D.C., 1924.

——, edit., *Diplomatic Correspondence of the United States concerning the Independence of the Latin-American Nations*, 3 vols., New York and London, Oxford Univ. Press, 1925.

——, edit., *Diplomatic Correspondence of the United States. Inter-American Affairs, 1831–1860*, 12 vols., Washington, D.C., 1932–9.

Marchant, A., *Boundaries of the Latin American Republics. An annotated list of documents 1493–1943 (tentative version)*, Inter-American Series No. 24, Dept. of State, Washington, D.C., 1944.

Moore, J. Bassett, edit., *A Digest of International Law*, 8 vols., Washington, D.C., 1906.

Obras do Barão do Rio-Branco, Questões de Limites, 9 vols., Ministério das Relações Exteriores, Rio de Janeiro, 1945–8.

South American Political Tracts, 1825–35, 1877–81; also *Miscellaneous Public Documents*, State Paper Collection, British Museum, London.

South American Political Tracts and *Miscellaneous Public Documents*, Institute of Advanced Legal Studies, Univ. of London.

Webster, C. K., edit., *Britain and the Independence of Latin America 1812–1830*, select documents from the Foreign Office Archives, 2 vols., London, Oxford Univ. Press, 1938.

Memoria del Ministro de Interior y Relaciones Esteriores presentada a las Cámaras de 1833, Chuquisaca, 1833.

Mensaje de S.E. El Presidente de Bolivia a las Cámaras Constitucionales de 1834, Chuquisaca, 1834.

Memoria que presenta al Soberano Congreso de Bolivia el Ministro de Estado en el Despacho de Interior y Relaciones Esteriores, Chuquisaca, 1837.

Exposición que el Ministro de Relaciones Exteriores de Bolivia presenta al Congreso Extraordinario sobre el estado de las Relaciones con el Perú, Chuquisaca, 1847.

Memoria dirijida a las Cámaras de 1849 en las Sesiones Extraordinarias por El Ministro de Relaciones Exteriores, a consecuencia de la conspiración el 21 de Febrero, La Paz, 1849.

Código Mercantil Santa Cruz dado por el Congreso Constitucional de 1834, Sucre (Chuquisaca), 1859.

Conferencias Diplomáticas de Arica entre los plenipotenciarios de Bolivia, Chile y el Perú con motivo de la Mediación de Estados Unidos, La Paz, 1880.

Memorandum sur les précédents et l'état actuel de la Guerre du Pacifique dans ses rapports avec la Republique Argentine presenté par la Légation Bolivienne, Buenos Aires, 1881.

Memoria que el Ministro de Relaciones Esteriores y Colonización presenta al Congreso Nacional de 1887, Sucre, 1887.

Documentos oficiales relativos a los límites entre Chile, Bolivia y la República Argentina en la región de Atacama, Ministerio de Relaciones Esteriores, Santiago, Chile, 1898.

Circular a las Legaciones de Bolivia en el extranjero, Ministerio de Relaciones Exteriores, La Paz, 1901.

Notas y el Memorandum de Bolivia contra el Tratado de Arbitraje Argentino–Paraguayo de 1876, Ministerio de Relaciones Exteriores, La Paz, 1929.

Memorandum que el Ministro de Relaciones Exteriores presenta al Congreso Nacional con motivo de los tratados celebrados con Bolivia sobre arbitraje de límites y demarcación de fronteras firmados en La Paz en 23 de Noviembre y 30 de Diciembre de 1902, Ministerio de Relaciones Exteriores, Lima, 1903.

El Arbitraje entres las repúblicas de Bolivia y el Perú y su última negociación sobre fronteras, Documentos diplomáticos, La Paz, 1909.

Arbitraje Argentino en la cuestion de límites entre las repúblicas de Perú y de Bolivia, libro azul, Ministerio de Relaciones Exteriores y Culto, Buenos Aires, 1909.

Libro Rojo, contiene los ultimos documentos de la Cancillería de Bolivia relativos a la reintegración marítima de la República, Ministerio de Relaciones Exteriores, La Paz, 1920.

Montes, I., *Blue Book Memorandum on the Rights of Bolivia to Tacna and Arica*, Paris and London, 1920.

Opiniones Chilenas y Peruanas sobre el Problema del Pacífico, Ministerio de Relaciones Exteriores, La Paz, 1927.

Visita efectuada por los Excmos, señores Representantes Diplomáticos de: Argentina, Brasil, Colombia, Costa Rica, República Dominicana, Ecuador, Estados Unidos, Guatemala, Haití, Honduras, México, Nicaragua, Panamá, Paraguay, Perú, El Salvador, Uruguay y Venezuela, a las obras de captación de una parte de las aguas del río Lauca en su naciente en las ciénagas de Parinacota y su aprovechamiento en el valle de Azapa, Ministerio de Relaciones Exteriores, Santiago, 1962.

La Cuestión del Río Lauca, Ministerio de Relaciones Exteriores, Santiago, 1963.

La Desviación del Río Lauca, Ministerio de Relaciones Exteriores y Culto, La Paz, 1962.

Rumbo al Mar, Ministerio de Relaciones Exteriores y Culto, La Paz, 1963.

(ii) Reports, Proceedings, and Principal Sources of the more recent and current statistical material

Commission of Inquiry and Conciliation, Bolivia and Paraguay. Report of the Chairman submitted to the Secretary of State of the United States of America, September 21, 1929, for transmission to the American Governments not represented at the Commission, and Appended Documents, Washington, 1929.

'Correspondence respecting the Treatment of British Colonial Subjects and native Indians employed in the collection of rubber in the Putumayo District, July 1910– June 1912' (Government Blue Book), *Miscellaneous Parliamentary Papers, No. 8* (1912) [Cd. 6266], London, 1912.

List of Sources

Division of International Law, J. B. Scott, edit., *The International Conferences of American States, 1889–1928*, New York and London, 1931.

—— *The International Conferences of American States, First Supplement, 1933–1940*, Washington, D.C., 1940.

Informe Final de la Comision Mixta Demarcadora de Límites Bolivia–Argentina, Buenos Aires, 1953.

Junta de Vías Fluviales, *Vías del Pacífico al Madre de Dios*, Lima, 1902.

—— *El Istmo de Fitscarrald*, Lima, 1903, 1904.

—— *Nuevas Exploraciones en la Hoya del Madre de Dios*, Lima, 1904.

—— *Ultimas Exploraciones ordenadas por la Junta de Vías Fluviales a los Ríos Ucayali, Madre de Dios, Paucartambo y Urubamba*, 2 vols., Lima, 1907.

League of Nations, *Dispute between Chile and Bolivia, Letters from the Chilean and Bolivian Delegations to the League of Nations*, Geneva, 1921.

—— *Dispute between Bolivia and Paraguay, Report of the Chaco Commission*, Document No. C 154, M. 64, Geneva 1934.

Patent Office, Library collection, London.

Report and Special Report from the Select Committee on Putumayo, together with the Proceedings of the Committee, Minutes of Evidence and Appendices, ordered by The House of Commons to be printed, 5th June 1913, 2 vols., London, 1913.

Research Association of British Rubber Manufacturers, Library and Archive collection, Shawbury, Shrewsbury, Shropshire.

Royal Geographical Society, edit., *The Peru–Bolivia Boundary Commission 1911–1913, Reports of the British Officers of the Peruvian Commission*, London, 1918.

United Nations, *Report of the United Nations Mission of Technical Assistance to Bolivia*, New York, 1951.

—— *Informe Preliminar sobre el Ferrocarril Arica–La Paz*, La Paz, 1955.

—— *Geological Report on the Mutún Iron Deposit*, La Paz, 1955.

—— *Consideraciones sobre el costo en divisas de los fletes ferroviarios para el comercio internacional de Bolivia*, La Paz, 1956.

—— *Transportes de Minerales a los Puertos del Pacífico*, La Paz, 1956.

—— *Los Transportes en Bolivia; Ferrocarriles, Caminos y Aereos*, 3 vols., La Paz, 1957.

—— *Conference on the Law of the Sea*, vol. VII, Fifth Committee, Geneva, 1958.

—— *Conference on Trade and Development, Report of the Committee on the Preparation of a Draft Convention relating to Transit Trade of Landlocked Countries*, New York, 1965.

Administración del Puerto, Antofagasta, Chile, Reports and Returns.

Administración del Puerto, Arica, Chile, Reports and Returns.

Aduanas de Bolivia, Ministerio de Hacienda y Estadística.

Bolivia Transport Survey, Final Report, Daniel, Mann, Johnson & Mendenhall, in association with Stanford Research Institute and Alan M. Voorhees & Associates, Inc., Los Angeles and La Paz, 1969.

Comision Mixta Ferroviaria Argentino–Boliviana, Interim Reports.

Consejo Nacional de Caminos y Transporte Fluvial, La Paz, Reports and Surveys.

Empresa Nacional de Ferrocarriles, La Paz, Estadística de los Ferrocarriles de Bolivia.

Estrada de Ferro Madeira–Mamoré, Guajará Mirim, Rondônia, Brazil, Monthly returns.

Ferrocarril Arica–La Paz, Arica, Chile, Monthly Returns.

Ferrocarril Guaqui–La Paz, Monthly Returns.
Ferrocarril La Paz–Antofagasta (Sección Boliviana, Sección Chilena), La Paz and Antofagasta, Chile, Monthly Reports and Returns.
Lloyd Aereo Boliviano, La Paz, Traffic Returns and Itineraries.
Ministerio de Agricultura, Ganadería y Colonización, La Paz – library collection.
Ministerio de Hacienda y Estadística, La Paz, Dirección General de Estadístaca y Censos.
United States Agency for International Development – Bolivia: Reports, Washington, D.C.; La Paz; Santa Cruz de la Sierra, Bolivia.

(iii) Newspapers and Periodicals

The Brazil and River Plate Mail, London, 1863–78; continued as *South American Journal*, 1879–1955.
El Diario, La Paz.
Financial Times, London.
The India-Rubber and Gutta-Percha and Electrical Trades Journal, London, 1884–1910; continued as *India Rubber Journal*, 1911–54; continued as *Rubber Journal*, 1955–7; continued as *Rubber Journal and International Plastics*, 1957–61; continued as *Rubber and Plastics Weekly*, 1961–
The India Rubber World and Electrical Trades Review, New York, 1889–99; continued as *The India Rubber World*, 1899–1954; continued as *Rubber World*, 1954–
Peruvian Times (*Andean Air Mail & Peruvian Times*), Lima, 1940–
Presencia, La Paz.
Press Cuttings Books: *Council of Foreign Bondholders, Bolivia Extracts*, 7 vols., 1872–1965, Guildhall Library, London.
The Times, London.

IV BOOKS AND ARTICLES

This list includes references cited in the footnotes to the text, and other selected material having a bearing on the theme.

Agassiz, L. J. R. and E. C., *A Journey in Brazil*, Boston, 1868.
Aguirre Acha, J., *De los Andes al Amazonas: Recuerdos de la Campaña del Acre*, La Paz, extended edit. 1927.
—— *La Antigua Provincia de Chiquitos; Limitrofe de la Provincia del Paraguay. Anotaciones para la defensa de los derechos de Bolivia sobre el Chaco Boreal*, La Paz, 1933.
Akers, C. E., *A History of South America, 1854–1904*, London, 1904. Second edit. 1912, third edit. 1930.
—— *Report on the Amazon Valley, its Rubber Industry and other Resources*, London, 1912.
Alcock, F., *Trade and Travel in South America*, London, 1903.
Alexander, R. J., *The Bolivian National Revolution*, Rutgers Univ. Press, New Brunswick, N.J., 1958.
Andrews, J., *Journey from Buenos Ayres, through the Provinces of Cordova, Tucumán, and Salta, to Potosí, thence by the deserts of Caranja to Arica, and subsequently, to Santiago de Chile and Coquimbo, undertaken on behalf of the Chilian and Peruvian Mining Association, in the years 1825–1826*, 2 vols., London, 1827.
Aramayo, A., *Bolivia*, London, 1863.
—— *Proyecto de una nueva vía de comunicación entre Bolivia y el Oceano Pacífico*, Sucre and London, 1874.

List of Sources

Aramayo, F. A., *La Cuestión del Acre y La Legación de Bolivia en Londres; documentos referentes al Contrato del Acre*, London, 1903.

Arenales, J., *Noticias históricas y descriptivas sobre el Gran Pais del Chaco y río Bermejo*, Buenos Aires 1833, Montevideo, 1849.

Arguedas, A., *Pueblo enfermo*, Barcelona, 1910.

—— *La Fundación de la República*, La Paz, 1920.

—— *História General de Bolivia, 1809–1921*, La Paz, 1922.

Armentier, N., *Navegación del Madre de Dios*, La Paz, 1887.

Arnade, C. W., *The Emergence of the Republic of Bolivia*, Univ. of Florida Press, 1957.

—— 'The Historiography of Colonial and Modern Bolivia', *Hisp. Am. Hist. Rev.*, vol. xlii, 1962, pp. 333–84.

Aubertin, J. J., *By Order of the Sun to Chile to see his total Eclipse*, London, 1894.

Ayala Z., Alfredo, *Geográfia Política de Bolivia*, La Paz, 1943 and 1956.

Balderrama M., Alfonso, *El Proyecto Otuquis*, La Paz, 1961.

Ball, J., *Notes of a Naturalist in South America*, London, 1887.

Ballivián, A., *Bolivia: her resources and future* (also as *La Bolivie: ses ressources, son avenir*), London, 1920.

Ballivián, M. V., trans. and annot., *La Exploración del Río Beni, revista histórica por el doctor Edwin R. Heath*, La Paz, 1896.

—— *Apuntes para la biografía de Mr. Edwin R. Heath*, La Paz, 1897.

—— and Pinilla, C. F., *Monografía de la Industria de la Goma Elástica en Bolivia*, La Paz, 1912.

Bandelier, A. F., 'The Basin of Lake Titicaca', *Scott. Geog. Mag.*, vol. xxi, 1905, pp. 582–91; also *Bull. Amer. Geog. Soc.*, vol. xxxvii, 1905, pp. 449–60.

Bates, H. W., *The Naturalist on the River Amazons*, 2 vols., London, 1863.

Baxley, H. W., *What I Saw on the West Coast of South and North America, and at the Hawaiian Islands*, New York, 1865.

Bee-Mason, J. C., 'Across Bolivia', *Discovery*, London, vol. xi, 1930, pp. 347–51.

Bennett, T. H., *A Voyage from the United States to South America, performed during 1821, 1822 and 1823. Embracing a description of the city of Rio de Janeiro, in Brazil; of every port of importance in Chili; of several in Lower Peru; and of an eighteen months cruise in a Nantucket whaleship. The whole interspersed with a variety of original anecdotes*, Newburyport, Mass., 1823.

Bertrand, A., *Memoria sobre las Cordilleras del Desierto de Atacama i rejiones limítrofes*, Santiago, Chile, 1885.

Bingham, H., 'Potosí', *Bull. Am. Geog. Soc.*, vol. xliii, 1911, pp. 1–13.

Blakemore, H., 'John Thomas North, the Nitrate King', *History Today*, London, vol. xii, 1962, pp. 467–75.

Blanchard, W. O., 'Foreign Trade Routes of Bolivia', *Journal of Geography*, Chicago, vol. xxii, 1923, pp. 341–5.

Bolivia, orijen de su nacionalidad y sus derechos territoriales, Buenos Aires, 1882.

Bolivia, its position, products and prospects. A Sketch compiled from original information and official returns, printed for private circulation, London, 1901.

Bolivia and the opening of the Panama Canal, n.p. [? Washington, D.C.], 1912.

Bolivia – August 6th 1825–1925. A Magazine published in commemoration of the First Centenary of the Independence of Bolivia (published by M. Urriolagoitia H.), London, 1925.

Un Bolivien, *La Bolivie; ses richesses, leur exploitation*, Paris, 1857.

Bollaert, W., 'Observations on the geography of southern Peru, including Survey of the Province of Tarapacá, and Route to Chile by the coast of the Desert of Atacama', *Journ. Roy. Geog. Soc.*, vol. XXI, 1851, pp. 99–130.

Bolland, E., *Exploraciones practicadas en el Alto Paraguay y en La Laguna Gaíba*, Buenos Aires, 1901.

de Bonelli, L. H., *Travels in Bolivia*, 2 vols., London, 1854.

Borchard, E. M., 'The Tacna–Arica Controversy', *Foreign Affairs*, New York, vol. I, 1922–3, pp. 27–48.

Bowers, Lieut. W., *R.N.*, *Naval Adventures during Thirty-five years' service*, 2 vols., London, 1833.

Bowman, I., 'The Distribution of Population in Bolivia', *Bull. Geog. Soc. Philadelphia*, vol. VII, 1909, pp. 74–93.

—— 'The Highland Dweller of Bolivia: an anthropogeographic interpretation', *Bull. Geog. Soc. Philadelphia*, vol. VII, 1909, pp. 159–84.

—— 'Trade Routes in the Economic Geography of Bolivia', *Bull. Am. Geog. Soc.*, vol. XLII, 1910, pp. 22–37, 92–104 and 180–92.

—— 'Geographical Aspects of the new Madeira–Mamoré Railway', *Bull. Am. Geog. Soc.*, vol. XLV, 1913, pp. 275–81.

—— *Desert Trails of Atacama*, American Geographical Society Special Publication No. 5, New York, 1924.

Boyd, R. Nelson, *Sketches of Chili and the Chilians during the War 1879–1880*, London, 1881.

Brabant, W. van, *La Bolivie*, Paris, 1908.

Brackenridge, H. M., *Voyage to South America, performed by order of the American Government in the years 1817 and 1818, in the frigate 'Congress'*, 2 vols., Baltimore, 1819, London, 1820.

Bravo, C., *La Patria Boliviana – Estado Geográfico*, La Paz, 1894.

Bresson, A., *Bolivia. Sept Années d'Explorations, de Voyages et de Séjours dans l'Amérique Australe*, Paris, 1886.

Brown, C. Barrington, and Lidstone, W., *Fifteen Thousand Miles on the Amazon and its Tributaries*, London, 1878.

Bryce, J., *South America – Observations and Impressions*, London, 1912.

Bulnes, G., *Chile and Peru: the causes of the War of 1879*, Santiago, Chile, 1920.

Caldcleugh, A., *Travels in South America during the years 1819–20–21, containing an account of the present state of Brazil, Buenos Ayres, and Chile*, 2 vols., London, 1825.

Campero, N., *Informe del General Narciso Campero ante la Convención Nacional de Bolivia como General en Jefe del Ejercito Aliado*, La Paz, 1880.

Campos, D., *Informe Incidental que presenta al Exmo – Gobierno de Bolivia su Delegado en la Expedición al Paraguay*, Buenos Aires, 1884.

Carpenter, F. G., *South America, Social, Industrial and Political; a twenty-five-thousand-mile journey in search of information*, New York and Chicago, 1900.

Carrasco, J., *Bolivia's Case for the League of Nations*, London, 1920.

Chandless, W., 'Ascent of the River Purus, and Notes of the River Aquiry', *Journ. Roy. Geog. Soc.*, vol. XXXVI, 1866, pp. 86–126.

—— 'An Exploration of the River Purus', *Proc. Roy. Geog. Soc.*, vol. X, 1866, pp. 103–7.

—— 'An Exploration of the River Aquiry, an affluent of the Purus', *Proc. Roy. Geog. Soc.*, vol. XI, 1867, pp. 100–2.

Chandless, W., 'Extract of a letter from Mr. W. Chandless, now exploring the Tributaries of the Amazons', *Proc. Roy. Geog. Soc.*, vol. XII, 1868, pp. 339–40.

Chávez, M., *Eldorado Boliviano*, La Paz, 1926.

Chávez Suárez, José, *Historia de Moxos*, La Paz, 1944.

Church, G. E., *Explorations made in the Valley of the River Madeira from 1749–1868*, London, 1875.

—— *The Route to Bolivia via the River Amazon. A Report to the Governments of Bolivia and Brazil*, London, 1877.

—— 'Northern Bolivia and President Pando's new map', *Geog. Journ.*, vol. XVIII, 1901, pp. 144–53.

—— 'Acre Territory and the Caoutchouc Region of South-Western Amazonia', *Geog. Journ.*, vol. XXIII, 1904, pp. 596–613.

Cleven, N. A. N., *The Political Organization of Bolivia*, Carnegie Institution, Washington, D.C., 1940.

Cobb, G. B., 'Potosí, a South American Mining Frontier', in *Greater America. Essays in honor of Herbert Eugene Bolton*, Univ. of Calif. Press, Berkeley and Los Angeles, 1945, pp. 39–58.

—— 'Supply and Transportation for the Potosí Mines 1545–1640', *Hisp. Am. Hist. Rev.*, vol. XXIX, 1949, pp. 25–45.

Cole, J. P., 'The Cochabamba–Santa Cruz Highway, Bolivia', *Geography*, Sheffield, vol. XLIII, 1958, pp. 273–5.

Conway, W. Martin, 'Notes on a map of part of the Cordillera Real of Bolivia', *Geog. Journ.*, vol. XV, 1900, pp. 528–9.

—— *The Bolivian Andes, a record of Climbing and Exploration in the Cordillera Real in the years 1898 and 1900*, London and New York, 1901.

Craig, N. B., *Recollections of an Ill-fated Expedition to the Headwaters of the Madeira River in Brazil*, Philadelphia and London, 1907.

Crampton, E. M., and Ullrich, L. F., 'Administration of José Ballivián in Bolivia', *Hisp. Am. Hist. Rev.*, vol. I, 1918, pp. 403–14.

Crespo, A., *Santa Cruz: el cóndor indio*, Mexico City, 1944.

Crespo, L. S., *Geografía de la República de Bolivia*, La Paz, 1911.

Crist, R. E., 'Bolivia', *Focus*, American Geographical Society, New York, revised edit. 1966.

Crossley, J. C., 'Santa Cruz at the Cross-Roads, a study of development in Eastern Bolivia', *Tijdschrift voor Economische en Sociale Geografie*, Rotterdam, vol. LII, 1961, pp. 197–206 and 230–41.

Cunningham, C. H., *The Audiencia in the Spanish Colonies*, Univ. of Calif. Press, Berkeley, 1919.

Curtis, W. E., *The Capitals of Spanish America*, New York, 1888.

—— *Between the Andes and the Ocean*, Chicago, 1900.

—— 'The Road to Bolivia', *National Geographic Magazine*, Washington, D.C., vol. XI, 1900, pp. 209–24 and 264–80.

Darwin, C., *Journal of Researches into the Geology and Natural History of the various countries visited by H.M.S. Beagle under the Command of Captain Fitzroy, R.N. from 1832 to 1836*, London, 1839.

Davis, W. C., *The Last Conquistadores; the Spanish intervention in Peru and Chile, 1863–1866*, Univ. of Georgia Press, 1950.

Delaney, R. W., 'General Miller and the Confederación Perú-Boliviana', *The Americas*, Washington, D.C., vol. XVIII, 1961-2, pp. 213-42.

Denevan, W. M., 'The Aboriginal Cultural Geography of the Llanos de Mojos of Bolivia', *Ibero-Americana*, No. 48, Univ. of Calif. Press, Berkeley and Los Angeles, 1966.

Dennis, W. J., *Documentary History of the Tacna-Arica Dispute*, Univ. of Iowa, 1927.

—— *Tacna and Arica*, Yale Univ. Press, 1931.

Díaz Machicao, P., *Historia de Bolivia*, 5 vols., La Paz, 1954-8.

Diccionario geográfico de la República de Bolivia, 1890-1911, La Paz.

Díez-Canseco, E., *Perú y Bolivia – pueblos gemelos*, Lima, 1952.

Díez de Medina, E., *La Question du Pacifique et la Politique Internationale de la Bolivie*, Paris, 1924.

Diffie, B. W., 'Estimates of Potosí mineral production, 1545-1555', *Hisp. Am. Hist. Rev.*, vol. XX, 1940, pp. 275-82.

—— *Latin American Civilization – colonial period*, Harrisburg, Pa., 1945.

Dingman, B. S., *Ten Years in South America, Notes of Travel in Peru, Bolivia, Chile, Argentine Republic, Montevideo and Brazil, comprising History, Commercial Statistics, Climate, Products, etc.*, 2 vols. known to have been published; vol. II, *Bolivia, Complete in Itself*, Montreal, 1876.

Dirección Nacional de Informaciones, *Bolivia – 10 Años de Revolución*, La Paz, 1962.

Dobson, A. A. G., *A Short Account of the Leach Bermejo Expedition of 1899, with some reference to the Flora, Fauna and Indian Tribes of the Chaco*, Buenos Aires, 1900.

Dreisbach, A. R., 'Mosquito Fighters of Guayaramerin aid Rubber Tappers', *Journal of Geography*, Chicago, vol. XLII, 1943, pp. 130-3.

Duffield, A. J., *Peru in the Guano Age*, London, 1877.

—— *The Prospects of Peru. The End of the Guano Age and a description thereof, with some account of the Guano Deposits and 'Nitrate' Plains*, London, 1881.

—— *Recollections of Travels Abroad*, London, 1889.

Duguid, J., *Green Hell, a Chronicle of Travel in the Forests of Eastern Bolivia*, London, 1931.

Edwards, H. A., 'Frontier Work on the Bolivia-Brazil boundary, 1911-1912', *Geog. Journ.*, vol. XLII, 1913, pp. 113-28.

—— 'Further frontier work on the Bolivia-Brazil northern boundary', *Geog. Journ.*, vol. XLV, 1915, pp. 384-405.

Edwards, W. H., *A Voyage up the River Amazon, including a residence at Pará*, New York, 1847.

El Derecho de Bolivia sobre El Chaco, desde el punto de vista geográfico, La Paz, 1930.

El Puerto para Bolivia: opiniones de personalidades bolivianas, La Paz, 1919.

Encina, Francisco A., *Las Relaciones entre Chile y Bolivia, 1841-1963*, Santiago, 1963.

Ericksen, G. E., 'Rhyolite tuff, a source of the salts of northern Chile', *Geological Survey Research Paper No. 230*, Washington, D.C., 1961.

Ertl, H., *Arriba, Abajo* (Bolivia in photographs), Munich, 1958.

Espinoza, L., *Después de la Guerra, las relaciones Boliviano-Chilenas*, La Paz, 1929.

Estigarribia, J. F., *The Epic of the Chaco; Marshal Estigarribia's Memoirs of the Chaco War 1932-1935*, edit. and annot. by P. M. Ynsfran, Univ. of Texas Institute of Latin-American Studies, No. 8, Austin, 1950.

Evans, J. W., 'Expedition to Caupolicán, Bolivia, 1901-1902', *Geog. Journ.*, vol. XXII, 1903, pp. 601-46.

List of Sources

—— 'The Rocks of the Cataracts of the River Madeira, and the adjoining portions of the Beni and Mamoré', *Quarterly Journal of the Geological Society of London*, vol. LXII, 1906, pp. 88–124.

Eyzaguirre, J., *Chile y Bolivia: esquema de un proceso diplomático*, Santiago, Chile, 1963.

Fawcett, P. H., 'Explorations in Bolivia', *Geog. Journ.*, vol. XXXV, 1910, pp. 513–32.

—— 'Further Explorations in Bolivia – the river Heath', *Geog. Journ.*, vol. XXXVII, 1911, pp. 377–98.

—— 'Bolivian Exploration, 1913–1914', *Geog. Journ.*, vol. XLV, 1915, pp. 219–28.

—— *Exploration Fawcett* (edit. B. Fawcett), London, 1953; also as *Lost Trails, Lost Cities*, New York, 1953.

Fernandez, C. J., *La Guerra del Chaco*, 3 vols., Buenos Aires, 1956.

Fifer, J. V., 'Arica: a desert frontier in transition', *Geog. Journ.*, vol. CXXX, 1964, pp. 507–18.

—— 'Bolivia's Boundary with Brazil: a century of evolution', *Geog. Journ.*, vol. CXXXII, 1966, pp. 360–72.

—— 'Bolivia's Pioneer Fringe', *Geog. Rev.*, vol. LVII, 1967, pp. 1–23.

—— 'The Empire Builders: a History of the Bolivian Rubber Boom and the Rise of the House of Suárez', *Journal of Latin American Studies*, Cambridge, vol. II, 1970, pp. 113–146.

—— 'The Plate Basin Project: new proposals for South American Economic Cooperation', *Geography*, Sheffield, vol. LV, 1970, pp. 209–14.

Figueroa, P. P., *Atacama en la Guerra del Pacífico*, Santiago, Chile, 1888.

Finot, E., *Historia de la Conquista del Oriente Boliviano*, Buenos Aires, 1939.

—— *Nueva Historia de Bolivia*, La Paz, 1944, Buenos Aires, 1946.

da Fonseca, J. G., 'Voyage made from the City of the Gran Pará to the mouth of the River Madeira by the expedition which ascended this river to the mines of Matto Grosso, by special order of His Faithful Majesty in the year 1749', *Royal Academy of Sciences*, Lisbon, 1826. (In *Explorations made in the Valley of the River Madeira from 1749–1868*, collected by G. E. Church.)

Franck, H. A., *Vagabonding down the Andes*, New York, 1917.

Francovich, G., *El Pensamiento boliviano en el siglo XX*, Mexico City, 1956.

Frezier, A. F., *A Voyage to the South Sea, and along the coasts of Chili and Peru, in the years 1712, 1713 and 1714, illustrated with 37 copper-cuts of the Coasts, Harbours, Cities, plants and other curiosities*, London, 1717.

Ganzert, F.W., 'The Boundary Controversy in the Upper Amazon, between Brazil, Bolivia and Peru, 1903–1909', *Hisp. Am. Hist. Rev.*, vol. XIV, 1934, pp. 427–49.

Gerstmann, R., *Bolivia* (in photographs), Paris, 1928.

Gibbon, Lieut. L., *U.S.N.*, *Exploration of the Valley of the Amazon*, vol. II, Washington, D.C., 1854.

Gibson, M. H., *Gran Chaco Calling*, London, 1934.

Gimenez Caballero, E., *Maravillosa Bolivia, clave de América*, Madrid, 1957.

Goblet, Y. M., *Le Crépuscule des Traités*, Paris, 1934; *The Twilight of Treaties*, London, 1936.

Greene, D. G., 'Revolution and the Rationalization of Reform in Bolivia, *Inter-American Economic Affairs*, Washington, D.C., vol. XIX, No. 3, 1965–6, pp. 3–25.

Grey, H. M., *The Land of Tomorrow – a mule-back trek through the swamps and forests of eastern Bolivia*, London, 1927.

18   273   F B L

Griess, P. R., 'The Bolivian Tin Industry', *Economic Geography*, Worcester, Mass., vol. XXVII, 1951, pp. 238–50.

Grubb, W. Barbrooke, *A Church in the Wilds*, London, 1914.

Guillaume, H., *The Amazon Provinces of Peru as a field for European Emigration*, London, 1888.

Guise, A. V. L., *Six Years in Bolivia: the adventures of a mining engineer*, London, 1922.

Guzman, A., *Geográfia de Bolivia*, La Paz, 1886.

Habig, M. A., 'The Franciscan Provinces of South America', *The Americas*, Washington, D.C., vol. II, 1945–6, pp. 335–56.

Häenke, T., 'On the Southern Affluents of the River Amazons: an official report addressed to the Spanish Government', trans. from a manuscript, dated 1799, on the advantages to be derived from the navigation of the rivers which flow from the Cordilleras of Peru into the Marañon or Amazons. Submitted to the Royal Geographical Society by Sir Woodbine Parish; see *Journ. Roy. Geog. Soc.*, vol. V, 1835, pp. 90–9.

Hall, Capt. B., *R.N.*, *Extracts from a Journal written on the Coasts of Chili, Peru and Mexico, in the years 1820, 1821, 1822*, 2 vols., Edinburgh, 1824.

Hanke, L., *The Imperial City of Potosí*, Sucre, 1954, The Hague, 1956.

—— *A Note on the Life and Publications of Colonel George Earl Church*, Institute of Latin American Studies, Columbia Univ., N.Y., 1965.

—— and Mendoza, G. (eds.), *Bartolomé Arzáns de Orsúa y Vela's History of Potosí*, 3 vols., Providence, R.I., 1965.

Hanson, E. P., edit., *The New World Guides to the Latin American Republics*, 3 vols., New York, 3rd edit., 1950. (Vol. II, Andes and west coast countries.)

—— *Bolivia*, American Geographical Society 'Around the World Program' publication, New York, 1959.

Haring, C. H., *The Spanish Empire in America*, New York and Oxford Univ. Press, 1947. Revised edit. 1952.

Heath, D. B., 'Land Reform in Bolivia', *Inter-American Economic Affairs*, Washington, D.C., vol. XII, No. 4, 1958–9, pp. 3–27.

—— 'Commercial Agriculture and Land Reform in the Bolivian Oriente', *Inter-American Economic Affairs*, Washington, D.C., vol. XIII, No. 2, 1959–60, pp. 35–45.

—— 'The Aymara Indians and Bolivia's Revolutions', *Inter-American Economic Affairs*, Washington, D.C., vol. XIX, No. 4, 1965–6, pp. 31–40.

Heath, E. R., 'Exploration of the River Beni in 1880–81', *Journ. Am. Geog. Soc. of New York*, vol. XIV, 1882, pp. 117–65; also *Proc. Roy. Geog. Soc.* (New Series), vol. V, 1883, pp. 327–41.

Helms, A. Z., *Travels from Buenos Ayres, by Potosí, to Lima*, London, 1806.

Herndon, Lieut. W. L., *U.S.N.*, *Exploration of the Valley of the Amazon*, vol. I, Washington, D.C., 1853 and 1854.

Herrara, F., 'An Official Report (1827) on the river Beni, and the countries through which it flows', *Journ. Roy. Geog. Soc.*, vol. V, 1835, pp. 99–101.

Hill, A. W., 'Notes on a Journey in Bolivia and Peru around Lake Titicaca', *Scott. Geog. Mag.*, vol. XXI, 1905, pp. 249–59.

Hinks, A. R., 'Notes on the Technique of Boundary Delimitation', *Geog. Journ.*, vol. LVIII, 1921, pp. 417–43.

Hoek, H., 'Exploration in Bolivia,' *Geog. Journ.*, vol. XXV, 1905, pp. 498–513.

Homenaje a Bolivia en el Primer Centenario de su Independencia 1825–1925, La Paz, 1925.

List of Sources

Hooker, M. R. ,*Adventures of an Agnostic, the life and letters of Reader Harris, Q.C.*, London, 1959.

Humboldt, F. H. Alexander von, *Personal Narrative of travels to the equinoctial regions of the New Continent, during the years 1799–1804, by Alexander de Humboldt and A. Bonpland*, Engl. trans. by H. M. Williams, 7 vols., London, 1814–29.

Humphreys, R. A., *Liberation in South America, 1806–1827. The career of James Paroissien*, London, 1952.

Ibarra Ardiles, C., *Esto Es Bolivia*, La Paz, 1956.

Instituto de Investigaciones Históricas y Culturales de La Paz, *Mesa Redonda sobre El Problema del Litoral Boliviano*, La Paz, 1966.

International Bureau of the American Republics, *Bolivia – geographical sketch, natural resources, laws, economic conditions, actual development, prospects of future growth*, Washington, D.C., 1904.

International Labour Office, *Labour Problems in Bolivia*, Montreal, 1943.

Ireland, G., *Boundaries, Possessions, and Conflicts in South America*, Harvard Univ. Press, 1938.

Iturralde, A., *Cuestion de Límites entre Bolivia y el Perú sobre la región de Caupolicán ó Apolobamba*, La Paz, 1897.

James, P. E., 'Latin America: State Patterns and Boundary Problems', in *The Changing World*, edit. W. G. East and A. E. Moodie, London, 1956, pp. 881–97.

Juan, J., and de Ulloa, A., *A Voyage to South America, describing at large the Spanish cities, towns, provinces, etc., on that extensive continent*, 2 vols., London, 1758.

Juaregui Rosquellas, A., *Geografía general de Bolivia*, La Paz, 1918.

—— *La Ciudad de los Cuatro Nombres*, Sucre, 1924.

—— 'La Audiencia de Charcas', *Bol. Soc. Geog. Sucre*, vol. XXX, 1933, pp. 1–53.

Kain, R. S., 'Behind the Chaco War', *Current History*, Philadelphia, vol. XLII,, 1935, pp. 468–78.

—— 'Bolivia's Claustrophobia', *Foreign Affairs*, New York, vol. XVI, 1937–8, pp. 704–13.

Karsten, R., *Indian Tribes of the Argentine and Bolivian Chaco*, Helsingfors, 1932.

Keller (Keller-Leuzinger), F., *The Amazon and Madeira Rivers. Sketches and Descriptions from the Notebook of an Explorer*, London, 1874.

Keller, F. L., 'Finca Ingavi – a medieval survival on the Bolivian Altiplano', *Economic Geography*, Worcester, Mass., vol. XXVI, 1950, pp. 37–50.

—— 'Institutional Barriers to Economic Development – some examples from Bolivia', *Economic Geography*, Worcester, Mass., vol. XXXI, 1955, pp. 351–63.

Kendall, L. C., 'Andrés Santa Cruz and the Peru–Bolivian Confederation', *Hisp. Am. Hist. Rev.*, vol. XVI, 1936, pp. 29–48.

Kerr, J. G., 'The Gran Chaco', *Scott. Geog. Mag.*, vol. VIII, 1892, pp. 73–87.

—— *A Naturalist in the Gran Chaco*, Cambridge, 1950.

Kirchoff, H., *Bolivia, its people and scenery* (in photographs), Buenos Aires, 2nd edit., 1944.

Klein, H. S., 'American Oil Companies in Latin America: the Bolivian Experience', *Inter-American Economic Affairs*, Washington, D.C., vol. XVIII, 1964, pp. 47–72.

—— '"Social Constitutionalism" in Latin America: the Bolivian Experience of 1938', *The Americas*, Washington, D.C., vol. XXII, 1965–6, pp. 258–76.

—— *Parties and Political Change in Bolivia, 1880–1952*, Cambridge, 1969.

18-2

Krause, A. E., 'Mennonite Settlement in the Paraguayan Chaco', *Univ. of Chicago Research Paper No. 25*, 1952; also *Geog. Rev.*, vol. LII, 1962, pp. 599–600.

Labré, Col. A. R. P., 'Colonel Labré's Explorations in the region between the Beni and the Madre de Dios Rivers and the Purus', *Proc. Roy. Geog. Soc.* (New Series), vol. XI, 1889, pp. 496–502.

La Foy, M., *The Chaco Dispute and the League of Nations*, Ann Arbor, Mich., 1946.

Lavandez, J., *La Colonización en Bolivia durante la primera centuria de su independencia*, La Paz, 1925.

Lelong, B., and Javal, J.-L., *Cordillère Magique*, trans. G. Sainsbury, *The Stars Weep*, London, 1956.

Leonard, O. E., *Bolivia: land, people and institutions*, Washington, D.C., 1952.

Lindsay, J. W., 'The War over the Chaco: a personal account', *International Affairs*, London, vol. XIV, 1935, pp. 231–40.

Lloyd, J. A., 'Report of a Journey across the Andes, between Cochabamba and Chimoré, to the westward of the Traders' Route, with remarks on the proposed communication between Bolivia and the Atlantic, via the Amazon', *Journ. Roy. Geog. Soc.*, vol. XXIV, 1854, pp. 259–65.

Los Derechos de Bolivia al Mar. Antología de Juicios Eminentes, Biblioteca de Clasicos Bolivianos, La Paz, 1962.

'Los Limites de Bolivia a través de un siglo', *Bol. Soc. Geog. Sucre*, vols. XXIII–XXV, 1925, pp. 138–79.

Lynch, J., *Spanish Colonial Administration, 1782–1810. The Intendant System in the Viceroyalty of the Río de la Plata*, London, 1958.

McBride, G. M., *The Agrarian Indian Communities of Highland Bolivia*, American Geographical Society Research Series No. 5, New York, 1921.

Macdonald, N. P., 'Bolivia', *The Fortnightly*, London, 1950, pp. 299–306.

Mallo, J., *Historia de la Fundación de Bolivia y lo que fué para ella la administración Sucre*, Sucre, 1871.

Mallo, N., 'Cuestiones de Límites Bolivia y el Paraguay', *Bol. Soc. Geog. Sucre*, vol. V, 1905, pp. 193–202.

Mance, H. O., et al., *International Transport and Communications*, 7 vols., London, 1943–7.

Manzon, J., Asturias, M.-A., de Medina, F. Diez, *Bolivia, an undiscovered land*, London, 1961.

Marcoy, P. (Laurent Saint Cricq), *A Journey across South America from the Pacific Ocean to the Atlantic Ocean*, 2 vols., London and Glasgow, 1873.

Markham, C. R., 'On the supposed Sources of the River Purus', *Journ. Roy. Geog. Soc.*, vol. XXV, 1855, pp. 151–8.

—— 'Sources of the River Purus, in South America', *Proc. Roy. Geog. Soc.*, vol. V, 1861, pp. 224–5.

—— *Travels in Peru and India while superintending the collection of Chinchona Plants and Seeds in South America, and their introduction into India*, London, 1862.

—— 'Railroad and Steam Communication in Southern Peru', *Proc. Roy. Geog. Soc.*, vol. XVIII, 1874, pp. 212–20.

—— *Peruvian Bark*, London, 1880.

—— *Peru*, London, 1880.

—— 'The Basins of the Amaru-mayu, and the Beni', *Proc. Roy. Geog. Soc.* (New Series), vol. V, 1883, pp. 313–27.

—— *The War between Peru and Chile 1879–1882*, London, 1883.

—— 'Recent Discoveries in the Basin of the River Madre de Dios (Bolivia and Peru)', *Geog. Journ.*, vol. VII, 1896, pp. 187–90.

Marsh, M. A., *The Bankers in Bolivia, a study in American Foreign Investment* (Studies in American Imperialism), New York, 1928.

Martin, L. D., 'Bolivia in 1956: an analysis of political and economic events', *Hispanic American Report*, special issue, Hispanic American Studies, Stanford Univ., Calif., 1958.

Mather, K. F., 'Eastern Bolivia – a land of opportunity', *Bull. Geog. Soc. Philadelphia*, vol. XVIII, 1920, pp. 49–55.

—— 'Exploration in the land of the Yuracarés, Eastern Bolivia', *Geog. Rev.*, vol. XII, 1922, pp. 42–56.

—— 'Along the Andean front in south-eastern Bolivia', *Geog. Rev.*, vol. XII, 1922, pp. 358–74.

Mathews, E. D., *Up the Amazon and Madeira Rivers, through Bolivia and Peru*, London, 1879.

Mathison, G. F., *Narrative of a Visit to Brazil, Chile, Peru, and the Sandwich Islands, during the years 1821 and 1822*, London, 1825.

Maúrtua, V. M., *Juicio de límites entre el Perú y Bolivia; prueba peruana presentada al gobierno de la República Argentina*, 12 vols., Barcelona, 1906.

—— *The Question of the Pacific*, Philadelphia, 1901.

Maury, M. F., *U.S.N.*, *The Amazon, and the Atlantic Slopes of South America*, Washington, D.C., 1853.

Melby, J., 'Rubber River: an account of the rise and collapse of the Amazon boom', *Hisp. Am. Hist. Rev.*, vol. XXII, 1942, pp. 452–69.

Mendoza, J., *La Universidad de Charcas y la Idea Revolucionaria*, Sucre, 1924.

—— *El Factor Geográfico en la Nacionalidad Boliviana*, Sucre, 1925.

—— *El Mar del Sur*, Sucre, 1926.

—— *La Ruta Atlántica*, Sucre, 1927.

—— *La Tesis Andinista, Bolivia y el Paraguay*, Sucre, 1933.

—— *El Macizo Boliviano*, La Paz, 1935 and 1957.

Mercado Encinas, M., *Esto es Bolivia*, La Paz, 1956.

Mercado M., Miguel, *Charcas y el Río de la Plata*, La Paz, 1918.

Miller, J., *Memoirs of General Miller in the Service of the Republic of Peru*, 2 vols., London, 1828, enlarged edit. 1829.

Miller, L. E., 'Across the Bolivian Highlands from Cochabamba to the Chapare', *Geog. Rev.*, vol. IV, 1917, pp. 267–83.

—— 'The Yuracaré Indians of Eastern Bolivia', *Geog. Rev.*, vol. IV, 1917, pp. 450–64.

—— *In the Wilds of South America*, London, 1919.

Minchin, J. B., 'Eastern Bolivia and the Gran Chaco', *Proc. Roy. Geog. Soc.* (New Series), vol. III, 1881, pp. 401–20.

Molina M., Plácido, 'Una nueva república en América: Santa Cruz de la Sierra', *Bol. Soc. Geog. Sucre*, vol. XXXII, 1938, pp. 204–8.

Moreno, J. L., *Geográfica, histórica y descriptiva de Bolivia*, Cobija, Bolivia, 1873.

Mulhall, Mrs M. G., *From Europe to Paraguay and Matto Grosso*, London, 1877.

Muñoz Reyes, J., *Bibliografía Geográfica de Bolivia*, Academia Nacional de Ciencias de Bolivia Publication No. 17, La Paz, 1968.

Bolivia: Land, Location, and Politics since 1825

Musters, G. C., 'Notes on Bolivia, to accompany original maps', *Journ. Roy. Geog. Soc.*, vol. XLVII, 1877, pp. 201–16.
Nordenskiöld, E., 'Travels on the boundaries of Bolivia and Argentina', *Geog. Journ.*, vol. XXI, 1903, pp. 510–25.
—— 'Travels on the boundaries of Bolivia and Peru', *Geog. Journ.*, vol. XXVIII, 1905, pp. 105–27.
—— *The Ethnography of South America seen from Mojos in Bolivia*, Göteborg, 1924.
de Oliveira Cezar, F., *La Vida en los Bosques Sud-Americanos. Viaje al Oriente de Bolivia*, Buenos Aires, 1891.
Olmos, J. L., *El Chaco*, La Paz, 1930.
d'Orbigny, A., *Voyage dans l'Amérique méridionale (Brésil, Uruguay, Argentine, Patagonie, Bolivie, Pérou) 1826–1833*, 9 vols. and atlas, Paris, 1835–47.
—— *Descripción Geográfica, Histórica y Estadística de Bolivia*, Paris, 1845.
Orton, J., *The Andes and the Amazon, or across the continent of South America*, 3rd. edit. rev. and enlarged, New York, 1876.
Osborne, H., *Bolivia: a land divided*, 3rd. edit., London, 1964.
—— 'Bolivia's New Path', *Geographical Magazine*, London, vol. XXVIII, 1955, pp. 193–9.
Ostria Gutierrez, A., *Un Pueblo en la Cruz*, trans. *The Tragedy of Bolivia – a people crucified*, New York, 1956.
Page, Capt. J., 'The Gran Chaco and its Rivers', *Proc. Roy. Geog. Soc.* (New Series), vol. XI, 1889, pp. 129–52.
Page, Lieut. T. J., *U.S.N.*, *La Plata, the Argentine Confederation, and Paraguay. Being a Narrative of the Exploration of the Tributaries of the River La Plata and Adjacent Countries during the years 1853, '54, '55, and '56, under the orders of the United States Government*, New York and London, 1859.
Palacios, J. A., *Exploración de los Ríos y Lagos del Departamento del Beni, y en especial el Madera, practicada de orden del Supremo Gobierno de Bolivia*, La Paz, 1852.
Pando, J. M., *Viaje a la Región de la Goma Elástica (Noroeste de Bolivia)*, La Plata, 1894.
—— *Expedición del Coronel Don José Manuel Pando al Inambary*, La Paz, 1898.
Pando Gutierrez, J., *Bolivia y el Mundo*, 2 vols., 2nd edit., La Paz, 1957.
Parish, Woodbine, *Buenos Ayres, and the Provinces of the Río de la Plata*, London, 1838, second edit. enlarged, London, 1852.
Peabody, G. A., *South American Journals, 1858–1859*, edit. J. C. Phillips, Salem, Mass., 1937.
Pearson, H. C., *The Rubber Country of the Amazon*, New York, 1911.
Pelleschi, G., *Eight months on the Gran Chaco of the Argentine Republic*, London, 1886.
Peña, A., and Escóbar, L., *Síntesis Geográfica de Bolivia*, La Paz, 1947.
Pentland, J. B., 'On the general outline and physical configuration of the Bolivian Andes; with observations on the line of perpetual snow upon the Andes, between 15° and 20° South latitude', *Journ. Roy. Geog. Soc.*, vol. V, 1835, pp. 70–89.
Philippi, R. A., 'Abstract of a Report made by Dr. R. A. Philippi to the Government of Chile, of a Journey into the Desert of Atacama in 1853–54', *Journ. Roy. Geog. Soc.*, vol. XXV, 1855, pp. 158–71.
Phillips, H. A., 'Bolivia – tin roof of the Andes', *National Geographic Magazine*, Washington D.C., vol. LXXXIII, 1943, pp. 309–32.
Pilling, W. (trans.), *The Emancipation of South America*, London, 1893.

List of Sources

Pinilla, S., *La Creación de Bolivia*, Madrid, 191?.

Piriz Coelho, R., and Barth, E., *Bolivia y sus riquezas*, La Paz, 1930.

Pissis, A., *Nitrate and Guano Deposits in the Desert of Atacama. An Account of the Measures taken by the Government of Chile to facilitate the Development Thereof*, London, 1878.

Platt, R. S., 'Conflicting Territorial Claims in the Upper Amazon', in *Geographical Aspects of International Relations*, edit. Colby, Univ. of Chicago, 1938, pp. 243–76.

Portman, L., *Three Asses in Bolivia*, London, 1922.

Prodgers, C. H., *Adventures in Bolivia*, London, 1922.

Raimondi, A., 'On the Rivers San Gavan and Ayapata, in the Province of Carabaya, Peru', *Journ. Roy. Geog. Soc.*, vol. XXXVII, 1867, pp. 116–51.

Ratzel, F., *Politische Geographie, oder die Geographie der Staaten, des Verkehres und des Krieges*, Munich and Berlin, 2nd edit., 1903, 3rd edit., 1923. (First published as *Politische Geographie*, Munich and Leipzig, 1897.)

Reeves, E. A., 'Note on Map of South Peru and North Bolivia', *Geog. Journ.*, vol. XXXVI, 1910, pp. 398–404.

Reid, W. A., *Bolivia, the heart of a continent*, Washington, D.C., 1916.

René-Moreno, G., 'La Audiencia de Charcas, 1559–1809', *Revista Chilena*, Santiago, Chile, No. XXIX, May 1877, pp. 93–142.

—— *Ultimos Días Coloniales en el Alto-Perú*, 3 pts., Santiago, Chile, 1896–8.

—— *Documentos Inéditos sobre el Estado Social y Político de Chuquisaca en 1808 y 1809*, Santiago, Chile, 1897 and 1901.

Revill, W., *Chaco Chapters*, London, 1947.

Rippy, J. F., 'Bolivia – an exhibit of the problems of economic development in retarded countries', *Inter-American Economic Affairs*, Washington, D.C., vol. X, No. 3, 1956, pp. 61–74.

—— and Nelson, J. T., *Crusaders of the Jungle*, Univ. of North Carolina Press, Chapel Hill, N.C., 1936.

Riquelme, D., *Bajo la Tienda, Recuerdos de la Campaña al Perú i Bolivia 1879–1884*, Santiago, Chile, 1890.

Riso Patron, L., *La Linea de Frontera con la República de Bolivia*, Santiago, Chile, 1910.

de Rivière, H. A., 'Explorations in the Beni Province', *Journ. Am. Geog. Soc. of New York*, vol. XXIV, 1892, pp. 204–14.

—— 'Explorations in the Rubber Districts of Bolivia', *Journ. Am. Geog. Soc. of New York*, vol. XXXII, 1900, pp. 432–40.

Romecin, E., 'Agricultural Adaptation in Bolivia', *Geog. Rev.*, vol. XIX, 1929, pp. 248–55.

de la Rosa, G., *The Boundaries of Chili in Atacama settled by History*, Lima, 1879.

Rudolph, W. E., 'The Río Loa of Northern Chile', *Geog. Rev.*, vol. XVII, 1927, pp. 553–85.

—— 'The Lakes of Potosí', *Geog. Rev.*, vol. XXVI, 1936, pp. 529–54.

—— *Vanishing Trails of Atacama*, American Geographical Society Research Series No. 24, New York, 1963.

Rusby, H. H., *Jungle Memories*, New York and London, 1933.

Ruschenberger, W. S. W., U.S.N., *Three Years in the Pacific; including notices of Brazil, Chile, Bolivia and Peru*, Philadelphia, 1834.

Russell, W. H., *A Visit to Chile and the Nitrate Fields of Tarapacá*, London, 1890.

Saavedra, B., *Defensa de los Derechos de Bolivia ante el Gobierno Argentino en el Litigio Fronteras con la República del Perú*, Buenos Aires, 1906.

Sagárnaga, E., *Recuerdos de la Campaña del Acre de 1903: mis notas de viaje*, La Paz, 1909.
Salazar Soriano, A., *Los Derechos de Bolivia sobre el Río Lauca*, Cochabamba, Bolivia, 1961.
Salinas Baldivieso, C. A., *Historia Diplomática de Bolivia*, Sucre, 1938.
Salinas, M. M., *Navegación de los Ríos de Bolivia confluentes del Madera y Amazonas y Colonisación*, Cochabamba, Bolivia, 1871.
Sanabria Fernández, H., *En Busca de Eldorado*, Santa Cruz de la Sierra, Bolivia, 1958.
Schurz, W. L., *Bolivia – a Commercial and Industrial Handbook*, Washington, D.C., 1921.
—— 'The Distribution of Population in the Amazon Valley', *Geog. Rev.*, vol. xv, 1925, pp. 206–25.
—— 'The Chaco Dispute between Bolivia and Paraguay', *Foreign Affairs*, New York, vol. vii, 1928–9, pp. 650–5.
—— 'Conditions Affecting Settlement on the Matto Grosso Highland and in the Gran Chaco', in *Pioneer Settlement*, edit. W. L. G. Joerg, American Geographical Society Special Publication No. 14, New York, 1932, pp. 108–23.
—— Hargis, O. D., Marbut, C. F., Manifold, C. B., *Rubber Production in the Amazon Valley*, Washington, D.C., 1925.
Schütz-Holzhausen, D. F. von, *Der Amazonas*, Freiburg-im-Breisgau, 1895.
Scott, P. H., *Bolivia – economic and social conditions*, Overseas Economic Survey, H.M.S.O., London, 1956.
Setaro, R. M., *Imágenes Secretas de la Guerra del Chaco*, Buenos Aires, 1935.
Siles Salinas, J., *La Aventura y el Orden, reflexiones sobre la revolución boliviana*, Santiago, Chile, 1956.
Sinopsis estadística y geográfica de la República de Bolivia, 3 vols., La Paz, 1903.
Stevenson, F. J., *A Traveller of the Sixties...in Brazil, Peru, Argentina, Patagonia, Chile and Bolivia during the years 1867–1869*, edit. D. Timins, London, 1929.
Stevenson, W. B., *A Historical and Descriptive Narrative of Twenty Years' Residence in South America*, 3 vols., London, 1825.
Suárez, N., *Anotaciones y Documentos sobre la Campaña del Alto Acre, 1902–1903*, Barcelona, 1928.
Suárez, P., *Notes on Bolivia*, London, 1902.
Temple, E., *Travels in various parts of Peru, including a year's residence in Potosí*, 2 vols., London, 1830.
Thomson, N., *Putumayo Red Book*, London, 2nd edit., 1914.
Thorlichen, G., *El Indio* (in photographs), La Paz, 1955.
Tigner, J. L., 'The Ryukyuans in Bolivia', *Hisp. Am. Hist. Rev.*, vol. xliii, 1963, pp. 206–29.
Tomasek, R. D., 'The Chilean–Bolivian Lauca River Dispute and the O.A.S.', *Journal of Inter-American Studies*, Univ. of Miami Press, vol. ix, 1967, pp. 351–66.
Tomlinson, H. M., *The Sea and the Jungle*, London, 1912.
Tschiffely, A. F., *Southern Cross to Pole Star: Tschiffely's Ride*, London, 1933.
Tschudi, J. J. von, *Travels in Peru, 1838–1842*, London, 1847.
Tucker, Q., *Seeking Rubber in Bolivia*, Dorchester, Mass., 1908.
Urquhart, D. R., 'The Bolivian Altiplanicie', *Scott. Geog. Mag.*, vol. x, 1894, pp. 302–12 and 360–71.
Vaca Diez, A., *Vías de Comunicación en el Noroeste de la República*, La Paz, 1893.

Vaca Diez, O., *Creación de Nuevo Departamento*, Riberalta, Bolivia, 1938.

Vacano, M. J. von, and Mattis, H., *Bolivien in Wort und Bild*, Berlin, 1906.

Vazquez-Machicado, H., *La Leyenda Negra Boliviana, la calumna dr la Borradura del Mapa*, La Paz., 1955.

—— de Mesa, J., and Gisbert, T., *Manual de Historia de Bolivia*, La Paz, 1958.

Virreira Paccieri, A., *Puerto propio y soberano para Bolivia*, La Paz, 1966.

Wallace, A. R., *A Narrative of Travels on the Amazon and Río Negro*, London, 1853.

Walle, P., *Bolivia, its people and its resources, its railways, mines and rubber forests*, London, 1914.

Weddell, H. A., *Voyage dans le nord de la Bolivie et dans les parties voisines du Pérou*, Paris and London, 1853.

Weeks, D., 'Bolivia's Agricultural Frontier', *Geog. Rev.*, vol. XXXVI, 1946, pp. 546–67.

Wickham, H. A., *Rough Notes of a Journey through the Wilderness*, London, 1872.

Woodroffe, J. F., and Smith, H. H., *The Rubber Industry of the Amazon, and how its supremacy can be maintained*, London, 1915.

Wright, M. R., *Bolivia – the central highway of South America*, Philadelphia and London, 1907.

Wrigley, G. M., 'Salta, an early commercial centre of Argentina', *Geog. Rev.*, vol. II, 1916, pp. 116–33.

—— 'Fairs of the Central Andes', *Geog. Rev.*, vol. VII, 1919, pp. 65–80.

Zalles, J. E., *Quinientas leguas a través de Bolivia*, La Paz, 1906.

Zondag, C. H., *The Bolivian Economy 1952–65*, New York, 1966.

Zook, D. H., Jnr (United States Air Force Academy), *The Conduct of the Chaco War*, New York, 1960.

INDEX

Physical features and place names, unless otherwise stated, lie wholly
or partly in Bolivia

Abaroa, Eduardo, 61, 90

Abuná (river), 92, 152; during rubber boom, and in boundary settlement with Brazil (1903), 129, 130, 132, 140; error in delineation of course (1903), 132n.; Brazilian penetration across, 139n., 155

Acre (river), 102; Brazilian penetration along, 101, 121, 128n., 139n.; crossed by boundary with Brazil (1867), 122, 122n.; Brazil's reservation upon its free navigation, 124n.; during rubber boom, 121–32 passim; part of boundary of independent State of Acre (1899), 125; part of boundary with Brazil (1903), 129–31; involved in boundary controversy, and later settlement, with Peru (1909–12), 145, 148–50; present-day activity along, 157–9

Acre Concession (Acre District), granted (1901) to Bolivian Syndicate of New York (also known as Anglo-American Syndicate), 123–30, 132n., 142, 143

Acre, Federal Territory of, later state of, Brazil, 128n., 155n. cont.

Acre, independent State of, 125–8, 142

Acre War (1902–3), 127–9

Agrarian Reform, in Bolivia, 81–2, 235, 261; in Peru, 82

Aguayrenda (Dept of Tarija), 199

Aiquile (Dept of Cochabamba), 229

altiplano (see also Titicaca), Marshal Sucre's march across, 14, 15; easier movement within cordilleran system afforded by, 26–7; routes across, 22, 25, 27, 49, 112, 166, by rail, 66–71, 88, 185, 200; its isolation from Pacific, 36, 61, 255; crossed by frontier, later boundary, with Peru, 39–40, 79; Bolivian new towns on (in relation to borderland contrasts with Peru), 82; its isolation from Oriente (northern sector), 93, 127–8, (south-eastern sector), 213; inaugural flights over, 211–12; nature of southern portion of, 226; smuggling across, 258; as part of a future regionally integrated area involving Bolivia, Chile and Peru, 263

Always Ready, 218n.

Amazon (river), Brazil, Portuguese/Brazilian expansion along, 31, 93–8, 130; problems of Bolivia's access to, 19–20, 28, 30, 100, 102–3; opened by Brazil to international navigation (1867), 103, 116, 137, 179; Brazil's reservation concerning free navigation on river Purus, 124n.; closed to Bolivian traffic (August 1902–February 1903, during Acre War) 126–9 (and during First World War) 139–40, 197; rights of navigation and transit for Bolivia confirmed by Brazil, 234

American International Products Co. (Paraguay), 184n.

Andean Group (Corporación Andina de Fomento), initiated by Bogotá Declaration (Aug. 1966); developed by Cartagena Agreement (May 1969): Acuerdo Regional Andino, Bolivia, Chile, Colombia, Ecuador, Peru, 262–3

Antofagasta, Chile, founded on coast of Bolivia (1868), 57; proposed British consular representation in, 239; replaces Cobija as capital of Bolivia's Litoral Department, 57n.; occupied by Chilean forces (1879), 61, 69; during nitrate boom, 56–61 passim, 74; captures Bolivia's Pacific trade, 70–1; Bolivia guaranteed commercial transit through, 66; port agents in, 245; in competition with other Pacific ports, 85–8; linked by rail to Buenos Aires (via Uyuni), 191; linked by rail to Salta, Argentina, 190n.; Bolivia's call for return of, 73, 90

Antofagasta (Chili) and Bolivia Railway Co. Ltd (see also Compañía de Salitres y Ferrocarril de Antofagasta), formation of company (1888) and extension of railway into Bolivia, 69, 247; its rumoured opposition to completion of Bolivia's rail link to Buenos Aires, 190–1; its association with the Bolivia Railway Co., 191, 248, 249n.; its strong controls over key sections of Bolivia's rail system, 248; thought to be pressing for British diplomatic representa-

Index

288

Index

Incas, their pattern of overland communications, 1; their use of guano, 52–3; settlement in the region of Lake Titicaca, 79, 81; a penetration road into the Yungas (for coca, bark, feathers, etc.), 100; their hunting expeditions in the western Chaco, 161n.; central plains Indians not incorporated into empire, 2

Ingavi, battle of (1841), 47, 49

Ingavi (Villa Ingavi or Caiza) (Dept of Tarija), 217

International Conference of American States (Pan-American Conference), 4th Conference (at Buenos Aires, 1910), 188; 6th Conference (at Havana, 1928), 210; 7th Conference (at Montevideo, 1933), 89; its Commission of Investigation, Conciliation and Arbitration. on hostilities in Chaco Boreal between Bolivia and Paraguay (at Washington, D.C., 1928–9), 209

Iquique, Chile, during guano boom, 53; during nitrate boom, 57, 74–5; blockaded by Chile during War of Pacific, 62–3; its proposed rail-and-canal linkage to Bolivian altiplano (1860–1), 43n.; its projected highway linkage to Oruro, 88

Iquiry (river), Brazil, 130, 131n.

Irindagüe (Bolivian fort), Paraguay, 216

irredentism (reivindicación, reivindicacionalismo), 73, 90

Isla Suárez, river Mamoré, 155–6

Islay, Peru, colonial port for Upper Peru, 24, 44; exporting Peruvian bark, 109

Itaú (Dept of Tarija), 199

Itaú (river), 187

Itenes (river), see Guaporé

Ixiamas, see Ysiama

Izozog swamps (Abapó–Izozog swamps), 209n. cont.; 233

Jackson, Sir John, 66, 198

Jaurú (Jaura) (river), Brazil, its confluence with river Paraguay a point on the Spanish–Portuguese colonial boundary (1750 and 1777), 94–5, 161, 177

Javari (river), Brazil/Peru, 92, 99, 115; part of San Ildefonso colonial boundary between Spanish and Portuguese claims (1777), 95, 101; its source remains part of boundary between Bolivia and Brazil (1867), 101, 122n., 127; attempts to locate source, 101–2

Jujuy (town and province), Argentina, on Potosí–Buenos Aires trail, 165–6; railway extended to, 190, 200; seasonal movement of Bolivian labour into, 224; Bolivian resident population in, 224; new oil and gas discoveries in, 223n.

Juliaca, Peru, 47, 71n.

Juruá (river), Brazil, 92, 99, 115; crossed by Bolivia–Brazil boundary (1867), and Brazilian penetration along, 101; part of boundary of independent State of Acre (1899), 125; steamer navigation on, 139

Keller (Keller-Leuzinger), Josef and Franz, 106n., 116n.

Kundt, Major, later General Hans, heads German Military Mission to Bolivia, later Bolivian Army Chief of Staff, 205–7; reorganises Bolivian Army Air Force, 211; dismissed and recalled, 212–13; dismissed again, 215

La Condamine, Charles Marie de, 111n.

Ladario, Brazil, 234

Lagunillas (Dept of Santa Cruz), its proposed rail link to Santa Cruz and river Paraguay (1879), 182; its proposed road link to Santiago de Chiquitos, and Lake Cáceres (1880), 182; oil exploration around (1920s), 199–200

La Noria, Chile, 57

Lanza (river), 147

La Oroya, Peru, 52n.

La Paz (city and Dept), city and province of Upper Peru, 10, 14–16, 44, 186; shows support for union with Lower Peru, 16, 22, 39; largest city in Upper Peru/Bolivia, 18n., 27; its rivalry with, and advantages over, Chuquisaca (Sucre), 26–7, 46, 48, 238, 252, 262; confirmed as de facto national capital (1898), 252; most economically served by port of Arica, 23, 25, 48–51, 57n.; projected rail link to Arica via Tacna (1850s), 51, (1870s), 67; as the major Bolivian market for Peruvian bark (1840s–1870s), 49n., 109; its remoteness from Oriente, 126, 130, 206; its proposed rail link to Riberalta, 133; its proposed rail link to river Paraguay (at Puerto Pacheco), 183; its proposed rail link to river Beni, 66n., 247; reached by rail from Guaqui (1905), 69, from Arica (to El Alto) (1913), 66–7, from Antofagasta via Oruro

Index

Index

Paposo, Chile, conflicting claims to, Bolivia and Chile, 32, 36, 53–4

Pará, see Belém do Pará

Paradero (Quijarro) (Dept of Santa Cruz), 231

Paraguay (river), problems of Bolivia's access to, and navigation of, 19–22, 30, 170–81, 218–20, 226, 229–36; part of San Ildefonso colonial boundary line between Spanish and Portuguese claims (1777), 28–9, 161–2, 174n., 176–8; Portuguese, later Brazilian penetration across, 163, 174–5; opened to international navigation by Paraguay (1852), 178; Bolivia relinquishes claims to right bank of upper Paraguay (1867), 127, 179, 182; Bolivia's attempts to consolidate claims to middle and upper Paraguay routeway, 182–3, 196, 198–9, 202–4, 219–21; rights of navigation and commercial transit for Bolivia guaranteed by Argentina (1868), 180n., 214; reservations by Argentina and Paraguay concerning navigation of Plate river system (1876), 214n.; Bolivia regains limited access to upper Paraguay's right bank (1903), 192–4, 231; rights of navigation and transit for Bolivia guaranteed by Brazil (1867, 1903, 1910, 1958), 179, 234–5; rights of transit and customs control for Bolivia at Puerto Casado guaranteed by Paraguay (1938), 218–19

Paraguay Land and Cattle Co. (Paraguay), 184n.

Paraná (river), Argentina/Brazil/Paraguay (see also Paraguay river), 30, 176–7, 214n., 222, 235

Paranaguá, Brazil, 218

Paranapanema (river), Brazil, 94

Parapetí (river), 164, 217; claimed by Paraguay to form part of 'natural limits' of Chaco Boreal, 209n. cont., 217n.; boundary of petroleum concession (exploratory) to Brazil, (1938), 227; bridged by Yacuiba–Santa Cruz railway, 223

Patillos, Chile, 62

Patiño, Father Gabriel, 175

Patiño Mines and Enterprises Consolidated Inc. (Delaware), 246

Pedro de Valdivia, Chile, nitrate and iodine plant, 75

Peñaranda, Colonel Enrique, 216

Pentland, Joseph Barclay, 18–19, 47n., 48n., 166, 238

peruleiros, 94

Peruvian bark (*Cinchona*), 49n., 104, 108–11, 118n., 142

Peruvian Corporation Ltd (London; nationalised by Peruvian Government, 1971), incorporating the Southern Peruvian Railway Co., 69–71, 84, 88

petroleum and natural gas deposits, early evidence of, 199–200; exploration for/exploitation of: (by Standard Oil Co. of New Jersey/Standard Oil Co. of Bolivia), 199–202 *passim*, 222, 247; (by Argentina) 192, 222–3, 225n.; (by Brazil), 227; (by Bolivia Gulf Oil Co.), 227–8; production centres (Y.P.F.B.), 222–4, 227–9; as part of Chaco Boreal dispute, 210–11, 217, 219–20; pipelines, existing or proposed: (trans-Chaco), 200, 202, 219–20; (to Argentina), 222, 228, 236; (to Ilo), 85n.; (to Arica), 85n., 227–8

Pilcomayo (river), 161–3; attempted navigation of, 162n., 175–6, 177; Argentina's and Paraguay's claims to, 176, 180–1; rumoured proposal by Argentina for Bolivian port on, 188n.; extension of forts down, 195–6, 207; its bridging-point successfully held by Bolivia during Chaco War, 217; bridged by Yacuiba–Santa Cruz railway, 223; triple boundary point on (Argentina–Bolivia–Paraguay), 188n., 218, 218n.

Pinasco Railroad, Paraguay, see under Puerto Pinasco

pipelines, oil and gas, see under petroleum and natural gas deposits

Piper, A. D., 106–7n., 123n.

Piray (river), 164

Pisagua, Chile, 61, 62, 74

Pisco, Peru, 24

Pitiantuta (Paraguayan fort), Paraguay, 212

Pizarro, Francisco, 1, 8, 9

Plate Basin Project, formalised by *Tratado de la Cuenca del Plata* (April 1969), Argentina/Bolivia/Brazil/Paraguay/Uruguay, 231–4, 263

plebiscite, proposed for solution of Tacna–Arica dispute, 64, 77

Pocitos, Bolivia and Argentina: boundary gully, 188; towns, 223–4, 258

Porongal (mt and river), Argentina, 187

Portachuelo (Dept of Santa Cruz), 236

Pôrto Acre, Brazil, see Puerto Alonso

Pôrto Esperança, Brazil, 209, 227

Pôrto Velho, Brazil, 134–5, 138n., 154n., 155, 234n.

Index

Porvenir (Dept of Pando), Suárez company town during rubber boom, 120, 128, 129n., 139n.; highway improvements from (existing and proposed), 152, 158-9

Potosí (city and Dept), city and Intendancy during colonial period, 1, 3, 6-11 passim, 13-16 passim, 18n., 22-3, 32n., 164-5; its links with port of Cobija, 36-7, 48; its links with Tarija and southern Andean centres, 169, 225; its improved highway link with Argentina, 225n.; its seasonal labour movement into Argentina, 224; railway extended to (1906-11), 66n., 248; railway extended beyond, 247

Principe da Beira (Portuguese fort on river Guaporé), Brazil, 95, 98n.

Public Works Construction Co. (London), 107-8

Puerto Acosta (Lake Titicaca, Dept of La Paz), 71n.

Puerto Alonso (Pôrto Acre), Brazil, founded by Bolivia (1899), 122; during Acre War, 122-8

Puerto Busch (proposed port on river Paraguay, Dept of Santa Cruz), 231-4

Puerto Casado, Paraguay, 208, 218-19, 226; Casado Railroad, 215, 218

Puerto Grether (river Ichilo, Dept of Santa Cruz), 222

Puerto Heath (confluence rivers Heath and Madre de Dios, Dept of La Paz), 141, 152, 159

Puerto Irigoyen (river Pilcomayo), Argentina, 214

Puerto Magariños (river Pilcomayo), Paraguay, founded by Bolivia (1843), 175, 177

Puerto Maldonado (confluence rivers Tambopata and Madre de Dios), Peru, 159

Puerto Pacheco (river Paraguay), Paraguay (see also Bahía Negra), founded by Bolivia (1885), 183; attacked by Paraguayan forces, 183, 194; Bolivia renews attempts to regain, 196-7

Puerto Pérez (formerly known as Chililaya or Cachilaya, Lake Titicaca, Dept of La Paz), 69-70

Puerto Pinasco, Paraguay, 184n.; Pinasco Railroad, 184n., 215

Puerto Quijarro (Lake Gaíba, Dept of Santa Cruz), 194

Puerto Rico (river Orton, Dept of Pando), 158; (U.S.A.), 66

Puerto Suárez (Lake Cáceres, Dept of Santa Cruz), founded (1880), 182; its development, 194, 196-8, 206; during Chaco Boreal conflict, 207, 209; its decline, 230-1

Puerto Sucre, see Guayaramerin

Puerto Villarroel (river Ichilo, Dept of Cochabamba), 222

Puna de Atacama, Argentina/Chile, 187, 190

Puno (Titicaca lake port), Peru, on colonial trail into Upper Peru, 44; part of independent State of South Peru (Peru-Bolivia Confederation, 1836-9), 44; occupied by Bolivian forces, 47; reached by railway from Mollendo (1874), 52n., 69, 241; its proposed rail extension to Guaqui and La Paz rejected, 71, 84; present-day activity in, 82-4

Purus (river), Brazil, 92, 158; crossed by Bolivia–Brazil boundary (1867), 101, 122n.; Brazilian penetration along, 101; A. D. Piper's attempt to colonize, 123n.; included in Bolivia's *Delegación* of Noroeste (1890-3), 113n., 198n.; during rubber boom, 112-15 passim; part of boundary of independent State of Acre (1899), 125; steamer navigation on, 139

Putumayo (river), Colombia/Peru, 115, 119, 138n.

quebracho, 161, 184, 213, 220n. cont.

Quechua language, 261, 261n.

railways, major period of growth in Bolivia, 247-8; Antofagasta–Oruro–La Paz (*see* Antofagasta (Chili) and Bolivia Railway Co. Ltd); Arica–Alto La Paz, 66-7, 69-71, 77, 198, improvements to, 86, 89; Arica–Tacna (Chile/Peru), 51, 63, 67, 78; Callao–Lima–Oroya (Peru), 52n.; Casado Railroad (Paraguay), 215, 218; Corumbá–Santa Cruz, 227, 229-31 passim; Guaqui–La Paz, 69, 249n.; La Quiaca–Villazón–Tupiza–Atocha, 190-1, 226, 250; Madeira–Mamoré Railway (Brazil), q.v.; Mollendo (later Matarani)–Arequipa–Puno (Peru), 52n., 67-71 passim, 84, 241; Pinasco Railroad (Paraguay), 184n., 215; Santa Cruz–Mamoré, 222; transcontinental, 3-4, 191, 227; Uyuni–Atocha, 248; Yacuiba–Santa Cruz, 223; proposed Andean centre links and extensions, 66n., 192n.; proposed Cochabamba–Santa Cruz, 66n., 133, 192, 227; proposed 'Great Central Railway', 105, 222; proposed Guayaramerin-

Index

railways (*cont.*)

Riberalta, 133; other proposed links in Amazonia during rubber boom, 112, 141; proposed Mejillones–Caracoles, 57n., 61n.; proposed Otuquis rail spur, 233; proposed link along Lake Titicaca shore (east), 71n., (west), 71, 84

Rapirrán (river), part of boundary with Brazil (1903), 130, 131n.; Brazilian penetration across, 139n.

Ratzel, Friedrich, *see* 'State-Idea'

República Bolívar, original name of independent Upper Peru (11 August–3 October 1825), 6, 16, 237

Reyes (Dept of Beni), mission at, 100; Peruvian bark trade at, 110, 118, 152; rubber production at, 110–11, 118

Riberalta (Dept of Beni), officially founded (1894), 152; Suárez company town, and regional centre, during rubber boom, 120, 140, 158, 243; Britain's refusal to place Vice-Consul at, 243; fails to acquire projected rail links, 133–4; loses administrative functions in Territorio de Colonias, 113n., 158; linked by improved highway to Guayaramerin (1968), 156; present-day activity in, 152–9 *passim*

Rio-Branco, José Maria da Silva Paranhos, Barão do, 128n. cont., 132

Rio Branco, Brazil, 155n. cont., 159

Riosinho, Brazil, 125

Ritter, Carl, 251, 251n.

Roboré (Dept of Santa Cruz), 21, 197, 206, 229

Rosario, Argentina, 189, 211; Bolivian transit and free zone facilities at, 235

Royal Dutch/Shell Group (London and The Hague), 210–11

rubber, boom period, 29, 110–34, 140–2, 147–9, 151, 185; collapse of boom, 136–40, 149–50, 152, 185, 206; its labour demands and conditions, 138, 138n., 139, 151n., 153; present-day production in Bolivia, 150–4

Saavedra, President Bautista, 191, 205–6

Saavedra (Bolivian fort), Paraguay 196

St John, Spenser, heads Special Mission to Bolivia (1875), 239–40

Salado (river), Chile, 32

Salamanca, President Daniel, 216

Salta (city and province), Argentina, on Potosí–Buenos Aires trail, 22, 165–8, 189;

on trans-Andean trail to San Pedro de Atacama, 189–90; its late colonial administrative tie with Tarija, 169; railway extended to reach, and extended beyond into Bolivia, 190–2; linked by rail to Antofagasta, 190n.; its air link with Tarija, 225; oil and gas fields in, 222, 223n.; seasonal movement of Bolivian labour into, 224; Bolivian resident population in, 224–5

Sama (cape), Peru, 37

Sama (river), Peru, 37, 73

Sama Grande, Peru, 37

Sanandita (Dept of Tarija), 192, 198, 216

San Antonio, Brazil, at lowest fall on river Madeira, 102, 105, 114–15, 119, 132, 134

San Ignacio (Dept of Santa Cruz), 197

San Ildefonso line (1777), delimiting Spanish and Portuguese colonial claims, 14, 28–9, 95–8, 101, 131, 161, 174n., 176

San Joaquin (Dept of Beni), 156

San José de Chiquitos (Dept of Santa Cruz), 21, 164, 197, 202, 204, 229

San Juan (Dept of Santa Cruz), 202

San Lorenzo, Argentina, 222

San Lorenzo (Abaroa), Peru, former Bolivian rubber *barraca* on river Manuripi, 149

San Lorenzo (Dept of Santa Cruz), 205

San Pedro de Atacama, Chile, 42–3, 58, 62, 189

Santa Ana (Dept of Beni), 156

Santa Cruz, President Andrés de, rejects Bolivian offers for port of Arica on behalf of Peru, 38; requests port of Arica on behalf of Bolivia, 39; attempts to develop the Litoral, especially port of Cobija, 40–2; establishes Peru–Bolivia Confederation (1836–9), 38–9, 44–7; exiled, 45, 242–3

Santa Cruz de la Sierra (city and Dept), founded, 164; part of colonial Intendancy, province, of Cochabamba, 11n., 14, 186; regional centre of Bolivian Oriente, 18n., 21, 176, 197, 236; its economy stimulated by rubber boom, 119, 185, 206; dispatches troops to Acre region (1903), 127; its regional depopulation resulting from Chaco War, 221; its isolation from principal Andean towns, 16, 26, 46, 206, 247; separatist movements in, 192, 206, 216, 238; its successive proposed rail, or improved road, links to the river Paraguay, 133, 182, 193, 202; linked by rail to

297

Index

Tarapacá (town and province), Chile, President Sucre's attempt to acquire from Peru, 38; part of independent State of South Peru (Peru–Bolivia Confederation, 1836–9), 44; nitrate production in, 57, 62, 73; Chilean ownership confirmed after War of Pacific, 62, 64

Tarairí (Dept of Tarija), 165

Tarija (city and Dept), officially founded (1574), 163; southern centre of Upper Peru, 8, 26, 161; its administration transferred to Salta (1807), 169; declares itself part of Bolivia (1825–6), 168–70, 185–6; its interest in promoting navigation of Pilcomayo, 175; city fails to acquire proposed rail links, 191, 192n., 247; its petroleum concession area, and production, 200, 222–4; political unrest in, 206, 238; seasonal and permanent migration into Argentina, 224; its improved highway link to Orán, Argentina, 225n.; its air link with Salta, Argentina, 225; present-day activity in, 224–6, 236

Tartagal, Argentina, on Salta–Santa Cruz foothill trail, 165, 185; its ownership contested by Argentina and Bolivia, 187–8; linked to Argentine rail system, 191, 201, 223; its commercial exchange with Bolivian border towns, 224

Tarvo (Bolivia–Brazil boundary point), 131–2

Territorio de Colonias, see Pando Dept

Tietê (river), Brazil, 94

Tiquina Strait (Lake Titicaca), 38, 83

Tirapata, Peru, 151

Titicaca (lake) (see also altiplano), 13; focus of settlement, communication and regional exchange between Upper and Lower Peru, 23, 26, 27, 44; subsequently forms part of frontier between Bolivia and Peru, 34, 38–9, 152, 226; reached by railway from Mollendo, 52n., 69; gunboats on, War of Pacific, 63; eventual delimitation of Bolivia–Peru boundary across, 78–81, 261; freedom of navigation by Bolivia and Peru on, 83n.; smuggling across, 258; present-day activity around, 81–2, 261; introduction of freight-train ferries on, 84

Toba Indians, 164, 166, 175

Tocopilla, Chile, port in former Bolivian Litoral, claimed by Peru, 34; occupied by Chilean forces (1879), 61–2; nitrate port, 74–5

Todos Santos (Dept of Cochabamba), 19

Tordesillas line (1494), delimiting Spanish and Portuguese colonial claims, 8, 31, 93

Toro, Colonel, later President José David, 216

Toro (Dept of Tarija), oilfield, 222

transit agreements, general, 4–5, 210, 235, 255–8; on air traffic, 255n.
  Bolivia–Argentina, 210, 214, 214n., 235
  Bolivia–Brazil, 103n., 124n., 124–5, 179, 215, 234, 234n.
  Bolivia–Chile, 66, 66n., 85n., 88, 209, 210, 214–15, 257
  Bolivia–Paraguay, 218–19, 257
  Bolivia–Peru, 49–50, 83n., 209–10

Transmarítima Boliviana, 262–3

Treaty, of Tordesillas (1494), Spain–Portugal (see also Tordesillas line), 93, 95; of Madrid (1750), Spain–Portugal, 94; of San Ildefonso (1777), Spain–Portugal (see also San Ildefonso line), 14, 28, 95, 98, 101, 161, 174n.; of Friendship, Commerce and Navigation (1837), Great Britain–Peru–Bolivia Confederation, 47, 238; of Friendship, Commerce and Navigation (1840), Great Britain–Bolivia, 47n., 238–9; of Boundaries, Commerce and Navigation (1852), Argentina–Paraguay, 176; of Friendship, Commerce and Navigation (1856), Argentina–Paraguay, 176; of Offensive and Defensive Alliance (1865), Argentina–Brazil–Uruguay (the Triple Alliance), 178–80; of Peace, Boundaries, Commerce and Navigation (1876), Argentina–Paraguay, 180, 214n.; of Peace and Friendship (Ancón, 1883), Chile–Peru, 64; of Peace between the Allied and Associated Powers and Germany (Versailles, 1919), 73, 205, 205n.; of Reciprocal Assistance (1947), Organization of American States, 89; of Montevideo, establishing Latin American Free Trade Association (1960), 262; of the River Plate Basin (Cuenca del Plata) (1969), Argentina–Bolivia–Brazil–Paraguay–Uruguay, 233, 263

Treaty: Bilateral Treaties between Bolivia and Neighbouring States (see also transit agreements)
  Bolivia–Argentina: of Peace, Friendship, Commerce and Navigation (1868), 180, 180n., 210, 214, 214n.; (as stipulated by Art. IX of 1868 treaty, Argentine Regulations respecting Goods in Transit from

Index